Hell on Wheels

CultureAmerica

Karal Ann Marling and Erika Doss, *Series Editors*

Hell on Wheels

The Promise and Peril of America's Car Culture, 1900–1940

David Blanke

 University Press of Kansas

Published by the University Press of Kansas (Lawrence,
Kansas 66045), which was organized by the Kansas
Board of Regents and is operated and funded by
Emporia State University, Fort Hays State University,
Kansas State University, Pittsburg State University, the
University of Kansas, and Wichita State University
Library of Congress Cataloging-in-Publication Data
British Library Cataloguing-in-Publication Data is
available.

Library of Congress Cataloging-in-Publication Data

Blanke, David, 1961-
    Hell on wheels : the promise and peril of America's car
culture, 1900-1940 / David Blanke.
        p. cm. — (CultureAmerica)
    Includes bibliographical references and index.
    ISBN 978-0-7006-1515-5 (cloth : alk. paper)
        1. Automobiles—Social aspects—United States—
History—20th century. 2. Popular culture—United
States—History—20th century. 3. Traffic accident
victims—United States—History—20th century. I. Title.

    HE5623.B58 2007
    303.48'32097309041—dc22   2007006216

Printed in the United States of America
10 9 8 7 6 5 4 3 2 1

The paper used in this publication meets the minimum
requirements of the American National Standard for
Permanence of Paper for Printed Library Materials
Z39.48-1992.

IN MEMORY OF

Vanessa McMath Allen

Contents

Acknowledgments

While some researchers and writers are blessed by natural talent, I am blessed by generous, insightful, and (thankfully) honest colleagues. I relied most heavily on Pat Carroll, Anthony Quiroz, and Robert Wooster, three of my professional associates at Texas A&M University–Corpus Christi. In addition, James Carter, Erika Doss, Joel Eastman, Tim Gilfoyle, Alan Lessoff, Karal Ann Marling, Peter Moore, Harold Platt, and Virginia Scharff read and provided many useful suggestions at various stages throughout the research and writing of the book. Jason DuBose and Ceil Venable read portions of the work and offered additional insights. I extend my thanks to the anonymous reviewers commissioned by the University Press of Kansas for their perspective. Combined, these critiques and creative suggestions helped me to better understand my own work and to better explain auto accidents within the broader contours of American history. In addition, I owe Pat, Anthony, and Robert my deepest gratitude for their time, advice, and friendship over these years.

I greatly valued and benefited from the feedback provided at several professional panel discussions, including those sponsored by the Organization of American Historians, the American Historical Association, the Popular Culture/American Culture Association, and the International Conference on Transit, Transportation, and Mobility. Nancy Scott Jackson, Hilary Lowe, Kalyani Fernando, Susan McRory, and Susan Schott at the University Press of Kansas kept me on track throughout the long process of researching, writing, and finalizing the book. They also provided timely and sound advice that substantially improved the final result.

Institutional support from Texas A&M University–Corpus Christi was essential to completing the research and writing. It remains my pleasure to teach at a public university committed to excellence in both teaching and scholarship. I greatly appreciate the financial support provided to realize these goals. A generous University Research Grant contributed funds to conduct much of the early work. In addition, the College of Liberal Arts offered timely and consistent course releases, travel funds, and other assistance. As a member of the College of Liberal Arts, my efforts to complete this study were sustained by the college deans, Paul Hain and Richard Gigliotti. I commend and express my gratitude to Marti Beck and Jan Geyer for their patience and help in guiding me through the many administrative procedures needed to take full advantage of these opportunities. Institutional support was also provided through the Jeff and Mary Bell

Library at Texas A&M University–Corpus Christi. The interlibrary loan staff—including Fiona Hibbert, Adriana S. Tomelloso, Krystle Zambrano, and Amber Stansbury—performed distinguished service in filling literally hundreds of book and article requests and by tracking down these sources, sometime with only limited information. Ceil Venable, Jason DuBose, and Les Henne helped early in the study by assisting me in collecting bibliographic information. Similarly, I owe my thanks to the research and library staffs at the Texas State Archives and Library, the Center for American History at the University of Texas, the Library of Congress, the Denver Public Library, the Chicago Historical Society, and the Widener Library at Harvard University.

My very special thanks is offered to Mrs. Margaret Turnbull, who generously funded the Frantz History Endowment Fund for the History Area at Texas A&M University–Corpus Christi. Frantz funds were essential in completing this project and in securing the rights to reproduce many of the photographs contained within this text. Mrs. Turnbull's commitment to excellence in research and teaching has significantly enhanced the quality of public education for all of South Texas.

I again (and again) offer my thanks and love to my wife and best friend, Janet. I am also grateful for the love, humor, and patience shown by our two children, Benjamin and Alexander (and for the patience they *will* show their parents as both boys learn to drive).

Introduction

*The oasis of the tiny hotel was filled with twenty motorists from ten states.
At supper a Michigan professor sat beside a Portland banker. . . . Like all
wanderers since Ulysses, we sat by the fire and forgot the mud and told lies. We
boasted how fast we could travel and how few blow-outs we had and how we
invariably "put it all over these fresh traffic cops." A few days ago, in office or
shop or study, each of us had been reasonably prosaic and standardized and
modern and dull. We had turned into soldiers of fortune gathered at a tavern
of the Low Countries in the days of Marco Polo. . . . Not merely to Montana had
the autohoboes driven, but to chivalry rediscovered.*

    "Adventures in Automobumming: Want a Lift?"

    Sinclair Lewis, 1919[1]

*To George F. Babbitt, as to most prosperous citizens of Zenith, his motor car
was poetry and tragedy, love and heroism. The office was his pirate ship but the
car his perilous excursions ashore.*

    Babbitt, Sinclair Lewis, 1922[2]

With the possible exception of Charles Dickens, no author created as unsympathetic a view of the upper middle class as Sinclair Lewis did with George Babbitt. A well-heeled real estate broker, Babbitt confused his self-centered, consumer-directed life with heroism, his possessions with character, and his lack of civic curiosity with wisdom.[3] Automobiles symbolized his success. Babbitt took great satisfaction in being served by the "dirtiest and most skilled of motor mechanics," feeling "himself a person of importance, one whose name even busy garagemen remembered—not one of these cheap-sports flying around in flivvers," a nickname for the inexpensive Ford Model T. His driving was more than just transportation, it was conquest. After securing a cherished parking spot on the crowded, rush-hour streets of Zenith, Babbitt claimed another "virile adventure masterfully executed."[4]

Yet barely three years earlier, Sinclair Lewis had projected a much more positive view of the automobile's effect on America's citizenry. In a three-part series for the *Saturday Evening Post,* Lewis chronicled his "adventures" traveling across the United States in his own flivver. Not unlike his fictional character, Lewis translated the freedoms of the open road into a statement about the integrity of the driver. For him, motoring authenticated personal values, "those humble sterling virtues that renew one's faith" in American society. Automobiles reproduced the spirit of rugged frontier individualism, of heartfelt cooperation, of democratic utilitarianism, and of the liberating hidden hand of the marketplace. Using imagery he returned to later in *Babbitt,* Lewis believed that the automobile "brought back the age of joyous piracy." Headed toward the horizon with the wind in his hair, he forgot his feelings of being "prosaic and standardized and modern and dull."[5]

Lewis celebrated the way the car leveled social divisions. While Babbitt expressed pleasure in employing working-class mechanics, Lewis enjoyed interacting with America's diverse motorized fraternity. For the writer, independent and resourceful drivers were, like Jefferson's yeoman farmers, the nation's freest citizens. One couple, in particular, caught Lewis's eye:

> Though they were under fifty they had done their work. They had brought up children, who were married and independent. They had saved enough money for a stake in old age. Now they were seeing the world. . . . Whenever he became restless, said his wife, "Pa comes home and grins at me and he says 'Ma, let's throw the skillet in the Lizzie [Model T] and go some place,' and we start next morning and hike round for three months. . . . They could travel a thousand miles on twenty dollars. . . . They had wanderlust and they satisfied it. They had beaten the game of civilization. They were supreme philosophers and people in high-powered cars passed them by, unseeing.[6]

Those unable to see these virtues were, like Babbitt, blinded by their class and cultural biases. Lewis recalled, as he and his wife were rescued for the third time by a pair of friendly strangers, an unforgettable scene:

> While we were working . . . a big car with eight cylinders and much upholstery passed by. The driver looked bored, but the woman beside him was more than bored; her contemptuous stare showed resentment at having to witness three greasy men working over a cheap automobile. That was three years ago and the woman took less than three seconds in passing, but I have not forgotten her glance or ceased to be sorry for her. I have no doubt that she is doing well socially. . . . But it must hurt her so to have to go on living among common people.

Experiences such as these no doubt influenced Lewis as he gave birth to the fictional Babbitt.[7]

Sinclair Lewis was a gifted writer. The first American to win a Nobel Prize in literature, he published such works as *Main Street* (1920), *Babbitt* (1922), *Arrowsmith* (1925), *Elmer Gantry* (1927), and *Dodsworth* (1929). Yet in spite of these gifts, he was concerned that his artistry failed to capture the motivations of his contemporaries. Writing about *Babbitt* to his friend and critic, H. L. Mencken, Lewis worried, "The book is not altogether satire. I've tried like hell to keep the boob Babbitt from being merely burlesque—hard tho it is at times, when he gets to orating before the Boosters' Club lunches. I've tried to make him human and individual, not a type." Given his personal experiences behind the wheel, nowhere is this difficulty more evident than in Lewis's views of motoring.[8]

While the automotive freedoms and potential for positive social interaction struck Lewis favorably, we might be forgiven today if these expressions appear as "merely burlesque" desires of simpler times. The thought that the car provides anything more than basic transportation appears naive. In contrast to the first decades of twentieth century, driving today is more routine than recreation. According to one commuter, modern traffic is "a form of imprisonment . . . like being caught in a huge crowd that is forever surging toward a narrow exit."[9] Yet, while often true, such an analysis misses the intoxicating atmosphere of unbridled mobility, freedom, personal expression, and raw power that still energizes the automobile age.

Obviously, these positive qualities form the core of what many term America's "automotive love affair." Overused and overgeneralized, the cliché was never an accurate description of how or why Americans adopted the automobile. But the affection between Americans and their cars did exist and continues today. We grew more skeptical of the term as the high costs of automobility became clear. The ugly, auto-induced urban sprawl, the pollution, and the vulgar excesses of planned obsolescence all sapped our faith in the car as a significant other.

The most painful and direct cost of mass automobility is the toll in human lives. Between 1899 and 2003, nearly 3.2 million Americans died as a result of auto accidents. In 2001 alone, motor vehicles were the single leading cause of death for Americans between the ages of four and thirty-four, and the eighth leading cause of death for all ages.[10] Auto fatalities were an even larger component of *accidental* deaths. In 2001, there were 157,078 accidental deaths, classified into five categories: traffic related, firearms, poison, falls, and work related (Table 1). On any given day, one in four of these accident victims, otherwise healthy Americans who expected to survive the day, were killed as a result of automobile use. Excluding murders, suicides, and terrorist attacks, in 2001 this ratio was closer to two in five (39.7 percent) of all fatal accidents.

This book surveys the social, political, and cultural repercussions of automobile accidents from 1900 to 1940. A central theme of the work contends that the "automotive love affair" emerged as a very real, meaningful, and shared cultural response to driving. A second theme explores the growing civic tensions exposed by the new (yet deadly) freedoms of the car and the collective risk of mass automobility. The combination of these two forces—the love affair and auto accidents—influenced reformers and average citizens alike. Americans debated the meaning of risk and safety, of inevitable and avoidable accidents, and of perfectible engineer-

While Americans were clearly smitten by the automotive love affair, the cost proved high. (Denver Public Library, Western History Collection, Harry M. Rhoads, Rh-381)

ing and flawed human nature. In examining the ways Americans resolved these dilemmas, we see how a democratic society came to terms with the accidental freedoms of the modern age.

Contemporary scholars, such as Ulrich Beck and Anthony Giddens, contend that risk now holds a central place in defining modern Western societies. Beginning in the late 1960s, citizens in the most-developed regions of the globe began realizing their growing vulnerability to uncontrollable risks. While, in the abstract, risk has always defined human culture (to be alive is to face the risk of dying), modern risk is qualitatively different than the risks assumed by pioneering settlers, industrial laborers, first-responders, or countless others who (more or less) willfully assume physical danger. Today environmental pollution, urban crime, corporate downsizing, and new biological threats (such as HIV) act indiscriminately upon the wealthy and poor, men and women, gay and straight alike. Those whom society once trusted to mitigate risks—technical experts, big business, and bureaucratic state authorities—are now charged with complicity in generating these threats. In recent years, individual citizens have found new

Table 1. Accidental Deaths in the United States, 2001

Cause of Death	Total Deaths (Total deaths, not counting murders, suicides, and 9/11/01)	Percentage of All Accidental Deaths (Percentage not counting murders, suicides, and 9/11/01)
Accidental deaths	157,078	100
	(106,777)	(100)
Traffic related	42,443	27.0
	(42,443)	(39.7)
Firearms	29,573	18.8
	(1,360)	(1.3)
Poison	22,242	14.2
	(2,980)	(2.8)
Falls	15,764	10.0
	(15,764)	(14.8)
Work related	8,303	5.3
	(5,477)	(5.1)

Source: *National Vital Statistics Reports* 52, no. 3, September 18, 2003.
Note: In actuality, traffic-related accidental fatalities are even more common than these numbers might indicate. Consider that 95.4 percent of all deaths due to firearms and 86.6 percent of poisonings were the result of either a homicide or suicide; hardly "accidents" when at least one individual can clearly be seen as having the *intent* to cause harm. In addition, the 2,826 lives lost on September 11 were categorized as "work-related" fatal injuries (true for fire, police, ambulance, transit, and other emergency service personnel killed at the World Trade Center and Pentagon, but certainly not a part of the job description for most others). Removing these from the tally means that nearly two of every five fatal accidents in 2001 involved a motor vehicle. One paradoxical twist is that traffic accidents and falls can be—and no doubt are—used for suicidal or homicidal purposes.

and more empowering sources of information than these progressive guardians of knowledge. By forming political interest groups, joining nongovernmental organizations, or tapping into new media outlets and the internet, contemporary society is fundamentally restructuring itself through the new risk paradigm. Beck's 1992 publication, *Risk Society,* spawned a host of intriguing and potentially revolutionary questions about the nature of this new (post)modern culture and the fate of institutions like the family and the state and traditional social distinctions such as race, class, and gender. While not intended to test Beck's thesis, this text examines automobile accidents with the same ends in mind. How did Americans respond to the new and dangerous personal freedoms of mass automobility?[11]

Exploring this question is a complicated process, but one that is aided by an abundance of direct evidence. The book relies on three main types of primary sources: auto-related safety studies conducted by numerous private, municipal, state, and federal agencies; an extensive reservoir of published periodical literature, especially national circulation magazines and newspapers, that records the everyday experiences and expressions of typical drivers; and enumerations from private, state, and federal agencies that cataloged driving conditions and auto accident trends. Where possible, I focus on regions—such as the West or the state of Texas—that have not received as much attention in the existing literature. Still, the book hopes to describe a national phenomenon. Collectively, these sources show that American drivers, from 1900 to 1940, possessed clear and achievable safety goals. They spoke and acted forcefully to improve the nation's roads and highways, to pass reasonable legislation, to enforce these laws, and to educate those willing to learn about the dangers beyond the curbside. Their assumptions defined their successes, just as their biases aided in their failures.

In probing the interaction among driving, safety, and reform, the study exposes a host of shared cultural values that define the automobile age. One of these is the deep and lasting sense of romantic freedom associated with driving. The merger of man and machine reanimated Americans' sense of themselves as pioneers poised to discover brave new worlds of motion, speed, and power. Even today, few activities provide as much raw freedom of choice as driving. The temporary excitement behind the wheel can rescue us from bureaucratized boredom, reclaim a sense of youthful adventure and vitality, and relieve our frustrations over society's many rules and regulations. Television advertisers and manufacturers rely on these same hopes and passions to sell their newest models. Ironically, this highly individualistic and liberating potential, captured in films as diverse as *Rebel without a Cause, American Graffiti,* and *The Blues Brothers,* supports strong, shared, and consensual ideals—our collective faith in technological progress, rugged individualism, and in a unique national character. These feelings are made manifest in the motorcar. It gives us a visceral confirmation that we are "Americans."

A second powerful and seemingly shared quality of car culture pertains to the public nature of driving. The roadway is a unique physical *place,* a sort of modern meeting hall where the public tests, refines, and validates its own rules and assumptions. The president of the American Automobile Association wrote in 1906 that "it is quite generally understood that roads are for the common use of all and not the private property of a few rich enthusiasts." These rights, he continued, "come to him through no statute law. The doctrine that streets are for the public is a part of our common law and is so old that we may safely hazard a guess that it is coeval with the existence of highways themselves." The automobile made the streets a place where Americans reexamined public rights in very new, exciting, and dangerous ways.[12]

Americans are familiar today with the social tableaux of the road. Much as before, the highways remain a contested terrain, one of the few physical locations where citizens are forced to meet each other stripped of the advantages of class, gender, race, or ethnicity. Regardless of whether one is behind the wheel

A trolley, pedestrians, and automobiles meet on Arapahoe and 14th Streets in downtown Denver, Colorado, c. 1920. (Denver Public Library, Western History Collection, Joe Langer, X-18355)

of a Lexus SUV or a '71 Pinto, drivers must act in accordance with the law and the expectations of others. Propelled by hundreds of horsepower, failure to do so is both discourteous and potentially lethal. Through Americans' physical experiences "on the road," drivers learn what they expect of each other. Ultimately it is this sense of trust, this code of civic morality, that gives motorists the confidence to repeatedly put their lives on the line. Failure to abide by these norms—through drunk or overly aggressive driving, cutting in and out of lanes, or a willful disregard for another's right-of-way—was frequently cited as the leading cause of auto accidents before 1940, and is still today.

Finally, overlaying the story of early auto use and safety is a series of compelling and powerful contrasts. The clash between risk and safety is the most important contradiction. Risk is a collective measurement that registers common threats to all of society. Safety, by contrast, is a personal assessment of danger to an individual. Following the terrorist attacks of 2001, for example, a series of measures were taken (such as a heightened presence of armed guards at airports or blockades around public buildings) that purportedly made many feel safer while arguably doing little to actually reduce the risk of such attacks. Quitting smoking lowers the statistical risk of many serious diseases but may not make the reformed former smoker feel any safer from these threats. Similarly, while lowering the collective risk of driving decreases the probability of accidental death, it does not necessarily change how safe one feels behind the wheel. Both risk and safety are "constructed" and both operate differently within the context of automobile accidents and reform.

Comparable contrasts abound. Where, for example, is the dividing line between the personal liberty of motorists and their social obligation to drive safely? How much control should society exert in enforcing traffic rules and how much of this power resides within the driver? Should there be a traffic cop on every street corner or simply harsher penalties for those who cause accidents? What responsibilities do free market providers have for public safety and why is it possible to purchase cars that can easily exceed the maximum speed limit or buy radar detectors designed solely to circumvent the law? Even our understanding of an auto accident is split into powerful contrasts. Are collisions the inevitable by-product of overcrowded streets or the avoidable sins of certain accident-prone drivers? These dichotomies place great importance on the personal decisions made by millions of individual drivers. Auto advocate Thomas Russell believed the driver, not the pedestrian or the police officer or the court system, was "obliged to take notice of the conditions before him and if it is apparent that by any particular method of proceeding he is liable to work an injury, it is *his duty* to adopt and follow some other or safer method."[13]

Throughout this period, personal character figured prominently in ascribing blame. By the late 1920s, reformers proved more willing to look into the human psyche to find the misanthropic "accident prone" driver than to blame the new and emerging social contract of the road. Harlan Hines, an educational psychologist at the University of Cincinnati, believed that the car could transform "perfectly normal persons" into "high-class morons." To Hines, it was the context of driving itself that defined risk and spawned recklessness. If "one is driving within the speed limit," Hines offered, the law-abiding motorist "may get tired of having so many cars go around him, and start out to do a little passing on his own account. Others can go fast and not be molested, why not he?" Appropriately Hines warned, "the real danger lies in the fact that our spells of confused thinking may become habitual."[14]

In many ways, reformers acted primarily to check these habitual episodes of confused thinking. Their collective approach, termed the "three E's" by the National Safety Council, established engineering, education, and enforcement as the fundamental tools of America's safety community. Experts and bureaucratic agencies designed better roads and cars, professional educators certified that young drivers acquired the appropriate values and skills before taking the wheel, and enforcement agencies tried to swiftly and fairly hold citizens to the law. Central to each was a heightened sense of personal responsibility; an acknowledgment that if "confused thinking" was not controlled in every driver then the roadways would devolve into anarchy.

Table 2. Automobile Fatalities, 1916–1966

Year	Auto Fatalities per 10,000 Vehicles	Auto Fatality Rate per 100 Million Vehicle Miles of Travel	Auto Fatalities per 100,000 People
1916	27.2	30.0	6.7
1926	10.0	15.8	18.9
1936	13.4	14.3	29.7
1946	9.7	9.4	23.9
1956	6.1	6.1	23.7
1966	5.5	5.5	27.1

Source: John B. Rae, *The Road and Car in American Life* (Cambridge, MA: MIT Press, 1971), 345; U.S. Department of Transportation, National Highway Traffic Safety Administration, "Motor Vehicle Traffic Fatalities and Fatality Rates," July 23, 2003.

On the one hand, this approach and these assumptions proved useful. The technical improvements and standardization of roads, laws, and the mechanics of the automobile significantly lowered collective risk over the decades (Table 2). Between 1916 and 1966, auto fatality rates per ten thousand vehicles and per one hundred million vehicle miles of travel (or VMT, a standard measurement of auto risk) fell by over 80 percent. But other fatality rates did not improve. The ratio of deaths per one hundred thousand people, for example, actually increased. Clearly, reform pursued in this way proved capable of correcting the *physical* deficiencies of streets and vehicles (deaths per car and per mile driven) but largely ineffective in changing the *behavior* of many motorists. The new social contract of the modern risk society remained unsigned.

As a result, the story of automobile safety is not solely one of progressive reformers, engineers, educators, and enforcement officials. Rather, it is bound by the individual opinions and behaviors expressed on the roads, in the marketplace, and through popular culture. Personal narratives and collective assumptions, such as those seen in the writing of Sinclair Lewis, remain essential in reconstructing this highly contingent atmosphere. Artist Grant Wood captured American' nervous gamble with disaster in his 1934 painting *Death on Ridge Road* (cover). Wood, an admirer of Lewis and the genius behind *American Gothic,* transferred the familiar anxieties of the car into a second visual masterpiece. The personal promise and perils of automobility are evident in the slow-moving yet dependable farm vehicles and the impatient yet exciting touring car, eager to pass. The contrasts among the geometric regularity of the countryside, the cartoonish swerving of the motorists, and the expressionistic mayhem of a potential collision (*will* the vehicles collide? which ones?) underscore the thousand of individual decisions that defined America's car culture.[15]

This book traces these thematic elements over an extended chronological arc. While generally following the narrative of events, the text approaches the challenge of auto safety in a particular sequence and makes certain theoretical assumptions. The first two chapters establish the broad context of automotive history and American life, from 1900 to 1940. The function, efficiency, and competitive setting of the country's transportation system during these years provided the internal combustion automobile certain historical advantages. Moreover, census data and numerous auto accident studies identified the composition of America's driving public: who drove cars, how they drove, and what types of accidents occurred in the first four decades of the twentieth century. I rely on a technology systems approach in these two chapters to better understand and place into context the rise of automobile transit, the auto industry, and the driving public. The purpose is to isolate some of these variables before examining the cultural response to cars and the accident crisis.

Chapters 3 and 4 define and explore the qualities of the automotive love affair. Grounded in notions of freedom, excitement, equality, and progress, the love affair concept proved highly resilient. Equally important, the normative qualities of the love affair made the concept useful as both an enticement for "good" drivers as well as a penalty for "bad" ones. Where many first-time motorists used the positive feelings of delight and amazement to justify their place as progressive citizens, subsequent generations used these same qualities to profile the motorized scofflaw—the "motor moron" or "flivverboob" who made driving dangerous. The book strives to show, through multiple perspectives, that these cultural values were present, well recognized, and generally accepted by a sizeable percentage of the driving public.

Chapters 5 and 6 trace the path of auto safety reform, the limits of these efforts, and reformers' inability to establish collective solutions to effectively curb dangerous behavior. These reforms established firm engineering, education, and enforcement standards as the backbone of this country's response to the threat of auto accidents. Here, the rise of institutional bureaucracies, such as the state bureau of motor vehicles, specialized traffic police squads and traffic courts, and numerous other safety "experts," mirrors the social dynamics first proposed by Max Weber over a century ago. Broadly speaking, Weber theorized that, in a modern society, citizens ceded power and cultural authority to bureaucratic experts in return for the rational, legal, and generally middle-class order that bureaucracies spawn. Weber held that "the parallel development of capitalism and bureaucracy is no accident; for modern Western capitalism rests on rational *calculation*. It therefore urgently needs a system of public administration and of justice where workings are predictable, like the workings of a machine." To be progressive, in Weber's time and over the span of this study, citizens accepted and strove to be part of this rational bureaucracy. In today's postmodern age we no longer have a choice.[16]

The book's concluding chapter examines these residual tensions between drivers and the safety bureaucracy they created and brings the question of auto

Automotive freedoms included easier access to urban shopping, dining, and entertainment, 1927. (Denver Public Library, Western History Collection, Harry M. Rhoads, Rh-77)

safety into a more contemporary focus. Using the theory of Ulrich Beck, the chapter compares earlier approaches to "perfect" the driver and rid the roadway of the "accident prone" with those in use today. Our "zero tolerance" of drunk driving, legally mandated safety specifications, and willingness to hold manufacturers responsible for safety at any speed contrast sharply with America's initial driving culture. Using Beck as a model, the public construction of the automotive love affair again looms large.

As with all historical accounts that examine the preventable loss of human life, the story of automotive safety touches on millions of personal tragedies. Indeed, statistics show that most American families will experience the direct financial, physical, and emotional loss associated with an accident. For the lucky ones, the encounter gives them a second chance; the opportunity to modify their behavior, to increase the odds that they or their loved ones might survive a future collision. For far too many others the encounter is sudden, irreversible, and tragic. This book is dedicated to Vanessa McMath Allen, who died in a single-car accident in 2003. But it is also offered to her parents, Charlie and Gwyn McMath, two friends and dedicated public educators. If their daughter's death is an unwanted symbol of the random horror of automobile accidents, then their lifelong commitment to public education is also a symbol of hope. The shared obligations of citizenship, civic trust, and social responsibility form the core of any reasonable solution to the accident crisis. If these civic concepts have any meaning to the vast majority of Americans it is largely due to the work of thousands of public educators like the McMaths. Charlie and Gwyn's grief joins a century-long chorus of lament. What have these experiences meant to America? How have we changed as a result and at what cost to our civic and personal liberties? As this book demonstrates, America's first generation of motorists earnestly and repeatedly engaged these questions. Their responses were contingent upon their times yet, just as surely, they inform our own.

1

The Car and American Life, 1900–1940

Auto camping, as the name implies, combines the freedom of driving with the romance of camping and was once an immensely popular recreation. In the early years, drivers stocked their cars with basic outdoor gear, such as tents, pots and pans, canned food, and fishing poles, and took to the open road. They pitched camps near wooded stretches of road, at local schoolhouses, or even in unsuspecting farmers' orchards (which afforded "free" firewood and, if lucky, an ample supply of fresh fruit). Later, municipalities established low-cost auto camps that, for about a quarter, supplied basic amenities such as bathrooms and running water. They soon added cabins, carports, and electric lighting. Entrepreneurs founded the commercial motel from these modest beginnings.[1]

One of the most famous autocamping excursions in America began July 21, 1921, near Bedford Springs, Pennsylvania. Automobile magnate Henry Ford and tire manufacturer Harvey S. Firestone, accompanied by their wives, three sons, and two daughters-in-law, began the trip nostalgically with a hearty "farm dinner" at the "old Firestone homestead." The two country boys who had made good then traveled via chauffeured limousine to the Cumberland Mountains for ten days of wood chopping, fishing, riding, cooking, hiking, and sleeping under the stars. The caravan met up with Thomas Edison, near Hagerstown, Maryland, and made camp July 22. The Wizard of Menlo Park expressed a desire to roam the "wildest sections" of the Blue Ridge and must have looked with skepticism at the "two automobile trucks containing complete camping paraphernalia" which accompanied the Ford-Firestone party. Edison was not the last to join the caravan. President Warren Harding and his secretary drove from Washington to join them on the afternoon of the twenty-third. The seventy-five-mile trip consumed nearly four hours of the President's time, although the *New York Times* reported he arrived "in his accustomed speedy way."[2]

Harding was a last-minute replacement for the late John Burroughs, the noted naturalist and one of the original "quartet of celebrated men" who regularly autocamped together. Perhaps the loss of Burroughs muted Edison's enthusiasm, for the inventor received limited attention from the press. Firestone fared little better. The press portrayed him as a typical, high-strung American business executive—dashing about tightening knots, straightening woodpiles, building and extinguishing fires—biologically incapable of relaxation. Henry Ford, by contrast, emerged as the darling of the reporter pool. They delighted in his enjoyment of the full spectrum of outdoor activities, from the sweaty pleasures of chopping wood to peaceful reflection beside the campfire. Already a popular folk hero, Ford, in turn, gratified the press's need for a good story. When asked to crank the starter of a nearby flivver, he informed the cameramen that the modern Model T was now equipped with a self-starter. Directed to "crank it anyhow," the proud father of the universal car grinned and obligingly bent to the task. The cameras clicked approvingly.

The location of the camp was idyllic. Known as "the Island," the ground was level within a gently valley, shaded by mature oak and sycamore trees, and bounded by a small stream and the peaceful Licking River. Fifteen miles from the Antietam battlefield, reporters guessed that "few except the natives" had seen the site "since the days of the 60's, when Unionists and Confederates operated back and forth across the Potomac in sanguinary conflicts. Doubtless the legends that they made their camps also where the President is sleeping are true." Combined, the setting and participants provided ideal propaganda for the many municipal chambers of commerce and auto clubs around the country who sought tourists' autocamping dollars. The story, which ran in most American dailies, smacked of local boosterism. The camp was described as "one of those secluded and lovely spots that abound in this country, but never are known to the motorist hurtling over the macadam from town to town. . . . No place could be imagined farther away from the strife and worry of Washington."[3]

As this last reference suggests, the president's adventures were the primary focus of the national press. One can't but feel pity for Harding, surrounded as he was by the *Übermenschen* of American science and industry. The published reports show him for what he was, an earnest yet unimaginative and completely average national politician making the most of a photo opportunity. While Harding attempted activities "that fitted the wood-chopping standard" of the day, he lasted less than thirty minutes on horseback and took only a few half-hearted whacks with the axe before turning his duties over to the Bunyanesque Ford. When the moment called for a politician, such as meeting dignitaries from Hagerstown or visiting a local country store (where Harding bought candy for a blue-eyed five-year-old girl) the president eagerly assumed the mantle of his office. Still, journalists reported that Harding "did not want to read a newspaper, like Mr. Edison, or think like Mr. Ford, or wander around the camp like Mr. Firestone. He wanted to go to sleep."[4]

The attention given to the Harding autocamping trip, at that time and by subsequent historians, is predictable. On one level it shows how four high-profile men and their families used the car for relaxation and gratification. On another level, the story is a powerful metaphor for the changes wrought by the automobile. Historian Warren Belasco argues that auto camping revealed a new "interface between business and culture, a material embodiment of tourist dreams of community, independence, equality, and spontaneity." Early drivers saw much

Auto Campers on the road to Taos, New Mexico, 1910. (Denver Public Library, Western History Collection, H. S. Poley, P-1411)

the same convergence. As one auto tourist remarked, in 1923, the "immense popularity of motor camping is easy to understand when one realizes that this pastime is romantic, healthful, educative, and at the same time economical."[5]

Indeed, these men seemed the physical embodiment of these four qualities. Like actors in a Greek drama, each possessed such obvious and well-publicized characteristics that their contemporaries might be forgiven for seeing the excursion as a modern American epic. Thomas Edison stood as the symbol of progressive education. Much like the car, the inventor harnessed science and engineering to improve the quality of daily life. Firestone was the manifestation of America's robust industry: broad shouldered, young, confident, with a dash of urban excess. Ford represented the iron laws of industrial capitalism: pragmatic, Darwinian, and unforgiving. The stentorian Harding acted as the guardian of America's romantic imagery. The soaring political ideals of republicanism seemed to be given physical form through the automobile—so much so that even a skeptical literary mind, such as that of Sinclair Lewis, could find few words other than freedom and independence to describe the experience.

Naturally, such unconditional adoration for the car did not survive into the modern era. While the costs associated with automobility were slow to be tolled, their ugly reality could not be avoided for long. Indeed, as early as 1921, daily published accounts of the dead and wounded acted as a Greek chorus predicting the fall of these Olympians. Appropriately, a second front-page *New York Times* essay, running next to that of Harding's travails in the woods of Hagerstown, detailed a series of horrific automobile accidents in and around Manhattan. Instead of individual freedom and romantic adventure, here the car represented recklessness, immaturity, and a willful disregard for the safety of others. Three young people died in a New Jersey crash. A four-year-old girl died in the arms of her father in another. The *Times* did not hide its indignation at the driver of the first accident. Intoxicated, he took the wheel from his sober brother. In this case, the car magnified the shoddy temperament of a man "determined to show that he was able to navigate the big machine. . . . [he] threw the gears into high and let her out for all the fast car was worth." It is precisely this separation between the two reports—the joy and self-congratulatory pride of the Ford-Firestone party and the bitter frustration in response to reckless citizens wreaking indiscriminate havoc—that defines the impulsive relationship between Americans and their cars.[6]

Context, of course, remains the key to understanding the burgeoning love affair, the deadly cost of automobility, and the ways that Americans perceived these events. Leading auto historian Clay McShane wrote that "One must examine the ways in which Americans discovered the car, and dreamed about its potential. . . . Only through this framework can one understand the pattern of automobility that emerged." This chapter looks at three key aspects of the automobile in American life to establish this broader context. The first is an understanding of the car as a technology that was introduced and developed within the specific context of the times. The second examines the relative success of the personal passenger automobile in comparison to existing transit options, most notably fixed rail. The third looks to the growth and development of the automobile industry in the United States and its effect on mass automobility.

A vast body of scholarship explores the multiple contingencies that led to the specific technological form of the automobile, the ways that the car bested other modes of mass transit, and the exponential growth of the American automobile industry that sustained a mass market. The work of McShane, James J. Flink, John B. Rae, and others establishes how the automobile bred a new and unique "technology system" within the United States, one that allowed for individual transportation but which also spawned new collective assumptions about life, risk, and citizenship in modern America.[7]

A technology system describes the complex relationship between mechanical innovations and the ways that human society makes use of these tools. The central question of such a system is whether modern and sophisticated implements determine new social patterns or whether existing human activities mold these tools to fit existing needs. Given the complexity of technology systems (and the vagaries of the historical record), most scholars wisely fall somewhere in the middle. Flink reasons that automobility reconciled these contradictory explanations "to achieve a social order based upon technical efficiency in which traditional cultural values would be preserved and enhanced." In short, we adopted *and* adapted to the automobile.[8]

"Automobility" was coined in the 1960s to describe the collective structures, cultures, and beliefs that pervade mass automobile use and includes the car, the road, manufacturers, the service sector, regulators, car owners, and drivers. The term focuses as much attention on the changing *consciousness* of the driving public as on the innovators, manufacturers, engineers, and reformers who hoped to shape public behavior.[9]

Understanding the car in systemic terms offers several advantages. First, it reduces the natural tendency to see change simply within the context of a specific national or regional identity. While American drivers justified their actions and beliefs based on their own national history and ideology, the automobile was flexible enough to fit within many national models. Advocates of the car used similar arguments on both sides of the Atlantic—efficient transportation, individualism, culture, health—to justify their passion. An early French *chauffeur* believed his countrymen were "seized" by the car, "filled with enthusiasm, with joy. . . . [at the] simple and naive pleasure of being in the midst of power, of strength. One participates in it. . . . One believes in it." The conventional wisdom today supports a view that while the car explained a good deal of modern American history it was "central to the history of [all] advanced capitalist countries in the twentieth century." Similarly, scholars of the American car have found that while northeastern urban locals were the first to begin changing to suit the needs of the motor car, all other regions of the country soon participated and contributed to the debate concerning its use and meaning. Thinking of the car as part of a broader technology system dissolves some of the mental barriers that naturally arise when comparing the United States to Germany, for example, or Ohio to Texas.[10]

Secondly, a systemic approach to the car makes it easier to assign meaningful dates to the story of the automobile. Rather than abide by subjective events— such as the founding of the Ford Motor Company or the first national conference on highway safety—the history of the automobile as a technology system reflects, first and foremost, a changing worldview. James Flink, in his essay "Three Stages of Automobile Consciousness," provides a chronology faithful to this approach. Americans before 1910 saw the car in terms of its limitless potential and pure individualism. Cheaper, faster, and more reliable than existing forms of mass transit, the car required no governmental assistance or large corporate investments to solve the problems of urban overcrowding and mass transit. In these early years car use was limited to a small number of rather wealthy and overwhelmingly urban individuals. The device appeared experimental and fragile. It was manufactured by hundreds of U.S. and European firms of varying quality and, generally, was very different than the vehicle people use today.[11]

In Flink's second phase, from 1910 until World War II, car use expanded dramatically and Americans fully accommodated themselves to an auto-based culture on a massive scale. In this stage, which is the focus of this text, the country willfully displaced entrenched customs, values, laws, and behaviors about individual and social responsibility to make room for the (increasingly deadly) freedoms of the car. As one 1915 writer suggested, the universal car "became first a reality and then a necessity—not a luxury, for it has taken its place with other utilities and inventions that have long been regarded as things which one could not do without." Conditions in the United States, including a high per capita income, a relatively equitable distribution of wealth, and vast geographic size, made mass utilization of the car possible. But it was the opening and unique operations of Ford Motor Company's Highland Park plant in 1910 that made the automobile a reasonable necessity.

By 1920, the effect of these changes became obvious. That year Americans registered more than 9.2 million motor vehicles. One automobilist marveled that the car had made "America one great crawling continent, as if it were inhabited by some lively and fast-moving beetles migrating hither and thither with no sense of direction, and no apparent community of interest. . . . As we slept in the shade of the gas pumps we wondered when America had had time to grow." While Flink's third phase, beginning after World War II, falls outside of the scope of this study, it too looks to the ways Americans made use of the automobile rather than relying on arbitrary dates to pace the history of the car in American life. Again, taking a technology systems approach clarifies rather than confuses the key issues influencing adoption.[12]

Finally, considering automobility as a technology system places proper emphasis on the cultural conditions that permitted universal automotive use. The period from 1900 to 1920 saw profound changes to many everyday technologies. Writing in 1936, one essayist marveled how the "generation now in its fifties has witnessed such changes that it is difficult to believe that there is much which can be added. The telephone, electric lights, sewerage, automobile, wireless, radio, all of these things which we accept now as a matter of fact have only come into general usage, to say the least, within the easy memory of those of us close to the half century mark." There was an equally profound contempt for those unwilling to embrace these changes. One recent scholar marveled at the high expectations of progressives and their "stunningly broad agenda that ranged well beyond the control of big business, the amelioration of poverty, and the purification of politics to embrace the transformation of gender relations, the regeneration of the home, the disciplining of leisure and pleasure, and the establishment of segregation." Americans' faith in science, technology, rational bureaucracies, and the marketplace to meet these challenges, like the popular adoration showered on men like Edison, Firestone, and Ford, was unprecedented.[13]

The car was understood fully within the context of progress and modernity and drivers quickly absorbed these values. The *President's Research Committee on Social Trends,* published in 1933, acknowledged that the "popular expression of 'hop in' has more than surface meaning; it typifies a state of mind." In the Teens and Twenties, motorists saw themselves in the vanguard of a brave new world. It was no coincidence that Aldous Huxley's futuristic novel of the same name elevated the appearance of Henry Ford's production line over the birth of Jesus as the seminal moment in Western Civilization. "Before Ford" and "After Ford" replaced BC and AD as the standard reference point for measuring historic change.[14]

The greatest challenge in understanding the car as a technology system is in appreciating the many contingencies of its history. As McShane shows, for example, the development of paved city streets was contingent upon urban planning, public health, and municipal regulations against the steam boiler. These events occurred within broad sociological contexts that were only partially related to individual transit yet had a profound influence on the car's ability to meet this need. Auto safety was equally relativistic, pursued by many groups with conflicting agendas.[15]

The place to begin reconstructing America's early car culture is with the automobile itself, the "definitive industrial and artistic expression of the modern age." The American dream machine was an immigrant, born in Europe. While designers on both sides of the Atlantic had theorized of a self-propelled vehicle, it was the Belgian mechanic Jean-Joseph Etienne Lenoir who built the first internal combustion engine in 1863. Others, such as Nicholas Otto, Gottlieb Daimler, William Maybeck, Karl Benz, Alphonse Beau de Roches, and Emile Constant Levassor, improved the performance and efficiency of both the engine and chassis so that, by 1895, a strong yet still small automobile market existed in England, Germany, and especially France. The basic design of the modern car, with the engine placed in front of the occupants and power transferred to the rear axle (the so-called *Systeme Panhard,* for the French manufacturing firm of Panhard and Lavassor) emerged before most Americans ever saw one in action. By 1900, half of all automobiles registered in the United States were European imports.[16]

The design of the car was never purely functional. Image and appearance were critical to closing the sale with wealthy sophisticates. In those early years, design elements focused on social graces: elegance, taste, and refinement. British firms, such as Rolls-Royce, Jaguar, and Bentley, conserved the fine carriage-making heritage of Great Britain. The more modern German and Italian designers, led by Mercedes-Benz and Alfa Romeo, emphasized speed and power. Bright colors, dramatic lines, extensive chrome piping and grillwork gave the impression of both muscle and loveliness. French designers, such as Louis Delage and Emile Delahaye, and the Milanese Ettore Bugatti endeavored to create custom-built works of art. These cars sold for thousands of dollars then and are nearly priceless today.[17]

With low overhead and surging demand, automobile assembly and repair shops proliferated across the United States. (Denver Public Library, Western History Collection, L. C. McClure, McC-4093)

Early American car designers, such as those at Cadillac, Duesenberg, Stutz, Packard, and Pierce-Arrow, matched the craftsmanship and detail of European automobiles but never aimed for high art. The top end of the American market projected a sense of prosperity and seriousness but with a flair for the sporting driver. Early model names included the Gentlemen's Speedy Roadster, the Success, and the Playboy. In later decades, these impressions were given substance by powerful engines and graceful design. The 1935 Duesenberg SJ "boat-tail speedster," for example, featured a supercharged 8-cylinder, 320-horsepower engine capable of accelerating to 100 miles per hour in only seventeen seconds. It more than justified the popular expression of describing something extraordinary as a "Duesey."[18]

For most consumers, however, the choices ranged from the comforting dependability of the large suppliers to the irregularity of lesser-known brands. By 1908, there were 253 domestic producers. Most of these firms, before 1910, were best described as assemblers of the multiple components manufactured by independent suppliers and sold through independent dealers. Liquidity and cash flow, the bane of any small business, were less of a problem because, in the words of one auto executive, "drafts against finished cars" provided by retailers "could be cashed as rapidly as the bills from parts makers came in." High demand, low production rates, and liberal credit arrangements kept start-up costs modest and made entry into the market relatively easy for entrepreneurs.[19]

While Ford Motor Company was properly credited with producing a profitable low-end automobile, many firms worked to build a cheap, mechanically simple, and reliable product. In addition to the Ford Model T (1908), serviceable and low-cost "runabouts" included the Curved Dash Olds (1901), the Buick Model 10 (1907), and the Chevrolet "490" (1915). Indeed, one early auto historian found that, even if "one takes the Ford figures out," low-cost vehicles represented anywhere from half to more than four-fifths of new car sales between 1912 and 1916. Where sales for cars ranging from around $2,275 to $4,775 (best understood as moderate to expensive prices, for truly elite autos listed for well over $5,000) made up almost half of the market in 1906, in ten years they accounted for less than 2 percent of all purchases. By 1916, cars selling for less than $675 constituted more than half of the total. Before the general availability of improved roadways, around 1920, these high-axled, stiff-riding motorized buggies were the most dependable way for the average American to enjoy automobility.[20]

The principal early variable in car design was the propulsion system. Early auto engineers disagreed over which system was best: steam, electric, or internal combustion. Electric cars, called "juicers," were clean, quiet, odorless, and easy to start. They had a touring range of about 50 to 75 miles per charge and traveled at a top speed of about 25 miles per hour. The batteries were large (adding nearly 1,000 pounds of dead weight), expensive, needed to be recharged daily, and had only a three-year life span. While electrics were costly, their ease of operation, status, and functionality as an urban runabout made them the ideal choice for wealthy female drivers. Ironically, the introduction of the electric self-starter, in 1912, eliminated one of the most vexing problems of the internal combustion engine: the need for appreciable physical strength to crank the motor. Additional gains in speed, comfort, and ease of use in the gasoline-powered machines led to an endless cycle of comparable "disappointments" with the slower advancements of the electric car. Technological improvements "created a moving target" of consumer expectations that the juicers failed to hit. The persistent limitations of battery storage and high cost sustained the public's view that the electric vehicle was a "technological failure."[21]

Steam power carried an even a greater historical burden. Plans for individual steam locomotion date back to the late eighteenth century. By the 1890s, steam-powered automobiles were easy to make, relatively inexpensive, technically simple, and powerful. The Stanley Steamer "Rocket" traveled at 127.66 miles per hour on a closed course in 1906. Kerosene, which was cheaper than gasoline, fueled the steam boiler, which came to full power after about twenty minutes. The critical and ultimately insurmountable technological problem facing the steamer was weight. The heavy load of fuel, water, and boiler ate away the engine's efficiency

A woman rides in an electric automobile (at left) while two share a gasoline-powered automobile (at right), c. 1910. Women constituted up to 20 percent of the driving public. (Denver Public Library, Western History Collection, Harry M. Rhoads, Rh-655)

(which was already compromised because the heat was generated outside the engine; internal combustion conserves this energy to a far greater extent) and made transit on the muddy American roads even harder. As with electrics, there was an ironic twist leading to the ill fate of the steam-powered passenger car. McShane shows that the early appearance of steamers, relative to electrics and internal combustion models, actually produced a competitive disadvantage for steam-powered autos. The fear of boiler explosions and live steam exhaust somehow seemed more frightening than more traditional problems of animal-powered vehicles. Moreover, residents were initially unwilling to cede control of the public streets to elite motorists, who alone had the financial resources to acquire steam automobility. City after city banned the steam car, drying up consumer enthusiasm and venture capital alike. McShane thus surmises that this early "public suppression was more important than mechanical inefficiency in explaining the failure of steamers."[22]

The gasoline-powered internal combustion engine had more than these contingent advantages in its favor, however. The device was anywhere between three and five times more efficient than steam or electric, allowing for much greater power and range of travel. The abundant supply of petroleum products, particularly after the 1901 Spindletop strike near Beaumont, Texas, which dropped the price of a barrel of crude oil to less than a nickel, further enhanced the gasoline-powered engine. Moreover, the early focus by European designers on internal combustion gave American mechanics a decided technical advantage in producing a reliable and inexpensive engine. The learning curve was substantially shorter than for its electric and steam rivals. Finally, by 1900, the public's acceptance of individual automobility, bought so dearly by the early steamers, lessened opposition to the noisy, new devices.[23]

A minor but bothersome problem for the internal combustion engine was the patent held by George B. Selden. In 1895, Selden patented an 1872 design for the 2-cycle, gasoline-powered internal combustion engine. As Flink noted, granting the license to Selden was "the most absurd action in the history of patent law." McShane justly calls Selden a "legal parasite." He never developed a fully functioning automobile using his engine yet demanded royalties from all who relied on internal combustion, even those who powered their cars with the Otto 4-cycle engine.[24] In 1899 the patent was sold to the Electric Vehicle Company, which charged a 1.25 percent royalty on all internal combustion motors. In 1903, the patent users formed the Association of Licensed Automobile Manufacturers (ALAM) to control competition in the increasingly promising automotive industry. After ALAM denied Henry Ford the use of the patent, Ford sued. He and his codefendants won in the U.S. Circuit Court eight years later. The Selden patent was considered binding only for the outdated 2-stroke engine. While the patent challenge had little long-term effect on the industry, it generated tremendous public goodwill for Ford, casting the uncompromising millionaire as defender of the "little man" and enemy of "restrictive trusts" such as ALAM.[25]

While internal combustion won out over the competing power plants, operating an early gas-powered vehicle still challenged the timid. Early ignition and engine timing systems were crudely and manually set by the driver. Both novice and expert drivers experienced frequent back-fires, stalls, sudden stops, and smoky accelerations. Simply maintaining forward momentum required hard work. Stopping in an emergency depended wholly on one's trained reflexes. In 1908, the veteran automobile essayist C. H. Claudy advised nervous first-time drivers when faced with an emergency to just "kick both pedals hard and jam down the brake lever" rather than "think about it first."[26]

There was a lot to think about. A typical driver needed to manipulate separate levers that controlled the spark (speed) and throttle (power), a hand brake, a shifter, and three pedals (clutch, a second brake, and the carburetor). Downhill driving was particularly difficult, for one needed to maintain control and continue to feed the proper mixtures of gas, spark, and air, without putting too much strain on the brakes and engine. One driver thought the "Ford charioteer" looked much like a man "smitten by the Charleston," a popular modern dance of young people.

> He steps on the low pedal. He releases this and lets it snap in high while he steps on the brake pedal. When he fears this is beginning to heat, he tramps on the reverse or else applies the emergency brake until it begins to scream

like a damned soul. Then he pushes down on the low speed pedal and begins all over again. By the time he has reached the foot of the descent . . . his machine, which has threatened, all the way down, to get away from him, smells like a fire in a tannery.

In addition, the average driver had to remain cognizant of the mechanical needs of the device, including the levels and temperature of oil, water, lubricants, and, of course, gasoline. Tire life was limited, often less than a hundred miles, and required the removal of the entire wheel. Before the Model T, it was not unusual for the early automobilist to employ a full-time chauffeur just to maintain and operate the complex new gadget.[27]

These burdensome conditions set the tone for early public perceptions of auto safety. It was not the poor streets, the lack of standardized rules, or the primitive cars that were faulted, but rather the "ill-prepared" driver. The public saw those unwilling—or, more than likely, financially unable—to acquire the necessary competencies to operate a car as irresponsible. Such an "ignorant driver" was "a menace, not only to the safety of the public, but also to that of his passengers. . . . there is no longer any excuse for his ignorance." One early driving instruction manual argued that "no man should attempt to drive a car of any size until he has informed himself pretty fully on its details of construction and methods of control." Individual drivers, not the public-at-large, had the primary responsibility to insure safety on the motorized streets.[28]

Concerns over technological ignorance took on normative qualities that had long-term consequences for U.S. car culture and auto safety. One of the most powerful of these was the belief that good driving reflected a man's progressive worthiness. If progress meant the effective use of modern technologies, then real men must master their tools. While everyone who sat behind the wheel probably "sought prestige and liberation through the new machines . . . men sought it more." One self-described "average driver," in 1907, advised the "finicky man" who "can't abide dusty clothes and . . . a little bit of grease on his hands" to avoid automobiling altogether. By contrast, worthy drivers embraced the challenges posed by the mechanical complexities of "planetary transmissions, sliding gears, jump sparks, and the hundred and one other parts of the gasoline engine."[29]

The reality, of course, was that technical competency was not gender bound. As historian Virginia Scharff notes, automobility "represented a new, movable field upon which women's struggles for power and autonomy would be played." Unable to vote and often unwelcome in the public sphere, women found a form of social acceptance by taking the wheel. Money and time limited the opportunity for many to achieve these progressive, technical competencies but did provide the chance for adventuresome, affluent women to participate in what was obviously a man's world. Many understood that minimal mechanical proficiency served as their passport to the real freedoms of automobility. One woman driver remarked, "I have often been asked what in the world a woman would do with a blow-out or punctured tire. From my own experience it isn't such a difficult task to jack the car up, spread a piece of rubber sheeting two yards square or a lap-robe on the ground, and then stoop down and get to work."[30]

The immediate safety concerns, which supposedly validated these biases about technical skill, intelligence, and gender, were soon made moot by Detroit engineers. By 1908, the typical automobile was fairly dependable. The development and adoption of the self-starter, the closed cabin, detachable wheels, and simpler methods of control reduced many of the physical barriers to driving. Shock absorbers, longer chassis frames, acetylene headlights, a less complicated transmission, and spring suspensions all added comfort and reduced the strain on car and driver, further weakening the claim that only the most progressive and intelligent of men should be behind the wheel. Seatbelts, included in some early models to simply prevent occupants from cascading out of their jostling machines, were actually removed as closed cabins became the accepted norm for most American autos.[31]

Technological change not only made driving easier but shifted some of the burden of safety from the driver to the engineer. Increasingly, by the 1920s, motorists of all classes rejected the demand to become mechanical experts. Instead, the expanding market engendered a sense of consumer entitlement as drivers placed their trust in the manufacturers, regulators, and (increasingly) advertisers of the 1910s and 20s. By 1929, driving enthusiast Berton Braley appeared quite different from the first generation of motorists in trusting that "when I step on the starter it starts, and when I step on the accelerator she accelerates. And if she doesn't I go to the garage and have her fixed." He understood nothing of how a starter or accelerator worked and "what's more, I don't care." Braley winked to his audience, sure that they too would agree that "I bought my car because I'd read the ads about it and they told me it was a good car that kept running." Braley added, even "if the ad writers wrote a lot of dope about hot points and cold points and balanced simplex gewhickets," their "words just rolled right over me. If they meant that the car ran a little better, that was all right with me, but I didn't have any curiosity as to any of those technical details."[32]

In addition to the mechanical development of the automobile, competing forms of mass transportation deeply influenced the means by which America adopted the car. The vast size of the country made other forms of travel, such as water and rail, much more cost efficient. Cars emerged within a society dominated by long-haul railroads and, at least until the 1956 Interstate Highway Act, they presented little challenge to the iron horse for this function. Rather, the car was stronger as a potential solution to the problems of interurban, short-haul rural, and suburban transit.

Historians have long noted the importance of America's recurring transportation revolutions. While technological improvements and productivity gains explain the early adoption of steam-powered ships and rail services, these devices did not replace existing solutions as much as create new possibilities for commerce and social interaction. In other words, there were no reasonable alternatives to the week-long railroad passage from New York to San Francisco other than not taking the trip at all. By contrast, the automobile emerged as an alternative to several existing options. Given the significant advantages of market priority (dependable rail service flourished for over fifty years before the appearance of the motor car), consumer familiarity, and its acceptable safety record, why did rail services soon wither "like a great and noble, but diseased oak tree" after the introduction of the automobile?[33]

One answer to this question is that they did not. Long-haul rail transit was not challenged by motorized trucking until well after World War II. It remains productive to this day. Moreover, the automobile did not take credit for the poor management and inefficiencies of regional rail oligarchies, the technological limits of rail transit (that travel only where the tracks lead them), or the unfair fiscal burdens placed on interurban lines, especially the mandate to retain the five-cent fare in light of growing operating expenses.

But in other respects, the automobile uprooted the iron horse. The relatively rapid acceptance of the automobile for local transportation remains well established.[34] The opportunity to replace light rail services appeared because, in the words of historian Paul Barrett, local transit was "a perennial urban crisis." This crisis emanated from a variety of factors, but the leading among them was the problem of overcrowding. Cities "emerged" as a convenience. Many people prefer to live near business opportunities, proximate to government and social services, affordable housing, leisure activities, and the rich and dynamic culture that cities provide. Proposals for transit solutions enjoyed wide support. By 1900, municipal investments for interurban trolleys alone exceeded three-quarters of a billion dollars. Moreover, significant legal, commercial, and governmental resources were spent annually to correct problems as they arose.[35]

For urban planners and land developers, the best solution was not further development of interurban transit but decentralization of the urban population. Relocation to the suburbs, beginning in the mid-nineteenth century and continuing to this day, satisfied four interrelated needs of urbanized Americans. First, it maintained the desired physical boundaries between the affluent and poor, working-class Americans and recent immigrants, and between whites and people of color. Subsequently, the suburbs supported a new domestic ideal that separated one's place of work from one's place of residence. Decentralization also decreased property values, making home ownership (and by extension, entry into the middle class) more affordable for millions of first-time buyers. Finally, single-family suburban homes were built on larger meadowy lots, which reduced the population density of the city. This, in turn, lowered the incidence of

The interurban trolley built early suburbs before being passed by the automobile. (Denver Public Library, Western History Collection, X-14780)

urban diseases and vice, heightened a sense of personal privacy, and raised the perceived "quality of life" for millions of progressive suburbanites.[36]

Convenient, reliable, and comfortable transportation was, of course, the limiting factor in realizing these bourgeois utopias. Here, again, automobility appeared quite compatible with progress. By contrast, many believed the existing streetcars generated more problems than they solved. They were an expensive liability for taxpayers, many of whom did not directly benefit from the lines. Slow to build, inflexible in operation, and predisposed to the whims of the corrupt urban machines that controlled them, trolleys, subways, and elevated trains posed deep structural problems for mass transit planners. Moreover, many argued that public money should not be spent to aid private land speculators and rail "monopolies." Finally, by 1900, urban growth in America was greatest in moderate-sized cities of around one hundred thousand people rather than the massive metropolis. These smaller locales had fewer resources to spare on mass transit, raising the political stakes over methods of taxation, the placement of transit lines, and the intended benefits to the city-at-large.[37] The salient point for automobility again provides a comparative interpretive context. The car was not a magic charm that solved the problem of urban overcrowding. As a technology, it functioned no better than fixed rail in moving people through space. Rather, the motorcar appeared at a time and within a context in which Americans, or at least those in a position to make such decisions, *believed* that individual mass automobile use represented a better option than continued rail expansion.[38]

The perception of personal freedom constituted the most direct social, or some might say psychological, benefit of automobility. The car was an exception to modern society, which favored and soon enforced predictability and structure. Early automobile scholars, like Lewis Mumford (no friend of mass automobility), recognized that the car "appeared as a compensatory device for enlarging an ego which had been shrunken by our very success in mechanization." Using cars to gain control over personal transportation from the hated rail monopolies—comprised of restrictive trusts, fat-cat owners, and persnickety accountants—provided a boost of remarkably powerful public goodwill. Furthermore, the car seemed to free Americans "from the restrictions of the railroad timetable, not to mention its limited route alternatives and unexciting facilities."[39]

The spatial transformation of travel by car gave substance to these gauzy perceptions. By the turn of the century, urban commuters were all too well acquainted with the awkwardness of mass transit. While streetcars physically expanded the geography of urban residence, literally creating the *sub*-urban bedroom community, commuting meant that upper-middle-class travelers now had an even longer transit from home to work. Passing through the ugliest sections of town, rubbing shoulders with the industrial working class, and following a schedule that did not provide flexibility, "commutation encapsulated, for the genteel Victorian urbanite, all of the tensions which accompanied the growth of industrial cities in the nineteenth century." Routine boredom and contact with the unwashed masses was made worse by transit strikes, overcrowding, delays and mechanical failures, smoke, soot, and the constant public cry for reform of the various urban "trolley rings." The combined effect of these displeasing contrasts—between home and work, between dirty and noisy trolley cars and the ideals of order and tranquility, between mass transit rings and trusts and the growing faith in the economic independence and agency of the middle-class— deflated Americans' confidence in public transportation and conditioned them to embrace a more individualized form of mass transit.[40]

The bicycle craze gave the first hint that Americans would trade their reliance on the rails for a new form of personal transportation. Sold by the millions in the 1890s, the idea of using safety bicycles as the solution to urban mass transit maintained a devoted following well into the twentieth century. Early cycling advocates formed a lobby, the League of American Wheelmen, to push for better roads and sing the praises of travel for individual commerce and pleasure. Combined with a surge in rural protest aimed against the rail monopolies, the league helped to form the Office of Road Inquiry (ORI) within the Department of Agriculture, in 1893. The ORI gave legitimacy to the search for transportation alternatives to fixed rail.[41]

The *experience* of biking was key. Gone were the inconveniences and boredom of mass transit, replaced by an apparatus that could easily change speed, maneuver, and go where one pointed it. The device didn't kick, bite, startle, or leave noxious waste strewn about the city streets. The fact that the bike required sustained muscular effort remained its central drawback. Physical endurance, and not a full gas tank, limited where or how far one could travel. Still, as auto pioneer Hiram Percy pointed out, the "bicycle created a new demand which it was beyond the ability of the railroad to supply."[42]

While transit consciousness emerged as an important factor in the relative success of the car, the lack of a functional road system limited mass automobility. Auto devotees expressed faith in an "if you build it they will come" theory of transit technology. But they avoided the obvious question: over what roads? As was made clear by the findings of the League of American Wheelmen and the ORI, road development over the vast American landscape was, at best, rudimentary. Most "roads" were mere traces, rutted dirt paths known only by locals and largely impassable in all but ideal conditions. Transit experts understood that "the poorest unit in any roadway determines the capacity of the entire road." But, by 1900, nothing but bottlenecks existed. In 1896, the ORI counted 2,151,570 miles of road in the United States, but only 153,662 (or 7 percent) of these were improved in any way. Of these improved roads, most were macadam or gravel surfaces within cities that functioned well in good weather but did not perform under wet or icy conditions, and which the elements soon returned to their primitive state. Asphalt paving covered only eighteen miles of America's entire road system. After more than a decade of reform, less than 9 percent of the nation's streets were surfaced when the Model T first appeared.[43]

Road improvement remains one of the traditional duties of local government. For most regions, this meant anachronistic and inefficient construction methods totally "unrelated to the needs of larger areas." Some local officials overseeing these public works were corrupt, wasted precious public resources and goodwill, and simply produced shoddy roads that soon proved unusable. Percy Whiting, writing about "Motoring Conditions in the South" in 1912, noted that anyone "who ventures on a trip to Florida or Texas and hopes to find smooth running is destined to be most bitterly disappointed. It takes bravery to make the trip to Florida and unparalleled heroism to risk a jaunt to Corpus Christi or El Paso." The commercial expenses of poor roads were obvious. As late as 1916, "it cost more for a Georgia farmer to ship a bushel of peaches twenty miles by road to Atlanta than it did for a California farmer to ship a bushel by rail across the country."[44]

Scholars have long disagreed over the relationship between road improvements and the rise of America's automobile culture. Ralph Epstein, in a 1928 study of the automotive industry, recognized this critical symbiosis when he observed that "it is sometimes said that the automobile has caused good roads; sometimes, that the construction of good roads has caused the development of the automobile industry." Automobility contained within itself a chicken-or-egg paradox: which came first, good roads or the cars that demanded them? The local nature of road building makes a definitive answer to this question impossible. What

A Studebaker-Garfield and another automobile mired on roads near Cheyenne, Wyoming, 1908. (Denver Public Library, Western History Collection, Harry M. Rhoads, Rh-634)

is clear is that good roads appeared first in America's cities, that these roads predated the adoption of the automobile, and that these roads existed for reasons only partially connected to individual transit.[45]

It was the federal effort to fashion a national *system* of roadways that led to the most dramatic change in universal car use. Aided by sustained public support for national coordination—initially driven by Progressivism and war and later by jobs programs during the Great Depression—real road improvement beyond the central business districts of America's great cities did not take place until after the passage of the 1916 Federal Aid Road Act. A major victory for the engineering arm of the auto safety troika (which included the "three E's" of engineering, education, and enforcement), the law authorized $75 million to, in effect, match state funds for local road construction. The policy required transparent accounting, to reduce fraud, and modern engineering methods, to insure that the resulting projects would last. By 1921, when the U.S. Congress replaced the 1916 bill with one providing $75 million *per year,* the formal design of a national network of major interstates was taking shape. By the end of the decade, more than 90,000 miles of roadway were improved as a result of these two statutes.[46]

State access to user fees, generated by gasoline taxes, licensing costs, and sales taxes, also led to significant new road improvements. Introduced first in the west and then quickly copied throughout the republic, the gasoline tax alone generated nearly half a billion dollars in revenue by the time of the Great Depression. Legal restrictions tied these funds to road improvements, although during hard times many sought to divert these revenues to other purposes. Historians note how user fees were, in effect, a direct public subsidy to the automotive industry. Cars needed improved roads in order to operate. Individual Americans paid taxes or, in many rural areas, provided manual labor as payment in kind for their local tax obligation. Railroads and streetcars similarly require "roads," in the form of steel rails, and proper annual maintenance. But by the twentieth century, light rail companies received little help from public funds; their expenses required private financing. By 1924, over a billion dollars in public money was spent at all levels of government to improve the roads. Only fifteen years later, an additional $1.4 billion was disbursed. By 1936, one tourist marveled how "the whole continent was netted with cement and asphalt roads, and the air above was beginning to hum with flying machines. . . . When did America ever build herself this immense system of transportation?" It is unlikely that the automobile would have prospered so spectacularly without this early public subsidy.[47]

Federal coordination also helped to coalesce associations of professional traffic and auto safety engineers, which soon acted as spokesmen for national highway-related reform. The men who made up the early state highway commissions regularly populated national safety commissions, reported to Congress, and lobbied the American public through the national media. In the words of historian Daniel M. Albert, they "laid down the laws which would govern motorized society and serve as a rational basis for subsequent traffic safety experts." The tangible substance of their work stands in stark contrast to the uncertain psychological forces that shaped the driving public's understanding of auto safety and justifies the intense scrutiny applied to them by automotive historians over the years.[48]

Two broad patterns characterize the regulation of the automobile from 1900 to 1940. The first maximized the commercial benefits of the car as a productive transportation technology. The influential leader of the Federal Bureau of Public Roads (formerly the ORI), Thomas Harris MacDonald, saw this duty as his "greatest public responsibility" and one that increased the "possibilities of enjoyment and happiness of life [more] than any other public undertaking." MacDonald's biographer, Tom Lewis, identified four interrelated components of the automobile and American commercial life under "Chief" MacDonald's long tenure: *agriculture,* or farm-to-town traffic; *recreation,* such as auto camping and tourism; *commerce,* strictly conceived as the transport of goods; and *defense,* the use of roads for military purposes. Engineers, regulators, and lawmakers focused their efforts on these practical concerns. They established appropriate speed limits, maximal traffic flows between, around, and within cities, technological improvements to both the road and car, and, of course, suitable bureaucratic standards and controls.[49]

The second type of regulation strove to make the roadways as safe as possible within the confines of this first and primary mandate. Often these duties overlapped. Those who wanted safer and more efficient auto transit as well as those interested in more efficient commerce both pursued traffic, speed, and licensing laws with equal zeal. Most, however, gave safety a subordinate position to commerce. Unlike the credentialed and nationally respected highway engineers, most safety advocates and traffic engineers remained legislative outsiders. The benevolent millionaire William Phelps Eno adapted the Gospel of Wealth to include traffic regulation along New York City's major thoroughfares. Eno's paternalistic view toward the average driver—he proudly proclaimed, in the second page of his self-published treatise on traffic control, that "I don't think I ever went on the streets of New York nor of any other city or town without being astonished at the stupidity of drivers, pedestrians and police"—typified the way that many reformers first approached the safety question: as an engineering puzzle waiting to be solved from the top down.[50]

Lastly, in addition to the contingencies of automotive design and competitive transportation options, the spread of automobility was deeply influenced by the unique history of the emerging auto industry. Given what we now know—how the industry grew to more than $3 billion in annual sales by 1926—the nervousness of early auto manufacturers seems laughable. But in reality, these first entrepreneurs had cause for concern. Their product was experimental and expensive. The roads they required were not yet built and the rail network they competed with was well established, funded from the deep pockets of huge transit corporations, and protected by influential politicians. Moreover, the faddishness of new transportation devices, such as the electric "juicers" and even the safety bicycle, did not auger well for long-lasting consumer confidence. Henry Ford, writing in 1906, reflected these fears as he defended his product against the charge of trendiness. Ford rejected the premise that "the automobile industry would go the way the bicycle went. I think this is in no way a fair comparison and that the automobile, which it may have been a luxury when first put out, is now one of the absolute necessities of our later day civilization. The bicycle was a recreation and a fad. The automobile, while it is a recreation, is in no way a fad."[51]

But the sudden rise and fall of the bicycle as a transportation alternative lent credence to the charge that these new, untested technologies were toys of the spoiled rich or specialized gadgets of wooly-headed tinkerers. The trick, as Ford noted, was in turning the recreation of personal automobility into a necessity. Many, like Ford, focused on the terminology. By World War I, industry executives and advertisers rejected phrases that identified the auto as a luxury item. The term "pleasure car," for instance, became "almost a taboo in the automobile fraternity." Advocates much preferred terms like passenger car or family vehicle, which denoted reliable, everyday commuting.[52]

While Ford fretted about the public's perception of the car, the relative strength of the American economy proved more important in determining the viability of the young industry. Industrial capitalism stormed into the twentieth century armed with aggressive new managerial and financial skills honed during the Gilded Age. Rae cites the preexisting trends in American business toward "concentration and oligopoly" rather than the "untutored geniuses working on the proverbial shoestring" budget as the leading factor for the industry's success. The wildcatting nature of the early entrepreneurs also prevented trust-busting progressives, focused on the established giants in petroleum, finance, and manufacturing, from meddling too much. Innovators certainly took advantage of the tons of inexpensive steel and other alloys, plate glass, petroleum, finished lumber, rubber, and coal that these robber barons produced.[53]

Bicycle manufacturers J. Frank and Charles E. Duryea founded the American auto industry, in 1893, when they drove the first internal combustion automobile constructed in the United States. Four years later, Ransom Olds developed an inexpensive yet reliable internal combustion vehicle that he mass produced in his Lansing, Michigan, factory. The industrial Midwest was an ideal location. Close to abundant hardwood forests and thriving carriage, wheel, and wagon manufacturers, the region was well suited to meet the rapid growth in automobile production. Midwestern engineers already showed a preference for internal combustion technology, giving the region an additional and, as time went by, growing advantage over its competition in New England. The success of the Curved Dash Oldsmobile helped concentrate auto production in southern Michigan. Introduced in 1901 for $650, Olds sold more than five thousand units in 1904 alone. The open-shop labor tradition of Detroit, which discouraged unions and collective bargaining, only quickened the pace as the region became America's auto production capital.[54]

Rather than compete with Europeans for the lucrative yet limited high-end market, many domestic suppliers focused their energies on meeting the untapped demand for an inexpensive yet dependable motorcar. While popular and more affordable, the low-powered, open-air "gas-buggy" design of these early cars confirmed a view held by many: when compared to their European counterparts, American motorcars were both inferior and vulgar. As a result, the initial test of the American auto industry was not whether its cars were as good as the Europeans' (they clearly were not) but whether an inexpensive, mass marketed auto could be reliable *enough* to justify buying one at all.

In response, manufacturers turned to marketing and promotion of their product through a series of highly publicized reliability contests. In 1901, Ransom Olds hired Roy Chapin to drive the Curved Dash 820 miles, from Detroit to New York, in order to appear at the prestigious New York Auto Show. Following the example of European road races, manufacturers also sponsored cross-country endurance events. In the summer of 1903, Americans followed the exploits of several cross-country treks and marveled as existing time or speed records were broken.[55] Tycoon Charles J. Glidden and the American Automobile Association (AAA) sponsored auto "reliability" tours, from 1905 to 1913, to showcase the soundness of the motorcar (twenty-seven of the thirty-four entries finished the first, 870-mile tour). In one of the last of these races, from Cincinnati to Chicago to Dallas, Glidden Tour organizer Frank Zirbes reported that the route rewarded "careful driving" and "a sturdy car," not the power or glittering chrome of most European imports. Still, as many were beginning to suspect, it was the danger and speed of these dashes, driven "so close to the brink of a precipice that care-less driving would result in sudden death," rather than reliability that seemed to hold America's interest. The movement began to wane soon after this race concluded. Manufacturers felt they had proven the car's reliability. Moreover, they had their hands full in simply meeting the demand of the marketplace. Car sales exploded, from less than four thousand units in 1899 to more than half a million by 1914, then to over five million by the start of the Great Depression.[56]

The business practices termed Fordism and Sloanism were largely responsible for these astounding production and sales figures. Ironically, neither Henry Ford nor General Motors CEO Alfred P. Sloan gained their renown though technical innovations. According to the adage, they didn't necessarily "build a better mousetrap" but rather built ones in such high volume, at such a low cost, and with such predictable quality that consumers preferred their products over more expensive or more unique competitors. In the most basic sense, "Fordism" refers to the advent of mass-produced automobiles and "Sloanism" to the birth of the organizational and marketing techniques needed to sell these high-volume, high-cost goods to a mass market. What Ford did for the shop floor, Sloan did for the executive suites; but Ford's innovation came first.

Henry Ford, a self-described automotive tinkerer, used his skills as a mechanic and auto racer to form the Ford Motor Company in 1903. The climate for a universal car was never more favorable, yet no one had perfected the method of producing such a car. The industry relied on an extensive network of part suppliers, skilled machinists and assembly mechanics, distributors, and dealers. Ford recognized that coordinating these efforts within a single organization, known as vertical integration, conserved the profits extracted between each transaction. Reinvested in the company, these funds made the economic efficiency of his firm even greater.[57]

But vertical integration only equaled the efficiency of existing manufacturers. In order for Ford Motor to "build a motor car for the great multitude," engineers at the firm, including C. Harold Wills, Charles Sorenson, and Joseph Galamb, needed to reinvent the process of manufacturing. Rather than rely on relatively slow and expensive skilled laborers to assemble each automobile, the parts and processes were standardized and automated. Ford's production method, which the world initially called Fordism but which Ford himself would later term "mass production," provided the necessary parts to semiskilled laborers just as they were needed in the assembly process. The constant or "rolling" assembly-line method was linked to these "just in time" supplies through an intricate series of cranes, belts, and slides.

Ford's genius was not in discovering these techniques but in ruthlessly *applying* them to the production of the automobile. Unlike his competitors, Ford refused to farm out various assemblies (for the chassis, transmission, or axle, for example) to more convenient yet less efficient contractors. Driven by a desire

The first Ford moving assembly line, Highland Avenue, Detroit, Michigan, 1913. (Courtesy of the Frances Loeb Library, Harvard Graduate School of Design, Acc. No. 16238)

to plow profits back into the assembly process rather than to stockholders, and from his much publicized quirky (even paranoid) personality, Ford demanded autocratic control. By 1926, Ford was reinvesting nearly a third of his firm's revenues back into the manufacturing process. This intense level of capitalization had an additional benefit. It forced competitors to follow Ford's lead or lose significant market share. The high cost of constructing such a massive operation as the Highland Park plant and the saturation of the new car market in the mid-1920s, effectively closed the window of opportunity for new entrants to the industry.[58]

Of course, autos produced by these methods ultimately had to meet the needs of the driving public. By this measure, the Model T was perhaps the most successful car in world history. The device proved easy to repair, had a high axle clearance (needed in order to travel America's deeply rutted roads), and was relatively easy to operate, at least based on then-current expectations. The 4-cylinder, 20-horsepower engine made the car deceptively powerful, capable of coaxing speeds of 35 miles per hour over smooth roads and of passing through all but the thickest mud. While the overall ride of a Model T was less than ideal—it certainly earned the nickname "flivver," so called because of the endless bouncing and shaking that was thought to be good "for the liver"—the total package suited a population that had seen cars in action but, as yet, could not afford one of their own.[59]

Ford opened his first just-in-time rolling assembly plant at Highland Park on January 1, 1910, with the Model T as his lone design. In only two years, Ford engineers had placed the entire assembly process on conveyor belts. That year, the firm produced more than 170,000 units of the Model T, six times more than his closest competitor. In 1916, construction began on the even larger (115-acre) and even more automated factory at River Rouge, which also included foundries to cast the engine block. The factories lowered production time for a finished automobile from days to only minutes. In 1915, one visitor to the Highland Park plant noted how Henry Ford allowed "favored guests" to place chalk marks on various wheels, fenders, and motor parts found in the warehouse. After a brief tour of the facilities, guests drove back to their hotel in a Model T made from the same chalked pieces. By 1923, 1.8 million vehicles rolled off his assembly lines. The unit price fell from $850 in 1909 to only $345 in 1916.[60]

While this proved to be a godsend to the average automotive consumer, Ford's workers felt justified in claiming that the devil was in the details. On the one hand, Fordism intentionally strove to de-skill his industrial laborer. Given the importance of skill in providing an individual with job security, high wages, and upward mobility, it is clear that Ford workers paid for the company's remarkable productivity. Moreover, routinizing the shop floor changed the satisfaction one could take in a day's labor. While this may seem a minor point for those of us raised with strong consumer values (where we work to live rather than live to work), it undermined the sense of purpose and social productivity that work provides. As Charlie Chaplin's 1936 film *Modern Times* humorously depicts, Fordism's effect on workers' psyche was profound. One Ford worker quipped, in 1923, "If I keep putting on nut No. 86 for 86 more days, I will be nut No. 86 in the Pontiac nuthouse." These psychological pressures were not imagined. Ford investigated his workers' private lives and restricted their freedoms while on the job. Union organizers and political radicals could expect rough treatment by Ford "Service Department" goons. Ford compensated for these indignities, in 1914, by raising the average worker's pay to five dollars a day (double the national average) and lowering the typical shift to eight hours. Although wartime inflation quickly devoured these gains, most workers swallowed their pride, reconciled their freedoms, and cashed their paychecks. In return, Ford maintained a steady, if not overly enthusiastic, supply of experienced laborers.[61]

The company also proved to be a difficult taskmaster to its national dealers. These local firms, more than 3,500 by 1912, provided the sales staff, maintenance, and customer support services needed to keep Ford customers happy. With the success of the T, this number ballooned to more than 10,000 dealerships and 26,000 authorized service stations by 1925. But to gain a lucrative Ford contract, dealers had to stock only Ford products and, in later years, to pay cash for all parts and vehicles consigned to their businesses. Ford stubbornly refused to negotiate with these all-important retailers, driving many into bankruptcy or the waiting arms of competing firms. Following his famous legal battle with stockholders in 1916, Ford borrowed heavily to buy out the remaining minority investors. When these bills came due, in April 1921, Ford mercilessly forced his dealers to pay cash for millions of dollars of unsold inventory, much of which was shipped without their authorization, to cover his expenses. Ford's famous quip that a client could choose any color "as long as it was black" suggests his managerial dogma. Top-down control of production, labor, investments, dealers, and consumers, what the *New York Times* termed industrial fascism, was the cost of producing the first universal car.[62]

But by the mid-1920s, Ford had lost his market magic. By then, the Model T was technologically out of date and no longer suited to the more refined demands of the auto-savvy consumer. Competitors copied and even improved upon Ford's production methods; his wage scale, eight-hour shift, and profit-sharing plans were no longer unique. The loss of managerial talent developed a problem of equal or even greater importance. While Henry Ford took credit for his firm's stellar rise, it was his talented stable of managers and engineers who made the system work. As Flink notes, "A complete list of the Ford executives who were arbitrarily fired or who resigned in disgust between 1919 and Henry Ford's retirement in 1945 would add up to a small town's telephone directory." The Model A, introduced in 1927 after a costly and much publicized shutdown and retooling of his production plants, did provide short-term relief but was soon deemed a disappointment. Ford's market share slipped against the competition. By 1936, Ford ranked third in auto sales (22 percent) behind Chrysler (25 percent) and General Motors (43 percent).[63]

Ford's relative decline was attributable not only to mismanagement but also to the marketing and organizational innovations made by his competition at General Motors. Ironically, while GM came to symbolize "the depersonalized, decentralized corporation run by an anonymous technostructure," it was founded by one of the auto industry's most temperamental and adventurous entrepreneurs: William "Billy" Durant. Throughout his career, Durant conquered and was invariably ousted from numerous automotive firms. His wisecrack to Walter Chrysler, in 1919, that he changed his management policies "just as often as my office door opens and closes," suggests just how different Durant managed his firm (and explains why he too drove talented auto executives like Chrysler from his company in packs). A successful carriage maker, Durant shifted to the automobile business in 1904 after he gained control of the failing Buick Motor Car Company. Placing it on sound footing, Durant then used Buick as leverage to acquire additional firms. In 1908, he proposed a merger of Buick, Ford, REO (owned by Ransom E. Olds), and Maxwell-Briscoe into a manufacturing trust called the International Motor Car Company. When Ford and REO declined, Durant created a new holding company, which he named General Motors. The firm controlled thirteen automotive lines, along with numerous ancillary parts and accessory firms.[64]

Durant's willingness to take risks was his greatest asset. It is still debatable whether this style rewarded Durant's skill or whether he was just plain lucky.

Unlike Ford, who specialized in producing one low-cost model, Durant favored a wide range of products, betting that one successful wager could cover losses from less profitable lines. What he forfeited in internal efficiency he hoped to gain in market share. Moreover, Durant speculated wildly on the stock market with GM assets. When he succeeded, as with the Buick Model 10 or the Cadillac line, or in raising venture capital from Wall Street, investors reaped windfall profits. But Durant's seat-of-the-pants managerial style made these same investors nervous. Following a business recession that led to a liquidity crisis at GM, in 1910, backers forced Durant from the firm. Durant would (vain) gloriously return to the helm of GM in 1916 by means of a buy-out scheme that inflated GM common stock from a high of $25 in 1914 to $790 two years later, but he soon re-created the same intolerable business climate. The firm again fired Durant in 1920. The interim leader, Pierre S. Du Pont, was better suited as a "silent" investor than CEO, and he willingly ceded control to Alfred Sloan in 1923. Durant continued on, in the industry and on Wall Street, until bankruptcy and ill health forced him to the sidelines by the time of World War II.[65]

Under Sloan, General Motors revolutionized the automotive industry in several ways. Business historians have long noted the firm's organizational and accounting innovations.[66] GM vertically integrated production capabilities and streamlined the decision-making processes of the various lines. The firm developed innovative marketing strategies and sales forecasting methods that supplied stability during hard times (GM actually earned profits throughout the Great Depression and issued record dividends to stockholders in 1936 and 1937). The firm assertively pressed its advantages in size during good times. GM divided its auto lines along perceived consumer segments: for example, with Cadillac at the high end, Buick in the middle, and Chevrolet at the bottom. The policy, termed "a car for every purse and purpose," enticed buyers to trade up in the product line as a visible symbol of their relative affluence. Advertising and credit sales, through General Motors Acceptance Corporation (GMAC), helped consumers attain the desired conspicuous consumption. After the American auto market reached its saturation point, GM's marketing innovations and annual styling changes became the norm for other suppliers. Competitors incapable of managing (or even marshaling) such vast resources soon faded from history. Ironically, what proved to be stabilizing for the auto industry actually undermined the health of the American economy. Flink argues persuasively that the saturation of the market and the development of these riskier consumer behaviors set the stage for (and even the severity of) the Great Depression.[67]

One important consequence of "Sloanism" was the greater emphasis placed on styling. By 1938, it was generally agreed that a "car that looks like a lot for the money is easy to sell." Novel design did not, by definition, mean a lack of safety or technical innovation. The lower, wider, and aerodynamic "streamlined" cars of the 1930s actually dropped the center of gravity of the heavier and faster machines, making them less likely to tip or skid than the higher-axled cars of the Teens and Twenties. But design changes were primarily intended to spur sales, not to safeguard the consumer. The trade journal *Automotive Industries* observed that "Gadgets and doodads appeal more . . . than things which would make cars safer and more economical to operate." As auto historian Joel Eastman adds, "the failure of the automobile industry to place significant emphasis on safety in the absence of government regulation becomes less of a conspiracy than an understandable response to the problems of marketing a technically complex product to a relatively uninformed consumer within an oligopolistic industry." To make matters worse, the stiffening competition for the dwindling new car market soon pivoted on more dangerous features such as speed and power. The 1932 introduction of the V-8 engine and the resulting surge in the average horsepower per motor vehicle (which grew more than 60 percent between 1925 and 1932) greatly increased the chance that a crash would result in serious injury. Innovative technologies, such as safety glass, power steering, or front-wheel drive, were implemented by the remaining firms only when the market forced them to do so.[68]

By the start of World War II, the automobile had fully realized the tantalizing potential dreamed of in the earliest days. As a technology, the car changed from an experimental gas buggy or expensive European dream machine to an everyday tool used by millions of average citizens. As a platform for the nation's transportation needs, the personal passenger car had not yet displaced rail for long-haul and daily commutation. But the device had carved out a market niche that would be accentuated by state and federal planning in the post–World War I era. The auto industry had changed the most. From its meek beginnings in the early decades of the century, the trade emerged as the central pillar of America's manufacturing and consumer economy. Barring these fundamental changes, all the hopes and dreams of early auto advocates would have amounted to very little. With these developments, however, the soaring ideals of individual automobility found few boundaries.

2

Auto Use and Auto Accidents, 1900–1940

Cars and driving possess a nearly universal cultural appeal. Since the first days of automobility, the image of a motorcar and its intrepid chauffeur promised liberation from the pale tedium of mass society. A driver's ability to master the technology of the car and to adapt to the ever-changing conditions of the open road became the standardized test of modernity. Emotionally, the car comforted those drawn to consumption. The intricate mechanisms, polished chrome, and bright colors caught the eye of an envious nation. Henry Ford's universal car, eventually available only in black, added hues to this cultural rainbow. With the low-cost flivver, even Americans of modest means could reap the practical and whimsical benefits of driving. The cultural expressions of America's automotive love affair were immediate, intense, and sustained. Advertisers, cartoonists, songwriters, artists, comedians, and dramatists imagined a thousand and one roles for the car in contemporary life. The device transformed work, play, sex, politics, consumption, and residency. It reordered our appreciation of gender, class, maturity, and progress.[1]

Take, for instance, early film and fiction. Movie producers took to the automobile for obvious reasons. The high-tech invention promised action and drama while at rest and delivered delightful surprises when in motion. Many of the narratives in early film followed a simple yet surefire plot: characters took the wheel, confronted the adventure and uncertainty of the road, and, in the process, resolved their personal dilemmas. Examining hundreds of early films, Julian Smith found that cars offered fictional characters and their audience "a form of emotional *transport,* the state or condition of ecstasy, of being enraptured." Smith concludes that "as Hollywood and Detroit came of age, they both learned how to supply dream vehicles that would carry us away from danger or boredom, transport us to better times and bigger adventures."[2]

Mack Sennett's Keystone Kops remains the best example of this type of modernizing cultural interpretation. Sennett formed the Keystone Film Company in 1912 and produced hundreds of comedy shorts (one- or two-reel silent movies that furnished about ten to twenty minutes of entertainment). His company made household names of actors like Charlie Chaplin, Mabel Normand, Gloria Swanson, and Roscoe "Fatty" Arbuckle.[3]

Sennett's Kops were simpleminded yet dogged pursuers of their prey. The films' narratives consisted of rowdy car chases that included fast driving, per-

Popular sheet music, jokes, cartoons, films, novels, and attire accompanied the automotive love affair, including this cover of Gus Edwards's best-selling waltz song, 1905. (Courtesy of the Sheet Music Collection, Rare Book, Manuscript, and Special Collections Library, Duke University)

ilous turns, and gut-tightening misses between pedestrians, buildings, and, of course, other vehicles. The energetic slapstick of the Kops never caused harm. Accidents solved problems or extricated characters from sticky situations. The format proved wildly successful. Sennett produced over five hundred Keystone Kops shorts before the media shifted to longer, more elaborate plots. Even then, the Kops often appeared in cameo. Sennett featured the gang in the country's first feature-length comedy film, *Tillie's Punctured Romance,* released by Keystone in 1914.

The cultural bearing of more reflective and calculated literary works contrasts sharply with the "lowbrow" appeal of the flickers. Whether considered high art or just another form of popular culture, novels written by William Faulkner, Sinclair Lewis, Booth Tarkington, and F. Scott Fitzgerald applied a more critical eye to the inherent values of automobile use. Typically, the car represented modernity, often with a hint of lowbrow hedonism. Fitzgerald's *The Great Gatsby* (1925), rightly hailed as a classic of modern literature, depicts the car as the vain possession of a lost generation, one desperately (and unsuccessfully) grasping for meaning in their consumer-ordered lives. The novel's central character, millionaire Jay Gatsby, assumed that his beautiful Rolls Royce, "a rich cream color, bright with nickel, swollen here and there in its monstrous length," displayed cultural sophistication and a decisive character. Yet, as the novel makes clear, consumer goods could not hide reckless immaturity. From the drunken "owl-eyed man," who mindlessly steers his luxury car into a ditch, then "washes his hands of the matter," to Gatsby and Daisy Buchanan, guilty of a hit-and-run homicide, the car aids and abets the worst excesses of modern social apathy. In the end, no heroes are saved or villains vanquished. Rather, readers are left to consider how exposed they are to the whims of a distracted, motorized society.[4]

Yet while both cultural representations still hold meaning for our contemporary appreciation of the automobile, they are symbols rather than reality. As David Laird writes of *The Great Gatsby*, "the point of interest here is the depth and comprehensiveness Fitzgerald brings to the analysis of the fateful *role* of the automobile, the possibilities it presents, the conditions and consequences it creates." The Keystone Kops or *The Great Gatsby* tell us as much about film, literature, and the audiences that consumed them as about the actual conditions on the road. It goes without saying that auto accidents do, in fact, produce injuries and that driving is not merely a mindless recreation for sauced sophisticates. The raw data of automobile use, compiled through numerous local, state, and national studies, places these vital cultural responses within a more objective framework. In short, they show who drove cars, how they drove, and what type of accidents occurred in the first four decades of the twentieth century.[5]

Even a cursory glance at the numbers confirms the remarkably rapid growth of auto use in America (Table 2.1; tables appear on pages 56–62). While the resident population of the United States nearly doubled between 1900 and 1940, the number of automobiles grew exponentially. Clearly, the 1920s were a pivotal decade. Low-cost, highly reliable autos combined with improved roads and services led to a threefold increase in the number of registered vehicles. The period also witnessed a sustained increase in the average number of vehicle miles traveled (VMT), which remained around eight to ten thousand miles per vehicle until 1940. A fair prediction for these years suggests that most Americans first read about the car by 1900, first saw one in action by 1910, first rode in one by 1920, and first owned a car by 1930.

The widespread diffusion of automobiles remains a distinguishing feature of U.S. car culture (Table 2.2). Compared with other developed countries, America far exceeded the comparable ratios of resident population to registered motor vehicles. Only New Zealand, Australia, and Canada (also nations with widely dispersed populations and better-than-average distributions of wealth) approached the U.S. rate. Others, like Argentina, France, Germany, the United Kingdom, and Brazil, exhibited only a fraction of the average density of American auto use.[6]

The United States' exceptional motor vehicle density was not concentrated in any particular region (Table 2.3). While the East and industrial Midwest were the first to experiment with autos, the tremendous growth in ownership quickly spread nationwide. One 1926 tally of state motor vehicle departments showed that low resident-to-vehicle ratios were shared across the country. Even large states, like the geographic giants of California and Texas or population leaders like New York and Pennsylvania, exhibited low proportions between citizens and auto owners. These figures support the widely held assumption that America quickly adapted to the automobile nationwide.[7]

But who owned all these cars? Many automobile advocates trumpeted the universal opportunity to own a motorcar. These enthusiasts equated automobility with egalitarian social values and democracy. The rapid decrease in the list price for a new car sustained these values. In 1903, expensive vehicles dominated the marketplace. Cars costing over $875 made up more than two-thirds of all autos sold. Those ranging from $875 to $2,775 constituted the bulk of this number, but cars priced over $2,775 represented a sizeable 10 percent of the market. Yet only thirteen years later the situation reversed itself. Nearly 70 percent of new car sales in 1916 were for vehicles priced under $875. The percentage of the mid-range models dropped by half to less than 30 percent of the total while top-of-the-line models (over $2,775) shrank to less than 1 percent. A 1928 study of auto sales in seven of Texas' largest counties confirmed the growing dominance of inexpensive lines. For the manufacturers of the cheapest models—including Ford, Chevrolet, Plymouth, and Whippet—year-to-year sales increased a whopping 72 percent. That year, Ford and Chevy alone accounted for two-thirds of all new car sales in the Lone Star state.[8]

But a low purchase price represents only a portion of the total expense of operating a motor vehicle. While these figures suggest that more Americans could initially afford automobiles they do not accurately measure the sacrifices required to maintain a car. By 1921, one report estimated that a citizen needed an annual salary as high as $2,800 in order to own, operate, and keep a motor vehicle. While this amount exaggerates the costs of car ownership, it does highlight the fact that few moderate-income Americans could reasonably expect to own a car in the early decades. U.S. census records indicate that, in 1921, annual incomes for most occupations (including farm laborers) hovered around $1,300 per year. As late as 1936, nearly four out of five American families reported annual earnings at or below $2,000. While a low-cost new car or, more than likely, a lower-cost used car remained within reach, even for Depression-era Americans, operational costs made ownership a considerable and ongoing burden. Annual expenditures for oil, gas, tires, and periodic maintenance averaged $112.85 per year per registered vehicle in 1930. This minimum (needed simply to run a car)

New models lined up at an automobile show in Chicago, Illinois, 1914. (Courtesy of the Chicago History Museum, DN-0062032)

represented 5.6 percent of the disposable income for families earning $2,000 per year. Data recorded for spending from 1934 to 1936 indicates that this constituted nearly all of the disposable money set aside for personal transportation. In other words, while poorer citizens could afford a car, the vehicle had to provide the entire family's transportation needs for the year. While "affordable," autos represented significant, and for some citizens, insurmountable economic burdens.[9]

Consumer credit assisted many in acquiring new and used cars. Spreading the cost of ownership over twelve or eighteen monthly payments lowered the initial expense of driving and lessened the pinch of operational expenses (gas, oil, tires, etc.). The census indicates that Americans purchased over $67 billion in goods using short-term unsecured credit between 1929 and 1940. Private financiers estimated that borrowers applied approximately a fifth to a quarter of all consumer credit for autos. By 1925, the reported average cost of a new car was less than $600, and used cars averaged around half this amount. In spite of these low figures, more than two-thirds needed credit to close the deal.[10]

The average age of the automobile owned also showed class deviations. In one national study, over half of all doctors, lawyers, and commercial travelers reported owning a car that was less than two years old. More than a third of

Night view of an automobile dealership displaying car, auto parts, and tires, c. 1920. (Denver Public Library, Western History Collection, L. C. McClure, McC-4094)

physicians' cars were less than one year old. By contrast, half of all farmers, laborers, and other wage workers owned vehicles older than three years. Moreover, as income decreased and the age of the car increased, owners reported a greater need for "necessity driving," or travel related specifically to work. Cars "of extreme old age," reported as nine years and older, were owned by the poorest Americans and used almost exclusively for economic activity. By contrast, wealthier Americans drove newer cars and used them, increasingly, for shopping and recreation.[11]

The popularity of automobile clubs mirrors these broad socioeconomic trends in car ownership. The elite Automobile Club of America (ACA), founded in 1899, counted more millionaires (including August Belmont, Alfred G. Vanderbilt, and Henry Clay Frick) than any other organization on the planet. The ACA staged a variety of high-profile tours and endurance races, lobbied to prevent restrictions on driving, and sponsored early auto shows. By contrast, local enthusiasts of more modest means founded the American Automobile Association (AAA) in 1902. While they too sponsored events, particularly the popular Glidden Tours that tested machine reliability, and promoted legislation favorable to the car, their goals were more practical and generalized: better roads and signs, quality service stations, and motorist aids like maps and lodging recommendations. In contrast to the ACA, the AAA welcomed the many newly formed regional motor clubs. While charter members still saw themselves as elites, the AAA's low registration fees and wide-ranging advertising drew patrons of more moderate incomes. By 1909 the AAA dwarfed its early rival, claiming over twenty-five thousand dues-paying members in thirty states representing over two hundred clubs.[12]

Gender also played an important role in constructing America's driving culture. An overwhelming body of evidence—including advertisements, songs, fiction, and the numerous published essays of automotive "experts"—indicates that gender remained central to many Americans' understanding of the automobile. As scholars like Virginia Scharff and Gijs Mom show, these popular attitudes limited the freedom of action accorded women drivers to a proscribed sphere of "appropriate" behavior. Municipalities often prevented women from purchasing more powerful steam or internal combustion cars because they were "unsuited for use in feminine hands." These cultural biases blended with economic limitations that denied many women the resources needed to purchase a car and the occupational opportunities to maintain it. Clay McShane concludes the car emerged as a "masculine status object" and "driving a masculine skill" for much of the period.[13]

Unfortunately, statistical sources only hint at the actual presence of women behind the wheel. Few analysts probed the number and nature of women drivers between 1900 and 1940. Some safety studies did address the supposed deficiencies of women, such as their relative strength, reaction time, and poise under duress as compared to the male norm. Occasionally, municipalities recorded the sex of early motorists. Combined, these reports suggest that, in the early decades, between 5 and 20 percent of drivers were women.

A 1913 directory of Bexar County, Texas, containing the city of San Antonio, listed the region's first 3,611 registered drivers. Of these, approximately 2,500 private citizens obtained individual license plates. The directory identifies 173 women (or about 7 percent of the total) as the primary "owner" of these vehicles. The guide identified twenty-seven of these women (or about 16 percent of women owners) as unmarried. A later statewide study, examining over forty thousand automobile collisions in Texas, reported that 11.5 percent of drivers were female. A similar investigation in Massachusetts concluded that women constituted no more than 8.5 percent of drivers involved in accidents. While it is difficult to know if these low numbers are an accurate reflection of overall women drivers (or rather a reflection of their lower mileage), studies in the 1920s and 30s bolster the conclusion that women represented up to one in five of the nation's drivers.[14]

Similarly, early cultural assumptions discouraged detailed analysis of the typical driver's age. Most motor vehicle bureaus did not limit licensing by age. It was not until the mid-1920s that many states first enacted minimum age restrictions.

Ford four-door sedan, with four passengers and a woman driver, c. 1923. (Courtesy of the
Library of Congress [LC-USZ62-46286 DLC])

As with sex, the most accurate statistical picture of driver age comes from auto
accident reports. Tabulating results from over a million auto collisions, in 1933,
the Travelers Insurance Company found that drivers under eighteen made up
less than 2 percent of all drivers on the road (Table 2.4).

As with class and sex, reformers took special notice of the relationship between the age of the driver and accident frequency. Many studies, such as ones
conducted by the states of Massachusetts (1934) and Connecticut (1938), the
Travelers Insurance Company (1933, 1938), and the AAA (1937, 1938), conclude
that younger drivers "had an undue proportion of accidents" because "their
judgement is poor and they lack consideration for others." The Safety and Traffic Engineering Department of the AAA reported that motorists aged sixteen
to eighteen showed a nine times greater likelihood of having an auto accident
than persons forty-five to fifty, statistically the safest group of drivers. These hot-
rodding, "troubled" youth emerged as another member of the motorized menace
and a chief source of society's accident problem.[15]

But national trends do not support the broad assumption that young drivers
were particularly accident-prone. By 1933, drivers between the ages of eighteen
and twenty-four were consistently underrepresented (when compared to their
presence in the general population) in the accident data pool. Comprising about
a fifth of the overall U.S. population, this group accounted for about the same

number of accidents (both fatal and nonfatal). By contrast, the large twenty-five to sixty-four group (48.0 percent of the general population) was responsible for three-quarters of all accidents. A more accurate analysis, again conducted by the AAA, avoids overly fine distinctions in age (and the bias inherent in these groupings). Their report, written by the respected safety researcher B. W. Marsh, concludes modestly that the number of miles driven (VMT) per fatal accident "steadily increases with each age level until the 45–50 year group is reached, at which time the . . . fatality [rate] begins to decrease."[16]

The broad trends in ownership, class, gender, and age support a fairly conventional view of mass automobility. While expensive, auto ownership was within the grasp of the typical working American family. Installment payments eased cash-flow burdens and the growing availability of low-cost runabouts and used cars dulled the sticker shock even further. Still, while financial barriers fell throughout the period, economics excluded a sizeable portion of low and medium wage earners from car ownership. As a result, it is likely that the bulk of automobile owners remained near or above the average annual income of the country as a whole. Second, no formal barriers prevented women or the young from driving. On the other hand, economic agency clearly limited their ability to consistently operate a motor vehicle. Moreover, if anecdotal sources can be trusted, women drove cars frequently but not as often or as far as their brothers. Gender and economic barriers appeared high enough to effectively constrain these populations' automobility.

The "typical" American driver also used the car in predictable ways. Before 1920, much of the information about auto usage remained anecdotal, often the recollections of upper-middle-class motorists using cars for recreation. In addition, during the first two decades of the twentieth century, the novelty of the car, the poor state of the roads, and the relatively high expense of owning and operating a vehicle circumscribed its use. As the country overcame these limiting factors, reformers sought a more consistent and accurate picture of auto use.

In 1923, the National Automobile Chamber of Commerce (NACC) undertook just such an analysis. Founded in 1914, the NACC emerged as a powerful trade association for the auto industry. The organization mailed questionnaires to motorists residing in states with large numbers of registered cars. They listed several auto-related activities and asked respondents to check those that applied. The survey reported the most common activities and the percentage of respondents by state for each category (Table 2.5). In contrast to the image of the early "pleasure" car, by 1923 "necessity driving" dominated Americans' time behind the wheel. In larger states, like California and Texas, where longer distances might limit the frequent use of the car, motorists expressed the consistent need to drive for business. While other activities, such as long-distance travel and weekly church attendance, remained optional it appeared that the car provided Americans with the ability to more regularly engage all of these practices.

The relatively low incidence of driving children to school, the study's authors argued, could easily represent no more than a statistical variant: underreported by parents who drove to work yet also shuttled their children in the process.[17]

Owners indicated that shopping was the most common reason for getting behind the wheel. In 1923, nearly three of every five drivers (the highest overall percentage) reported that they frequently used their cars to shop. By 1940, based on a survey of over 76,000 drivers, this number ballooned to over 86 percent. Moreover, nearly four in five American drivers claimed that they used their cars to shop at least once a week (Table 2.6).

The strong and symbiotic relationship between shopping and cars resulted in profound changes. Numerous and influential studies, including Robert and Helen Lynd's *Middletown: A Study in Modern American Culture* or the report *Recent Social Trends* (1933), commissioned by President Herbert Hoover, show how the automobile greatly altered traditional leisure activities and social "habits." The Lynds noticed how frequent shopping trips affected Americans' views on saving, visiting, clothing, religious observances, and vacationing. One respondent believed she "never felt as close to my family as when we are all together in the car." According to the authors in *Recent Social Trends*, everyday driving created a new "automobile psychology," closely connected to consumption, which became the "dominant influence" in restructuring modern life. Demographic patterns, including a shift away from shopping within the cities' central business districts and the rise of suburban malls (the first auto-centered mall was built in Kansas City in 1922), aided the flight to the suburbs and accelerated changes in work patterns, settlement, and a host of other market-oriented behaviors.[18]

Significantly, rural America displayed as much if not more acceptance of these new consumer-related activities as urban citizens. Historians Ronald Kline and Hal Barron agree that farm communities adapted to the new possibilities of the automobile, in Kline's words, "on their own terms [which] allowed them to weave the car into the fabric of rural life." As in the cities, automotive shopping patterns disrupted traditional activities and timetables. Where suburban consumers now avoided the hustle and flow of the busiest retail districts, rural shoppers moved away from the small general stores that dotted small town crossroads to the larger, better stocked, and nationally advertised chain stores appearing in medium-sized towns. As Barron concludes, cars "increased rural access to consumer culture and had a dramatic impact on the economic geography of rural society."[19]

By 1940, driving was an inescapable ingredient of modern citizenship. Necessity driving constituted over half of all miles driven and three-quarters of all trips taken in an auto. Fully 96 percent of the 26 million cars on the road were used for necessity driving on a weekly basis. The cumulative miles driven (not including recreational driving) counted more than three and a half times that of all other forms of automated transportation (Table 2.7). The pervasiveness and uniformity of auto use across the continent support the assumption that by 1940 the car was king (Tables 2.8, 2.9).[20]

But patterns of automobile usage shifted between 1900 and 1940. Most obvious was the fact that local transportation became essentially automotive. Nearly three-quarters of all people drove to reach the central business district and more than 2,100 cities reported no interurban mass transit system of any kind. Most driving remained within five miles of home. While rural drivers averaged fewer round trips per year than urban motorists, the ratio between necessity use and recreation proved nearly identical. Driver occupation had little effect on these norms. One study separated drivers by those who required an automobile to conduct their vocation (physicians, lawyers, commercial travelers and other salesmen) from those who used cars to reach their place of employment but did not use the car while working (laborers, farmers, clerks). Comparing occupations, researchers found that while annual mileage and number of trips for business drivers, like physicians, was much higher (12,932 miles, 947 round trips) than for nonbusiness drivers, like farmers (5,750 miles, 392 round trips), "on a percentage basis 66.8 per cent of the doctor's mileage and 66.8 per cent of the farmer's mileage . . . are [equally] for economic purposes." In short, there was little difference in the percentage of economic use across occupation. The results were so uniform that the report stressed the need to reassess stale assumptions about class. While workers and clerks may not be the largest percentage of drivers in America, their driving was consistent with other motorists. The authors concluded that "the picture of workers' homes clustered about mill or factory is obsolete. On the contrary, 70 per cent of workers in car-owning families go to work by automobile."[21]

As with class, sex, and age, auto usage patterns show standardizing trends in American automobility. While the first two decades of the new century display the widest variance, mass automobility eventually produced a "typical" car journey. With slight regional variations, most notably in the higher incidence of recreational travel, few actual differences were evident between the driving of rural and urban dwellers, between the upper class and workers, or within large cities or small towns.

A statistical picture of the "typical" auto accident is also informative. Here again the data supplied by commercial, municipal, state, and federal agencies needs to be treated carefully. The greatest challenge remains the complexity of an auto accident. Collisions are best understood as an accident *process* involving dozens of interrelated events rather than a single or isolated incident. Human decision-making skills are the critical variable. Recent studies place driver agency as the "probable or definite" cause of nearly 95 percent of all accidents. As a result, the presence of variables affecting decision making, such as traffic congestion or rate of speed, are crucial to the overall accident rate. These two variables changed dramatically over the period from 1900 to 1940. With more vehicles to hit and (with higher speeds) less time to think, an increased incidence of auto accidents logically followed. By contrast, the segregation of animal-powered vehicles, electric trolleys, and pedestrians from the roadways simplified the driver's decision-making process and lowered the potential for an accident.[22]

A second complication is the method used to record auto accident information. Investigators frequently provided confusing or overly general categories to describe collisions. For example, in 1924, Connecticut (a progressive bellwether in auto-safety reform) listed at least three distinct accident causes—skidding, speeding, and driver "miscalculation"—for accidents that could easily have been the result of a single activity: excessive speed. As with the economic and demographic data, tallies of accidents and accident causes can only loosely approximate the real conditions that Americans faced on the roadway.[23]

The tabulation of auto fatalities, from 1900 to 1940, tells several tales (Tables 2.10, 2.11). The raw number of auto fatalities shows a steep increase beginning around 1915, about the time that Henry Ford opened his River Rouge assembly plant and ushered in the era of the low-cost, reliable "universal car." The total peaked in 1937 at 37,819 fatalities. This infamous record would stand for another twenty years, surmounted in 1957 when more than twice the number of cars were then on the road.

Changes in fatality rates are particularly interesting. When measured by the number of *vehicles* in use or the number of *miles traveled* per vehicle, fatality rates fell consistently throughout the era. Using 1915 as a baseline, by 1940 the fatality rate per 10,000 vehicles and per 100 million VMT fell by 62.7 percent and 68.6 percent, respectively. By contrast, the fatality rate per 100,000 *residents* mushroomed over 400 percent, from 5.90 per 100,000 people in 1915 to 25.00 per 100,000 people by 1940.

These conflicting trends, which continued throughout much of the twentieth century, expose a social dynamic that lies at the heart of this study. From one perspective, it appeared possible to enact reforms to reduce the risk from both the car and road. Falling rates for fatalities per vehicle and per mile driven certainly justify this view. Engineers, manufacturers, and reformers could (and did) claim that they lowered the overall risk of American mass transit. Conversely, one might conclude that individual drivers were no safer. Reform lowered fatality rates per car and per mile, but every year Americans owned more cars and drove more miles. Moreover, the rate of 25.00 deaths per 100,000 people remained consistent for most of the twentieth century. Except for a stretch during World War II, when gas rationing and the suspension of new car manufacturing curtailed driving, the rate never fell below 20 deaths per 100,000 citizens. While cars and roadways carried less risk, individual citizens were no safer from the threat of accidental death. Stricter penalties and law enforcement measures designed to remove "unsafe" drivers appeared justified.

These perspectives—between collective risk and individual safety—directly affected the nature of auto safety reform. Many assumed that unsafe behaviors, such as speeding, reckless or intoxicated driving, and ignorance of basic motoring skills, reflected deficiencies in the character of the motorist rather than collective risk of mass automobility. As a result, reformers initially acted to isolate or remove these menaces, the so-called "accident prone" drivers, so that their personal recklessness would not affect others. These debates—between "inevitable" and "avoidable" fatalities, between blameless "accidents" and reckless "collisions," and between the relative perfectability of the car or road and the stubbornly hazardous driver—captured the core consideration of America's struggle to manage the public risk of mass automobility.[24]

More importantly, these growing concerns led to the perception of an "accident crisis" around the end of World War I. Certainly, the higher number and rate (per person) of auto-related injuries and fatalities justified these feelings. But the changing culture and demographics of the modern roadway added an intensity, even urgency, to the public response. As Americans returned to normalcy they turned away from a more inclusive vision of U.S. society (as indicated by tough new immigration restrictions, the Red Scare, the rise of the KKK, and other infamous examples of the Tribal Twenties). The perceived accident "crisis" seemed to reveal America's unraveling social network, a culture under attack by motor morons and flivverboobs. Reformers questioned whether women, the working class, immigrants, and the young possessed the character to properly assume their civic responsibilities. Max Weber's proposals—that modern, capitalist societies turn to bureaucracies to legitimize and standardize majority values—predict the rise of a structured and professional "community" of safety experts.

Unfortunately, the data used by these experts to perfect society remained flawed. Auto accidents can be studied only after they occur. The data recorded, such as the rate of speed or traffic congestion, is often isolated from the context in which they occur. Driving 70 miles per hour on a flat, straight highway is a very different risk than the same rate of speed through residential or commercial streets. Early auto safety reformers understood these complications. They worked to establish uniform accident reporting procedures as a means to overcome the contingencies of auto collisions. Then-Secretary of Commerce Herbert Hoover, who chaired an influential and much-discussed series of national commissions on auto safety, cited the lack of standardized reporting as the most pressing need for state regulators. Still, by 1938, the U.S. Bureau of Public Roads admitted that in each of the thirty-eight state highway commissions it examined, no two used the same accident reporting methods or monthly summary forms. They found this "utter lack of uniformity" the primary obstacle to effective safety reform.[25]

"Lack of uniformity" certainly cast a cloud over the reliability and comparability of accident statistics before 1940. As the Automotive Safety Foundation observed in 1941, data collection inconsistencies only accentuated "the kaleidoscope nature of the problem." For example, one 1936 study examined 892 fatal accidents and reported 2,524 separate causes. Table 2.12 lists the most common types and incidence of auto accidents found in seven separate studies, between 1918 to 1939. The four most common accidents involved cars striking other cars, pedestrians, other nonautomotive vehicles, and fixed objects. More than likely, the variations indicate divergent methods of reporting accidents rather than significant regional recklessness. Still, some useful conclusions can be drawn. The first is the high incidence of collisions between cars and pedestrians, which constituted more than half of all accidents in two studies and a third in two others. Indeed, in the early years, the auto accident problem is best understood as a contest over appropriate street usage. Secondly, car-to-car collisions outpaced all other vehicular crashes by a sizeable percentage in all but two studies. Highway and traffic engineers made great strides in reducing both of these trends. The formal segregation of pedestrians and other nonautomotive traffic as well as the use of one-way streets and divided highways did much to limit the opportunity for disaster.[26]

As state accident investigations became more sophisticated and consistent, the data collection and reporting split into two distinct groupings. The first recorded the factual conditions of the crash, such as time of day, weather, and physical location. They captured basic sociological data, such as sex, age, and race. But the reports also included interpretative data, such as the mental condition, attitude, or driver behavior that may or may not be related to the cause of the crash.

Information more relevant to accident causes shows a predictable dispersion across time and conditions. Time of day, weather patterns, and road conditions changed the likelihood of experiencing a collision. Dawn and dusk remained the deadliest periods reported, largely because they combined dense traffic patterns (from commuting) with shifting visibility (as sunlight grew or faded). A Grand Rapids, Michigan, study ingeniously compared traffic congestion and accident patterns. They reported times when collisions exceeded the average or expected rates, based on street usage. Rates spiked during the evening commute, around 6:00 p.m., followed by a period of several hours where accidents continued to outpace traffic volume. During these hours, the roadway was the riskiest for Michigan drivers. This relationship reversed itself around 1:30 a.m., when accidents occurred less frequently than predicted. These favorable conditions lasted until the next evening's rush hour when the cycle renewed. Pedestrian danger also peaked at 6:00 p.m., with about six times greater danger than in the morning.

These same "common sense" findings were reported for weekly rates: accidents peaked on Friday and Saturday, and annual rates dipped in the cold-weather months as people wintered their cars and refrained from pleasure driving. A sixteen year monthly average, from 1921 to 1937, on Texas roads saw nearly double the number of fatal accidents in December than in February. The fall (October through December) proved the deadliest months and the coldest part of the year (January to early April) the safest. Weather certainly affected traffic conditions, but national reports indicated that a vast majority (84.06 percent) of fatal accidents transpired in "clear" weather. Only one in eight accidents happened in the rain. Summary national data on weather is even less reliable since the incidence and reaction to a rainy day in Los Angeles or Phoenix is quite different than one in Seattle or Honolulu. One interesting conclusion indicates that the lethality of a crash (or the likelihood that a fatality would occur in any given collision) was greatest in rainy conditions, appeared not affected by clear or snowy weather, and actually decreased in the fog. Apparently drivers made allowances for occasional foggy days but were not as ready to adapt to the more common weather hazards of rain and ice.[27]

Sociological data such as sex, age, and race add more substance to the portrait of a typical accident. Men were overwhelmingly behind the wheel of most accidents. One Texas study, of over forty thousand collisions, found that 88.5 percent of accident drivers were male. A similar report for Massachusetts found the number to be slightly higher (91.5 percent). Age was also important (Table 2.13). A longitudinal study of Ohio fatalities shows that safety reform efforts, aimed at keeping young children out of the path of automobiles, were effective (Table 2.14). Children and young adults (aged 0–19) made up more than a third of all fatalities in 1911, but less than a quarter only two decades later.[28]

Researchers rarely recorded race or ethnicity in their cumulative statistics. When they did, the findings suggest some of the hidden costs of a segregated society. Comparing accidental deaths per one hundred thousand people in Ohio, from 1910 to 1933, the Buckeye State reported that the rate for blacks ran one-fifth to one-quarter higher than for whites. A similar survey of pedestrian accidents in the city of Dallas, from 1935 to 1938, shows that Hispanics also suffered. The study marks no significant racial or ethnic differences in the causes of pedestrian accidents (they noted that all groups jaywalked and played in the streets). Still, a marked difference existed in the incidence of young Hispanic victims as compared to the white and black populations of the city (Table 2.15). A similar jump in the average percentage of Mexican Americans involved in accidents suggests that safety reforms proved less effective in the "Mexican colony" of Dallas and that, in the words of the report, "much work is needed among the Spanish-speaking people of Dallas in view of a condition that is getting worse all the time." While the report does not directly state the obvious conclusion, it is likely that Mexican-American residents had less access to motor vehicles. This meant they walked the streets more frequently and for longer periods of time, exposing the group to greater risk.[29]

Assessing the qualitative causes of accidents remained the central goal of these reports. Here again the idiosyncrasies of each report make comparison difficult. One 1930 report of accidents in Washington, D.C., classified a mere 1.5

percent of its 10,822 accidents as the result of "exceeding the speed limit." Still, the authors continued, 22.5 percent of accidents were due to "reckless driving," 6.5 percent from skidding, and 5.3 percent from "lost control." In each of these instances it is hard to imagine that speed was not a proximate cause. Moreover, in spite of the contingencies of an auto accident, many reports injected morality into their analysis of causes. One 1925 Michigan study described the accidental driver as a "thoughtless, selfish motorist who, with the disregard for others, violates the rules of safe driving." Accordingly, the authors reported a much higher incidence of "reckless" driving when compared to other behaviors (Table 2.16). Common to all was the high incidence of speeding (ranging from one-eighth to one-third of all accidents) and drivers who neglected the right-of-way of others (ranging from one-eighth to one-quarter of all accidents). Regardless of drivers' supposed *moral* failings, those who broke the rules of the road clearly caused a large number of collisions.[30]

A 1934 survey of Massachusetts drivers confirms this lackadaisical attitude by motorists toward the law. Researchers observed and recorded over 450,000 driving situations in all weather conditions, at all hours of the day, and at various points of the year. The authors claimed they actively looked for "driving habits which might lead to accidents." In their findings they believed they had found these habits. For example, at the nearly 75,000 stop signs observed they determined that half of the motorists merely slowed to three miles per hour, a third slowed to only 15 miles per hour, and fully 17.6 percent completely ignored the law. One in ten regularly violated traffic signals "regardless of day of week or time of day" and more than half took the "right of way illegally, or raced to achieve it." A third habitually sped, with "no variance for time of day or day of week." Collectively, drivers *averaged* more than 20 miles per hour over the posted limits in residential areas and near schools. Spotters timed individuals doing up to 81.0 miles per hour on straightaways and 68.1 miles per hour on long-radius curves. Massachusetts motorists themselves, in a questionnaire completed by 12,000 drivers, confessed they often held "no regard for the rights for others," displayed abject "carelessness" behind the wheel, drove with "negligence," showed "indifference to laws," and took "too many chances." Few supported efforts to more strictly enforce the law (which seems logical, given their reported behavior). Over half thought it a bad idea to formally "examine operators at stated intervals." Only 973 respondents indicated the need for driver exams and, of these, 63 percent wanted the analysis limited to a simple physical or vision test. Nearly all (over 85 percent) rejected subjective exams designed to evaluate a driver's knowledge of the law.[31]

This statistical portrait of auto use and accidents suggests several important trends for the first four decades of the twentieth century. Most notably, by the 1920s, motor vehicles dominated personal transit for a sizeable percentage of the population. While other forms of mobility, such as trolleys and interstate rail, remained viable, the availability and relatively low cost of cars meant that the foundations of the "automobile age" were secure. Increasingly, Americans drove cars to conduct their everyday affairs.

Equally important, reformers and state officials appeared increasingly concerned with identifying the multiple causes of auto accidents. Certainly the climbing injury and fatality statistics demanded action. Studies helped identify the persistent dangers from grade crossings (between the highway and rail lines), at intersections, with pedestrian walkways, and from roadside obstructions, giving road engineers and state motor vehicle bureaus actionable data upon which to spend their limited resources. As the Grand Rapids study shows, many activists used the raw (if flawed) figures as a launching point to discuss the attitudes and assumptions of the driving public and propose normative values of "good" driving. The resulting tensions, between the perception of avoidable and inevitable accidents, emerged as the dividing line between positive and negative attitudes about the car and driver in the modern era. Existing at the intersections of these two perspectives, the emerging American automotive love affair symbolized both the potential for significant safety reform as well as a formidable barrier to the methods that regulators could employ.

Table 2.1. U.S. Automobile Statistics, 1900–1940 and 2000

Year	U.S. Resident Population	Registered Motor Vehicles (thousands)	Vehicle Miles of Travel (millions)	Average Travel per Vehicle (miles)	Ratio of Resident Population to Motor Vehicles
1900	75,994,575	8	100	12,500	9500:1
1910	91,972,266	469	3,580	7,633	196:1
1920	105,710,620	9,239	47,600	5,152	11:1
1930	122,775,046	26,750	206,320	7,713	4.6:1
1940	131,669,275	32,453	302,188	9,312	4:1
2000	281,421,906	225,331	2,781,462	12,177	1.25:1

Source: U.S. Census Bureau, *Statistical Abstract of the United States: 2003* (No. HS-41, Transportation Indicators for Motor Vehicles and Airlines, 1900 to 2001), 77–78; U.S. Bureau of the Census, *Historical Statistics of the United States, Colonial Times to 1957* (Washington, DC, 1960), 462.

Table 2.2. Ratio of Resident Population to Motor Vehicles, 1926

	Registered Motor Vehicles, 1926	Ratio of Resident Population to Motor Vehicles
United States	20,051,276	6:1
Canada	715,962	13:1
New Zealand	99,443	14:1
Australia	29,121	20:1
France	735,000	53:1
United Kingdom	815,957	55:1
Argentina	178,050	55:1
Germany	323,000	193:1
Italy	114,700	346:1
Brazil	63,650	530:1

Source: Ralph Epstein, *The Automobile Industry: Its Economic and Commercial Development* (Chicago: A. W. Shaw, 1928), 318; U.S. Bureau of the Census, *Historical Statistics of the United States, Colonial Times to 1957* (Washington, DC, 1960), 12.

Table 2.3. States with Most Registered Motor Vehicles, Ordered by Ratio of Resident Population to Motor Vehicles, 1926

State	Resident Population, 1920	Registered Motor Vehicles, 1926	Ratio of Resident Population to Motor Vehicles
California	3,426,861	1,600,475	2.1:1
Michigan	3,668,412	1,118,785	3.3:1
Iowa	2,404,021	698,998	3.4:1
Ohio	5,759,394	1,480,246	3.9:1
Wisconsin	2,632,067	662,282	4.0:1
Texas	4,663,228	1,049,869	4.4:1
Illinois	6,485,280	1,370,503	4.7:1
New York	10,385,227	1,815,434	5.7:1
Massachusetts	3,852,356	690,190	5.6:1
Pennsylvania	8,720,017	1,455,184	6.0:1

Source: Ralph Epstein, *The Automobile Industry: Its Economic and Commercial Development* (Chicago: A. W. Shaw, 1928), 318; U.S. Bureau of the Census, *Historical Statistics of the United States, Colonial Times to 1957* (Washington, DC, 1960), 12.

Table 2.4: Ages of Drivers Involved in Accidents Resulting in Persons Killed or Injured, 1933

Age Group	Percentage in U.S. Population, 1933	Number Involved in All Accidents	Percentage Involved in All Accidents	Number Involved in Fatal Accidents	Percentage Involved in Fatal Accidents	Number Involved in Nonfatal Accidents	Percentage Involved in Nonfatal Accidents
Under 18 Years[1]	26.1	15,050	1.4	830	2.2	14,220	1.4
18 to 24 Years[2]	20.1	245,360	22.5	10,160	27.4	235,200	22.3
25 to 64 Years	48.0	817,860	75.0	25,150	67.9	792,710	75.3
65 and over	5.8	12,070	1.1	910	2.5	11,160	1.1
Total	100.0	1,090,340	100.0	37,050	100.0	1,053,290	100.0

Source: U.S. Bureau of the Census, *Historical Statistics of the United States, Colonial Times to 1957* (Washington, DC: 1960), 8; Travelers Insurance Company, *The Great American Gamble* (Hartford, CT: 1934), 16, 17, 44.
[1] The U.S. census divides this age group as "under 14 years."
[2] The U.S. census divides this age group as "14 to 24 years."

Table 2.5. Motor Vehicle Use in States with Most Registered Motor Vehicles, Ordered by Ratio of Resident Population to Motor Vehicles (1926) (in percentage)

State	Ratio of Resident Population to Motor Vehicles, 1926	Drive to work	Daily Use in Business	Long-Distance	Church	Children to School	Shopping
California	2.1:1	55	45	55	29	16	44
Iowa	3.4:1	46	29	55	57	11	55
Wisconsin	4.0:1	42	26	49	54	17	52
Texas	4.4:1	60	57	58	81	29	67
Illinois	4.7:1	52	45	45	64	27	63
New York	5.7:1	36	45	50	44	14	63
Massachusetts	5.6:1	59	50	59	37	11	54
Pennsylvania	6.0:1	50	42	56	42	17	54
Total		52	46	51	52	18	58

Source: "What Do Folks Use Their Cars For?" *Literary Digest* 79 (November 17, 1923): 66–69.

Table 2.6. Use of Vehicles for Shopping in Automobile-Owning Families, 1940

Frequency	Percentage Reporting
Daily	23
More than Once a Week	32
Once a Week	24
1–3 Times a Month	4
Less than Once a Month	3
Never	14

Source: Automobile Manufacturers Association, *A Factual Survey of Automobile Usage* (Detroit, c. 1941).

Table 2.7. Passenger Miles by Type of Transportation, 1940

Type of Transportation	Passenger Miles (in millions)
Passenger Cars	274,000
Electric Railway	26,780
Steam Railway	23,700
Buses	21,000
Airlines	1,042

Source: Automobile Manufacturers Association, *A Factual Survey of Automobile Usage* (Detroit, c. 1941), 7.

Table 2.8. Types of Round Trips in Urban and Rural Areas, 1940

Region	Necessity Trips (%)	Other Use (%)
Rural Areas	77.70	22.30
Urban Areas	76.36	23.64
Other Areas	23.27	76.73

Source: Automobile Manufacturers Association, *A Factual Survey of Automobile Usage* (Detroit, c. 1941), 10.

Table 2.9. Average Annual Mileage and Necessity Mileage per Car by Population Group, 1940

Population Group	Average Annual Miles per Car	Necessity Mileage	Necessity Mileage (%)
Unincorporated Areas	6,606	4,331	65.6
Less than 1,000	7,436	4,404	59.2
1,000–2,500	7,843	4,399	56.1
2,500–5,000	8,236	4,431	53.8
5,000–10,000	8,221	4,363	53.1
10,000–25,000	8,293	4,267	51.5
25,000–100,000	8,360	4,311	51.6
100,000+	8,994	4,636	51.5
All Areas (31 States)	7,796	4,417	56.7

Source: Automobile Manufacturers Association, *A Factual Survey of Automobile Usage* (Detroit, c. 1941), 14.

Table 2.10. Motor Vehicle Usage and Fatalities, 1900–1940 and 2000

Year	U.S. Resident Population	Vehicle Miles of Travel (millions)	Total Motor Vehicles (thousands)	Average Mileage per Vehicle (miles)	Fatalities
1900	75,994,575	100	8	12,500	36
1905		970	79	12,278	252
1910	91,972,266	3,580	469	7,633	1,599
1915		19,530	2,491	7,840	6,779
1920	105,710,620	47,600	9,239	5,152	12,155
1925		122,346	20,069	6,096	20,771
1930	122,775,046	206,320	26,750	7,713	31,204
1935		228,568	26,546	8,610	34,494
1940	131,669,275	302,188	32,453	9,312	32,914
2000	281,421,906	2,781,462	225,331	12,177	42,116
Total (1900–1940)					622,756
Annual Average (1900–1940)					15,189

Source: U.S. Census Bureau, *Statistical Abstract of the United States: 2003* (No. HS-41. Transportation Indicators for Motor Vehicles and Airlines, 1900 to 2001), Mini-Historical Statistics, 77–78.

Table 2.11. Fatality Rates, 1900–1940 and 2000

Year	Fatality Rate per 100 Million VMT	Fatality Rate per 10,000 Motor Vehicles	Fatality Rate per 100,000 Residents
1900	36.00	45.00	0.05
1905	25.98	31.90	NA
1910	44.66	34.09	1.74
1915	34.71	27.21	5.90
1920	25.54	13.16	11.50
1925	16.98	10.35	17.10
1930	15.12	11.67	25.42
1935	15.09	12.99	26.90
1940	10.89	10.14	25.00
2000	1.51	1.87	14.97
Average (1900–1940)	24.56	20.93	15.57

Source: U.S. Census Bureau, *Statistical Abstract of the United States: 2003* (No. HS-41. Transportation Indicators for Motor Vehicles and Airlines, 1900 to 2001), Mini-Historical Statistics, 77–78.

Table 2.12: Type and Incidence of Auto Accidents (in percentages)

Type of Accident Reported	MA 1918– 1919	CT 1924– 1927	MI 1925	IL 1926	OH 1929– 1933	US 1933	TX 1936– 1939
Car Hitting Pedestrian	31.87	15.00	8.49	53.81	59.83	37.14	13.88
Car Hitting Car	52.39	65.83	63.81	8.20	25.29	44.87	57.16
Car Hitting Other Vehicle (Trolley, RR)	9.20	9.90	25.53	29.72	8.60	3.80	5.21
Car Hitting Fixed Object	6.54	9.28	2.00	4.46	6.26	6.13	7.41
Accidents (Total 969,590)	34,197	111,007	5,996	1,548	5,651	756,500	54,691

Sources: Massachusetts: *Twin Mutual's Primer of Automobile Insurance* (Boston: Pinkham Press, 1920); Connecticut: Richard Shelton Kirby, *A Study of Motor Vehicle Accidents in the State of Connecticut* (New Haven, CT: Hartley Corporation and Yale University Press, 1926), subsequent studies published in 1927 and 1928; Michigan: James Sinke, *Think: An Analysis of Automobile Accident Causes* (Grand Rapids, MI: Department of Public Safety, 1926); Illinois: "Automobile Fatalities Becoming One of Our Deadliest Scourges," *American City* 35 (September, 1926): 341–342; Ohio: State of Ohio, Division of Vital Statistics, Department of Health, "Report of Fatal Accidents from 1910 to 1933," Library of Congress, Washington, DC; United States: Travelers Insurance Company, *The Great American Gamble* (Hartford, CT, 1934); Texas: Texas Department of Public Safety, Driver's License Division, *Texas Highway Accidents, 1938* (Austin, TX: n.p. 1938), subsequent study published in 1939.

Table 2.13. Deaths and Injuries in Auto Accidents, United States, 1933

	Age 0–4	Age 5–14	Age 15–64	Age 65 and Over
Killed	1,630 (5.46%)	3,220 (10.75%)	21,010 (70.27%)	4,040 (13.52%)
Injured	41,430 (4.87%)	138,750 (16.31%)	640,240 (75.26%)	30,280 (3.56%)

Source: Travelers Insurance Company, *The Great American Gamble* (Hartford, CT: 1934), 16, 17, 44.!

Table 2.14. Fatalities due to Automobile Accidents, by Age, Ohio, 1911–1933 (in percentages)

Age	1911	1916	1921	1926	1928	1929	1930	1931	1932	1933
0–9	24	18	25	19	15	14	13	12	11	11
0–19	13	11	12	12	11	12	11	12	11	12
20–34	16	23	17	19	19	21	22	22	21	22
35–55	17	28	23	22	27	25	27	26	26	26
56 and Over	30	20	23	28	28	28	27	28	31	30

Source: State of Ohio, Division of Vital Statistics, Department of Health, "Report of Fatal Accidents from 1910 to 1933," Library of Congress, Washington, DC, 14.

Table 2.15. Pedestrian Accident Victims, by Age Group and Designated Race, Dallas, Texas, 1935–1938 (in percentages)

	Total Population	Anglo American	African American	Hispanic American
0–4	7.8	7.4	5.9	9.9
5–14	26.6	20.0	21.5	37.9
15–24	12.7	12.5	14.3	11.3
25–64	44.4	49.4	50.0	33.4
65+	8.6	10.4	8.4	6.8
	100.0	100.0	100.0	100.0

Source: Dallas Bureau of Traffic Education, "Survey and Report of Pedestrian Traffic Accidents in the City of Dallas, Texas. A Complete Analysis Covering 1935, '36, '37, and together with 1938 Supplemental Summary," Center for American History, University of Texas–Austin.

Table 2.16. Activity Reported to Have Caused an Accident (in percentages)

Activity Reported	CT 1924	CT 1925	MI 1925	CT 1926	CT 1927	US 1933	US 1936–37
Excessive Speed	15.10	17.80	19.70	17.90	12.80	25.57	32.60
Wrong Side of Road	8.00	6.80	9.30	5.80	2.60	12.44	15.00
Off the Road	NA	NA	1.00	NA	NA	11.96	14.50
No Right of Way	24.50	21.20	24.60	21.00	16.80	24.04	13.90
Reckless, Inattentive	29.00	33.20	45.40	36.20	29.70	6.43	12.90

Sources: Connecticut: Richard Shelton Kirby, *A Study of Motor Vehicle Accidents in the State of Connecticut* (New Haven, CT: Hartley Corporation and Yale University Press, 1926); Michigan: James Sinke, *Think: An Analysis of Automobile Accident Causes* (Grand Rapids, MI: Department of Public Safety, 1926); United States: Travelers Insurance Company, *The Great American Gamble* (Hartford, CT: 1934); U.S. Department of Commerce, *Accidents and Opportunity* (Washington, DC: Government Printing Office, 1937 and 1938).

3

The Dysfunctional Love Affair

Extracting a meaningful understanding of Americans' early relationship with the automobile is complicated. Drivers wrote a lot about their experiences and expectations behind the wheel; yet their narrative accounts varied widely. What some essayists viewed as strengths of the motorcar—such as its speed and power—others recognized were liabilities. Some trusted the technology to leap beyond the contemporary problems of the day—such as traffic congestion and urban overcrowding—where others felt only apprehension for the potentially dangerous personal freedoms unleashed by mass automobility. Historical hindsight heightens this debate. Americans know that the automobile "won" the contest over mass transit. Filtering this certainty from the views expressed by the first generations of drivers is difficult, but essential in order to understand why the car was so successful in capturing the trust of the American public.

Robert Bruce's October 1900 essay for *Outing* magazine, "The Place of the Automobile," provides a fine example of both the wild speculation and the powerful associations early drivers made about their cars. Bruce offered no evidence to explain how the automobile could replace the nation's fixed-rail transit system nor was he concerned (or seemingly aware) over the need for billions of dollars in new highway construction, the massive coordination required by federal, state, and local government agencies, or the significant technological limits contained within the basic design of early cars. His unswerving faith appears, today, more delusional than prophetic.[1]

Bruce's defense of the new technology did not rest on its practicality but on its emotional appeal. Unlike rail or animal power, car travel made Americans *feel* different. The auto appealed to citizens' "genuine interest in engineering and mechanics," their "search for adventure," and their quest for personal authority. As one motorist gushed, driving made him feel like "the most independent and absolute monarch locomotion ever produced." These qualities, for Bruce, appeased America's "natural instincts" for excitement, freedom, social equality, and progress. In the end, it was not the capacities of the automobile as a technology system that ultimately satisfied the public. Rather, it was the "feeling of independence which so consciously possesses . . . the seasoned motorist," the "love of sustained speed and endurance," the sensation "of being lifted up and along," and "of gliding down and of bounding up" the roadway that remained the source of the car's consummate appeal.[2]

Robert Bruce's words reflected, of course, the emerging love affair between Americans and their cars. Given the obvious inconsistencies of this relationship, automotive scholars are hesitant to rely too heavily on this concept in their effort to explain automobility.[3] Perhaps the greatest hurdle to overcome is the irrational nature of the love affair. To love a thing we need to give it character, identity, and spirit. Nothing better illustrates this point than the habit of naming and ascribing personalities to cars. In 1924, after purchasing a second-hand Model T, one motorist noted the "curious phenomenon which, doubtless, many car-owners have observed" where "the moment you buy or even consider any sort of automobile, it at once assumes a distinct personality." The closest analogy the author could draw was siring a child. While "most babies look exactly alike . . . their parents assure me that is not the case. Well, so it is with automobiles." Five years earlier Sinclair Lewis defended the uniqueness of his own mass-produced T, saying, "You know how it is. Your flivver is different from all other flivvers. It is smarter and racier and sportier and a lot more powerful. The only reason you have such difficulty in picking it out from the others at the parking space is because you have dust in your eyes."[4]

In later years, as the relationship matured, cars assumed more demanding and fickle persona. Frederic Van de Water, who traveled cross country with his family in 1926, named his automobile Issachar, one of Jacob's twelve sons described in Genesis and whose descendants became slaves of the Egyptians. Van de Water's car acted as both his servant and his master. When conditions turned difficult it seemed that his car took on a decidedly confrontational personality. The family began to notice how the more they adored the vehicle the more it disappointed them. "If I praised him to his face, it was always a forerunner of calamity. He took a cold and sardonic delight in making me out a liar. If I boasted of his prowess in camp, sooner or later the next day, he picked up a nail or blew out a tire with a defiant and contrary zest." While Van de Water loved his car, the machine "always regarded me with sullen disdain and a clenched teeth expression." Irony and abuse, rather than triumph and love, defined the relationship. In the end, Van de Water practiced a form of reverse psychology on himself and in his association with Issachar. He came to believe that the car "thrived on contumely and physical abuse. It became my ritual on rising to kick him in one of his balloon tires and mutter disparaging epithets to guarantee a good day's run."[5]

These projections of personality also existed in U.S. popular culture. Early songs, jokes, and advertisements granted cars an optimistic, can-do personality. The auto was the "snappiest, pluckiest, happy-go-luckiest" device ever created. Authors described early flivvers and other runabouts in Disneyesque-terms, as "stubby" creatures "with scrawny springs and wobbly wheels, with a rattle and a bang as they chug-chugged down the road." One 1909 song chorused: "I am the fizzing, the buzzing, and whizzing, Redoubtable Motor Car! I am the puffing, and chugging, and chuffing, Redoubtable Motor Car!"[6]

In later decades, horror writer Stephen King updated this anthropomorphized vision of the automobile to reflect a more modern sensibility. King gave his 1958 Plymouth Fury, named Christine, a bitchy and vindictive personality. Where, in the early years, Americans once dreamed about the potential of the automobile, today they fear an automotive nightmare. Obsession replaced love. Collective civic values are overshadowed by petulant individualism. For her part, Christine simply slaughtered those who defied her driver's desires.

The frequent use of humor and satire to describe the relationship offers another clue of the irrationality of the early love affair. Comedy functions when an audience shares the unexpected awkwardness of everyday life. Car humor conserves these tensions, between the rational and emotional impulses of driving and between the individual and collective assumptions about a motorized society, to soften the fears we have about the car. Consider the following tale. A senior citizen was driving down the highway when his cell phone rang. Answering, he encountered his wife's frantic plea: "Herman, I just heard on the radio that some damned fool is driving the wrong way down the highway! Please be careful!" "Hell," replied the man, "It's not just one car, it's hundreds of 'em!" Given the unsettling frequency of similar accidents caused by drunk drivers or even the elderly, the humor here is clearly dark. The comedy reflects our own generation's more cautious yet shared perceptions about risk and the roadway.

The uninitiated are often shocked to find these same hard-edged and somewhat cynical perceptions early in the history of mass automobility. Sidney Strong, an essayist for *Collier's* magazine, writing less than five years after the introduction of the Model T, observed that car humor had already shifted considerably. He noted that

only a few years ago the professional humorist's conception of an automobile was of an object that *refused* to move. . . . the comic automobile always stood still, and the driver, holding a monkey wrench, lay on his back under it. To-day the machine is represented with its wheels in the air, and the driver sits dazed in a ditch with one of his legs in the lunch basket, and a spare tire around his neck.

Americans have whistled past the graveyard for over a century.[7]

The novelty and immense popularity of the Model T created a cottage industry in Ford jokes. Most of these revolved around the supposed cheapness of the product or the owner. Speculating on what F-O-R-D might stand for, one wag guessed Funniest Of Recent Discoveries, Filler Of Roadside Ditches, or Fine Old Rattling Device as likely candidates. Others used the flivver to parody current events (one sticker plastered across an engine hood read "I do not choose to run in 1928," a quote taken from the lips of departing single-term president Calvin Coolidge). Regardless, as the authors of the book *Oh, That Funny Ford!* remarked, "our aim is not merely to amuse the scoffers, but to give pleasure to Ford owners themselves . . . goodness knows they need it." The jokes duplicated the shared civic bond that invited all Americans to laugh *with* and not *at* these owners.[8]

Early travel accounts remain the best sources to find the rich experiences, perceptions, and frustrations that constituted the automotive love affair. These usually took the form of published articles and books intended to entertain and enlighten the reader. Many used a self-deprecating humor or presented their efforts as "against all odds" dramas that harked back to the pioneering adventures of preceding generations. While the bias inherent in commercial publishing—most notably, the desire to sell books or secure additional freelance articles—is certainly present in these sources, the accounts provide substance to the collective emotional bonds established in these early years.[9]

Travel narratives were most popular as the automobile shifted from an experimental technology to one that was more easily acquired and used by the middle class. The real strength of these sources is in the ways that they describe Americans' relationship with the car. For most, the car was the crucial difference between exciting and romantic recreation and disappointment or even life-threatening danger. They evangelized for a new automobile culture that promised freedom and life-altering experiences. Melville Ferguson wrote to "persuad[e] the reader who has longingly but hesitatingly contemplated" taking to the open road "that the price to be paid in discomfort or actual hardship is negligible and the rewards in wholesome and instructive experience rich." He believed himself less of an author than "an enthusiastic volunteer organizer and proselytist for the Amalgamated Order of Motor Campers."[10]

One of the best examples of this genre was the work of Winifred Hawkridge Dixon, who drove 11,000 miles across the American southwest with her friend Katherine "Toby" Thaxter in 1922 and wrote *Westward Hoboes: Ups and Downs of Frontier Motoring* in 1924. Her account is lively, charming, intelligent, and paced by the exciting experiences of two young Bostonian women as they explored Texas, New Mexico, and Arizona. Searching for automotive freedom and mobility, the pair plunged into the back country with optimism and determination. One stretch of an Arizona trail summarizes their many misadventures. While they had followed their only reliable guide, the Southern Pacific Railroad tracks, "with dog-like devotion," they soon became lost "in a crooked maze of wagon tracks . . . and had to drive back ten miles to the nearest house to ask directions." To make up for lost time, and "in the bitter, reckless mood every driver knows, when nobody in the car dare speak to him," Dixon "raced for two hours at forty-five [miles per hour], through sandy, twisting tracks, with the car rocking like a London bus." She knew "each turn was a gamble, but the curves were just gentle enough to hold us to our course." Confident that her white-knuckled driving had put them back on schedule, Dixon grimaced when the air "ooze[d] gently out of

The automobile gave many Americans access to a nearly pristine wilderness, seen here at Berthoud Pass on the border of Grand and Clear Creek Counties in Colorado, c. 1920. (Denver Public Library, Western History Collection, Harry Lake, L-396)

the rear tire." Such narratives, where everything that can go wrong in fact does go wrong, only added to the adventure and uncertainty of early motoring.[11]

The pair exhibited all the traits of pioneering American autoists. They marveled at the civic equality and warm hospitality that they experienced throughout their trip. They counted expenses and were pleased to find that the cost did not restrict auto travel to the upper class. They cheered their victories over the miles of rutted and muddy roads, the inaccuracies of local maps, and frequent mechanical breakdowns. They gave enchanting personality traits to their car, nicknamed "the Old Lady," that included bravery, persistence, style, and even vanity. Dixon believed the car, a Cadillac Eight, projected a male "rakish hood" but a "matronly tonneau" making the front "intimidating, its rear reassuring." Completing the first and most arduous part of the journey, across the boggy furrows of rural Texas, the pair stopped in El Paso to "sleep, shop and have the car overhauled." There, they also took time to have the muddy "gumbo of Texas, now caked until it had to be chipped off with a chisel, washed from its surface." Toby wanted the "Old Lady" to "to leave Texas as she had entered it,—with clean skirts." Washed and well-oiled, the car "seemed to feel the difference from her former draggle-tailed state; she pranced a bit [and] . . . shied around corners."[12]

Both Dixon and Thaxter loved speed, noting honestly that the happier they felt the faster they drove. Approaching Houston at 70 miles per hour, Dixon was arrested by the local police and brought to court. She acknowledged being distracted by the two male hitchhikers, both servicemen, whom the girls picked up along the road, but maintained she was doing nothing out of the ordinary. Forced to pay her fine, Dixon took one last dig at the local judge. She pled "I wouldn't have done it for worlds, your Honor, if I hadn't seen all the Texas cars going quite so fast, so I thought you wouldn't mind if I did the same."[13]

The two took pride in controlling their destiny. They relied on their technical proficiency, solved peculiar problems, and responded to emergencies with cool reason. Dixon admitted that her automotive skills were decidedly unconventional, even positively gendered—she relied mostly on hairpins and woman's "intuition"—but she used these skills to correct the many "defective batteries, leaky radiators, frozen steering wheels, cranky generators, wrongly-hung springs, stripped gears and slipping clutches" that plagued them throughout the journey.[14]

Travel accounts such as this, as well as numerous shorter pieces in the popular press and newspapers, give substance to the emotional bond between Americans and their cars. They were humorous, ironic, self-effacing, and often whimsical. Enthusiasts freely equated the experiences behind the wheel with their deepest personal and civic values. The love affair they describe shared four distinct characteristics: the exciting experience of driving, the freedom of automobility, the civic equality of the open road, and the fulfilling sense of progressive mastery over this new technology. Two of these qualities—the sensory excitement and the liberty of driving—changed little over time. The others—a belief in the civic equality and the therapeutic, progressive nature of automobiling—shifted noticeably during these years and in the decades since. All four profoundly influenced the ways that the nation came to understand and then address questions of auto safety.

The most immediate, sustained, and universal quality of America's love affair with the car was the excitement occasioned by individual mechanized travel. Drivers marveled how the auto allowed them to "whirl along at a pace now fast now slow; the machine will respond to his slightest touch, the fresh wind will cause his blood to rise and tingle with exhilaration and in experience of a brief day he will realize what years of reading and theorizing could not teach him regarding the fascinations of motoring." "Next to flying," another thrilled, "there is no sensation to compare to the glorious vagabondage of the open road and the skinning motor car." Auto advocate Leon Vandervort saw this as the most compelling characteristic of the automobile age. He wrote "If Saint Paul should arise and attempt to characterize us as he did the Athenians, he would say . . . that our chief delight is to know some new sensation." In 1924, a first-time driver gushed that he and his wife now "had the world and all these newly discovered thrills to ourselves. Heaven must feel something like those enchanted hours" behind the wheel.[15]

The Motor Car is the Magic Carpet of Modern Times

LEXINGTON MOTOR COMPANY
CONNERSVILLE, INDIANA, U.S.A

Advertisement for the Lexington Motor Company, c. 1920. (Courtesy of the Advertising Ephemera Collection [A0012], Rare Book, Manuscript, and Special Collections Library, Duke University)

Logically, most compared these new sensations to the familiar experiences of rail and animal-powered transit. Vandervort acknowledged that while the typical American may have traveled rapidly in the past, it was "never when he could look directly down on the onrushing road, with no horses or engine to interfere, nor when he rushed about in a carriage drawn by nothing and with no tracks or trolleys." Others noted, unlike rail where one was merely a passenger, the car was "easily controlled" by the operator: "Try it. A touch of the accelerator and the machine jumps to thirty miles an hour. Up with the spark, down with the pedal, and in another minute it is doing fifty-five or sixty." Julian Street concluded that the car provided "more sustained sensations, more picturesqueness and dramatic value" than any other activity.[16]

This rush of adrenaline and sensory stimuli supported the view that driving altered reality and transformed the operator. In 1907, one *Harper's Weekly* contributor expressed "no consciousness of jarring or any other suggestion of coming in contact with the ground." Automobiling was like "running on a thick, endless cushion of air." Many claimed driving produced a calming effect, particularly for the suburban commuter. Everyday commuting was "just the relaxation and exercise that [one] needs, for the running of the car calls into play the muscles which are most needed in relaxation and . . . affords a zest that can be appreciated only by the man who has tried it and felt the effect of its stimulus." The surreal experience led to a "subtle intoxication" that "creeps into the veins . . . as all the world swims past him in swift, silent, glorious panorama." The overall experience was unnatural, "like the magic of some conjurer's trick—when the lamps flicker and dance and the road spins by beneath you like some Titanic ribbon spun for your pleasure, and is reeled into the machine by magic hands beneath; when the hands grip the seats and the hair blows back—when the roar of the air in the ears precludes all other sounds, and the consciousness of the exhaust is but that of vibration." Only after experiencing this new sensation could "then at last you know for what you live, and why, and the meaning and the riddle of your life are made clear."[17]

In addition to the physical sensations of driving, the potential for adventure inherent in the automobile stirred drivers' emotions, recalling visions of an earlier frontier America. Unlike the fixed schedules and destinations of the railroad, cars allowed motorists to *seek* thrills. The road acted "like the stream to the born canoeist"; it became "the pathway of adventure." Motorist Henry Griffin reminded drivers that, in the car, they owned "a veritable Aladdin's carpet, an open sesame to wide countryside, strange roadways, and the wonderland of all outdoors." Often, these magical sprees were nostalgic. In 1907, an admitted "anti-motorist" converted to the cause because he could now revisit regions that he "hadn't seen since I was a boy." In an ironic contrast between his reminiscences and reliance on modern technology, the driver remembered, as he drove home on a warm September afternoon, "the fate of Lot's wife and did not look back."[18]

For the auto tourist, driving delivered the adventure of pioneering and a romantic escape from civilization. Diarists like Sinclair Lewis believed this freedom allowed them to experience life anew, "It was sheer magic, slipping through the steely air over macadam roads. Nothing could ever halt us; we flew, as in a dream . . . not mere getting somewhere but going for the sake of going." He felt transported to "the quiet place of the elder gods" and likened his journey to that of Ulysses. Melville Ferguson stated what was quickly a popular assumption: "there is always adventure just around the corner. That is the basis of its widening appeal."[19]

While the search for adventure was a constant theme of early twentieth-century travel, the car delivered on this promise in ways that other forms of transit could not. Frequently, this excitement was generated by the many mechanical breakdowns experienced along the way. For those crossing mountains or deserts, the sheer drama of surviving in the unforgiving wilderness was quite real. Invariably, authors included their encounters with larger mammals like bears and cougars as rites of passage for the auto tourist. Many, like Winifred Dixon, consciously avoided more settled and commercialized parts of the country, especially those serviced by the rail network. She and her friend made only one premeditated decision about their itinerary, "we would *not* visit California. California was the West, dehorned."[20]

But by the mid-1920s, diarists recognized that the "old spirit of romance [was] fading." Long-distance travel was becoming more commercialized and shorter trips more routine. One disappointed driver believed that the "sentimental phrasing" of these early experiences, "its fervor and emotion—lacks actuality and seems forced and artificial in our matter-of-fact age." While the sensory exhilaration of driving remained, it was less frequently bundled with mythic allegory and exotic destinations unreachable by the masses. Rather, the unique operation of the vehicle itself, especially its speed and power, became the primary means of exhilaration.[21]

From the very beginning, automobilists expressed a love for speed. In the words of one pioneer, he was "conscious of only one wish—to go faster." Another wrote that "no one can ride in an automobile without wanting to go fast. The desire for speed is as natural as the desire for breath. We are all subject to it." But there were limits. Like a narcotic, the thrill of speed was obtained only through greater and greater doses. Many learned that satisfaction was "always just beyond reach. . . . Perhaps it is always flying on, this riddle." The public's love of speed was also curtailed by the rising incidence of auto accidents. By the close of the first decade of the new century, drivers comprehended that "few epidemics of late years are more destructive of human life than the mania for speeding automobiles." While some assumed that the car had secured a lasting place in American society, speed critics fretted that the auto "will certainly not stay unless [it] can be brought under rigid control. If it should appear that it is impossible to reduce the rate of mortality, the automobile will be driven off our highways."[22]

Because speed was such a determining and negative factor in auto safety, the love of speed became more muted in the everyday expression of affection for the car. While the allure remained, fewer were willing to admit their lead foot. The market was not so shy, however, and commercial auto racing soon emerged as a popular spectator sport. By the start of World War I, racing legends like Barney Oldfield earned $40,000 to $50,000 per season from national tours, prize money, and special exhibitions. Lesser celebrities might collect anywhere from $2,000 to $20,000 a year. Long-distance endurance racing emerged first, but these exhibits served more accurately as a function of automotive testing, like research and development. Public interest, which was initially very high, waned for endurance racing. The car was no longer a novelty. People could experience cross-country travel on their own rather than from the sidelines. Closed-track speed racing, by contrast, offered the best of both worlds. Highly skilled drivers used specially designed, high-performance vehicles over courses that were strictly intended for high speeds. While Europeans preferred longer road races, Americans embraced the closed-circuit track, such as the Indianapolis Motor Speedway, founded in 1911. Promoters favored "bringing the car past the grand stand as often as possible." If there was to be an adrenaline rush, the American public wanted a front row seat.[23]

These positive experiences behind the wheel were critical to the initial success of the device as a means of individual transportation. The feelings of adventure, speed, and power provided an immediate and visceral response. While significantly modified over the years, even today (if advertising is to be believed) many Americans seek these qualities through the purchase of an automobile.

A second characteristic of America's automotive love affair was the sense of personal freedom. While closely linked to the physical excitement of driving, notions of freedom and independence offered a slightly more rational justification for the growth of personal automobility. "The man who gets the best out of his motor car," one 1914 essayist wrote, gains "a liberal education in the university of the open spaces and the open air." The belief that the car validated an American's civic freedom remains strong. While modern readers understand auto-related liberties in more qualified terms—as with Bruce Springsteen's "suicide machines" in "Born to Run," where cars provide only a temporary escape from boredom, a dead-end job, or a troubled marriage—in the first decades of the twentieth century the idea carried less baggage. Then, the car offered the freedom to explore new places, to get away from the clock, or to break away from dreary Victorian formalities.[24]

The rhetoric of those who chronicled this faith was studded with references to adventure, romance, and independence. Armed with only a "supply of gasoline to last for a run of two or three days," one autoist believed, a driver could "break away from all civilization and spend a long period in complete retirement." Another explained, "You are your own master, the road is ahead; you eat as you please; sleeping when you will under the stars, waking with the dawn; swim in a mountain lake when you will, and always the road ahead. Thoreau at 29 cents a gallon." Gotham's Melville Ferguson fully "expected to have to make our night stands in isolated spots and depend entirely upon our own resources." He saw himself as the typical "jaded city-dweller" who "longed for the open spaces, the

American auto racing began as endurance testing over many miles. By the 1910s, closed-course ovals like the Indianapolis Motor Speedway or Overland Park in Denver, Colorado, shown here c. 1920, favored vehicle speed and driver daring. (Denver Public Library, Western History Collection, Harry M. Rhoads, Rh-5801)

scent of the moist forest, the wide sweep of the wind across the stark prairie. . . . He knew that he must go."[25]

These expressions must, again, be understood in the comparative context of the times. Car travel was clearly different than railroad or trolley passage. After an initial period of experimentation, where many Americans felt liberated by the extension of fixed-rail commuter services, the experience of "strap hangers" turned sour. Much like airline travel today, common concerns with rail were delays, missed connections, corporate rate fixing, boredom, inefficiency, and frequent carrier unavailability (due to strikes or technical problems).[26]

Accordingly, drivers expressed freedom not in absolute terms but relative to the social restrictions that they knew all too well. Motorists marveled at how the car facilitated feelings of traveling "care free," "on a crusade of joy," and "released" from the burdens of traditional travel. These freedoms carried with them some sense of social responsibility, but this was far from universal and, notably, carried no penalty or provisions for enforcement. When the American Automobile Association published its "Creed of the Open Road" in 1931, it acknowledged that the "love [for] the freedom of the open road" was the leading factor in the amazing growth of auto tourism. But "the open road is not policed, except by the honor of the traveler" and the auto group warned drivers not to "permit freedom to degenerate into license," or to "be so boorish a guest as to leave [the roadways] in disorder and uncleanliness." Even then, the AAA understood what was an important paradox in America's love affair: that individual liberty existed as a privilege that entailed obligation.[27]

The earliest motorists did not feel these twinges of social guilt. The most avid drivers considered themselves gypsies or vagabonds, freed from traditional forms of mass transit and the strict burdens of Victorian morality. As one 1908 autoist remarked, "The care for the morrow should be left for the new dawn. It is a heart-free, care-free trip that one is planning." They reveled in the folksy charm of backcountry inns, poor roads, and the new culture of the highway. Melville Ferguson "learned . . . how to cook a course dinner in a tomato can." Casting a disdainful view at a family of travelers who were so dependent on the comforts of home that they brought along their butler and maid, Van de Water declared that on the road "you work your own passage. Otherwise you don't belong."[28]

This "new brood of American gypsies," however, did not last long. Perhaps this was inevitable. Early long-distance traveling proved feasible for only a limited number of the upper middle class. For them, class distinctions were essential in justifying their place near the top of America's cultural hierarchy. Van de Water, for example, considered his behavior on the road scandalous, compared to life back home. On one occasion, he found himself "sit[ting] in the public park of Lyons, Iowa, within six feet of the main street and shav[ing] himself in plain view of the citizenry on their way to work." Had he predicted such "crude" behavior before starting out on the journey, he later admitted, he "probably should have abandoned the trip."[29]

This awkwardness offered an ideal market opportunity to someone who could preserve the perception of freedom while erasing the class hardships of life on the road. In 1920, Sinclair Lewis essentially predicted the rise of motel chains, like Howard Johnsons, in observing that

> somewhere in these states there is a young man who is going to become rich. . . . He is going to start a chain of small, clean, pleasant hotels, standardized and nationally advertised, along every important motor route in the country. He is not going to waste money on gilt and onyx, but he is going to have agreeable clerks, good coffee, endurable mattresses and good lighting; and in every hotel he will have a least one suite which, however small, will be as good as the average room in a great modern city hotel.

As historian Warren Belasco writes, "Ultimately, the gypsy gave way to the consumer, not because the urge to stray off the beaten path was insincere or unimportant but because the bourgeois route was safer and easier."[30]

The result bred a form of independence stripped of its capacity for radical social change. Drivers confined their activities to those that were once done elsewhere but were now more practical behind the wheel of an automobile. In the case of sexual practices, this meant one row behind the steering wheel. As historian Beth Bailey reports, while the "automobile certainly contributed to the rise of dating as a national practice, especially in rural and suburban areas, . . . it was simply accelerating and extending a process already well under way." The preference and availability of inexpensive closed cars (those that covered the driver and passenger compartments, rather than the open runabout) in the 1920s provided new opportunities for sexual activity. Some, no doubt, "made love in cars because they found it exciting, sometimes dangerously so, and [a] change from familiar surroundings." But just as with creature comforts for auto camping, the market responded to the "couples trade" with convenient and low-cost cabins available for more pleasurable liaisons.[31]

Freedom from time and fixed schedules was another goal that motorists prized. Traveling cross-country in 1908, George Walsh felt "independent of town and cities and all the rush and turmoil of strenuous business life." Even daily commuters found that the car made them "wholly independent of the necessity of catching trains morning and evening." The autoist "may run upon his own time-table and in his own special train with even greater independence than the president of the railroad himself." Others thrilled at how the automobile exposed their dependency on railroad time, teaching them how to relax. One admitted he "had laid down . . . a schedule of daily runs" that mirrored the railroad schedule across the country. He soon realized that such a "schedule was a great mistake" and "the consequence was that, being always behind time, we ever felt obliged to rush through places where we should have liked to linger. . . . Time-card regulation of a gypsy tour is incongruous. It was our worst blunder." Winifred Dixon actually planned her voyage to be "uncertain." She and her traveling companion intended "to drift, to sketch and write when the spirit moved." Dixon explicitly contrasted this type of freedom to the confines of railroad travel, which "implie[d] time-tables, crowded trains, boudoir-capped matrons, crying babies and the smell of bananas, long waits and anxiety over reservations." All told, the automobile liberated those who "hated alarm clocks . . . and the faces of the conductor who twice daily punched his ticket on the suburban train."[32]

The feelings of freedom and independence, like that of sensory excitement, had long-lasting effects on the relationship between Americans and their automobiles. On one level, the limits of mass transit over the rails justified both qualities. Not only was motoring a thrilling new sensation, but the lone driver controlled and directed the action. His will determined his destination, not the conductor, the schedule, or the company mangers who laid down the tracks. But there was something more than a comparative advantage to automobiles. The *potential* for freedom unbound—to go where one wanted, when it was convenient, as fast or as slow as one wished, to suit the driver's tastes and not those of his neighbors—seemed equally unlimited. Even in the early years, when the complexity and high cost of motoring worried consumers more than the accidents or congestion of later generations, the promised benefits of automobile freedom obliterated concern. In his 1913 essay "Motor Car 'Don'ts,'" *Collier's* contributor A. G. Johnson presented a long list of problems awaiting the neophyte driver. Still, he concluded,

> Don't forget . . . that there is a credit-item which far outweighs any expenditure that you have made. You have spent some money on the car, but the car has taken you out into the sweetness and light of God's out-of-doors; has filled your lungs with good clean air; has browned your cheeks with the caress of the sun; has steadied your nerves; has added twenty years to your life, and by the same token has made every minute of the time better worth living.

These feelings of excitement, adventure, and freedom remained strong throughout the era and sustained America's love affair with the automobile.[33]

In contrast to these two more enduring aspects, the concepts of social equality and progress changed rapidly from 1900 to 1940 and are certainly not universally embraced today. One obvious reason for this difference is that sensory excitement and impressions of freedom are highly individualized, whereas equality and progress require a broader, more inclusive view of the driving public. It was, and is, easier for drivers to feel good about their own skills and character than to grant the same attributes to others. In the earliest decades of the twentieth century, the popular understanding of automobility strongly supported notions of civic equality and social progress. By the 1920s and 1930s, however, accidents, aggressive driving, and market forces shifted these perceptions in considerable and consequential ways.

Civic equality has shown itself to be an enduring ideal of American society. From the Declaration of Independence to the present day, the nation has defended the principle that all are created equal and that this natural right should be upheld by law. While it is foolish to suggest that the country consistently honored this promise, the ideal remains part of the backbone of America's civic and political ideology.

Economic equality, however, is much less consistent. In a capitalist country, economic equality is not an ideal to be achieved (all citizens earning the same amount of money, for example) but rather an *opportunity* to be grasped (all have the chance to achieve wealth). While economic opportunity, in concept, does not necessarily clash with civic equality, the two concepts rest on very different principles: one is a possibility while the other is a natural right. The changes from a rural, agrarian, and producer economy to an urban, industrial, and consumer one, largely accomplished around the turn of the century, radically altered the opportunities for economic equality. These shifts aggravated long-standing national rivalries, justified and empowered materialist doctrines like socialism and communism, and spawned dynamic organizations like the corporation and the industrial union. The period from 1900 to 1940 was one of the most violent eras for labor, racial, international, and political strife in modern times. For the most part, this ferocity was driven by a desire to maintain or augment one's economic advantage over others.

The concept of automotive equality was influenced by both of these contradictory definitions. Universal civic equality meant that the freedoms of driving should be secured for all Americans and that all shared in the collective responsibility to preserve this right. Economic equality, by contrast, supported the view that only those who had the "opportunity" to drive, meaning enough money or free time, were legitimate "citizens" of the road.

Within this context, the appearance and spread of Fordism was one of the most stabilizing social events in modern American history. Universal access to low-cost luxuries like the automobile provided economic equality to millions and justified the claim of civic equality in capitalist America. As historian David Harvey argues, Fordism provided very little real economic power to laborers or the middle class, but it essentially fused the two notions of equality in American culture. What was good for GM was now good for America because the values of both economic and civic equality were one. For American drivers and, more generally, American culture, the change was profound.[34]

Before Ford, most Americans did not drive and generally resented the pampered elite who did. The civic inequality exposed by driving was politically dangerous. Princeton University president Woodrow Wilson, in an often-cited 1906 speech, argued that "possession of a motor car is such an ostentatious display of wealth that it will stimulate socialism" in America. Newspapers and periodical accounts reveled in printing stories of elite motorists running down pedestrians and generally disregarding the safety of others. Most assumed that these first car owners were "rolling in wealth" and, in reality, they were not far from the truth.[35]

Early auto culture did little to minimize these class tensions. The Automobile Club of America was comprised of and controlled by the nation's elite, like William G. Vanderbilt, who constructed his own private expressway on Long Island and raced his many cars both domestically and abroad. The ACA sponsored auto shows and road races (the most popular run over Vanderbilt's personal course) that only reinforced Wilson's view of the car as "ostentatious display." Unlike the perception today of NASCAR fans, racing then was "a pastime . . . [that] only the very wealthy can indulge." Given "the great costs of these racing cars, the expense of their upkeep and the fabulous expenses of the racers themselves, many people very naturally gained the impression that cars were wholly beyond their reach." As late at 1924, many believed that the man "who travels in a closed car," which was the original meaning of the term *limousine,* was "repugnant" and simply wanted "to display his rank and wealth."[36]

The appearance of the mass-produced, inexpensive "Tin Lizzie" changed economic necessity into civic virtue. Model T drivers like Sinclair Lewis and Frederic Van de Water marveled at how their jalopies broke down the barriers between complete strangers. Van de Water's flivver, Issachar, went "a long way toward establishing this comradeship . . . [it] disarmed suspicion and resentment . . . [and] was a guaranty that all men were at least our equals." He later wondered whether he would have been greeted as warmly in "a high-priced car," but was content to know that "the dustier and more disreputable we appeared, the more hospitable and warm-hearted people grew." One tourist expressed this as a "democratizing agent, that it should bring back to us something of the wide and intimate acquaintance."[37]

As Fordism spread throughout the auto industry, car ownership became a possibility for most of the middle-class, some of the working-class, and nearly all farming families. By 1939, the typical car owner looked a lot like the typical American. Statistically, one writer summarized, he was "43, married and the father of two children, earning $20 to $30 a week and owning a second-hand car. His present car, worth about $238, is four to five years old, but capable of meeting travel requirement of 8,500 miles a year, with consumption of 600 gallons of gasoline." Most would laugh if told their cars represented an "ostentatious display of wealth."[38]

Certainly car culture was not alone in defining equality in terms of consumption. The parallel growth of the suburbs gave the middle class even more reason to define themselves through their possessions and less by their status as producers. R. H. Van Court, writing for *American Homes and Gardens* just two months before Woodrow Wilson became U.S. president, believed that "the practical advantages of motoring are within the reach of just the class most in need of its help—the hard working business man of moderate means and his family." The automobile made it "possible his working in the city and living with his family in the country . . . it secures for them the fullness of the enjoyment of country living."[39]

The merger of civic and economic equality was soon expressed by drivers in more subtle ways. For example, the equality of the open road supported a greater sense of national unity as drivers began to interact more directly and randomly. Part of this experience came, no doubt, from the act of travel itself. Whether by horse, train, or automobile, tourists noticed a comparative sense of regionalism as they left the comfort of their homes. Moreover, the turbulent times—which included two world wars, a great depression, and several strong periods of anti-ethnic fervor—engendered a powerful cultural need to see the country as one great melting pot, whether this existed in reality or not. Auto touring provided the mobile middle class direct contact with new communities and numerous opportunities to consider national diversity. Even state license plates, which preserved a sense of regional distinctiveness, reminded many of a broader national unity. Ike Ashburn, the publisher of the auto advocacy magazine *Texas Parade,* noticed this during his trip to the Gettysburg battlefield. Ashburn found "a Georgia car and a Massachusetts car parked side by side as signifying the dissipation of the bitterness that once existed between North and South, and the reunion on these battlefields of citizens of the United States who, while expressing their reverence for their dead, nevertheless have reached an accord and understanding *largely attributable to the fact* that highways have made these sections easily accessible to each other." Winifred Dixon was similarly fascinated by how her Boston roots accentuated her bonds with rural Texans. Frederic Van de Water's voyage deeply affected his family's notions of citizenship. As a result of driving, they "were no longer New Yorkers, but Americans, which, they learned, is something surprisingly and hearteningly different." His wife's disdain for western culture disappeared, "to her, they are awful no longer but instead folk who can be respected and admired by even a dweller in Manhattan." Summarizing, he intoned that "To us 'America' no longer is an abstract noun, or a familiar map of patchwork, or a flag, or a great domed building in Washington. It is something clearer and dearer and, we think, higher. It is the road we traveled."[40]

The popularity of auto camping fully merged these perceptions of civic and economic equality, much as the earlier Ford-Firestone excursions had absorbed the broader themes of American automobility. The period between 1915 and 1923 saw the greatest activity. Before then, the services needed by an average driver to take an extended trip—such as garages, filling stations, and good roads—were not in place. By 1923, the father and son team of "automobummers," John C. Long and John D. Long, estimated that "thousands play golf each year, tens of thousands play tennis, hundreds of thousands engage in baseball, but in the past few years millions have gone in for motor camping." While avid enthusiasts, the two were not wrong in their estimate of auto camping's popularity. More than 2,000 camps and "a considerable literature on the art of motor camping" existed by 1925. The low cost of gasoline and supplies, assuming one had access to a motor car, kept the excursions within the budget of the middle class. As early as 1908, motorist George Walsh wrote, "few are so restricted in their vacation expenses that they cannot make arrangements to go touring for a few weeks." Expenses ranged from $25 to $75 dollars per trip.[41]

But consumerism soon put a price tag on the egalitarianism of the open road. In crossover states, those between northern cities and the western national parks, local communities saw the economic potential of auto tourism. One cross-country tourist noted that "Camps east of the Alleghenies are comparatively scarce. On the other side of the rampart there are few towns that have not at least one camp. Frequently there are two or three, while many houses in addition, advertise their willingness, even eagerness, to welcome wanderers for over night."

A study of Iowa, in 1923, found that more than "two hundred towns and cities" maintained some sort of auto camp in that state alone. The "Evergreen Playground" surrounding Puget Sound claimed over seven hundred camps and, by 1930, 5,450 individual cabins. While campers perceived a sense of civic solidarity with the locals, it was their purchase of local retail goods that kept the good times rolling. Researchers at Iowa State College estimated that each carload of travelers spent up to $5 a day in local cash purchases. It appeared as if Ford Motor Company's $5-a-day salary had trickled down to the tourist trade.[42]

The heightened role of consumption changed the experience of auto camping. For example, the amount of gear "needed" to gypsy increased dramatically. In the words of Sinclair Lewis, it was "camping for the sake of showing off the delightful equipment." No Conestoga wagon was better stocked. Lewis recalled a doctor from Chicago with enough paraphernalia to make an "army division—with tanks—look like a tramp with one spare shirt button." Another long-distance traveler purchased an assortment of stoves, buckets, blankets, poles, cameras, a rifle, a spade, four spare tubes, fishing gear, a crowbar, a trench pick, boots, a phonograph, records, water, and an Airedale named "Swive" before setting out on the road. Certainly a camping trip that spanned days or weeks at a time required many of these devices. But it was also the act of consuming and the visibility of these goods that made such a lasting impression. Winifred Dixon best captured the pleasures of accumulating gear when she concluded: "The charm of an article which collapses and becomes something else than it seems I cannot analyze nor resist."[43]

A similar commercialization took place in the camp itself. Warren Belasco found that the entire feel of the camps changed as services, such as bathrooms, running water, and cook stoves, appeared within individual cabins. What was once a community experience sustained by civic equality was now a consumed and highly individualized affair. Officials with the "Paradise Camp," an auto camp established in the Mt. Ranier National Park, found, in 1930, that

few years ago when the auto camp was just starting it was looked on with little favor by the majority of better class travelers; this of course was before the days of modern cabins with running water, lights and the high type of equipment now available. . . . Paradise Camp was available for those who were financially unable to meet the prices of the hotel, and a census of the cars parked near the tents at the camp would have shown the majority to be those vernacularly known as "crates." Now it is not at all uncommon to see Packards and Cadillacs and other expensive cars parked near the tents.

To Belsaco, the original and authentic appeal of the camps was soon replaced by "style and advertising: New England, Virginia, or Spanish colonial architecture; innlike signs and names; homey lace curtains, rocking chairs, and window boxes with flowers. The tourist camp was still a 'home away from home,' but it resembled more a suburban bungalow than a humbler farmer's cottage."[44]

What was first evident in auto camping soon characterized American car culture. Drivers demanded a lot of stuff. This included a variety of goggles, dusters, hats, boots, and gloves. Individualizing the mass-produced car was also an essential task. Retailers encouraged motorists to personalize their cars through custom kits, just as they aggrandized their personal wardrobes. These consumer values gained strength from the structural shifts in the auto industry and the loosening of consumer credit. General Motors successfully replaced Ford's low-cost universal car with multiple automotive lines that played off of these personal desires to impress the neighbors. Historian Pamela Walker Laird noted how aggressive auto advertising "set a new pace for the field with dynamic images and copy about power, speed and fun." Modern advertising used latent elitism, of snobbish self-importance (in Laird's view, "for lively, youthful adventurers, or those who perceived themselves as such"), to sell speed, power, exclusivity, and a record number of new cars by 1929.[45]

Conspicuous consumption was certainly not limited to the automobile. But the very visible and public nature of driving heightened the public consciousness of the car. In the earliest years, when few perceived much difference between the "pleasure in engine riding than buggy riding," one clear reason to make the switch was "because everyone saw you when you drove about town." One 1906 essayist resolved "I ought to have [a car]. I can just see myself in one going to the grocery around the corner. . . . I'd put on my leather clothes and my goggles and my cap and I'd honk-honk around . . . on one wheel." His rationale, "I owe it to myself," became the consumer's creed of the twentieth century. The *Saturday Evening Post* wrote, in 1923, that "a majority of people . . . will go into debt to buy an automobile much more readily than they will to buy anything else. They will also agree to larger monthly payments." This willingness to buy "more car" than needed was no longer confined to the anxious urban middle class, but also the "people who live in villages and small towns who like to look prosperous."[46]

Excessive consumerism, particularly when it seemed only to glorify the "latent arrogance and selfishness of its driver," undermined the spontaneity and authenticity of travel. As early as the 1910s, many lamented the explosive growth of roadside signs that advertised for local garages, rest stops, or regional attractions. One frustrated traveler noted how contrived references to scenic attractions or "a little local history" were typically used only "to sugar the pill of a tire advertisement." The modern motorists no longer discovered America but purchased prepackaged experiences along the roadside. One tourist party was asked whether they stopped at a particularly charming village, Chocorua, New Hampshire, along their route. The passengers recalled for "a vague moment; then one of us pipes up: 'Oh, yes, of course. I remember. Chocorua was where we got the ice-cream cones.'"[47]

Consumer elitism and the commodification of the roadways had predictable effects on the supposed leveling egalitarianism of the automotive community. Even the image of the Model T, once the great symbol of America's equal access to automobility, changed. By the 1920s, many people owned second- or third-hand runabouts. Model T jokes, which once sought to ease the fears of new automobilists of moderate means, now reflected the consumer values of a more assertive and class-conscious bourgeoisie. Instead of positive values, like practicality and frugality, the flivver now suggested crudeness and inferiority. Some of the "cheap" humor was still just slapstick, like the Ford dealer who thought his agent had sold twelve cars to New York City's elite "Four Hundred" only to find it was "a dozen Ford cars for $400." But other jokes cut deeper, like the businessman who fell on hard times and wore "a wig and false whiskers" rather than be seen driving a Ford. Even the day laborer now expressed embarrassment at driving a flivver. In one joke, when told by his suburban boss that he should never drive the family T without permission, the handyman responded with an indignant "You bet I won't."[48]

While few people openly expressed their class biases, auto camping confirmed a pronounced shift in the ideal that all were equal behind the wheel. The recession that followed World War I hit both the rural population and unskilled laborers particularly hard. Large numbers of displaced workers took to the roads, relying on the camps for low-cost and convenient shelter. An Iowa state college study cautioned that "the greatest source of trouble is from peddlers and itinerant workmen, who desire to remain more or less permanently at the camp in order to reduce personal expenses while working in the community. These classes usually tend to predominate at the beginning and end of the camping season." In the Puget Sound region, camp owners heard "complaints . . . made against the camp. Undesirable people made their abode there and demanded that wood be hauled and light furnished." As expected, these transients were frequently blamed for such common nuisances as increased garbage or noise, which were more than likely the result of increased usage. Auto-tourist Melville Ferguson unsympathetically viewed these nomads as "professional hoboes who are so skillful at panhandling that they can afford the luxury of motoring in fourth-hand flivvers." Others categorized them as a "sinister, frowzy, none too honest lot" and proposed stiff increases in user fees or legal restrictions. Gypsies no longer represented the freedoms of automobility, but rather the supposed laziness and vice inherent in lower-class transience.[49]

The legal provisions covering auto camping changed as a result of these perceptions. Early codes, like those in California (1921) or Iowa (1922), specified services that the camps must provide to all motorists. These included access to water and sewage lines, flush toilets, paid garbage removal, and a permanent, on-site caretaker. The California statute warned local communities that "every effort should be made to keep the grounds and equipment in an attractive and sanitary condition. To the tired stranger a cordial invitation and a hearty welcome are important—but neatness and cleanliness mean more."[50]

But by the middle of the decade, ordinances shifted from insuring the equality of all motorists to securing the rights of those who were able to pay higher user fees. These changes harmed many penny-pinching travelers, down on their luck and looking to make a fresh start. Camps banned activities that implied homelessness, such as cooking over open fires or allowing children to roam free. The minimum charge rose from a quarter to up to a dollar a day and stays were limited to two weeks or less. Camp managers showed less concern for neatness and cleanliness than with maintaining order. In one case, the superintendent was granted "full police power subject to the orders of the chief of police" to deal with any trouble. Private camp owners also placed political pressures on municipalities to close their low-cost, government-run facilities. Clinton Ambrose, the secretary of the Oregon Auto Camp Association, reported in 1928 how the "Association continues its protest against the subsidized city operated tourist camp—camps maintained in competition with private enterprise which are taxed directly or indirectly for their maintenance." As Belasco has shown, such protests were effective in first curtailing then killing the publicly owned auto camp.[51]

John Steinbeck's 1939 novel *The Grapes of Wrath* eloquently captures the hardships that accompanied these changes. Following the ill-fated Joad family on their automotive odyssey from Oklahoma to California, Steinbeck uses the camps as both a case study and metaphor for Depression-era poverty. Forced to migrate to find jobs, the family is also forced into the role of undeserving poor through their camp experiences. Entering a commercial auto camp for the first time, the Joads were quickly apprised of their feeble civic rights beyond the marketplace:

> The proprietor said: "If your want to pull in here an' camp it'll cost you four bits. Got a place to camp an' water an' wood. An' nobody won't bother you."
>
> "What the hell," said Tom. "We can sleep in the ditch right beside the road, an' it won't cost nothin."
>
> The owner drummed his knee with his fingers. "Deputy sheriff comes on by in the night. Might make it rough for ya. Got a law against sleepin' out in this State. Got a law about vagrants."
>
> "If I pay you half a dollar I ain't a vagrant, huh?"
>
> "That's right."

The tense negotiations broke down completely after the owner concluded that the family lacked the money needed and were simply a bunch of "goddamn bums." Tom angrily replied "when'd we get to be bums? We ain't asked ya for nothin'. All of us bums, huh? Well, we ain't askin' no nickels from you for the

Depression-era Americans often relied on their cars for mobility and shelter. Here a migrant woman is camped in Lincoln County, near Prague, Oklahoma, 1939. (Courtesy of the Library of Congress, Prints and Photographs Division, FSA-OWI Collection [LC-USF34-033486-D DLC])

chance to lay down an' rest." For Steinbeck, only the nonprofit government-run camp, affectionately known as the Weedpatch, supported the civic values that motoring once espoused. At this camp, the family found simple amenities, like running water and flush toilets, community governance, entertainment, and even speed bumps to protect children from the constant traffic. The one dollar per week charge was paid in labor; the family helped clean and maintain the camp. Here, equality was sustained by communal solidarity, not market forces, a theme that Steinbeck returns to throughout his novel.[52]

While privatization was certainly not confined to nor caused by the automobile, consumerism clearly changed the concepts of equality within the love affair. Where drivers were once thought of as equal participants in a broad social network, society was now physically and intellectually segmented by the burgeoning marketplace. The strong sense of civic duty implicit in the notion of equality was equally shorn away by consumption. For safety reform this change was critical. Privatized automobility allowed many to situate the causes of auto accidents within equally individualized problems, and often within the context of age, class, gender, or ethnicity. In short, the problem shifted from an increasingly complex social interaction to one that blamed an increasingly ill-prepared "problem" driver.

A final component of the love affair was the progressive nature of automobility. Like equality, the concept of progress contains both public and private meaning. Civic progress meant social evolution. A progressive society uses modern technologies and methods more efficiently than previous eras. It actively encourages rational planning, bureaucratic control, and the scientific method to identify and propose solutions to society's ills. The car was one of many technologies introduced around the turn of the century that offered the opportunity to modernize America through progress. Clearly, the stated intent of civic progress is *improvement*; a judgment that the "old ways" are inferior or less progressive than the new.

The private meaning of progress was even more predisposed to normative and moral judgments. A progressive individual was someone who demonstrated the ability to adapt to modern society. One proved his or her mettle by mastering new technologies and bending these tools to meet one's personal needs. Moreover, such a person embraced the challenge to conquer these changes. "Good" progressive citizens succeeded in this transition while "bad" ones did not.

The technological sophistication needed to maintain and operate a motor vehicle seemed a tailor-made opportunity for progressive American society and the driving public. Accounts of "good" and "bad" driving were dotted with references to how a driver must master the technology, control their own impulses, and use the car to advance past others too stupid or ill equipped to do the same. Writing near the conclusion of World War I—perhaps the most serious challenge to the concept of progress in Western culture—John Eustis argued that the automobile was "the great civilizing agent of modern times. The Great War has set civilization back many years and the motor vehicle will be a big factor in helping it to catch up with the progress of the time. Pessimism as to the future of the nature of that vehicle is unthinkable."[53]

Technical mastery was the initial prerequisite for the progressive motorist. Robert Bruce wrote that, in driving, a "premium is placed not only upon mental and mechanical dexterity in management, but also upon careful and accurate judgement in such prosaic matters as equipping and refueling." He argued that a "considerable knowledge, if not indeed a technical command, of the principles" of the car were "essential to so complete a mastery." Those who demonstrated this proficiency, such as auto mechanics, were highly esteemed. Lewis joked that "garage men are not merely topics of discussion" among motorists, but closer to "principles of ethics." This faith initially lent automotive progress an optimistic rather than elitist tone; one based on the premise that individuals could choose to act or to ignore this pressing opportunity.[54]

Advocates made no pretense that the internal combustion motor car was a simple device to understand. They did, however, assume that any motivated amateur could safely master the basics and, in the process, demonstrate their command over the car and their own lives. In the words of one educator, "the entire joy of motoring" was not "simple driving; a lot of it is in *knowing* your car." Another warned that while a motorist "will find himself from the very beginning on a small island of Possibility, completely surrounded by a sea of 'Don'ts,'" careful application and training could elevate them to the ranks of the technically savvy. The early literature certainly provided a lengthy list of motoring "don'ts." Much like the popular books that educated the emerging middle class on proper manners, these tracts established the minimal competencies and attitudes that progressive drivers must display. Typical was a 1910 *Harper's Weekly* essay titled "Motor-car Don'ts for Neophyte Owners," which listed fifty-four prohibitions. These spanned from simply "seeing you have plenty of oil, gasoline, and water" to behavioral advice like don't "'hog' the road" or "don't lose your head; keep cool."[55]

The tone of these essays hints at the social hierarchy contained within progress. Many wrote as if they were tolerant schoolmasters instructing particularly dim-witted students. The new driver was not an adult, but rather like a child "enter[ing] upon a new stage of his existence." Some essayists, like C. H. Claudy, dispensed advice as a venerable "Old Motorist" to characters that clearly misunderstood the true nature of the automobile. Others developed a more mystical approach to progress, likening technical skills to an art or athletic prowess. Progressive drivers learned to "control their muscles and make them obey instantly and accurately the commands of their brains," proving their "mastery over the car and over oneself." There were signs "visible to him," the trained motorist, "invisible to others." Some, like Herbert Harrison, hinted at a near evolutionary change in the experienced driver who, "having grasped [the] elementary points. . . . will find himself growing into a very close sympathy and understanding of the motor—the ear, eye and sense of touch will become highly developed and sensitive to even the smallest details of its mechanism. This feeling will lead to a certain sense of justice—to a loving care for the car and an unwillingness to work it beyond its capacity." In the end, as *Scientific American* surmised in 1919, "almost any person of average intelligence can learn to drive a car" as long as they make the "modern motor car . . . obey its masters." The frequent repetition of terms like *mastery* and *control,* in describing the automotive love affair, was not coincidental.[56]

Auto manufacturers turned to this explanation—a lack of technical sophistication in drivers—to explain many mechanical troubles. Executives from various car companies found the greatest fault not with their products or the ways they were educating the public in their use, but with those unable to adapt to the more demanding technical requirements of automobility. Packard blamed a general "lack of attention" for most glitches. Officials from the Dayton Motor Car Company believed that "More than 95 per cent of the troubles" came from simple "carelessness and ignorance." One Cadillac executive reported finding "the remains of a cigar in the pump strainer" as evidence of the idiocy one could expect from the typical motorist. Only through the benevolent skill of the engineer and mechanic, the author concluded, could "inexperienced and ignorant people" find a reasonable degree of satisfaction. This early link, between problems with the auto and the guilt of technical ignorance, would develop into an important explanation of auto accidents in the years to come.[57]

Learning to drive converted many fears to pride. Driving skills were not simply methods of self-preservation but an indication that one had the personal character needed to "master" their machine. Terms like character, honor, and responsibility were frequently used to support these technical skills. Writing a fictional account of a conversation between a father, considering buying his children a car, and a pool of experienced drivers, C. H. Claudy highlighted the "character-building" qualities of the automobile as its chief advantage. Car ownership sharpened a son's "self reliance; it will develop his taste for mechanics. Give him a car on condition that he care for it himself . . . put the car in his hands as a trust to be administered, not as a toy for his amusement, and see if it doesn't do him a lot of good."[58]

The truest test of how effectively the automobile developed character was in the changes shown in women drivers. One female driver, who had logged over 80,000 miles behind the wheel, believed that "the real pleasure" for her sex was in "realizing the power she is now able to control, she will learn to love her car almost as a living being and will only with the greatest reluctance ever take any seat except the one at the wheel." Claudy's fictional advocates told one man, concerned with his daughter's driving abilities, how "the gas car has made even greater headway among women than these improvements would warrant. It is the women who are changing, too, as well as the cars. And it is the cars themselves, and their use by women, which has made the development possible." Virginia Scharff, in her study of women drivers in the earliest years of automobility, noted how the car helped women to act independently within the confines of a masculine culture. In her words, "the auto was born in a masculine manger, and when women sought to claim its power, they invaded a male domain." Claudy would agree, noting that when women drivers "go out in the country and have a puncture they no longer sit on the fence and cry, waiting for some masculine rescuer to come along and fix it for them—they go pluckily to work with jack and wrench and . . . are soon on their way rejoicing." They can "take pride in the accomplishment rather than the shame in the soiled hands. It is a development of character as well as of machine which makes it possible!"[59]

Clearly, women faced substantial prejudices, which extended well beyond the curbside. Rather than contest these biases, though, many simply assumed that progressive driving would harness the "natural" tendencies of women to more positive ends. Fred Jopp reassured readers that "The hand that rocks the cradle is quite as steady and sturdy at the wheel of a car" as that of a man. He considered women drivers much "less inclined to take chances that have dangerous possibilities." Many female drivers agreed, such as one in 1908 who argued that the "spirit of recklessness that often comes with the potential power and speed of a car is . . . far more a trait of man than of woman. A man has more of a spirit of bravado than a woman." Dr. Katherine D. Manion, the former president of the National Medical Women's Association, speaking before the American Medical Association in 1924, argued that women easily adapted to the car, making the "modern girl . . . the healthiest, happiest girl the world has ever known." She "wouldn't exchange the modern flapper, as you call her, for any other girl of any other time."[60]

But much of the discussion about women focused on stereotypical qualities that were ill suited to the car. Vanity was often cited, such as among those who purchased their cars to match fabric samples rather than their technical competencies or those who took to the streets despite "a natural disinclination to do any work that will soil hands or clothing." A female essayist, writing in 1910, believed women "worshiped more ardently at the shrine than any man. Something about this showy, sputtering immensity, or else all of it—its size, its noise, its display— appealed mysteriously to the sex that loves gems that shine and silk that rustles." Another caustically surmised that the "only thing about a car which a woman does not have to teach herself with patience and skill is how to dress for it."[61]

Age-old prejudices were widely applied to diagnose the woman driver. Kate Masterson, who despised the loosening morals of the auto age, believed that women "have made guys of themselves, donning dresses of leather, hideous goggles, shapeless veils and hoods, and so attired they have displayed themselves . . . like disheveled Bacchantes, talking the lingo of the motor and eating and drinking voraciously." The new female driver, Masterson held, once "the creature of smiles, tears, and moods, now hugs her chains of cogs, bolts, levers, cranks, all of which she knows better than her prayers." Others suggested that women lacked the innate capacity for driving. *Outlook* contributor Montgomery Rollins stated,

> She is not trained to think of two things at once. . . . The boy is trained from earliest youth in playing baseball, where he has to watch two or three bases at once, to say nothing of the home plate and numerous other points; he is trained in a thousand and one ways to act quickly and in emergencies. . . . With a few exceptions, a woman seldom reaches this peculiar phase of mental activity, called for time and time again in automobiling. . . . a woman is not to be compared to a man in level-headedness.

These and other prejudices would return to describe the "accident prone" driver in later years.[62]

But such strong bias also indicates just how deeply progressive values pervaded America's car culture. On the one hand, it was assumed that even women, portrayed collectively as scatterbrained, immature citizens, could be trained to properly operate a motor vehicle. They simply needed to apply themselves to the task and to control their natural (and in this case, ill-serving) instincts. Manners maven Margaret Emerson Bailey, like C. H. Claudy, believed that cars had the power to overcome the limits of gender. Bailey mocked the indecisive, demure, and nervous female driver as well as the badgering, backseat wife. To Bailey, these stereotypes were relics of the past rather than representatives of the day. The modern female driver displays "tact and confidence! She seems certain in the . . . knowledge of the roads. . . . [and] certain of our ability to drive." Another advocate argued that these traditional biases against women were "not insurmountable, and as a matter of fact are much more imaginary than real, and that there is no good reason why thousands of women should sit quietly in the tonneau and let the men have the keenest enjoyment of the greatest sport of to-day." Ann Murdock, in a girl-to-girl chat with fellow *Journal* readers, cheered "it is all up to you. It's your moment, and whether you are going to become panicky or prove yourself to be a self-confident, independent, resourceful and intelligent American girl, the next hour will determine." Women willing to take on the modern challenge could gain a full appreciation for, and participate in, the love affair as equals.[63]

The negative repercussions of these progressive values, on the other hand, were equally significant. Coupled with the triumph of consumer values, the highly individualized and judgmental nature of "progressive driving" shifted responsibility for auto accidents away from the car, the state, and society-at-large toward the irresponsible old-fashioned driver ill suited for modern times. In addition, even though advocates themselves reveled in the subjective pleasures of automobility—a key aspect of the love affair—these same irrational qualities were just as often ascribed to the "problem" driver. As the safety crisis deepened, progressive reformers used this double standard against those they believed to be incapable of civic or personal improvement. They argued that personality profiles and IQ tests administered by progressive psychologists would identify and remove these lone nuts behind the wheel once and for all.

The automotive love affair between 1900 and 1940 was very real. Americans of all types and backgrounds expressed a common appreciation for the excitement and freedom of the car. While the more elastic concepts of equality and progress shifted considerably during these same years, drivers frequently returned to these ideals to describe the allure of the nation's automotive culture. The qualities, by themselves, are not particularly "American." Other nations developed similar rationales for their relationship with the car. But close analysis of the love affair establishes a unique cultural context for how people understood and described their relationship to technology, the roadway, and to their fellow citizens. Indeed, Americans found the concepts so flexible, yet clear, that they applied them in their understanding the *problems* of mass automobility. Automotive citizenry was a two-way street.

Avoidable Accidents and the Challenge of

Automotive Citizenship

On the night of May 5, 1938, six people lost their lives in an automobile accident just outside of Dallas, Texas. The collision occurred near the town of Kleberg, at the intersection of State Highway 15 and Belt Line Road. Billy Mullins, an employee of the Terrell State Hospital, was hurrying home from a Dallas minor league baseball game in his 1936 Ford Model A with another member of the psychiatric hospital's staff, Bill Roach, and three African American inmates, Leonard White, Andrew Monroe, and August Chandler. Gus Darst, returning from a night at the movies with Aubrey Welch, his sister Dorothy Welch, and her friend Alva Pruett, was driving south on Highway 15 when his 1934 Model A entered the same intersection, around 11:18 p.m. In all likelihood, both Fords housed the new 65-horsepower V-8 motor, introduced in 1932. At top speed, the engine propelled the 2,400-pound machine to over 120 miles per hour. Some considered the V-8 Model A the company's finest complete package of styling, economy, and power. The outlaw Clyde Barrow observed, in 1933, "For sustained speed and freedom from trouble the Ford has got [every] other car skinned . . . what a fine car you got in the V-8." Investigators estimated that both vehicles were doing well over 60 miles per hour when they collided. The impact spun Mullins's car 105 feet in the air and pitched Darst's vehicle twice that distance down the center of Belt Line Road. The collision instantly killed White, Monroe, and Chandler, from the first car, and Dorothy Welch from the second. Alva Pruett, who sustained a basal skull fracture, and Darst, who suffered multiple lacerations and internal injuries, died within hours.[1]

Darst was an experienced but foolhardy and aggressive driver. Witnesses testified that he rarely yielded to other motorists, routinely sped, and never stopped at the posted signs. Darst and his friends were found to have been drinking before attending the movies, after the show at a roadside tavern, and then from the bottles of whiskey and white wine that were later found in the wreckage. The investigation ruled that Darst "legally should have yielded the right-of-way" at the fateful intersection. He did not and the collision occurred.[2]

Mullins presents an equally unsympathetic portrait. He regularly drove in excess of 90 miles per hour. One passenger, driving with Mullins to a previous ballgame, "tried to point out the dangers of such speeds" only to be "rebuffed with sullen silence." This petulant attitude could not have been helped by the beating that the Beaumont Explorers inflicted on Mullins's beloved Dallas Steers on that clear Cinco de Mayo night. The Dallas *Morning News* lamented the Steers' woeful performance, who lost nine to two, and their sinking chances to creep out of fifth place in the Texas League standings. In the end, Gus Darst's dying words to Bill Roach were typical of the carelessness and indifference that characterized both drivers. Lying with his face bloodied and body mangled by the sheer physics of the crash, Darst wisecracked, "I hear that you lost your Negroes, I lost my ear, and Dallas lost the ball game."

One obvious conclusion drawn from these events is that the accident was wholly avoidable. Alcohol, poor attitudes and driving skills, habitual recklessness, and high speed indicate a complete disregard for the dangers of automobility in both drivers and passengers (although it is unlikely that the three black inmates had much influence in their guard's driving). Even minimal efforts to correct these shortcomings might have prevented the tragedy. The official report concluded that the collision was caused by a simple "gamble against error." Moralizing that no man "attained such perfection as never to err" they agreed that driving "at such speeds [was] suicidal, if not criminal." Reporting their findings to the public on the 13th, the members of the investigating team dramatically placed the empty whiskey bottle in the middle of the conference table, a solemn reminder of the folly of men.[3]

Yet while the report made mention of these emotional details, the final conclusions of the investigation proved decidedly different. In an "unprecedented action," Texas governor James V. Allred called for a high-profile investigation by a panel of traffic safety experts the day after the crash. His actions were certainly not prompted by public outrage over the accident. Indeed, while the crash was front page news in Dallas, it was barely mentioned—only twelve lines—in the Austin *American* and received no notice in other regional dailies. It was the accident's banality, its "everyday-ness," that drew the investigating committee's attention. According to chairman C. J. Rutland, speaking a day after the crash, their work was "not to fix the blame primarily upon the driver of either automobile but to determine what fundamental cause or causes resulted in this accident, so typical over the state."[4]

The country certainly once worked hard to "fix the blame" for auto accidents on the reckless and unthinking driver. From the late 1910s until well into the 1930s, Americans reacted to what they termed an epidemic of automobile fatalities. For over two decades, activists and reformers hoped to identify, improve, or abolish poor driver behavior, including speeding, recklessness, and a disregard for the rights of others and for the law. Public opinion, at least as registered by the printed page, shared in the recognition of an accident crisis. In 1923, the city of St. Louis constructed a public monument to the victims of auto accidents "sacrificed on the altar of haste and recklessness." At the dedication, the mayor

The rising toll of dead and injured led reformers to identify the root causes of "avoidable" automobile accidents. (Denver Public Library, Western History Collection, Harry M. Rhoads, Rh-1381)

voiced the common perception that "Many an accident is caused by the mental condition of the driver." Many assumed that this psychology could be "cured," like an infectious disease, and auto accidents lessened.[5]

But neither the "mental condition" of Darst or Mullins nor the driving culture of America were of interest to the Allred commission. The committee members—including the presidents of the Texas Safety Association, the Public Safety Commission, the State Highway Commission, and the Dallas County Commissioners' Court—certainly understood these very vocal and emotional public debates. The Dallas accident, no doubt, tore at old emotional wounds of Governor Allred, who had lost his sister to an auto accident barely two years earlier. In an eerie coincidence, the Dallas region experienced a rash of fatal auto accidents following the formation of the panel. A train struck and killed a family of four at a nearby grade crossing, two young men burned to death after their vehicle crashed into a bridge railing (one of the victims, William Morton, had lost his uncle to an auto accident less than a week earlier), and a prominent clubwoman, Adalyn S. Bryson, died in a collision on her way to Palacios, Texas, for a Mother's Day visit. Twelve were killed and ten injured in less than seventy-two hours which, in the words of the Dallas *Morning News,* "added greatly to interest in the investigation." The petitions, monuments, public safety campaigns, and complaints about character in years past had not resulted in safer streets. The committee concluded that "the entire traffic control movement is yet groping in the dark for solutions." A new perspective was needed.[6]

This new perspective suggested that traffic accidents were, in a word, inevitable. Reform, if it were to proceed with any meaning, must go beyond simply blaming poor character and, instead, identify and then correct structural problems. In the first substantive paragraph of the report, the committee described its own purpose by "ask[ing] itself this question: If an industrial accident in some factory had snuffed out six lives, what would be an investigating procedure?" In this scenario, the accident reflected a breakdown in efficient management. The report continued,

> In this accident, isn't it logical to assume that the State of Texas . . . corresponds to the management of the factory and the motorists correspond to the employees? . . . Has the State failed to provide safe-driving conditions through traffic engineering improvements, adequate warnings of dangers ahead, and proper mechanical restrictions and safeguards? Has it neglected to properly inform motorists of the regulations it has set up to govern motor vehicular traffic? . . . These are the questions that this Committee has asked itself, and on the succeeding pages of this report the answers will be found.

Accidents could be limited, but not eliminated, if the State acted on these conclusions.[7]

The Darst-Mullins crash provided a goldmine of "inevitable" problems. While both drivers displayed a history of speeding and recklessness, neither was legally licensed to drive nor ever took a course in driver instruction. In spite of their known behavior, the evidence indicated that Mullins never was "arrested and properly penalized for speeding," or that Darst "had ever paid a fine for running a stop sign." Even if cited for reckless driving, the court system was so arcane that "there is only an even chance that they would be forced to pay any penalties." Collectively, the drivers broke five distinct statutes of Texas highway law yet, the committee concluded, Darst and Mullins "proceeded with such a degree of assurance and confidence of escaping punishment and all consequences that they were caught wholly unprepared for the contingency brought on by their disobedience." The Highway 15–Belt Line Road intersection was, itself, poorly maintained. As early as May, the Johnson grass and wild oats were tall enough to obscure traffic in both directions. Likely, both drivers first laid eyes on each other, and their startled passengers, a mere second before impact. The crossroad had seen several accidents over the past three years, including three other fatal collisions, but received no additional police coverage. The committee found that "the sum total of enforcement effort at this location consists of a State Highway Patrolman passing once in every two days, remaining in sight of this intersection for about one-half minute." The failure was systemic. It transformed typical human weaknesses into life-threatening "habits." After "word soon gets around that traffic law enforcement amounts to nothing," the committee surmised, it was inevitable that, eventually, men like Darst and Mullins would meet at the wrong place and time.[8]

The "inevitable" conclusion was widely accepted by most safety experts. Surveying the damage of the previous four days, the Dallas *Morning News* called, on Monday, May 9, for "further tightening in examinations, enforcement and procedure for removal of licenses," for greater "legislative attention," and for "stricter enforcement of existing laws." They expressed hope that "eventually the construction of boulevard-type highways, with central stripes separating lines of traffic," while not preventing collisions, "will give added protection against some kinds of accidents." The staff cartoonist provided a suitable illustration for this new perspective, that of a brainless (indeed headless) motorist speeding past a warning sign with the caption "The Headless Driver Haunts the Road."[9]

Throughout the first four decades of the twentieth century, Americans openly debated the merits of both the inevitable and avoidable causes of auto accidents. Both sides agreed that the uncertainties of automobile driving were real enough. Licensing and drivers' education was poor nationwide, many roads were narrow, unpaved, and ill-maintained, and the rising popularity of automobile use made the roads more congested. Driving attitudes, like those displayed by Mullins and Darst, were typical of many who willfully sped, disregarded traffic signs, and drove while impaired by drugs or alcohol. Both explanations were legitimate and, in most cases, both helped to explain why any single auto accident occurs.

The inevitable view did not slight the human tragedy of the auto accident, any more than the avoidable argument ignored the need for good roads, cars, and regulations. Inevitability simply directed the blame for these tragic events away from individuals and toward the entire automotive technology system. The development of automobility was highly contingent on a variety of very elastic factors—such as the evolution of the motorcar, the appearance of serviceable roads, and successful free market providers—but the *system* that emerged was soon rigidly deterministic. General Motors and the American highway system were made, not born. The failure of alternate-fuel automobiles, of competing mass transit options, and of open competition in the automobile market were only the most obvious examples of how these structures helped determine the shape of America's auto culture. From this perspective, motor accidents were the unfortunate but inescapable by-products of personal automobility. "The best we can expect of our most valiant efforts," one reformer wrote, "is to hold the killings down to an irreducible number. The trouble lies deeper than in bad driving. It lies in the *fundamental incompatibility* of machines and man, steel and flesh, in a running mix-up on the highways. Nothing on earth can make their intimacy safe."[10]

Two bystanders calmly examine the aftermath of what could be considered an "inevitable" accident. As also suggested by Table 4.1, identifying the inevitable or avoidable causes of car crashes directed early safety reform. (Denver Public Library, Western History Collection, Harry M. Rhoads, Rh-1721)

A wide variety of auto safety advocates supported this view. Herbert Croly's *New Republic* editorialized, in 1926, that "much of the present waste of life is inevitable and will continue no matter what preventive measures are taken. It is part of the price we have to pay for the new era which, whether it is worth what it costs or not, is certainly here to stay." Those who failed to recognize this new reality were either willfully ignorant or stuck in the past. Another lamented the "incoherent protests against motor killings" that "reveal us as still horse-minded, still quite unable to grasp the wholly changed character of the highways, and not yet ready to accept the fatalities as a necessary feature of motoring." While certainly engineers, reformers, and essayists alike all worked to lower automobile fatalities and, no doubt, grieved at the loss of human potential that did take place, they lacked the sense of optimism and faith in social progress present in the avoidable argument. One mused that the "best we can hope to do" for the victims "is to send or omit flowers, as the relatives request."[11]

The champions of this new auto-safety culture were traffic engineers. Men like Julian Montgomery, a Texas State Highway Chief Engineer, reminded drivers that "Death Never Takes a Holiday." While painful, the "cold facts . . . reflect the day-to-day death and accident toll taken by traffic." Making the process of data gathering and reform "a matter of unemotional routine," he argued, regulatory agencies should "provide a basis for a scientific engineering solution to the safety problem." In later years, Montgomery's successor at the Texas Department of Public Safety confidently displayed "death maps" that predicted the demise of future motorists. They knew that "whenever a new stretch of road is opened up, we can be sure someone will be killed on it within the first two months." While a "foolproof" system remained impossible, Montgomery assured his readers, "Everything possible is being done by the engineers within the limits of funds available to make the highways safe."[12]

But the tragedy of the auto accident resonated with another, less deterministic yet equally valid perspective: that of the love affair. Powerful, often conflicting, experiences, emotions, and civic values defined the automotive love affair. These included the excitement of driving, the freedom of the open road, the relative equality of U.S. car culture, and the progressive nature of the modern driver. From the standpoint of the love affair, it was not cars but drivers that lost their way. While the overall transportation system had improved by leaps and bounds (most roads and cars were both better and safer by 1920), the rising number of fatalities suggested proliferation in personal carelessness. As the *American Auto News* opined in 1930, "Practically all automobile accidents are avoidable—if drivers would play SAFE—all the time." From this perspective, accidents were viewed as avoidable, not inevitable.[13]

Significantly, Americans used the same terms and civic values to describe the problems of automobility as they used to sing its praises. The exhilaration of driving could devolve into "speed mania," the freedoms of the open road into the reckless liberties of drunk driving, the equality of driving into a world segregated by autoists and pedestrians, and the progressive pride of high-tech citizenry into the childish tantrums of road rage. This consistency, in terminology as well as ideology, reinforces the importance of fully understanding the many-layered love affair between Americans and their autos.

Herbert Towle's 1925 article "The Motor Menace" wistfully recalled an era when motorists embodied the civic values essential to safe driving. Then there were fewer operators and "ownership implied both skill and earning power, usually with the responsibility that those qualities bring." By the 1920s, however, cars were cheap, driving was easy, roads were plentiful, and consumers wanted no other responsibilities beyond filling the gas tank. Towle frowned that these conditions acted "like a drug on the market," unleashing fools who simply sought speed and power rather than "the tonic effect of rapid motion and changing scenes" enjoyed by an earlier, more refined cohort of motorists. He groused that "any young fellow may purchase an old high-power car for a few weeks' earnings, and 'burn up the road.'"[14]

This new demographic, of younger more aggressive drivers, carried the weight of a more critical and apprehensive American culture. By the 1920s, the fervor of the Progressive Era had cooled. The "Lost Generation" of Ernest Hemingway, Gertrude Stein, and F. Scott Fitzgerald, scarred by World War I, rejected the "truths" that their parents used to define values like honesty, character, and morality. Immigrants, the urban working poor, and these disaffected youths seemed to willfully reject mainstream culture. Towle imagined a fictional motor menace, named "Nick Belloni," who nurtured "a disposition to think himself above the law" and who was unable to even comprehend the social responsibilities of his driving. As a "hot-headed" immigrant, Belloni never stopped to consider that his weekend speeding took money away from the possibility of home ownership, "next winter's coal, or shoes for the *bambini*." Towle generalized about the affluent, too: "The new-rich owner, made arrogant by success, and the spoiled sons and daughters of rich parents, have property, but without responsibility. . . . they are thoughtless and selfish rather than willfully criminal." Both stereotypes displayed an utter lack of civic responsibility that made up the core of the automotive love affair. Towle reasoned that "Instead of money and a taste for mechanics, the greatest need of the owner to-day is . . . courtesy and fair play to one's neighbors on the road. It is the lack of this quality, among a minority of the newer class of motorists, that accounts for most of the avoidable accidents."[15]

It was not just nostalgic romantics and moral reformers like Towle who championed the "avoidable" argument, nor was their criticism limited to the individual character of the driver. Academics, jurists, engineers, and elected officials argued that personal integrity mattered both behind the wheel and in society at large. For example, John J. Maher, a professor of law, municipal judge, and a frequent participant on panel investigations in the 1920s and 30s, wrote *Mind over Motor,* in 1937, as an appeal to the "thinking man and woman" to "build up public opinion and consciousness that care and caution in the little things in the daily life of the average person will contribute invaluably to reduce the staggering total of all accidents." To Maher, the auto was simply a tool with "a power for good and, conversely, a great power for evil" if the driver "feels he has no responsibilities toward his fellow man." While the vast majority of automobilists were conscientious and fair, too many others courted trouble and, in so doing, rejected their public responsibilities. He classified these latter miscreants as "mentally unfit to drive, antisocial, or downright careless and indifferent." Maher, like many others, saw the contest in military terms, with competing armies staffed by gunners, captains, and grunts like "Private Reckless Operator, Corporal Heavy-Foot, Sergeant Drunk Driver, and Captain Indifference." These drivers were not simply poorly trained or ill equipped (although this was often the case), but a "new enemy" that society must ostracize or eliminate.[16]

These differences between the inevitable and avoidable argument also had important implications for how one understood the concept of risk. Risk is a relative term. We compare our chance of injury based on the options available. For example, horse-drawn vehicles once proved much riskier than automobiles.

Horses kicked, shied, tired, and acted according to their own needs in ways that often had dangerous consequences. But as auto speeds and congestion increased, motorized traffic soon surpassed the risk of the dray horse. Were it simply a question of getting from one point to another, it would have been "logical" to return to animal-powered vehicles. But the car provided additional benefits that modified our assessment of risk. The love affair suggested that a motorist was more modern, more active, and more alive behind the wheel of a car than in guiding Old Dobbins down the country lane. These benefits, conveniences, and pretensions helped to lower the assessed risk of automobility in the minds of many drivers. Even today, most Americans assume that the potential damage from cars is "worth" the risk.

Current researchers note how this shifting definition of risk alters our appreciation of an accident. Rarely are accidents "'natural' or 'neutral.'" They are constructed from the social and political values of the day. Robert Campbell, exploring the changing meaning of an accident, notes how this conceptual pliability affects our appreciation of the cause of tragedy:

> An accident is not something which *cannot* be foreseen, but something which *was not* foreseen. Just because something *can* be foreseen does not mean that it will be. Accidents are not uncaused events; an uncaused event is a miracle, not an accident. On the contrary, we expect an accident to have causes. We frequently try very hard to determine the causes of accidents, in the hope of preventing them in the future.

An accident is "accidental" only if the collective risk is not anticipated and actively avoided. But defining this risk for the automobile meant defining a collective standard that was at odds with the individual nature of driving. This was the paradox that America faced in the automobile age. Using the love affair to define risk was logical—for its values were established and accepted well before the accident crisis emerged—but it did not effectively address this tension between collective responsibility and individual freedom.[17]

This internal conflict was evident even in the types of metaphors used to describe the problem. Unlike the first motorists, who saw only the vast potential of automobility and likened the opportunity to the rubbing of Aladdin's lamp, many soon came to see the car as a demon unleashed. Some described this evil as a Frankenstein's monster—a mechanical nightmare created by the vanity of mankind. Others preferred the lessons of Dr. Jekyll and Mr. Hyde, where the individual driver's character was the source of the problem.[18]

More writers, possibly less comfortable with Victorian science fiction, preferred the metaphor of conflict. Fresh from their experiences in World War I, Americans understood both the inevitable and avoidable aspects of mortal combat. On the one hand, safety advocates used the war motif to convey the vast

Table 4.1. Fatality Rate for Selected Infectious Diseases, 1906–1940, per 100,000 Population

Year	Syphilis	Tuberculosis	Whooping Cough	Typhoid Fever	Motor Vehicle Accidents
1906	14.1	175.8	16.1	30.9	0.4
1910	13.5	153.8	11.6	22.5	1.8
1915	17.7	140.1	8.2	11.8	5.8
1920	16.5	113.1	12.5	7.6	10.3
1925	17.3	84.8	6.7	7.8	16.8
1930	15.7	71.1	4.8	4.8	26.7
1935	15.4	55.1	3.7	2.8	28.6
1940	14.4	45.9	2.2	1.1	26.2

Source: U.S. Department of Commerce, Bureau of the Census, *Historical Statistics of the United States, Colonial Times to 1957* (Washington, DC: Government Printing Office, 1961), 26.

scope of the problem. The Pittsburgh *Gazette-Times* in 1926 marveled "were our Army to lose over 10,000 men a year in battle the 'horrors of war' would be on our minds constantly, and we should demand that it be stopped." But given that "automobiles pick off one, or two, or three at a time, we take little note of them." The Texas investigators of the Darst-Mullins crash, like countless other essayists, reformers, legislators, and enforcement officials, lamented "if this nation had a foreign foe that was killing 40,000 of our people every year and wounding over a million annually there would be no question about a united front on the part of our people. Adequate troops would be called into action . . . [and] a wartime emergency would be proclaimed." Still others used the war metaphor to foment the moral outrage they felt society needed to combat the problem. The *Outlook* argued that "the victim of an automobile accident dies to no purpose."

> To the forty-eight thousand Americans killed in the World War a grateful country has erected public monuments to record their service; but to the twenty-four thousand dead of automobile accidents last year there are no public memorials, but only those gravestones that testify to personal grief and loss. An armistice brought the war to an end; but there is no end to the killings on our highways and in the onslaught of the machine upon human life there is no armistice.

The problem was defined as both inescapable and avoidable.[19]

By far the most prevalent and revealing metaphor was that which compared auto accidents to a plague or epidemic. As with the grim realities of war, the growing number of annual auto fatalities gave substance to this comparison. Moreover, the relative decline in deaths due to infectious diseases, compared to the increased risk from collision, made for a powerful analogy (Table 4.1). No doubt, the connection between auto reforms and the medical and scientific

Grisly descriptions and dire warnings of auto accidents—much like contemporary America's cultural fixation on postmortem forensics and crime scene investigations— accompanied a growing anxiety over personal safety. (Library of Congress, Prints and Photographs Division, FSA-OWI Collection [LC-USF344-003362-ZB])

community lent legitimacy to the public health metaphor. Cloaked in the mantle of science, reformers suggested that the country could be "cured" of motor madness. They demanded that drivers be educated on the behaviors that "spread" auto fatalities, much like a sexually transmitted disease. Once isolated, offenders could either be healed or kept from infecting others. Accidental deaths could be prevented.[20]

As these metaphors suggest, expressions of public fear over auto fatalities were on the rise. Initially, this was considered to be a natural and beneficial change. One writer observed in 1911, "too much fear in motoring is better than too little. Fear only makes one uncomfortably alive to the dangers of the road; fearlessness is apt to make one uncomfortably dead to them." But the lack of consensus on the causes of modern accidents—preventable or inevitable—soon turned this fear into a minor hysteria.[21]

The 1935 *Reader's Digest* article "And Sudden Death" was an extreme example of this passion. Written by J. C. Furnas, the essay recounted in gory detail the physical carnage of a high-speed accident. Furnas provided "picturesque tales of how a flying human body will make a neat hole in the [windshield] with its head—the shoulders stick—the glass holds—and the raw, keen edge of the hole decapitates the body as neatly as a guillotine." Similar broken bones, mutilations, and sudden death awaited anyone who allowed their guard to fall. In what would look very much like a casting call for one of George Romero's *Dawn of the Dead* films, Furnas imagined a scene where, "If ghosts could be put to a useful purpose, every bad stretch of road in the United States would greet the oncoming motorist with groans and screams and the educational spectacle of ten or a dozen corpses, all sizes, sexes and ages, lying horribly still on the bloody grass."[22]

The strength of the article was Furnas's willingness to expose, with frightful clarity, the real risks that Americans took behind the wheel. Stripped of the rationalizations of the love affair, these risks did not seem "worth it" any longer: "you've stopped screaming [and] it all comes back—you're dying and you hate yourself for it. That isn't fiction either. It's what it actually feels like to be one of the 36,000. . . . Take a look at yourself as the man in the white jacket shakes his head over you, tells the boy with the stretcher not to bother, and turns away to somebody else who isn't quite dead yet. And then take it easy." Only after experiencing "the pain and horror of savage mutilation" could the public's perception of the problem "rate something more than a perfunctory tut-tut" as they turned from sanitized newspaper accounts of the crash "back to the sports page." One wonders how easily Billy Mullins turned to the Dallas Steers' box-scores after living through his ordeal.[23]

Americans did not shy away from the intense anxiety and fear of Furnas's vision. Rather, they embraced it. The essay was wildly popular. *Reader's Digest* reported more than 3.5 million requests for reprints by January 1936 and more than ten times that number in subsequent years. The article was distributed in traffic courts, at toll booths, and by highway patrolmen. A short movie was produced and, for a brief time, a syndicated cartoon appeared in many hometown newspapers. A similar tough-love approach was taken by magistrates, who sentenced offenders to a day of observation in the children's trauma ward of the local hospital or, more ghastly still, to remain with the corpse of their victim while it was prepared in the morgue.[24]

But talk of monsters, wars, germs, and fear of decapitation did little to identify or reform the reckless driver. Motivated by these compelling human tragedies, reformers set out to correct the perceived chaos of the highway. Dana Hubbard, a physician working under the auspices of the Bureau of Public Health of New York City, argued that careful "motorists have ample justification in shifting blame from themselves when very many of these accidents are caused by the negligent and abusive use of the automobile." By contrast, the accident-prone drivers were, according to New York City Traffic Court magistrate W. Bruce Cobb, "persons who are grossly illiterate, reckless, habitual criminals, drug addicts, inebriates (chronic or occasional), feeble-minded or partly insane, deaf, or [of] defective vision, over-excitable or nervous, and un-trained." Reformers called on citizens' groups to attack the problem as one would fight war or disease. People should "unite in assisting in [the] detection, capture, and punishment" of the reckless driver. These criminal types "should be hunted down as vigorously as bank absconders are hunted . . . They are as dangerous as lunatics with loaded guns."[25]

The accusatory tone of these and many other offensives against the character flaws of the reckless driver were, in part, influenced by the contentiousness of the times. Even a cursory glance at the titles of leading accounts written about the Progressive Era gives a sense of the raucous climate. The period saw sustained and fundamental change, arguably more than any other era in U.S. history. Historians have defined the decades as an "Age of Reform," an era of "New Citizenship," or as "Pivotal Decades." Citizens faced "status anxiety," numerous "struggles for justice," saw the collapse of their "island communities," and felt themselves to be "standing at Armageddon." David Kennedy's historical synthesis of the Great Depression and World War II describes America's exit from this time as a collective longing for a "Freedom from Fear."

These titles are not simply catchy phrases, but accurate reflections of the heightened rhetoric and tensions of the early twentieth century. Americans frequently used harsh terms like chaos, collapse, and failure to describe the country's social ills. They sought control, stability, and morality in their society. Others feared rings, trusts, and monopolies in business and trusted efficiency, order, and hierarchy in government. While Progressivism meant many things to many people, Americans of this time were highly conscious of the contentious shifts in personal values that accompanied modernization.

While it would be impossible, and highly inaccurate, to condense the Progressive Era into a few key policies, understanding the life cycle of the movement places the public mood about the auto safety crisis into the context of the times. Early progressivism, evident in the last two decades of the nineteenth century, was a multifaceted and generally local phenomenon that energized thousands of people who may otherwise have never engaged in the public debate. Progressives embraced modernity while conserving aspects of their society and culture that best suited their talents, economic advantages, and worldview. As historian Michael McGerr writes, progressives "intended nothing less than to transform other Americans, to remake the nation's feuding, polyglot population in their own middle-class image."[26]

The political power of the movement was its most potent from the late nineteenth century until America's involvement in World War I. From Teddy Roosevelt's Pure Food and Drug Act and Taft's "trust busting" to Woodrow Wilson's domestic "New Freedom" and international "New World Order," it seemed that nothing was beyond the reach of progressive reform. During these two decades, interest groups and elected officials modified public education, public health, economic competition, voting rights and governance, fiscal policy, labor relations, popular culture, and the rights of children, women, immigrants, and minorities. On the international scene, they pushed forward an aggressive agenda of American expansionism and agonized over the country's role in the burgeoning European crisis. During the Great War, blind patriotism and real national perils stifled public criticism, the fuel that drove Progressivism, and aided in the politically conservative "return to normalcy" of the 1920s. Yet this chill was as much an indication of the exhaustion of an activist generation as a formal rejection of their progressive goals and ideals. The popular yet numbing attractions of the new mass consumer culture further distracted the public and sapped the potency of reform. When the Great Depression forced Americans to again take up the unresolved inconsistencies of industrial capitalism in a democratic republic, it was with a decidedly less zealous longing for structural reform. Political savant Franklin Roosevelt guided the country through a New Deal that was both radical (in the scope and scale of federal activism) and conservative (in its hesitancy to challenge America's economic gospel in the face of clear class inequalities). Significantly, the New Deal shifted the "liberal" agenda away from moral reformation of the electorate (as seen in the repeal of Prohibition) and toward a new definition of citizenship bound by economic opportunity and consumer "rights." As McGerr more succinctly writes, the new "task of government was to make sure Americans could afford pleasure, and then get out of the way."[27]

But the moral outrage over highway fatalities was neither artificial nor the empty shell of a dying progressive movement. Concepts like character, duty, and public virtue, while battered by the war and the narcotic effects of consumerism, still mattered greatly. Given the deep penetration and diffusion of "progressivism" in the preceding decades, it would be illogical to assume that these ideals did not still resonate with the American public. Yet the sense of political impotence was particularly evident in those who viewed auto accidents as preventable. Harvard president Charles William Eliot noted that if one doubted "Americans have made the worst botch of government in the recorded history of the world, you should study the daily report of automobile accidents. . . . In no other civilized land could you find such a record of official incompetence or indifference as the figures will show." L. F. Wynne, of the Georgia Railway and Power Company, lamented the "callous disregard of all the amenities of life, and that the theory of survival of the fittest is the only principle by which our actions should be governed."[28]

This pessimistic public mood undermined many people's faith in traditional progressive solutions. In 1923, political essayist Mark Sullivan perceived a growing "mood of resentment against those who are in office and supposed to look out for the public good." Others agreed, noting that while the "present temper of the public, which has caused, as these lines are written, some sixty bills to be presented to the legislatures of twenty-seven States," they gained little substantive progress. Fittingly, much of this state legislation was aimed not at making the roads safer (prevention of avoidable accidents) but at securing "financial re-sources to victims of motor accidents" (compensation for inevitable accidents). Fearing, correctly, as it turned out, that much of the auto safety acts simply seg-regated pedestrians, children, bicyclists, and other nonmotorized travelers away from the roadway, Sullivan sounded bitter and resigned: "Any community which permits itself to be driven off the streets, or any part of them, by the entrenched power of the small number of persons who have a material interest in seizing the streets for the automobiles—any such community has reached a degree of supineness about its rights that is pretty menacing in a society organized on the theory of upholding the rights of the individual." C. E. Pettibone, the President of the National Safety Council, surmised that, by 1930, Americans lacked "struc-ture in community life" making it nearly impossible to mount an effective moral campaign against the scourge of auto deaths and injuries.[29]

Commonweal magazine ironically compared the unresolved problems of auto accidents with those of the era's greatest experiment in progressive social en-gineering: Prohibition. Contrasting the decrepit moral outrage expressed over traffic deaths to the massive public outcry against the "kings of beerdom," who exchanged gunfire on the crowded streets of New York City's lower East Side, the magazine noted that the "Gangland shooting brought death to one" whereas "automobiles are fatal to thousands." Americans seemed indifferent to the loss that "summons to mind ancient and terrible images of gods to whom babes were tossed in sacrifice, of hideous Molochs grinning above a mound of smoking in-fant flesh." Rather than waste ink and paper calling for a crusade that would no longer materialize, the essay simply called attention to the "sinister modern plague which might not improperly be termed butchery and socially condoned mass murder."[30]

Cultural pessimism was also on the rise. Writers lamented the ways that loos-ened sexual norms, rising divorce rates, the popularity of "degenerate" mass cul-ture, and the cult of consumerism all ate away at consensual visions of public duty and civic responsibility. Kate Masterson despaired that society had "learned to glory in the dangers of the automobile and laugh at the narrow escapes from smash-ups." Rather than witness the birth of a brave new world, "No doubt we will pass on to our reward unenlightened as to what our emotional palpitations on the subject of the motor-car may be symbolic of—what sex-rush may follow in the future, carrying the generations over some awful brink into Chaos." Even the trendy clothes and automotive gear, which once suggested confident opti-mism, now signaled cultural decline. The modern driver was a brutish "creature . . . sitting on the small of his back, and so sunken that the crown of his head is almost on the level with the shoulder of the person by his side." Others wrote as if describing a new species, "Take note of him as he crouches down behind the wheel, dodging in an out among the city's throng. . . . He looks like a drunk and disorderly rowdy. . . . He is proverbially lazy. . . . pampered with the luxury of soft upholstery." Comparisons between recklessness and the new social freedoms of the Jazz Age connected accidents directly to the supposedly debauched state of American culture. The new driver will "think nothing of going out to some roadhouse and get [sic] liquored up on a lot of bootleg." The Chicago *Tribune,* never bashful about dishing out moral instruction, expressed the need to "counteract and counterbalance the social effects upon our youth of the jazzed and joyriding life of to-day." Searching for "moral and religious inspiration . . . not a multiplication of regulations," the daily surmised that "the pastor is needed, not the policeman." Such was the state of the once-optimistic Progressive Movement during the height of the accident crisis.[31]

The recognition of an auto "accident crisis" arose during these contentious times. As noted in Chapter 2, contemporary debates about falling fatality rates can cloud our understanding of the historical context that generated and sustained public anxieties. Where today we see long-term trends that limited the lethality of auto accidents, in the immediate postwar years and Tribal Twenties, the social construction of risk was deeply influenced by fears of waning moral character, race suicide, and the absence of individual self-control. The end of the Progressive Era, as scholars note, witnessed profound shifts in the nature and apprehension of the modern social order. Where early progressives, like Jane Addams and John Dewey, identified global or environmental threats to modern living (including poverty, ignorance, overwork, and disease), social commentary during the 1920s looked again to Social Darwinism and the moral environmentalism of personal choice to fashion a response. It was within these unique times and shifting perspectives that safety reformers turned assuredly to the argument that auto accidents were avoidable.[32]

Evidence of this shifting perspective was seen in the way Americans constructed the "character" of the typical reckless motorist. Early in the history of American automobility, two broad categories classified poor drivers into groups that essayists, in the spirit of early auto humor, labeled "flivverboobs" and "motor morons." Critics considered the flivverboob, at worst, an immature pest. While potentially deadly, this species seemed more threatening to themselves than society at large. Like "jaywalkers" (another neologism coined at this time), flivverboobs were driven by "mischievous maliciousness." They enjoyed hearing "women scream as the mud spatters on their new fall gowns and the men rave as the dirty water splashes over their clothes." They refused to adjust their speed to suit traffic conditions, changed lanes and turned without warning, failed to yield to streetcars and pedestrians, and otherwise displayed "rude" public behavior. In general, these jerks represented social annoyances rather than life threats. Still, it was their character, their utter lack of concern about the rights of others or their responsibility to society-at-large that constituted their principal failing.[33]

By contrast, the "motor moron" emerged as a far more criminal menace, for his recklessness was intentional and clearly very dangerous. Motivated by arrogance and ego, these motorists rejected the idea that driving demanded civic responsibility. To critics, the motor moron "either doesn't know the rules of the road or wants to 'take a chance' with them, to save a second or so." In defining these miscreants, reformers often used legal or quasi-medical terminology, such as "lunatic," "idiot," "sociopath," and "psychotic," as substitutes for the more farcical "motor moron." While many of these delinquents did not "know very much about cars or driving," many others were categorized as "just plain crazy." Clitus Jones, who reportedly purchased the first car ever sold in Dallas in 1907, remarked thirty years later that he now "always assumes that every person I meet on the road . . . is a stark, raving maniac and totally irresponsible for what he may do." These "morons on the macadam" had changed the image of the auto from an instrument of liberation to a stalking menace.[34]

The central pillars of the avoidable argument were a belief that the character of the individual driver was critical to safety, and that those with reckless personalities could be identified, reformed, or removed from the road. As late as 1944, driver instruction manuals placed behavioral problems, such as a lack of "courtesy and consideration," a tendency towards "bluffing the other fellow," or a desire to "take a chance," as more serious infractions than legal misconduct, such as driving on the wrong side of the road, speeding, illegal passing, or a failure to yield. References to "human faults" like selfishness, a lack of responsibility, carelessness, and an "unwillingness to conform to reasonable driving regulations necessitated by public safety" suggested to many that the "driver is in need of a thorough overhauling." Notable auto safety advocates, like Paul Hoffman and Robbins B. Stoeckel, agreed, citing "recklessness, selfishness, and faulty judgement" as "the major cause of automobile accidents." Americans understood, absorbed, and applied these moral lessons through the prism of the much-discussed love affair. Embracing the automobile through these values and experiences—the enervating excitement and freedom of driving, the equality and progress of auto culture—they tackled automobile accidents as a necessary evil rather than a disease that could be completely eradicated. Logically, reformers drew upon these same values and experiences in order to frame their arguments.[35]

Speed was, and remains, a critical component of this experience. In the earliest days, driving speeds were limited by the reliability of the car, the condition of the roads, and the driver's exposure to the elements (particularly for the low-cost, open-carriage runabout). While the Model T could easily exceed forty miles an hour on the open road—more expensive models could just as easily double this rate—only a fool drove faster than twenty-five to thirty miles an hour under these primitive conditions. By the late 1910s and early 1920s, road improvements and new car design made speed more manageable. Manufacturers enclosed cabins, which limited the annoyances of noise, wind, and flying debris. They enhanced the suspension system and tires to absorb the bone-rattling jolts and bumps and made more powerful engines. Federal and state governments funneled money into road improvements, making stretches of highway safer and more reliable. By the mid-1920s, consumers demanded vehicles that could easily exceed 50 to 65 miles per hour, and the desire for "top speeds of 70 m.p.h. or more, [was] growing every day." Writing for *Automotive Industries* in 1927, Norman Shidle observed that the typical buyer's first question was how fast the new car could go. "Even the most conservative and safe of drivers," he argued, "probably gets something of a thrill out of being able to answer that question with a figure just a few miles higher than his friend's car will go."[36]

While speed was often identified as a likely cause of avoidable accidents there was justifiable ambiguity about the exact nature of the problem. Undeniably, speed magnified the severity of a crash: the physics of force is measured by mass times acceleration. But many recognized that a more powerful motor also prevented potentially dangerous situations. Using "speed for safety," drivers were able to conquer hills without dangerously snarling traffic, could pass with greater confidence, and could use acceleration to safely merge with faster traffic. Even Shidle admitted that "speed and unsafeness are not in any sense synonymous; that many factors other than speed *per se* are responsible for a goodly proportion of accidents."[37]

The problem was that increased speed had the potential to change the experience from one of controlled excitement to a frenzied quest for greater stimulation. In the earliest years, essayists portrayed these lead-foots humorously and often sympathetically. C. H. Claudy's fictional characters professed, in 1913, that constant speeding was a "tonic" that restored character and a sense of accomplishment. "When I started to drive," the "Speed Maniac" vouched, "I was a nervous wreck—a panic, a lost business, and a mental breakdown were responsible. I got a car and spent five hours a day in the country. In six months I was made over."[38]

Instead of characterizing speeders as playful rascals, however, the rising auto-related death count turned habitual speeding into a character flaw. Addicted speeders were the "same type that speculates in more stocks than he is able to carry, eats and drinks more than he can assimilate, covers himself with gaudy jewels, and makes an objectionable exhibition of himself on every possible occasion." Others saw them as "criminaloids" with a "very slight capacity for self-restraint." Such an obsession "might with greater logic be regarded as morphine and cocaine are. Possession and ability to use, when combined with an inborn passion, create a temptation that many are unable to resist." Significantly, driving instructor John Floherty cautioned young people that all Americans carried the "latent mental deficiencies" that were then exposed by the accelerator. Those incapable of controlling their worst excesses would soon "show their true colors to the world as they tear recklessly along the highway."[39]

While early critics frequently associated the dangers of speed with the foolhardiness of young drivers, the extensive "hot rod" culture of the late 1940s and

1950s (captured in films like *Rebel without a Cause* and *American Graffiti*) had yet to develop. Still, as early as 1913, the Los Angeles police arrested over one hundred juveniles a year for "joy riding" in stolen vehicles. In the 1920s, speed enthusiasts in Southern California used the neighboring alkaline lake beds, like Muroc Dry Lake (about one hundred miles from downtown Los Angeles), to challenge other drivers. Driving over the firm, flat surface, which stretched ten miles in width and twenty-two miles in length, racers took about three miles to reach full acceleration before being electronically timed over a quarter-mile stretch. Participants also raced in groups, as many as twenty cars at a time, rather than to beat the clock. The thin layer of alkaline dust that settled on participants was not washed away but rather worm proudly on the streets of L.A. as a badge of honor.[40]

In the 1930s, hot rod culture began to take shape. The low cost of used cars and ease by which young mechanics could modify stock engines and chassis made "hot rods," "hop-ups," and "gow jobs" more popular and affordable. Traditional hot-rodders raced only over the salt lakes and focused on timing records rather than personal or club rivalries. Most frowned upon street racing and often penalized club members who were arrested for urban speeding. Still, the long drive to the salt beds and their seasonal availability (they flooded in the winter) drove competitive speeding to more convenient locales. Meeting at local drive-ins (which served as informal clubs for neighborhood racers), teens agreed to a specified, yet secret, time and place. By word of mouth, dozens of participants and often hundreds of spectators appeared to block side-street access, man police lookouts (using flashlights to signal if the law was close), and to record the victory. While over five hundred cars were reportedly present at one such contest, on L.A.'s Lincoln Boulevard, dozens or scores of vehicles were more common. Hot-rodders also used less-traveled rural or suburban roads, such as Fifth Avenue in La Puente or the highways to Yorba Linda and Placentia to avoid arrest. *Collier's* reported that the eventual arrival of the police only "added to the hazards" of street racing. At "the first sound of the [police] siren," at one 1938 contest, "cars darted into side streets in all directions, whipping around blind corners on two wheels. The resulting traffic accidents made the public, the press and the law loudly vocal in condemning the menace."[41]

While hot-rod culture fully developed only after World War II, critics responded to these pioneer hot-rodders' brand of lawlessness in ways that resonated with earlier fears. *Life* magazine lamented how "on the open highways and in the crowded suburbs of the US teenagers and their post-graduate friends have been killing themselves in jalopies with sickening regularity since 1932." Others decried the daredevil stunts that seemed a natural extension of the speed thrill. "Playing chicken" happened when a driver let go of the steering wheel while on the highway. The first to grab the wheel and correct the steering "lost." In another variation, two oncoming cars drove while keeping their left tires on the center line. The "chicken" veered off. Similar games, like "pedestrian polo" and "crinkle fender" (known as "bumper thumping" in the Midwest), sought to lightly strike other cars or pedestrians without causing too much damage. As Moorhouse reports, their motto was "just brush 'em, don't hit 'em." These attitudes confirmed the "criminal intent" of speed demons and led New York State's director of motor safety to conclude that, not only was mere "possession of the 'hot rod' . . . presumptive evidence of an intent to speed," but "a deliberate and premeditated idea to violate the law." As with their flivverboob fathers and motor moron uncles, these younger operators were "confused into believing that driving is a competitive sport. They have a feeling of superiority in recklessly darting in and out of traffic in their attempt to out-speed other cars on the road."[42]

Unlike other poor driving habits, such as recklessness or road rage, critics held auto manufacturers partially responsible for speed mania. Detroit simply provided consumers with too much power. Even worse, advertisers seemed determined to sell the capacity for speed as the principle attraction of their new models. This resulted in the possession of cars "which will go faster than necessary and which creates a desire on the part of the purchaser to try it out accordingly." Auto manufacturers certainly used speed figures as inducements to buy their brands. Ad copy frequently highlighted the speed records that each model had set and prominently featured endorsements by speed exhibitionists and race car drivers, like Barney Oldfield. By 1927, the president of Elcar Motor Company noted that "Many buyers that would [once] never think of speed . . . are today asking for it and demanding it, undoubtedly due to the cause that speed has been advertised so promiscuously during the last eighteen months or two years." The absurdity of much of the advertisements, which one critic groused gave drivers "the idea that an 80-mile-an-hour car could be driven through a brick wall without so much as spoiling the driver's hair comb," made for an easy target of reform.[43]

Manufacturers responded to this criticism by hosting a series of academic conferences that investigated the effect of "speed advertising." In September 1927, dozens of safety experts met in Chicago with industry leaders to discuss speed advertising at the Annual Safety Congress of the National Safety Council (NSC). W. H. Cameron, the managing director of the NSC, flatly stated that "I certainly cannot agree that speed advertising is harmless. Looking at accidents from the point of view of the car driver, speed is the third largest contributing cause of motor vehicle accidents. Accordingly, when you emphasize speed, even this so-called 'speed for safety,' you are handling a dangerous weapon." Knight Dunlap, a professor of psychology at Johns Hopkins University, agreed, concluding that "human curiosity and daring will lead most drivers of high-power cars to test out the advertised speed. In other words, the driver of a car which is sold as a fast car wants to be sure it *is* a fast car." Executives, like Studebaker's Paul C. Hoffman, publicly expressed their concern and promised to reform their companies from within.[44]

In reality, little was actually accomplished except the forestalling of governmental intervention. While many stopped featuring overt references to top speeds, there was no acknowledgment that advertising encouraged recklessly fast driving. Even Hoffman, a man committed to increased auto safety, dismissed the link. He compared the connection between speed ads and speeding to ads by a national watch manufacturer who promised one could freeze their product in a block of ice and still expect it to tell the correct time. To Hoffman, speed ads "can no more be taken as an invitation to the public to use the speed of which these cars are capable than the practice of a watch maker can be interpreted as a suggestion that all watches be kept in ice." Others, like the Auburn Automobile Company, which recently ran a series claiming tops speeds of well over 100 miles per hour, shifted the blame back onto the driver. Auburn ads only "told the public that such speed proves our product capable of many years of average use and that the breaking of records was merely incidental."[45]

Public reformers and safety agencies were less convinced. In 1926, the Better Traffic Committee of Pittsburgh was one of the first to claim that speed advertising placed "onto the minds of automobile drivers a craze for speed which is being reflected in the mounting traffic accident toll." Talk of government intervention to mandate mechanical speed governors or national speed limits faded quickly from the headlines, though. Speed ads were deemphasized but, as one essayist astutely observed, the decline was probably due to the fact that promoters "have simply exhausted one appeal and are off hot on the trail of another."[46]

Just as the exhilarating sensations of motoring were used to frame the problem of habitual speeding, so too were the beneficial freedoms of driving used to understand recklessness. While speeding was a form of recklessness, the two categories were generally considered separately by safety reformers. Most auto safety reports listed speeding and recklessness as unique causes of auto accidents. The debate could, legitimately, go either way. But recklessness was a broader term, suggesting a willful desire to abuse the freedoms of driving and to disregard the safety of others in the pursuit of individual gratification.

Again, the early humorous flivverboob transfigured, under the influence of mounting auto fatalities, into a menacing and slightly demented "motor menace" or "moron of the macadam." Fear replaced amusement as the typical reaction to these uncontrollable egoists. Julian Street expressed an increasingly common view: "I am becoming more and more afraid of the other fellow and his car, whether I be his passenger or only happen to run into him upon the road, as one might put it." One driver actually sold his car, and advocated that others do the same, because "he valued his life, and the lives of others who ride with him, too highly to take the risk in pursuit of the pleasure, especially when the danger arose from the recklessness of others."[47]

As with the love for speed, some countered that human nature included, inevitably, an element of recklessness. They held that many drivers simply "don't seem to understand" that reckless freedom was "practically in the category of premeditated acts." Others removed the "practically" and advocated summary justice. Recklessness showed certain drivers to be inevitably flawed and "morally deficient." Many agreed, believing that "the logical conclusion of such disordered lives as these is in State's prison or the electric chair."[48]

But most safety advocates were more likely to see recklessness as a choice and an expression of character rather than innate criminality. They believed that people could learn to control their behavior, could change their character, and, thus, could avoid many of the accidents attributed to recklessness. The title of John Maher's 1937 work, *Mind over Motor*, suggested just how closely the problem was attributed to attitude. Maher argued that reckless driving was a sign of immaturity. As with a child, reckless drivers lacked the emotional development needed to safely interact with others on the highway. He also likened the growth of recklessness to the hedonistic freedoms of mass consumption. Reckless drivers were like spoiled adolescents who "receive many gifts, appreciate them little, and destroy or lose them in no time. The psychology of the whole thing is very simple." Other critics drew equally sharp distinctions between the immaturity of the driver and the cold realities of driving. While "the automobile of today is as nearly perfect as science and industry can make it. . . . the driver, figuratively speaking, is still wearing rompers. He just hasn't been able to keep up with improvements made on the road and the machine."[49]

Drunk driving was the most obvious example of how unrestricted automotive freedoms could prove deadly. The problem of alcohol or drug abuse was, of course, not caused by the automobile. Still, the mixture of alcohol and the motor vehicle created a deadly combination of poor attitudes and physical capabilities. Driving under the influence of alcohol was a well-known and recurring problem in all regions of the country. By some estimates, nearly 20 percent (fittingly, a fifth) of all auto fatalities involved alcohol. By 1939, many cities routinely collared fifty to seventy drunk drivers a month with a conservative estimate that more than ten times this number went undetected. One Tennessee newspaper sarcastically asked drivers who drank to pin their names to their clothes or send a short obituary to the editors if they planned to "take a few quick snorts of fire-water before getting into the car to drive to grandma's or the football game."[50]

Ironically, it was Prohibition, the great moral experiment in progressive social engineering, that abetted the rise of drunk driving in the 1920s. Responding to a 1926 survey that asked law enforcement officials to list the principal causes of traffic accidents, one New Jersey police chief simply wrote "THE VOLSTEAD ACT." The law made it illegal to distill, transport, or sell alcoholic beverages. Still, it was relatively easy for most to find bootleg hooch and beer. Lacking the public spaces to consume this liquor, many retreated to the relative privacy of the personal passenger car (and the very public roadways).[51]

Those concerned about drunk driving noted two distinct problems. The first was the obvious disregard for public safety by "wet" motorists. While many also considered reckless drivers immature, their faults appeared more innocent and childlike than the drunk driver. The intoxicated motorist, by contrast, was "obstinate, defiant of all social responsibility, he stands poised—an enemy to all mankind, an enemy to himself."[52] The Raleigh (NC) *News & Observer* claimed that "the gangster, the murderer, the kidnapper are trifling menaces compared with the killing motor corps of drunkards on the highways." Given the numbers killed by both inebriated drivers and mobsters, they were right.[53]

Second, for planners to credibly claim that alcohol-related accidents were avoidable they needed to show how to remove drunk drivers from the roadway. In short, society must force citizens to accept the responsibility of their personal freedoms. Some suggested that social pressures could do the trick. Curtis Billings, writing for the *Atlantic Monthly* in 1935, believed drunk driving was simply a "social custom" and that "people of influence and strength" could end the practice if they expressed their disapproval strongly enough. Elites needed to "set a proper example if drunken driving is to become in the popular mind as reprehensible a practice as it actually is." To Billings and many others, the driver could reform himself. The Texas Safety Association reported much the same conclusion in 1940 when it surmised that drunk driving was a problem largely because the public tolerated this behavior and failed to condemn obvious examples of drunk driving. The authors concluded "this lack of acceptance by the public is the weakest link in the chain of enforcement necessary for conviction" of those who break the law.[54]

Others demanded greater police protection and stricter enforcement of existing codes. Most states had laws on the books making driving under the influence illegal. But one writer noted how his state of Massachusetts "hasn't the pluck" to enforce these laws and "put a stop to the murderous threat of the drunkard on the streets and highways of the Commonwealth." The Kansas City *Star* expected "vigorous enforcement of the law" and the superintendent of the California Highway Patrol vowed that "intoxicated drivers will not be tolerated." Between 1935 and 1941, the state of Connecticut issued no fewer than six special reports with titles like "If You Drink, Don't Drive," "Intoxicated Operators," and "Alcohol and Traffic Accidents" for both the public and the state highway enforcement agencies to consider.[55]

But the freedoms of the car seemingly overrode the demands of public safety. Drivers refused to abide by the rules. Drunk driving statutes were "flagrantly disregarded, and so futile were the attempts of law officers to enforce the unpopular edict that similarly feeble efforts were made to enforce other laws." Weak laws and, more importantly, reluctant juries made prosecution a pointless exercise. One Texas county saw nearly two hundred arrests for drunk driving over a two-year span. Of these, only a quarter were prosecuted and, of these, only two were punished. While the law called for a maximum sentence of two years in state prison, the judge placed both men in the county jail for five days.[56]

The response to these criticisms was unpredictable. Many, it seemed, took the scolding to heart and honestly endeavored to improve their driving (or at least that of their children) through state-mandated training programs and regular governmental inspections of their capacities and their vehicles. But many others proved unwilling to trade the freedoms of the car for lowered risk. Attitudes toward lawbreaking and respect for enforcement officials were noticeably different for traffic violations than for other forms of social deviancy. The ill-humored relationship between drivers and traffic cops stands in stark contrast to the view of other public officials and agencies created to insure the safety of the American public.

In addition to sensory excitements and freedom, the automotive love affair promised Americans a tangible demonstration of civic equality. The relative ease of access to a low-priced, reliable automobile and the democratic culture that soon emerged sustained this perception well into the 1920s. But, as with the other positive traits, the rising accident rate caused many to reassess the relationship between automotive equality and public safety. Again, the qualities of the love affair were used to differentiate between the competent and the "problem" driver.

In terms of social equality, the most obvious aberration was the inherent bias against pedestrians. Early auto reformers, like William Eno, hoped to physically redesign the streets to allow for peaceful coexistence. Safety lanes—where pedestrians crossed busy intersections and boarded streetcars—met with initial resistance but were soon an accepted practice in most cities. But the contest between the rights of the motorist and those of the pedestrian went unresolved. New Jersey governor Harold Hoffman saw the questions dividing the roadway "as much opposed in viewpoints as were the North and South in '61. They are the drivers and the pedestrians." Since there was literally no contest in the collision between man and motorcar, driver attitude was the single most important variable. Motorists who failed to grant the "lowly pedestrian" equal rights to the road were the source of the problem. In the words of one, these drivers saw pedestrians as "an unspeakable being; a furtive, deceptive, dodging target whose peregrinations, if they are to be tolerated at all, should be confined strictly to the footpaths designed for them."[57]

Drivers who terrorized pedestrians cultivated an "air of superiority" that transformed the Golden Rule—of treating others equally—into the Law of the Jungle. Assaying the problem, in 1936, one safety advocate believed that drivers acted out "the primordial traces in Man's mentality" in a Darwinian contest on the streets that allowed "the strong to attack the weak." Such a view made the road a contested terrain where pedestrians scurried within a space set now aside for the motorcar. As one exasperated reformer noted, "the pedestrian is entitled to *at least* five feet of the street when the motorists have thirty." This attitude abetted a warped ego already inflated by horsepower. It led "seasoned gentlemen," who behaved with polished manners and civility when afoot, to make the pedestrian "jump for his safety."[58]

Still, pedestrians also have the right to use the roadway. If motorists were made to see the equality of their positions, it was hoped, they could avoid deadly interaction. To achieve this, motorists must accept that "according to all law and precedent, on sea and land, it is the duty of the stronger to take care of the weaker. Until the automobile made its appearance there was never a question but that the pedestrian has the right of way on the street. Why should this law be nullified, and at such a cost?" Mark Sullivan argued in 1923 that "most of the automobiles are on the streets and roads for pleasure, just as the roller-skating children." If any obligation existed, "let it be by all means the pleasure automobile. The child on roller-skates does no harm and is a danger to no one. The automobile kills, maims, and is a constant instrument of terror and danger."[59]

But pedestrians also struggled to adjust their behavior. Governor Hoffman reminded his constituents that "Careless drivers are not alone to blame; the foolish, contrary walker has much to answer for. Death moves on unthinking feet—in the face of red lights; it steps from behind parked cars; it straggles across the street in the middle of the block; it walks with its back to oncoming traffic on dark highways." Only foolish rustics, or "jays," indiscriminately crossed traffic at any point along the road. Such "jaywalking" infuriated motorists who, logically, bore the brunt of society's disgust of pedestrian fatalities. In such circumstances it was "the pedestrian who invites the accident and is largely responsible for it." Many complained that it was the pedestrian who failed to observe civic equality; one essayist wrote in 1923, the pedestrian who "thinks and acts as if he owns the streets," just like "the motor road hog dismounted . . . is a menace to the safety and comfort of others."[60]

But children posed a unique problem. It could not be assumed that they understood their civic obligations nor that they could reform their character. "It is wrong, deeply and viciously wrong," wrote the *Commonweal* editors, "for the motorist to assume that little boys and girls take the same risks he does." While drivers complained that they had rights in the streets, typically "the child can make no reply. He is usually at fault—and therefore dead." Given the emotional and intellectual immaturity in children, the driver had complete responsibility. The *St. Louis Post-Dispatch* found the driver's plea of "unavoidable accident" when children died simply "the perjury of a murderer."[61]

Finally, just as many praised the progressive qualities of American motorists—their ability to master and adapt to driving, the car, and traffic conditions—they also blamed the accident problem on those who lacked these modern attributes. Certainly, the automobile and roadways were placed under stricter "scientific" scrutiny. State and federal investigators examined the properties of tires, head-

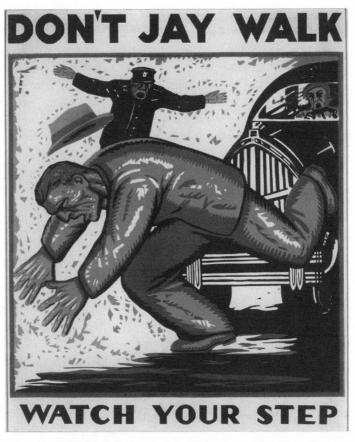

DON'T JAY WALK

WATCH YOUR STEP

Pedestrians who ignored the rules of the road were considered as guilty as
the motor morons who drove them down. (Library of Congress, Prints and
Photographs Division [LC-USZC2-1100 DLC])

lights, brakes, safety glass, road obstructions, and pedestrian walkways. Funded
by the 1917 Federal Road Aid Act, state highway departments standardized and
upgraded road construction materials and methods. Grade crossings, the intersection of roads and rail lines, received particular attention. One such department claimed "good engineering and common humanitarianism imperatively
demand that all plans for highway construction be amended so that an under-
pass or overhead crossing shall be substituted for the grade crossing. The added
expense is inconsequential when compared with the loss of human lives." Over
the next twenty years, states either eliminated or circumvented their most dangerous grade crossings, improved thousands of miles of neglected highway,
widened the roads, segregated the pedestrian, and removed obstructions that
contributed to fatal collisions.[62]

With such an impressive record of change many wondered why the roadways were becoming more rather than less deadly. Study after study showed that "a surprising small proportion of the casualties result from material imperfections, such as signals out of order, defective cars, or poor roads." Critics blamed the driver for this lack of progress. In California, a motorist's paradise because of its good weather and open roads, activists marveled how one found "automobile accidents in spots where you are forced to wonder how such an accident could possibly happen." The Maryland State Roads Commission found that the vast majority of fatal accidents occurred on the most modern, flat, and relatively straight stretches of road. By contrast, "in the western half of the State, where the inclines are naturally steep and the gradings curve abruptly, only eight accidents have happened in three months" without a single fatality.[63]

While the problems of speed, reckless freedom, and pedestrian inequality were correctly faulted for their role in the carnage, others noted how some drivers seemed incapable of fulfilling their duties as progressive citizens within a modern, risk-laden transportation system. Here, again, safety advocates cited childish, immature motorists as the chief source of the problem. Unlike the reckless speed maniac, however, these fools seemed incapable of recognizing the risks presented in automobile use. For example, at railroad crossings, where one could assume that any competent adult would accurately assess the increased risk, engineers erected lights and oscillating signs, like "over-grown baby rattles," that acted as "grotesque wooden arms set to wigwagging in mid-air, after the manner of the fond mother who waves colorful objects before the eyes of her offspring." Seth Humphrey, a vocal critic of these "motorized morons," suggested with "every one of these silly devices [erected] at grade crossings we acknowledge an uncounted number of hopelessly infantile grownups." Humphrey mischievously mused "if this precaution were carried to its limits of usefulness there would be other signs, such as 'Slow Up! Several Absent-minded Professors Live on This Street,' or, at certain intersections, 'Look Out! Morons Usually Plentiful Around Here.'" Clearly, to Humphrey and others, some of the driving public lacked a minimal level of progressive competency (even innate intelligence).[64]

Critics pointed to the growing incidence of dangerous emotional outbursts, temper tantrums, and aggressive or even malicious driving, what we today term "road rage," as evidence of deeper psychological disorders. Collectively, these activities—cutting off drivers, racing to beat or jump the traffic light or bell, aggressive driving, excessive horn blowing—were often cited as simple "bad manners." One motorist observed, in 1927, that it was "hardly possible to drive fifty miles on the crowded highways to-day without having dozens of opportunities to display modesty, courtesy, and self-control." A lack of restraint demonstrated a lack of character, and proved that one "not only is a 'road hog' but is obviously not a gentleman." Progressive driving required maturity and patience, the ability to tolerate "the driving and walking shortcomings of others" and, most importantly, the ability to "control one's temper."[65] One particularly honest essayist admitted "there are many times when I feel inclined to make it uncomfortable for other motorists because I am simply yielding to the very human desire to 'get even' for the thoughtless things men and women do when piloting a motor car. It is this spirit of getting square with each other which is going to send an alarming number of motorists to the hospitals and to the courts and police stations."[66]

The accelerating pace of change made the collapse of public courtesy particularly alarming to this generation. The roadway gave them an unsettling glimpse of a future where mass society had no use for civility, manners, or civic progress. Frank Wiggins, the secretary for the Los Angeles Chamber of Commerce, observed that citizens would never act as poorly "in public . . . in a line at a theater ticket window or at a cafeteria" as they were willing to do behind the wheel of an automobile. Another asked "what the world would be like if a man could get away with the incivility of tripping up a pedestrian whenever he felt inclined to see someone annoyed. . . . such perversion of common decency wouldn't be possible in our enlightened age. But are we not witnessing a striking analogy in the attitude of present-day drivers toward one another?" Frequently, the notion of the "woman driver" was bundled with this sense of pending social chaos. Why did a woman, who normally "feels shy and timid when walking among men and women on the streets often becomes a regular cave lady the moment she steps on the gas?" Simply "give her a motor car, five gallons of gas and one lesson, and she is apt to be telling the most experienced veterans of the wheel where they get off."[67]

The growing use of car horns as an emotional release for the frustrations of driving seemed to exemplify these juvenile temper tantrums. While certainly preferable to running someone down, the car horn changed from being a reasonable means of warning others of an approaching vehicle into a statement of possession and control. Particularly when used against pedestrians, the car horn evolved into a tool that intentionally startled and intimidated. One driver claimed "when the autoist sounds his horn for the pedestrian to clear the way, he is doing precisely what the ancient kings use to do when they sent their criers before them, shouting, 'Make way, make way for his Majesty,' and enforcing their demands with whip or staff." With the horn, emotional drivers were transformed into screaming children demanding attention: "He blows his horn. He puts his hand on the button and keeps it there. He crowds and pushes and shoves—in a manner of speaking. He yells at those he passes, honks at those ahead. And glares at all the rest. . . . he scares nervous old ladies and women with baby carriages into fits by blasting his squawker in their ears."[68]

Predictably, those who saw auto accidents as avoidable showed little sympathy for drivers who lacked the capacity to contain their rage. As one editorial concluded, "we ought not to fool ourselves. Automobile fatalities are not inevitable. They are a species of murder or suicide." Some, like Seth Humphrey, believed that the "new life-saving geegaws are practically useless for stopping people so obtuse that glaring signs, shrieking whistles, and thundering trains do not impress them." Another concluded that "their own recklessness [was] responsible for their undoing," they "usually kill themselves or their friends. In such cases the responsibility is their own." Steeped in the restrictive racial and ethnic policies of the times, many concluded that "the law of the survival of the fittest is at work, both among drivers and pedestrians, as the slowest-witted and the most stupid are killed off." In a chilling yet fairly accurate portrayal of this assessment, the *New Republic* sarcastically "await[ed] expectantly a brochure on this theme by some eminent biologist under the title, *The Automobile: The Friend of Eugenics*."[69]

Understanding the causes of automobile accidents, like the Darst-Mullins crash in 1938, presented Americans with a paradoxical problem. On the one hand, the public wanted to understand the attitudes that contributed to fatal accidents. Using the same terminology and logic that justified the love affair, safety activists hoped to arouse public interest, modify behavior, and ultimately protect the unlimited use of the automobile. They argued that the thrilling experiences of driving should not excuse "speed mania." The liberties of the open road did not grant motorists the freedom to drive recklessly or under the influence of alcohol. Pedestrians deserved separate but equal access to the nation's streets. Society must prevent the willful abuse, by emotionally unstable operators, of these modern and potentially lethal technologies. This arousal was widespread, heartfelt, and believed to significantly lower the incidence of accidents and the general risks of automobility.

But evidence of recurring character deficiencies suggested that structural change was more effective than moral suasion. Human nature resisted reform. As a result, accidents could be classified as the inevitable fate of automobility. Road and traffic engineers, in particular, were frustrated by the impractical solutions posed by those who hoped to reform the character of the driver. One Texas highway engineer, Charles E. Simons, recalled in 1937 how "For many moons, particularly since the public has become aroused over the critical situation existing on the nation's highways, much has been said and written about improving safety factors." Yet, in spite of these efforts, accidents remained a daily occurrence. Rather than redouble efforts to isolate the "motorized moron," Simons reasoned, the country needed to commit itself to the "three E's" of traffic safety: engineering, education, and enforcement. Without these structural modifications, he believed, it was "humanly impossible, without calling out all the armed forces of the commonwealth, to patrol the highways and streets in such a fashion that the foolish, daredevil driver will be kept in check. . . . It [was] unreasonable to expect any set of enforcement officers to watch every fool who gets behind a steering wheel."[70]

Simons's perspective was widely shared by others who viewed accidents as inevitable. The weak, pleading, and largely ineffective nature of moral reform, intended to correct avoidable lapses in character, left many frustrated. Ray Sherman, who participated in several national auto safety conventions and wrote widely on the subject, saw these "campaigns of horror" as more of a "menace rather than a help. Dangling a collection of mangled remains before the eyes of a driver generally succeeds only in shaking his morale and makes him a worse driver than he was before." Sherman worked, briefly, as a panelist on the much-publicized 1924 auto safety commission chaired by Secretary of Commerce Herbert Hoover. He recalled his frustration over an exchange with another contributor who wanted to better "understand the character" of the average motorist. After hearing the testimony of a highway patrolman, who described the "inattention" of one particular driver, the following exchange ensued:

"Ah," said the professor, "let's find what caused the inattention."

"What difference does it make?" I asked. "It might have been a billboard in the field."

"Ah," he said, "let's find that out too. Let's find out the causes of the inattention."

"What good will it do?" I asked. "If the driver was the type who would be inattentive he would have looked at a cow instead of a billboard. . . . You can't remove all the billboards and cows in America."

Similarly, Sherman, Simons, and many others came to believe that the country could not remove all the drunk, immature, or reckless drivers from the roadway. Sherman renounced the conference and left that night, frustrated by the committee's approach and the lack of leadership shown by Secretary Hoover, who was "evidently hoping that somehow, somewhere, somebody would find out something about what was wrong with traffic." Unlike those who believed that character was the key to avoiding accidents, discussions of freedom, equality, and progress were, to Sherman, "just words. Useless words and wasted hours trying to find out what everybody already knew, and paying no attention to what, it was obvious then and now must be done to reduce the number of traffic accidents." Gradually, this view of the inevitability of accidents took deeper root in the various state and federal highway agencies. Rejecting moral lectures, these reformers turned to the "three E's" of road and car engineering, public education, and law enforcement to stem the flow of innocent blood.[71]

5

Perfection and Perfectibility in Auto Safety Reform

The gathering of twelve hundred prominent city, state, and national auto safety reformers on January 7, 1937, in Dallas, Texas, at the posh Adolphus Hotel looked, felt, and acted like scores of similar meetings held throughout the country from 1915 to 1940. Tuxedoed dignitaries, such as Texas governor James Allred, director of public safety for the National Safety Council (NSC) Sidney Williams, Automobile Manufacturers' Association safety chairman Paul G. Hoffman, and the state Citizen's Traffic Commission manager Carl J. Rutland sat at the head table behind elegant crystal and silver place settings long enough for the *Dallas Morning News* staff to snap a photo for the next day's front page. Leaders of the Dallas city police department and the newly created Texas Department of Public Safety (DPS), adorned in their full dress uniforms, occupied separate tables. The partition between the two enforcement agencies was intentional. Tensions smoldered since the legislature gave the DPS expanded jurisdictional powers and control over traditional policing bodies, such as the revered Texas Rangers. No doubt, simple jealousy between local and state officials played a part. The media portrayal of the dauntless, motorcycle driving "T-Men" of the DPS (a name for state "traffic men" drawn from the federal government or "G-Men" made popular by J. Edgar Hoover's FBI and Edward G. Robinson's Hollywood) gave State Highway Patrol Chief L. G. Phares and his men a heroic public persona that most local traffic cops clearly lacked. But this was a night for unanimity, not petty rivalries. Most of the guests expected an evening of good food, assertive pronouncements, and tough but practical recommendations for auto safety reform.[1]

On this score, the conference disappointed no one. The program featured "the cold hard facts of the traffic menace" told by men "who based what they said strictly on experience over many years of battling hand to hand the demon that deals death on wheels." Williams encouraged perseverance in the NSC's campaign, begun in 1915, to bolster the "three E's" of automotive reform: engineering, education, and enforcement. Governor Allred presented safety awards to the Dr. Pepper Bottling Company, the Hormel Company, and Humble Oil for their record of safe driving. Hoffman tried to correct public misconceptions that auto accidents were due to a few careless drivers or the poor mechanical condition of the nation's aging fleet of automobiles. The program also rallied the troops. Carl Rutland used the popularity of a recent film and the nation's preoccupation with Depression-era outlaws like John Dillinger and Bonnie and Clyde to rechristen auto accidents as "Public Enemy No.1." He theatrically vowed to "fight to the end." The Texas chairman of the State Public Safety Commission, Albert Sidney Johnson, went a step better—providing journalists with a partial headline for the next day's front page—in declaring a "permanent war on traffic accidents." In sum, the congress congratulated itself on its collective work to date and promised concerned citizens that, with continued "sustained effort," they could expect up to a 50 percent reduction in auto fatalities over the next two to three years.[2]

Three grade school girls quickly deflated the confidence and bravado of these men. One can imagine the well-fed reformers smiling affably, loosening their coats, and brushing crumbs from their uniforms as the children walked nervously to the dais. Representing approximately 60,000 Dallas children, the three read from a tightly scrolled paper. They asked for protection of themselves, their parents, and their futures. They cited well-publicized safety statistics that showed "one out of every three children is killed or injured before the age of 21" by auto accidents. "This means that one of us standing here must some day suffer this fate—unless there is a change." Solemnly presenting the scroll to Dallas city manager Hal Moseley, the girls pled "we want to live." Moseley accepted the parchment, attempted to respond but, finding himself mute before such honesty, simply resumed his seat without comment. Allred, a seasoned politician, regained his composure and addressed the moment. He quipped that he may need "these three little girls [to] deliver their message to the Legislature" as he introduced a bill on "this driver's license business." The *Morning News* turned the responsibility back to where it was originally directed. The next morning's headlines read: "Three Little Girls Ask Crowd of 1,200 for Life."[3]

After the fact, Albert Sidney Johnson defended the silence of the city manager. "I don't blame Mr. Moseley for saying nothing," Johnson said, for "there is no answer to be given." But the opinion of historians who examine early auto safety reform efforts suggests that this lack of a meaningful response was typical of the years from 1900 to 1940. They conclude that most reformers' understanding of the problem was narrow and naive, their actions muddled and misguided, their pronouncements too emotional, idealistic, or incomplete. In short, reform during the era accomplished little more than stirring public opinion, scaring little children, and distracting the nation from strategies that might have had a real chance at improving auto safety.[4]

Neither callousness nor ignorance created this chaotic state; the complex nature of the problem did. In the earliest years, few envisioned a world dominated by these expensive, inefficient, and once delicate machines. Initial "reforms" were mostly restrictions placed on the freedom of young urban elites. Exclusive motor clubs challenged these barriers and early regulation degraded into a form of class conflict. Confusion also multiplied due to the many competing modes of transit, which included the car, streetcars and trolleys, animal-powered vehicles, pedestrian traffic, heavy rail, and bicycles. Conflicting municipal, state, and federal oversight further confused the issue, adding multiple layers of regulation and scrambling the authority and responsibility for public safety.[5]

Historians are also sympathetic to the fact that auto accidents represented extremely complex events not easily controlled by casual reform. Robert Baker argues that the "simple cause-and-effect assumption[s]" fail to appreciate that "conditions are never that simple. Different parts of the system are weak in one place and strong in another." Problems of congestion, poor road design, and poorer road conditions plagued America's highways, increasing the potential for a catastrophe. Multiply these circumstances by the surging number of new drivers and decisions each novice must make to avoid a collision and one can begin to appreciate the staggering numeric probabilities of an accident. Combined, these considerations suggest that the sheer complexity of the problem overwhelmed a political and regulatory system born in the horse-and-buggy days.[6]

Collectively, historians advance two general patterns for auto safety reform from 1900 to 1940. The first suggests serendipitous or accidental safety. The work of road and car engineers, traffic and licensing officials, and driver educators did lower the risk of driving (as measured by fatality rates per million vehicle miles of travel or VMT). But these gains were not the result of an organized or coordinated policy. Highway and traffic engineers improved roads simply to allow more efficient use. Detroit built simpler and more reliable cars to spur sales. Politicians passed restrictive laws and levied fines to placate angry constituents (and fill local coffers). While all desired safer public transit, rarely did these motives and measures link directly to a systemic response to the problem. Clay McShane and Gijs Mom, for example, cite the growth of suburbs and changing urban traffic patterns as far greater causes of accident reduction than bureaucratic reform. As McShane notes elsewhere, the "great irony of traffic control" was that the *failure* of reformers to control congestion actually made urban streets safer. The tremendous growth in traffic overwhelmed most plans, which resulted in slower average speeds and reduced the severity of the typical auto accident. Historic fatality rates fell almost in spite of reform.[7]

A second and related analysis blames the failure of long-lasting auto safety on early reformers' tendency to address only the moral inadequacies of the driver. Certainly poor or reckless driving contributed to the accident problem, but the lone motorist represented only one piece of the puzzle. The road, car, auto regulations, and type of traffic all factored into the computation of an accident. For a number of scholars, this obsessive hunt for the amoral, accident-prone driver directed reformers toward a target that could not be changed. Activists used "pleading, shaming, harassing, frightening, and imprisoning" to cure impatience, immaturity, and motorized aggression. Historian Daniel Albert persuasively posits that these reformers conflated the growing accident crisis with their fears of social disorder in the modern age. To combat the depersonalization of the city and the potential for deadly accidents, reformers demanded drivers display "moral uprightness, maturity, intelligence, physical ability, and respect for the rule of law." Activists used tactics like psychological testing and moralizing as means to this end. Their inevitable failure led to a vicious cycle of blame and cynicism. Aggressive driving, habitual speeding, and law avoidance continued unabated and undermined any sense of progress on the nation's highways.[8]

But the assumption that reformers, before 1940, either ignored the problem or expected to change human nature is inaccurate. While many scholars assume that "no one seemed to notice" the rising death tolls of the Teens and Twenties or that "public interest in traffic safety was slight until the middle 1930s," this simply was not the case. As early as 1910, *Collier's* expressed a common and expanding refrain of the early auto age: "What is needed just now is less fussing about speed maniacs and more diligence in enforcing the law of the right of the road." In the first of his high-profile Conferences on Street and Highway Safety, in 1924, U.S. secretary of commerce Herbert Hoover noted how "today over two hundred great newspapers are [already] cooperating with the National Associations in a daily study and analysis of the accidents happening in their respective communities." Already a well-respected national reformer and activist, Hoover concluded, "I dare say there is not a progressive newspaper in the United States which is not making an organized drive on traffic conditions in their cities."[9]

Moreover, activists before 1940 acknowledged the limits of their own initial safety efforts. Today we are well aware of the critical difference between *suggested* national safety standards and firm *mandates* backed by federal law. We also acknowledge the financial constraints of the free market that bind many suppliers. Manufacturers certainly do not wish to see harm come to their clients. But their primary focus remains selling cars rather than insuring safe driving. Americans, before 1940, were not ignorant of these pressures. Members of the 1937 Dallas convention, for example, showed a keen appreciation of their past failures. Albert Johnson cautioned his audience not to start "another sporadic campaign" of moral outrage against the traffic scofflaw. Paul Hoffman expressed his doubt that sentimentality, preachy moralization, and additional "horror campaigns will stop accidents." Nearly all supported stronger engineering standards, greater legal uniformity, and regulatory simplicity. Twelve years earlier, traffic expert Miller McClintock admitted amazement that "so little restrictions [were] placed on the drivers of motor cars." He concluded that simple legal barriers— such as licensing and registration—were "the first step[s] toward gaining effective control" over auto accidents. Few believed that these changes would be easy. Victory in the "war" against traffic fatalities, Hoffman noted, would not come "in a single battle but in a fight that is carried forward on many fronts with a sustained effort." He concluded, pragmatically, "there is nothing spectacular about accomplishing" these goals. It was "all tough spade work."[10]

Finally, and perhaps most significantly, early reformers did not place undue emphasis on *changing* human nature. As understood through the automotive love affair, "good" driving provided an opportunity to display one's commitment to social equality and individual freedom. "Bad" drivers, the so-called flivver-boobs and motor morons, came under heavy criticism for their lack of civic honor and low moral character. Yet the use of morality in describing the problem of auto accidents was not the same as suggesting these drivers could be *cured* of their antisocial behavior. As early as 1914, auto advocates admitted that driving was not an exceptionally difficult task to master. For the driver of "average human intelligence," the car was "an easy thing to handle." This ease of operation allowed anyone, even those handicapped by poor character, to get behind the wheel. Americans understood that "with twenty-odd million drivers on the roads, a certain number of fools can be counted on to do the wrong thing."[11]

Reformers worked not to change the nature of these "fools" but rather to accentuate the moral obligations of the sane driver, to sharpen their skills, and to praise the actions of those who "fool-proofed" mass transit. They explicitly recognized their inability to reform most flivverboobs. A typical editorial, appearing in a 1925 *Collier's* magazine, praised the "perfection" of the car and highway, but grimly warned its readers that "some drivers are fools." While others hoped to create "a new mentality" in the American drivers, for the most part this meant increased safety consciousness. Good drivers would be those who "think safety and practice safety as second nature." Thus, reformers sought a moral arousal rather than the unrealistic dream of changing fundamental flaws in human nature. The two most active areas of early safety reform—engineering and education—both pursued methods that effectively *ignored* the amoral driver. Auto and roadway engineers worked to perfect their products so that personal character mattered very little. While educators spoke of the perfectibility of the driver, they focused their efforts almost exclusively on the young; not the drivers who already possessed unsafe habits or questionable ethics. Six months after the Dallas auto safety conference concluded, the Texas Good Roads Association held that "we should feel encouraged at the suggestion of traffic scientists that ninety percent of the people are safety-minded—that only one-tenth chisel on public safety. In other words, the situation is nine-tenths licked, and nothing but persistency will materially reduce the other tenth."[12]

Indeed, far from hoping to rejuvenate this untalented tenth, the growing consensus of many reformers was that dangerous drivers remained immune to positive change. Rather, the motor moron required firm legal restraint. Following the successful implementation of a demanding new municipal policing policy, the *San Diego Union* opined, in 1923, that the "personal liberty" of the habitual traffic offender "should be seriously infringed upon. This is meant literally. The driver of an automobile is under strict obligations to the public—to the large body of taxpayers who furnish him with roads and highways, and to all others to whom, if he is not regulated, he can become so serious a menace." Others called for more authoritarian enforcement, longer jail terms, and generally "more teeth" in state and local laws. Just as the market compelled industrialists to improve safety or face economic penalties, safety enforcement coerced drivers to obey the laws or confront the costs of imprisonment, the revocation of their license, or society's displeasure. In an address before the National Safety Council, long-time auto safety advocate A. W. Koehler admitted that "Enforcement is the most necessary thing of all. Not drastic punishment, but a *certainty* of punishment. Not a drastic enforcement, but a *certainty* of enforcement." As such, the belief in the ability of moral suasion to change human nature rarely contented early safety reformers.[13]

The real problem with the historic interpretation of auto safety reform—to the extent that one exists—concerns the concepts of risk and safety. Rather than debate the metaphysics of inevitable or avoidable accidents (for clearly they favored the former), early auto reformers considered the relative merits of risk (the *probability* of an unwanted event occurring within a defined set of characteristics) and safety (the *perception* by individuals that they effectively limited or controlled the variables that produced risk).[14] The paradox between risk and safety clearly confounded participants at the Dallas safety conference. The men who championed solutions through engineering, education, and enforcement envisioned a transit system that lowered the collective risk of driving for the average American. However, early auto reformers did little to tap into the public's hopes for improved personal safety. Focused on reducing collective risk, they argued that character mattered very little. But the love affair was powerful. It validated a set of qualities that, the public believed, connected driving to civic duty. As a result, safety efforts pushed by reform experts veered away from the very definitions of *safe* automobiling that made the most sense to mobile Americans. In a parody of the bureaucratic "three E's," one 1931 essayist countered with the very individualized "three C's"—"concentration, caution, and consideration"— as a better guide to personal driving safety. Unlike the NSC model, which sought lowered risk, the "three C's" linked personal driving behavior to safety. Rather than statistical risk, these three terms reflected perceptions of safety. Drivers derided "attempt[s] to salve the injured feelings of the dead by quoting statistics showing that they were and are getting more and more mileage before dying." Reduced risk "gives little comfort either to [the dead] or to those of us who stay behind and grieve." The three young girls who silenced the twelve hundred conference attendees stated this sentiment more clearly: they wanted to live.[15]

America's early auto safety community hoped to untangle the various threads of safety, risk, and the perfectibility of the problem driver. Throughout the period, activists from a variety of regional and national safety associations struggled to define the purpose of auto safety reform. They wrestled with traditional anxieties—such as the proper role of public regulation over private industry and the respective constitutional prerogatives of state and federal government—but also with new worries about the power of modern science and progressive education to address these troubles. In the end, it was neither the reformers' lack of vision nor their hopeless idealism that led to frustration. Rather, a lack of effective enforcement arose as the missing link that connected the powerful love affair to meaningful safety reform.

The broad narrative arc of safety reform from 1900 to 1940 appears both remarkably simple and strangely complex. On the one hand, legislative solutions followed a pattern typical of other progressive reforms: local activists, aided by the popular press, drove municipalities and state governments to pass basic restrictions on auto usage, such as speed limits and rights of way. These rules then formed the agenda for national associations and eventually federal legislators. In a similarly straightforward pattern, the private sector standardized the operation of the automobile. While manufacturers installed automatic starters, higher powered and more reliable engines, and standardized controls to spur sales, these had the added benefit of simplifying the operation of a car and thereby lowering accidents. Finally, road and traffic engineers applied their skills to the most obvious road hazards, such as grade crossings, dangerous intersections, and road obstructions. While these solutions took on greater complexity through the sheer volume of cars and drivers, the process of reform remained orderly and rational.[16]

Yet safety reformers found the devil in the details. Traditional tensions between federal, state, and local authorities stymied efforts to unify driving and manufacturing standards. Even after five national safety conferences, advocates grudgingly concluded that the "accident problem is national only in the sense that it represents the aggregate of thousands of local problems, each the product of peculiarly local conditions." Ethical and legal problems over business regulation also distracted and distorted safety reform. States could not force corporations, legally considered as individuals, to redirect their assets without a full consideration of their Constitutional rights.[17]

Competing perspectives of what automobility meant to American society further complicated the picture. Three nodes of government (local, state, and federal), private industry, and the driving public each exhibited discrete and, at times, mutually exclusive philosophies over the meaning and purpose of individual mass transit. For some it meant freedom and individuality. Others saw mass transit as an opportunity of the free market. By the 1920s, the growth of road-related public works and a dramatic increase in public money—from gas taxes and user fees—meant patronage and political power. It was no small wonder that auto reformers' actions exhibited redundancy and ambiguity. Pleasing all of these interests proved impossible.

Three key developments shaped the image and substance of early safety reform: the creation of the National Safety Council, increased federal road funding, and national advisory councils convened to provide uniformity.

Growing concern over on-the-job safety in hazardous industries like mining and the railroads spurred initial reformers into forming the NSC. The birth of modern industry, with its focus on product throughput, efficiency, and economies of scale, provided business executives the financial justification to finally protect their workers. Accidents slowed production rates, harmed skilled employees, opened firms to liability lawsuits, justified ruinous strikes, and generated bad publicity.[18]

In 1907, the Association of Iron and Steel Engineers formed the first independent safety committee to study the hazards of industrial work. The 1908 Federal Employers' Liability Law provided businessmen with the legal and financial incentive to cooperate with the safety movement. As momentum swelled, partly a result of the public outrage over the Triangle Shirtwaist fire of 1911, a mixture of safety engineers, labor leaders, and businessmen formed the Co-operative Safety Council, in October 1912.[19] When a second safety congress convened a year later in New York City, the assembly formed the National Council of Industrial Safety. They soon rechristened the organization the National Safety Council. The NSC was chartered as a nonprofit, nonpolitical interest group dedicated to publicizing safety information. Its motto, "Safety First," suggested a broad appeal intended to influence government agencies, businesses, and workers.[20]

In an effort to reach the public, the NSC focused much of its resources on safety propaganda. Its 1913 inaugural safety poster promoted safety glasses and featured an eyeless worker with the caption "Why take a chance and be maimed for life? Safety First." As private industry internalized on-the-job safety engineering, the NSC shifted more forcefully toward the general public. They publicized information about traditional accidents—such as home fires and falls—but took advantage of the opportunity afforded by the rising number of traffic accidents. The NSC formed a Public Safety Section specifically to address auto safety. In 1915, Julien Harvey provided the Council with an easy-to-remember slogan when he coined the "three E's" of auto safety: engineering, education, and enforcement. The agency published magazines, like *Public Safety* and *Safety Education*, that focused attention on the traffic menace. They sponsored dozens of youth organizations (called Junior Safety Councils) and enrolled over eight hundred cities in national traffic safety contests. The NSC also formed an "Education Section" sponsored by leading advocates of John Dewey's "social adjustment" methods of progressive education, including former Dewey students Harold Rugg, William Kilpatrick, and staunch ally E. George Payne.[21]

The industrial roots of the NSC biased their safety reform initiatives. Using a cost-based analysis (which argued that safety is economically efficient), the council suggested that safety reform was most effective when it emerged from industry itself. This "business model" provided auto manufacturers with a free pass to self-regulate. But the approach was consistent with the legal, business, and political predilections of pre–New Deal America. The NSC justified its meth-

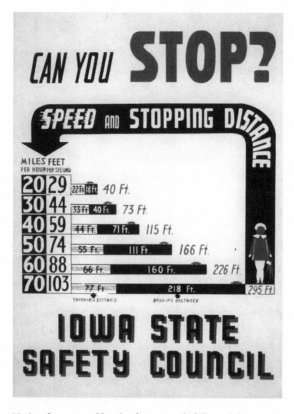

National, state, and local safety councils followed the "business model" of safety. They provided motorists with rational information, such as reaction times and braking distances, in an effort to perfect the motorist and reduce avoidable collisions. (Library of Congress, Prints and Photographs Division [LC-USZC2-5254 DLC])

ods by the tremendous decrease in the average incidence of fatal or debilitating accidents. Accidents per million man hours worked in the steel industry, for example, fell from 44.1 per year, in 1910, to 11.7 per year in 1939. Census records indicate similarly dramatic drops in accidents for mining and railroads. The economies of scale made the larger, more powerful industries particularly responsive to the safety movement. Historian Mark Aldrich notes the irony: had reformers been more effective in disbanding these large firms, worker safety would have suffered.[22]

The public goodwill generated by industrial self-regulation also lowered the likelihood of external meddling by government and labor groups. Internal safety reforms promoted trust in management's benevolent care of the workforce and suited the long-standing institutional goals of unions like the United Mine Workers and American Federation of Labor. As one safety advocate reported in 1937, the "feeling among the industrialists today is that safety is the greatest morale builder they can secure. A protected employee becomes a loyal employee; and loyalty, definite records show, is the biggest factor in low production costs." The business movement also created a cadre of new professional safety engineers, many of whom soon staffed the NSC.[23]

The council's primary focus—risk reduction—became a staple of their auto safety initiatives. C. W. Price, an early industrial safety advocate and later secretary, vice president, and then president of the NSC, argued that Detroit must lead the fight against auto fatalities. While the automotive industry should not "go into the business of conducting safety campaigns" or public safety education, they should recognize the fiscal imperatives of safety. "Entirely aside from humanitarian considerations," Price argued, "aside from any moral obligation, but purely on a basis of sound principles, the automotive industry should take the lead in any safety movement." Specifically, reformers wanted manufacturers to test their products for passenger safety, replace hazardous materials and designs, and continue to instruct the public on the safe use of their products. The resulting benefits, it was thought, would only spur demand. Carl Rutland, as president of the Texas Safety Association and featured speaker at the 1937 Dallas conference, saw the auto safety movement as one "initiated and motivated by the economic savings to come through a reduction in the accidents." Perhaps this is why Rutland, who led the investigating team of the infamous Darst-Mullins crash, placed their work squarely within the business model. The committee asked itself this question: "If an industrial accident in some factory had snuffed out six lives, what would be an investigating procedure?" The financial efficiency of safety, proven so conclusively in industry, emerged as the grail of the auto safety community because "only when transportation is safe is it economical, profitable, and desirable." The roots of the NSC and the early efficacy of industrial safety initiatives lent auto safety a distinctly corporate appreciation for the accident problem. Risk dominated their thinking.[24]

But the business model proved poorly suited to safety reform on a number of levels. Most importantly, as auto safety historian Edward Tenney writes, it involved "no sacrifice." Industries saw clear economic incentives to reform their private operations; steel was cheaper or worker productivity grew. But auto accidents disconnected the costs from these benefits. While some cautioned that car sales would fall dramatically if the accident problem was not solved, events did not bear out this warning. Detroit sold faster and deadlier vehicles to a public which valued automotive freedom and the visceral excitement of driving. Sales were unaffected and automakers not pressured to respond in any meaningful ways.[25]

Second, the business model, almost by definition, required minimal public oversight. To work effectively, proponents argued, safety reform must emerge from within industry. Firms that provided the safest product would garner the greatest economic benefits. Governmental interference only muted the power of the hidden hand. While the NSC did call for greater legal restrictions on driving and full enforcement of automotive laws, there was no legitimate place for a central governmental authority. *Scientific American* believed that "Congressional discussion of any proposed uniform automobile and traffic laws would degenerate into an orgy of bickering and log-rolling." For their part, most drivers agreed that accidents were socially "painful and unpleasant." But few proved willing to surrender their individual freedom to pay these collective costs. Indeed, most Americans understood the accident crisis in terms of flivverboobs and motor morons, not as a function of an unregulated and massively expanding motorized citizenry.[26]

Still, the National Safety Council established the first major link to effective auto safety reform. The agency defined the problem, proposed a solution, and kept the issue before the public. But the business model of safety reform—so well justified by the experience of industrial safety—proved ineffective for America's roadways. While reformers claimed that auto and highway engineers "perfected" their product, and that educators did the same to young drivers, their inability to link the costs of accidents with the financial benefits of safety reform doomed their approach.

A second broad development in automotive safety was the sudden and substantial increase in federal road funding. From a practical standpoint, the 1916 and 1921 Federal Road Aid Acts provided the economic resources that many states needed to begin building a modern road system. The 1916 act authorized $75 million over five years while the second apportioned more than $75 million *annually* as well as the transfer of military surplus equipment such as trucks and tractors. President Hoover raised the ante to more than $125 million annually, and the combined contributions of New Deal agencies, specifically the Works Progress Administration, Public Works Administration, and Reconstruction Finance Corporation, added more than $1.8 billion from 1933 to 1940. The U.S. Department of Commerce reported that 13.8 percent of all construction funds for state-administered highway projects between 1916 and 1920 had come from the federal treasury. By 1940, this number had increased to over 40 percent.[27]

While one might assume that these funds significantly increased the amount of road mileage in the United States, in reality the money was spent improving and redesigning the existing system. Regulators spent federal money on an increasingly large part of the nation's roadways, from 169,007 miles of improved highway in 1923 to 235,482 miles in 1940. But during these same years the overall mileage of public roads grew by less than 2 percent. In other words, the work did not add mileage but rather improved the quality of existing roads. Engineers eliminated dangerous curves, removed obstructions, abandoned old section-line roads for more efficient routes, and updated surfaces. In some regions, the change was dramatic. In Mississippi, the state surfaced only 8 percent of its roads by 1917. Five years later, more than 40 percent of the highways were improved. In Texas, federal aid paid for the construction of nearly three hundred miles of concrete highway and fifty-six modern bridges between 1917 and 1925.[28]

But while the total road mileage in the United States went largely undisturbed, the "administrative responsibility and quality . . . changed substantially." Tom Lewis's study of federal highway construction shows the dramatic transformation that the Road Aid laws had on state and federal highway authorities. Men like Thomas MacDonald modernized the federal Bureau of Public Roads, replacing political cronies with highway engineers and policy "technocrats" who sustained the federal program even through the lean Harding and Coolidge administrations.[29]

The acts also encouraged the professionalization of the state highway departments. While some Eastern and Midwestern states formed commissions staffed with trained engineers and transit experts well before 1916, the provisions of the federal law mandated "a highway department capable of administering the funds" and constructing modern thoroughfares. This required appropriate accounting and, more importantly, engineering standards. The professional association of these state regulators, the American Association of State Highway Officials (AASHO), stood with the most powerful lobbying groups in Washington and exerted considerable influence over the safety community. Federal and state engineers oversaw the construction of every project that received federal funding. The very first meeting of the Texas State Highway Department, June 4, 1917, focused on the hiring of University of Texas engineer George Duran and the proper reporting procedures necessary to track spending decisions. The committee, appointed by the governor, planned to meet one day a month. Their minute books, however, record activities that spanned more than seven full days of every month. Activities included planning, commissioning professional advice and construction supervision, evaluating proper building materials, placing directional signs, and issuing license plates. The state published, as ordered on the second official meeting, 150,000 copies of the recently amended Texas Automobile Law. Of the $269,705 in salaries and travel expenses appropriated from 1920 to 1922, costs for "engineering" claimed fully $162,823 or 60 percent of total expenditures.[30]

The vast increase in funds also attracted professional and business interests. In addition to manufacturers, federal oversight involved firms that sold cement, rubber, insurance, brick pavers, and petroleum. The celebrated Hoover Conferences, for example, were supported by contributions from the American Automobile Association, the American Railway Association, the National Association of Taxicab Owners, the National Bureau of Casualty and Surety Underwriters, and the Rubber Manufacturers' Association. Professional highway and traffic engineers played prominent roles within both state and national safety organizations.

Highway engineers siting a transit for a new grade crossing at
Independence Avenue and 14th and 16th Streets SW, Washington,
D.C. As with safety educators, engineers hoped to perfect America's
roadways in order to eliminate avoidable accidents. (Library of
Congress, Prints and Photographs Division, FSA-OWI Collection [LC-
USF34-011418-D DLC])

The efficacy of their methods led to a stable and long-lasting relationship among
industry, government, and the professions that served the purpose of road improvement quite well.[31]

By the close of World War I, and the rise of the national accident crisis, the
safety reform movement displayed two of its three most important characteristics. The NSC emerged as the leading advocate of driver safety. The council's
principles of the "three E's" addressed the primary causes of accidents. Moreover, prominent professional safety communities (particularly those of the private sector) supported the NSC's philosophies. Finally, state and federal funding
initiatives for road development established the working and fiscal structure of
safe road design. The success of both the NSC and the state highway programs
rested on their tacit agreement in the inevitability of auto accidents and the de-
sirability of collective risk reduction. Whether termed a business model or not,
both approaches assumed that reducing driving hazards led to fewer collisions
and better overall transit efficiency.

Whatever impact these associations might have had on risk, for the driver the system appeared increasingly unsafe. More reliable, modern roads abetted the rapid growth of automobility and added further opportunities for disaster. Given the local and individual experiences of drivers, it was logical that their frustrations turned to the seemingly chaotic state of local motoring ordinances. Depending on where one lived, one might, on an average day's drive, pass through several distinct legislative districts all with unique and often conflicting laws. Even those intent on obeying the law inadvertently broke local customs when they traveled beyond their neighborhood, thus creating the unintentional lawbreaker. "In a good many cities," one confounded driver complained, "you go to the right of a traffic officer when making a left-hand turn. . . . [but do this] in some other cities and [you] will witness some lively and arresting action on the part of the cop." The same proved true of speed limits, directional signals, rights of way, pedestrian restrictions, traffic lights, parking laws, and a host of other regulations. Like the popular ketchup, critics charged that conflicting motor laws and regulations presented drivers with "fifty-seven varieties" of reform resulting in "one of the most thoroughgoing muddles in [legislative] history." It got so bad that one motorist suggested in 1922 that drivers accept a set of uniform directional hand signals proposed by the popular press, not those of competing state authorities. The author of the Harriss-*Collier's* signal system promised better safety "without waiting for the necessarily slow process of lawmaking." While concerned about losing their cherished automotive freedoms, "we must realize that with twelve million cars on the road to-day . . . we are facing a problem, the solution of which lies only in proper and suitable legislation."[32]

The smaller New England and Mid-Atlantic states faced the question of contradictory state laws sooner than most. In a meeting of chief executives in 1910, Massachusetts governor Ebenezer Draper complained of the many conflicting state mandates. Reciprocity, or the recognition of certain common state statutes, cut through red tape. A spate of legal changes, such as New York's Callan Law (1910) and New Jersey's Stickel Law (1912), provided limited reciprocity but also increased the legal requirements for driving in both states. State road funding proved the greatest obstacle to more uniform legislation. Simply stated, local motorists objected to paying for roads used freely by out-of-state motorists. Some legislators proposed temporary license fees for visitors. One driver, in 1910, totaled the cost of out-of-state registration fees for a planned cross-country trip at $125.75. "It would be manifestly unequal and unfair," another wrote, "for the people of New Jersey to grant the citizens of other states the unrestricted privilege of using her highways out of mere courtesy." Pennsylvania and New York, by contrast, charged all drivers a user fee (tolls) for the privilege of using their newest highways. The problem emerged from the mixture of these funding plans. Should New Jersey drivers, for example, be expected to pay tolls while traveling abroad but allow others the free use of Garden State roads and highways?

"Considered purely from the economical standpoint," one essayist concluded, "the burden of maintaining her highways would be vastly increased without anything like an equivalent return. [Our] problem is not an easy one."[33]

Lawmakers agreed that legal and fiscal uniformity saved "a lot of uneasiness and trouble." As early as 1909, activists dreamed of a uniform federal law. Certainly, the passage of the Federal Road Aid Acts mitigated the financial burden on any single state and suggested that a national solution was possible. Beyond the popular press, proposals also emanated from a variety of institutional sources. In addition to the NSC, the National Automobile Chamber of Commerce sponsored uniformity conferences through the Traffic Planning and Safety Commission, led by Studebaker vice president Paul G. Hoffman in the early 1920s. In October 1921, New York City hosted a meeting of local State Motor Vehicle Administrators. They saw their goal as the "absolute uniformity of motor vehicle laws; the day when a small manual of regulations covering both equipment and road rules will apply in all States from Maine to California." The group held quarterly meetings with the anticipation that drivers would soon have no "fear—as is often the case now—that they will be arrested for some trivial offense which is within the law in their own State." *Scientific American* echoed these sentiments and threw its full support behind a conference to establish federal highway standards for traffic legislation. Standardization of laws, they held, prevented the sane, law-abiding driver from "becoming a danger both to himself and others."[34]

These efforts culminated in a call by Commerce Secretary Herbert Hoover to hold the First National Conference on Street and Highway Safety, which met in Washington in December 1924. Four subsequent national conferences, in 1926, 1930, 1935, and 1938, fleshed out an ambitious agenda of reform that included standardized accident reporting, uniform traffic controls, highway construction and engineering specifications, city planning and zoning laws, insurance, public education, and motor vehicle standards.

Political considerations curtailed reformers' ability to act uniformly. The Republican administrations of Coolidge and Hoover clearly distrusted the growth of federal powers. In his plenary speech at the inaugural meeting, President Coolidge sternly reminded participants that they met merely to conduct a "comprehensive study of the causes." He cautioned,

> The solution does not rest in national action. Highway control is primarily for the states, and it is best that this is so. We cannot regulate local traffic by Act of Congress. Means to overcome the difficulties, to keep our complex traffic moving with order and safety, must be found by the states. It is a proper function of Federal authority to mobilize the best experience. . . . But uniformity, while of the greatest value and highly advisable, so far as shifting local requirements will permit, should not be imposed by the inflexible fiat of central power.

Hoover repeatedly reaffirmed this sentiment in subsequent conferences. Even in later meetings, renamed the Accident Prevention Conference by Franklin Roosevelt's secretary of commerce Daniel C. Roper, New Deal Democrats held to the principle that "the sole purpose in organizing had been to serve the needs of the various states by coordination and an interchange of ideas and methods." Roper vowed that the new administration "had no desire to take over any of the activities now performed by existing accident prevention groups." With the business model as the operating assumption, most participants expected little real federal enforcement of their proposals.[35]

With the tone of localism and voluntary cooperation established, participants set to work laying out the principles of uniformity. In short, they wanted to simplify the law in order to prevent accidental violations. Over the span of the five conferences they published a host of ambitious recommendations, including a Uniform Vehicle Code, a Model Municipal Traffic Ordinance, and a Manual of Uniform Traffic Control Devices. Many maintained high hopes for substantive change. Immediately after the conclusion of the 1924 conference, twenty-three states adopted portions of the Uniform Vehicle Code and some borrowed wording from the conference's "Rules of the Road." One contributor to *The Saturday Evening Post* predicted that the "Hoover safety conference not only set a new style in national conferences, but its practical results to the American people will, perhaps, outweigh those of any other conference in this country."[36]

But little substantive change resulted. Many local governments took the recommendations to heart, but without federal enforcement there was no sustained effort to coordinate state statutes. In 1926, editors of *The New Republic* concluded that "the efforts of Secretary Hoover's recent National Conference on Street and Highway Safety are not a very happy augury." Even the conference's policy on universal hand signals failed to eclipse the private Harriss-*Collier's* system of 1922. By contrast, critics charged, the federal meeting "contended itself with the opinion that when a driver puts his arm out, it should be understood that he intends to do *something*, other than roll straight along at a uniform speed"; hardly the leadership needed to confront the growing auto accident crisis. Hoover himself conceded as much when, as president, he lamented that "in view of the emphatic and widespread demands for uniform and effective traffic laws, it must be said that progress to date appears far from adequate." Subsequent conferences proved little more effective. By 1938, the U.S. Department of Agriculture concluded "despite recent improvements resulting from partial adoption of the vehicle code recommended by the National Conference on Street and Highway Safety, there is still an utter lack of uniformity."[37]

The commissions' willingness to blame the driver proved equally problematic. Rather than fault weak public resolve or hold the private sector accountable for selling dangerous vehicles, the specter of the lone reckless driver haunted the conferences. Again and again, the "inconsiderate, the careless, and the incompetent" motorist emerged as the advisable target of reform. Based on their reading of the first commission's findings, editors at the *Washington Star* concluded that "the real death-dealing monster is our national ignorance of traffic and highway safety." As late as 1935, five of the seven key goals, considered "imperative to accident reduction" by the Accident Prevention Conference, dealt with poor driver behavior, including reckless speeding, poorly maintained vehicles, and law avoidance, and called for better "driver consciousness and respect of law." The result was an unnecessary and fruitless battle between auto enthusiasts and state legislators. Auto clubs rejected the charge of wholesale recklessness by their members and bitterly opposed state and federal laws that limited their automotive freedom. The Chicago Motor Club, for example, led efforts to repeatedly defeat legislation for a uniform drivers' license law in Illinois from 1927 to 1935.[38]

To be fair, the conference reinforced and sustained several important national trends in auto safety reform. First, it affirmed the structure of the NSC's "three E's" campaign. Reform must improve engineering standards, better educate American drivers, and enforce uniform driving codes (if only at the state or local level). FDR's Accident Prevention Conference even went so far as to suggest that Detroit (voluntarily) redesign its products to "protect the reckless motorist against his own folly."[39]

Second, the conferences confirmed that the various auto-related "communities," including highway and police authorities, educational institutions, insurance agencies, engineers, city planners, the NSC, labor, and local chambers of commerce, must work consistently to reduce the number of auto accidents. By 1939, the institutional rhetoric against the habitually reckless driver softened as reformers recognized that "the primary responsibility for traffic safety rests with public officials." Their "effective and balanced official programs" merely required the passive support of the driving public.[40]

Lastly, their recommendations spurred state officials to pass more uniform motoring laws. By 1935, "strong independent state safety committees" operated in twenty states and only eleven states remained without any driver licensing provisions. While, by that time, State Highway Patrols existed in all but four states, enforcement of the law "appear[ed] to be the major function of the patrol organizations" in only twenty-two states. Reformers augmented these policing functions in both manpower and oversight to match the growth in traffic. In any event, policing bodies that "consist[ed] of a very small personnel concerned primarily with the collection of revenues" from speed traps and traffic court fines must be revised. The proposed Uniform Vehicle Code (1939) was an amalgamation of the five conferences. Its provisions called for uniform registration, licensing, liability, financial responsibility, and rules of the road.[41]

The combined efforts of the NSC, federal aid, and the various national safety commissions gave substance and standing to the auto reform community. When men like Sidney Williams, Paul Hoffman, and Thomas MacDonald spoke about accident prevention, most listened. Their collective work also thickened state and federal government support for the professional safety community. The growth of influential professional organizations, like AASHO and the American Society of Civil Engineers (ASCE), further strengthened and streamlined their recommendations. The broad philosophical goals of the "three E's" remained at the heart of their efforts. Accordingly, it was through engineering and education (and later, enforcement) that their work must be measured.

Of all the reforms proposed, improved engineering demonstrated the greatest reduction of overall risk. The NSC's use of the term *engineering* actually refers to three distinct types of technical design: automotive, highway, and traffic engineering. Each benefited from the Progressive Era's affection for science and technology. Each demonstrated a strong belief in the inevitability of auto accidents. But each retained an unshakable optimism in their craft; a progressive confidence shared by the public-at-large. Engineers, particularly mechanical and civil engineers, represented Promethean figures exemplified by Thomas Edison and George Westinghouse who literally distributed lightning stolen from the gods. Indeed, progressive science and engineering promised to provide the tools needed for efficient modern living with the lowest possible risk.[42]

Low expectations and quick results placed early auto engineers high in the public's regard. Perhaps auto designers had it easy. Early cars, with their persnickety levers and throttles, troublesome tires, and stiff handling characteristics not only presented real safety concerns but, more importantly for Detroit, real marketing problems. In their drive toward greater reliability, engineers erased much of the confusion in operating a car. By making cars simpler, more reliable, and more appealing to all-year use, they corrected many of the troubling nuisances of the original open-wheeled flivvers. Henry Ford's ability to turn the engineering genius of men like Harold Wills and Charles Sorenson into market share established a cyclical, reinforcing financial relationship between improved design, greater reliability, lowered cost, and rising consumer demand.

By the 1920s, as the new-car saturation point neared, marketing innovators like GM's Alfred Sloan shifted this equation away from the more marginal engineering gains (at least in terms of the public's expectations for a vehicle that would start, go, turn, and stop) to more attractive styling and brand packaging. As Joel Eastman shows, in the competition between styling and safety, styling easily triumphed.[43]

While, on balance, manufacturers were not held responsible for most auto accidents, safety advocates assumed that auto engineering represented the key to any overall solution. For their part, state public reform agencies conducted limited product testing on only the most obvious safety hazards, such as brakes, windshield glass, head and tail lamps, and tires. But aside from acetylene headlights and the lenses used to project light upon the roadway, few regulations required specific and uniform safety standards. Even fewer suppliers factored normal wear and tear into their specifications. Many manufacturers admitted that, for example, "the braking effort originally built into any car has, at the end of 5,000 miles, been lost to a degree which may run to as much as fifty per cent." This loss, of course, was rarely "apparent to the average driver until it [was] forcibly brought to his attention" through a collision.[44]

Whether manufacturers "sense[d] the changed attitude" toward public safety or simply desired more marketable cars, the presence of reassuring essays by auto engineers in the popular press expanded during the 1920s. Studebaker's Paul G. Hoffman and the visionary Walter P. Chrysler, for example, expounded on engineering improvements as a key to the cure. Others wrote of the "unremitting efforts of the manufacturers to furnish us with a safe car. No expense has been spared to obtain, through their research departments, accurate and impartial information concerning the car reaction in every conceivable accident." *Scientific American* profiled GM's engineering genius Charles Kettering in the weeks immediately following the first Hoover Commission. Appearing like the "bearded alchemist of medieval times," Kettering managed over four hundred engineers and mechanics at his six-acre research laboratory in Dayton, Ohio. Their meticulous testing identified "invisible forces" not "perceived by the five senses." The result, the correspondent comforted nervous readers, was as "if we could rub the magic lamp and wish for the ultimate in automobiles." Engineers produced an "automobile in the test tube!"[45]

By the mid to late 1920s, most agreed that the motorcar "has come to be accepted as a highly perfect product." A 1937 driver's manual for teens expressed what was a commonly held assumption: "The automobile of today is as nearly perfect as science and industry can make it. . . . Neither time nor effort has been spared by the builders in their efforts to make the automobile a safe and enjoyable means of transportation."[46]

But, of course, engineers had not perfected the safe car. Even conservative estimates concluded that defective equipment was responsible for 9 to 15 percent of all automobile collisions. Periodic "safety lane" inspections found that a *majority* of American drivers operated defective automobiles. One 1936 study of ten Michigan cities stopped over thirty thousand cars. They found that 40.4 percent ran with defective brakes, 39.8 percent with faulty lights, and 59.0 percent with some substantive mechanical problem. As Eastman shows, by that time design elements featured streamlined windows and doors and long hoods and sleek profiles that reduced driver visibility to the barest minimum threshold. Balloon tires, introduced in the 1930s, enhanced comfort but severely limited braking effectiveness and steering controls, particularly when treads were worn thin. Engineers developed power steering in 1924 to compensate for this loss, but companies refused to implement the device until 1951. Moreover, many firms began to withdraw simple safety devices like seatbelts from circulation. Fearing the perception that their products were unsafe, Detroit removed any indication that it agreed with this assessment.[47]

Based on the logic of auto engineers, much like that of later opponents of gun control, it was not the car that killed but rather the driver. Judge John Maher, comparing the rattling gas-buggies of the 1910s to the cars "of today which possess streamlines . . . hydraulic brakes, electric lights, free wheeling, automatic clutches, and balloon tires. *The astonishing thing is that the development of the cars has far outstripped the development of the drivers.*" He lamented that while the "modern automobile is one of the finest products of a mechanical age, . . . no amount of engineering skill can make it safer than its operator." Miller McClintock, traffic engineer and Director of the Albert Erskine Bureau for Street Traffic Research at Harvard University, claimed that "defects in humanity run so far ahead of the defects in the automobile as to make it instantaneously obvious that we have only ourselves to blame" for accidents. Another concluded that good auto design actually facilitated poor driving, for "in fact, the perfection of the car has a tendency to make a driver careless and reckless."[48]

But the best test of Detroit's desire to engineer for safety rather than sales was seen in the industry's pursuit of speed. While early expensive autos easily exceeded 50 to 60 miles per hour, it was not until the 1920s that affordable cars and good roads brought these rates to the masses. If the prevailing logic was correct—that many drivers lacked the necessary skills to operate a motorcar at this speed—then responsible engineers and regulators must respond. The insurance commissioner of the Commonwealth of Massachusetts, Francis J. DeCelles, spoke "vigorously and at length" at the Accident Prevention Conference in 1935 on the dangers of speed. Using statistics compiled over the years, DeCelles demanded action "which will enable us to cut down the present enormous loss of property and life—the avowed purpose of this organization."[49]

The speed debate was primarily about marketing. While advertising speed raised a storm of protest, it also sold cars. Even some industry leaders, like Glenn A. Tisdale, president of Franklin Motor Car Company and the Automobile Dealers Association of America, agreed that "It is time for [us] . . . to stop fighting any and all legislation for the regulation of automobiles and to unite upon some means of bringing an end to the accident menace. The truth of the whole matter is that we have got too much speed." Others, such as Roy Chapin, president of the National Automobile Chamber of Commerce, averred that "our industry is committed to every sound policy that will increase safety upon the highway, and we are glad to have suggestions" for limiting the "craze for speed."[50]

While some—such as Buick, Dodge, Chrysler, and Wilys-Overland—did restrain their ad copy (for a while), the industry did nothing to *engineer* limits on the technology. Reformers toyed with goofy mechanical devices that indicated if a driver exceeded the posted speed limit. In 1921, *Illustrated World* described a gadget, prominently installed on the radiator hood, that lit three lights based on the speed of the vehicle: a white bulb lit when below 15 miles per hour (the typical city speed limit), a green bulb lit between 15 and 25 (the rural limit), and a red bulb lit for anything over that. Others proposed passive safety systems that cut the motor, threw out the clutch, and sounded the horn when danger approached. One essayist reported a "practice commonly indulged" by supposedly high-minded automakers: rigging "speedometers so that they will register anywhere from 5 to 12 percent more than the rate at which the car is actually traveling." In theory this cut down on speeding yet retained the speed thrills demanded by the consumer.[51]

By mid-decade, a simple and saner solution appeared: a mechanical speed governor. The device did nothing to inhibit the rapid acceleration that many speed advocates argued was the primary benefit of a more powerful motor. A governor held "the speed down to whatever number of miles the law stipulated." While some suggested that "such a step as this would seem to be a drastic one . . . isn't it [also] a drastic act to take the lives of unoffending fellow citizens wantonly through a mere mania to 'step on the gas'?" Frustrated by the inability to keep motorists below the 50 miles per hour speed limit, the New York Automobile Commissioner concluded that automobilists must either "drive at reasonable speeds or be compelled to do so" by speed governors. A Texas official likened extra-legal speed to a children's toy and cautioned, "when a mother sees her child playing with something that is dangerous, she quickly takes that plaything away." Mechanical speed governors not only limited the fool behind the wheel but acted as a strict enforcer of the law. "Under such mechanical control," one 1930 essayist offered, "the duties of 'traffic cops' would become mainly duties of inspection of cars and a patrolling of regions within which speed limits are to be enforced."[52]

Auto manufacturers never installed speed governors into American automobiles, nor did legislators require them to do so. While Detroit certainly (and dramatically) improved the quality of its product between 1900 and 1940, manufacturers did little to respond to the greatest safety needs of American motorists. Although the prevailing logic of both safety experts and the love affair suggested that foolish drivers generated the most accidents, engineers did nothing to limit the damage that fools could cause. Following the "no sacrifice" business model, automakers lowered risk in ways that did not impinge on their sales. Although they did respond to state mandates—such as installing safety glass and nonglare headlights—the lack of uniform federal laws left the "perfect car" with a conspicuously poor safety record.[53]

As with the car, reformers also heralded the perfection of road engineering. Unlike the private purview of automotive manufacture and design, however, road building long existed within the legitimate jurisdiction of public agencies. Governments designed, maintained, and funded all public thoroughfares. Moreover, credible universities and professional bodies, such as the ASCE, established well-known procedures for proper surveying, construction, and testing of materials necessary for these streets and highways. Road engineers certainly suffered from the same lack of administrative uniformity and centralized control. Safe design, many lamented, remained "a matter of state and local control." The inefficiencies and redundancies of federalism, the 1930 Hoover Commission concluded, prevented the public from "reap[ing] the benefit" on a "nation-wide scale." Road engineering reform, they cautioned, "will require some yielding of state and local preferences; it will require devotion of increased resources which no state or community can afford to withhold; it will in many jurisdictions require the setting up of more adequate administration; [and] it will require the loyal effort of enforcing authorities."[54]

Clearly, the existing American road system proved ill prepared to handle the rapid increase in mass automobility. Poorly maintained and unsuited for the car, streets and highways remained a perennial barrier to local commerce and a constant source of accident and disease. In the early years, auto advocates vacillated in their condemnation of the muddy ruts and the health threats that the mire (or, in dry conditions, the particulate fecal matter carried by the wind) spawned. Cataloging the "worst roads in America," one driver remarked, "I have never seen or even imagined that there were such streets in any city, as the black, oozing filth and foul smelling mud of South Chicago. It was not on account of bad weather—it is a regular thing. The natives are used to it and the children wallow in it." Poor conditions, illogical design, dangerous grade crossings between roads and rail lines, and general confusion led another to conclude, simply, that most auto accidents were due to "poorly constructed highways, and the censure in such cases should be placed where it justly belongs."[55]

The most important challenge facing road engineers was not the scope of the problem, but rather the professional split that appeared between rural highway engineers and urban traffic engineers. This division carried important consequences. Scholars have long debated the relative importance of good roads in facilitating the rise of mass automobility. Simply stated, did road reform sustain the demand for the car, or did the car (and bicycle) spawn improved roads? This distinction depends largely on locale. Scholars like Eric Monkonnen, Clay McShane, and Peter Hugill show that urban traffic and street usage justified the improvement of cities' streets well before the automobile. By contrast, Tom Lewis, Howard Preston, John C. Burnham, and Jeanette Keith argue that rural interstate highways arose in response to the growth of automobiles. The question became (largely) irrelevant after World War I, as money poured into the states from the Federal Road Aid Acts with the specific intent of developing the rural highway system. But the parallel paths taken by rural and urban road engineering split the reform community in ways that produced a lasting effect on automotive safety.

The chief problems facing rural road designers appeared obvious: most "highways" could not handle the growing volume or speeds of modern motor vehicles. The solution for highway engineers proved equally clear. Relying on the deep pockets of the federally funded state highway departments and their scientific professional standards (as defined and supported by universities and the ASCE), highway engineers commenced surveying, preparing roadbeds, and building roads to provide the most efficient motorized transit possible. The National Highway Traffic Association in 1923 cited fourteen specific priorities. They each shared four simple goals: to secure good engineering specification for new roads, to improve old roads, to reconstruct existing roads that proved "especially dangerous," and to "improve the location of the center line on dangerous curves and elevations." Accordingly, highway engineers widened existing roads, cleared obstructions, banked curves, built guardrails, controlled private advertising (such as billboards that obstructed sight lines), and improved bridges. In later years, engineers incorporated designs that strictly segregated traffic (such as divided highways or cloverleaf interchanges). In sum, highway engineers focused on efficiency as a means to reduce risk rather than relying on driver training or law compliance as the surest path to public safety.[56]

By contrast, urban traffic engineers offered a competing vision of efficient street design. As detailed by historian Daniel Albert's careful study, traffic engineering arose from the foment of urban progressivism in the first two decades of the twentieth century. They were an odd mixture of elite philanthropists, such as William Phelps Eno, and urban planners, like Frederick Law Olmsted and Daniel Burnham, who generally viewed municipal traffic patterns as a form of social engineering. Unlike in the countryside, here it proved impossible to tear down obstructions like factories and skyscrapers, avoid busy intersections, or move streets that existed for decades. Rather than focus on the street itself, reformers hoped to change urban transit *patterns* to take full advantage of mass automobility. Albert argues these engineers sought, in Eno's words, to bring "order out of chaos."[57]

The early history of traffic engineering supports Albert's contentions. The paternalist millionaire Eno used his money and influence in New York City to promote a philosophy that favored traffic efficiency over individual safety. Through "continuous flow" traffic circles, by widening the main avenues, and narrowing feeder streets, Eno designed city roads that privileged the automobile and rapid movement over traditional (largely pedestrian) street activities. Eno, like others of his class, saw nonmechanical street behaviors as disorderly, even bordering on the criminal (such as those activities conducted by the newly christened "street walkers"). Outdated, inefficient, and morally corrupt social patterns would not stand in the way of progressive auto transit.[58]

Eno stands as an ironic architect of the traffic engineering community. For one, Eno displayed little concern for public safety. Elevating auto traffic over pe-

Traffic engineer Miller McClintock of the Erskine Bureau for Street and Traffic Research conducted traffic flow and street use studies to improve the efficiency of urban transit. This lantern slide shows vehicular traffic volume in Boston, 1927. (Frances Loeb Library, Harvard Graduate School of Design, Acc. No. 19968)

destrian street uses led to outrageously high pedestrian accident rates that Eno simply ignored. Moreover, his strategies of continuous flow and traffic segregation (through one-way streets) soon emerged as credos of the highway engineer's craft, not of urban traffic planners. Still, Eno's early championing of auto movement studies—which physically observed urban traffic patterns in an effort to identify bottlenecks and inefficiencies—gave later and more serious practitioners the opportunity to establish the "science" of traffic engineering.[59]

The more studied work of Miller McClintock shows the enthusiasm that urban traffic engineers took in distancing themselves from the basic principles of their ASCE counterparts. Unlike the amateur Eno, McClintock was a Harvard-trained professor of public management at the University of California (later UCLA). His 1925 book, *Street Traffic Control,* became the most widely read study on traffic engineering. He developed the critical framework for efficient traffic flow that included a host of specific regulations—such as one-way streets, parking laws, speed limits, and mechanical traffic controls—and, especially important, a critical reliance on the concept of the "good driver." To McClintock, "a good driver may be said to be one who has an ability to catch and correlate impressions which affect him." Not only does this operator require "a knowledge of the traffic regulations," he also must "possess the will to act lawfully and in accordance with the rules of safety." For traffic engineering to work, McClintock argued, the driver must actively cooperate (or be forced to cooperate) with the system.[60]

But efforts by McClintock and Studebaker vice president Paul G. Hoffman to institutionalize and legitimize traffic engineering ended in failure. Hoffman convinced company president Albert Russell Erskine to commit $10,000 a year to create the Bureau for Street and Traffic Research. Housed initially at the University of California, the agency moved to Harvard and eventually to Yale University. While the bureau conducted several noteworthy urban traffic studies from 1927 to 1932 and benefited from its close ties to the National Safety Council, it never secured a solid institutional footing. Studebaker's insolvency in 1933 dried up the bureau's funding. Moreover, the Automobile Manufacturers Association formed a competing pseudo-academic agency, called the Automobile Safety Foundation, in 1936, which focused on highway safety rather than urban traffic design. Adding to the uncertainty, engineering academics at Harvard and Yale, highway professionals, and the ASCE disdained the upstart field of traffic engineering. McClintock's background in urban management and the general feel of progressive social reform fit poorly within the firm mathematical rigor of civil engineering. When McClintock left Yale University in 1942 the experiment in traffic engineering left with him.[61]

The traffic/highway engineering rift left a profound legacy for early auto safety. For one, it legitimized the philosophical split between auto risk and auto safety. While their professional brethren in the ASCE focused on the more mundane aspects of risk reduction—such as straightening roads and grading curves—traffic engineers highlighted the role of the good driver and called for restrictions on the bad. Significantly, traffic engineers like McClintock demanded uniform "rules of the road" and strict enforcement of the law. Like reformers who wanted engineering limits placed on the speed of automobiles, traffic engineers placed accidents within the context of driver safety rather than overall risk. In addition, while auto and road engineers served different constituencies and followed different paths, both assumed that engineering perfection was possible. Highway engineer Charles Simons wrote that with modern "smooth, level twenty-foot highways, with no physical obstacles, no curves, no ditches and a wide, sloping right-of-way, engineering cannot be held at fault. Engineering made the road as technically perfect as it could be and, if accidents occur, certainly they must result from some other cause." But auto safety advocates like John Maher still warned, "no engineering approach to the highway safety problem is complete without the admission that the human equation holds the ultimate key to its solution."[62]

As engineers delivered the "perfect" automotive infrastructure, progressive educators argued that they could do the same for American society. Like engineering, the term *education* refers to an assortment of distinct components of safety reform, each pursuant of different aims. In one sense, drivers needed a basic knowledge of local, state, and federal driving regulations. In another, operators required the skills necessary to safely control a motor vehicle. Similarly, an educated automobilist understood the basic physics of the car (braking distances, the effect of weather and lighting conditions, turning radii, and so on) but also the common psychological states—such as aggressive speeding, recklessness, and driving while intoxicated—that increased risk. A critical division in education appeared between existing ill-trained drivers and young people who had yet to acquire "bad habits." These two populations presented distinct challenges and opportunities and the response, by educators, suggests that auto reformers retained very different expectations of the potential for public education. As with engineering, the differences between collective risk and individual safety remained unresolved.

By 1920, progressive educators had already reassessed the fundamental goals and tactics of their profession. In 1893, the National Education Association's (NEA) distinguished "Committee of Ten," led by Harvard's Charles William Eliot, claimed that secondary school education best served the burgeoning public school population by requiring content mastery. Students studied the classics, basic mathematics, and composition skills in order to prepare themselves for entry into college. Given the small number who pursued a university degree, the Ten rationalized that the curriculum offered the remaining majority a taste of the "mind culture" that signified refinement and intelligence. By 1911, the NEA reconstituted its steering committee, this time as the "Committee of Nine." The new group rejected these earlier goals as too elitist and shifted the primary purpose of secondary education toward practical social skills. By 1918, with the publication of NEA's *The Cardinal Principles of Secondary Education,* progressive education imbued public schools with the ambitious mission "to lay the foundation of good citizenship." Under this directive, driver education now found a home in public schools.[63]

With evangelical zeal, progressive educators like John Dewey at the "Laboratory School" of the University of Chicago stressed social adjustment to a modern world. Their faith in the power of education was absolute. Richard Hofstadter concludes that their "breathless" progressive idealism appeared "more certain than ever" by the 1920s, "because it seemed to be vindicated morally by the needs of democracy and intellectually by the findings of science." By introducing an NSC-sponsored safety curriculum into the classroom, educators promoted several agendas: life adjustment, the new pedagogy, and lowered collective risk. But it was hard to identify their *primary* mission.[64]

Regardless of these problems, activists viewed education as an essential component of safety reform. Most agreed that drivers, like good citizens, "are trained; not born." By 1938, over thirteen hundred articles and scholarly essays on driver education existed in print. Fostered by the crusade for social adjustment, safety educators believed that "when the proper appreciation of the motor vehicle in the general scheme of this modern world is thoroughly drilled into an individual, especially a child, it constitutes a long stride toward a permanent solution of the safety question."[65]

As with engineering, education professionals lamented the lack of national uniformity. While pronouncements on the potency of safety education were widespread, little consensus existed on the most effective course of action. A 1938 study by the American Automobile Association found that only twelve states had laws mandating the teaching of auto safety in secondary schools. Most of these, like Connecticut, Indiana, New York, and South Carolina, had done so only recently. While nine state boards of education required the teaching of general "life safety," the curriculum was, at best, loosely organized. Given the comments of the NEA, which indicated that safety instruction was a means to an end, this was not surprising. Few shared a common textbook, theme, or method for measuring the legitimacy of safety instruction. For a pluralistic concept like auto safety education, this meant that teaching methods shifted for each population.[66]

The education of current, mature drivers was even more sporadic and anecdotal. Rarely did educators express much confidence in adults' ability to change. New York driving instructor William Stewart likened his full-grown clients to "boneheads" and recalled humorous stories of novices who attempted to stop their cars with a loud and vigorous "Whoa!" The NSC's managing director, W. H. Cameron, believed that "the training of the adult mind" to auto safety "seemed almost hopeless . . . from the standpoint of actually diminishing accidents." With few exceptions, only voluntary organizations or private instructors existed to promote better driving by motorists who actually took to the streets. These included the typical hometown associations of the day, such as the Rotary Club, Kiwanis, private motor clubs, and various Chambers of Commerce. While the Hoover Commissions placed special emphasis on driver education, they contented themselves, in the case of adult drivers, to leave this duty "a fundamental purpose of motor clubs, . . . Safety councils and other special organizations." Their approved list of "methods for the education in safety of the general public" included such passive voices as public posters, motion pictures, lantern slides, and by "reaching parents through school children" (which assumed that all bad drivers had children in public school).[67]

In contrast to this passive resignation, plans for the education of young people *before* they ever drove was especially enthusiastic. Exploiting the intense desire by youth to get behind the wheel, progressive educators saw an opportunity to perfect America's civic culture through driver education. Simons observed that safety instruction for children was "predicated in the theory that a young mind is more receptive to training; it accepts without question a reasonable interpretation of rules of safe driving." Children proved less "inclined to argue and challenge" authority because they were "not set in their ways as are older drivers who are driving by habit, rather than as trained and intelligent beings." The NSC's Cameron believed "that the solution of the public accident problem lies in the human brain." Through the council and the public schools "we will develop a generation which will prove the theory" of driver safety education.[68]

Early youth safety propaganda reflected these assumptions. The NSC published a series of stories written by Roy Rutherford Bailey that first appeared in 1915. They featured a quirky, impish character named "Sure Pop" who recruited young "Safety Scouts" to warn others of the dangers posed by cars. Bailey's characters were young, typically in grade school. The hazards of automobility, particularly as a pedestrian, represented only one (albeit the most important) of the life lessons these children had to absorb in order to survive to become productive citizens.[69]

By the 1930s, as the country gained better control over the child pedestrian problem, the propaganda shifted away from youngsters to young adults learning to drive. For example, Ralph Henry Barbour's tale, *For Safety!* (1936), strongly supported the progressive "perfectibility" argument. Future drivers learned not only to be safe but to be morally just. Barbour's main characters accepted safety reform as an aspect of good citizenship and rejected the jaded resignation of the adult population. Deriding grown-ups who seemingly held vested economic interests in the continued reckless abuse of the car—interests the children specifically identified as the auto and insurance industries, the popular press, the police, politicians, and lawyers—one young female character conceived a "reform movement" to "teach [adults] by example, we'd educate them." She believed that other young people would participate not simply in order to drive but because "belonging to the League is a duty they owe to their community and an honor to themselves. Because I really believe that's just what it is. I believe it's a noble effort in—in the cause of Humanity."[70]

Safety education certainly suggested that drivers could be perfected, but the methods remained haphazard. The work of two leading safety educators, E. George Payne and Albert W. Whitney, gives useful examples of the broader tensions and contradictions contained within this branch of the "three E's." Both Payne and Whitney committed their life's work to auto safety education and deeply believed in the positive power of progressive education. Payne, past president of Harris Teacher's College in St. Louis and later dean of the School of Education at New York University, accepted the vice chairmanship of the NSC's Education Section in 1919. He wrote numerous essays on driver safety and authored the NSC-supported *Education in Accident Prevention,* the standard text on auto safety education from 1918 to 1937. Whitney, the permanent chair of the Education Section of the NSC, was an executive with the National Bureau of Casualty and Surety Underwriters. He sponsored Payne within the NSC and even contributed a chapter to Payne's safety primer.

The two parted ways in 1936 because of their conflicting philosophies toward auto education. Whitney, who by then co-authored a competing treatise titled *Man and the Motor Car,* felt that education alone would be insufficient to rectify the problem. Relying on his experience in the insurance industry, Whitney charged that market forces, stronger and more consistently applied than the moral messages conveyed in the classroom, best corrected poor driving behaviors. Hinting at the powerful automotive love affair, Whitney believed the nation had "shown little fighting spirit in the face of the hazard that the automobile has created,—perhaps because we have not been willing to discipline ourselves, perhaps we have felt that the pleasure and convenience that it has brought us was something that we could not have except at a price." His blueprint was, of course, the business model where "twenty-five years ago, accident conditions in industry were as intolerable as they are in the case of traffic today." Risk assessment and avoidance compelled manufacturers, through direct costs, to reduce "their accidents eighty and ninety percent, and with this has come increased efficiency." Central to Whitney's assessment of the problem was the absence of stiff financial penalties levied against the traffic menace. Increased education of the young led merely to "indifference" in adults. His solution stressed that the "motorist should be made legally responsible for the quality of his driving."[71]

For his part, Payne charged that market forces alone had not nor would not substantially change poor driving habits. In a 1937 essay for the *Journal of Educational Sociology,* Payne doubted whether the past business campaigns of the NSC "affected the situation favorably at all." He did not question their commitment or concern, but rather their "lack of an intelligent attack upon the problem." Specifically, Payne felt, safety education needed to be effected within the construct of citizenship rather than consumerism. Economic penalties and strict enforcement only proved that the driver received a poor education. Payne bemoaned that the "leadership of the safety movement," including his old friend Whitney, "has been for a long time in the hands of an agency which has the appearance of a professional society or public-service agency." The NSC "is actually more nearly a trade association primarily interested in saving money for its members and incidentally in saving human lives."[72]

The differences between Payne and Whitney reflected more than the hurt feelings of a soured professional relationship. Their respective approaches indicate two very different ideas about the proper function of auto instruction. Whitney's way was more direct and best termed driver *training*. His outlook favored vocational-style driving instruction; time spent behind the wheel or in simulators getting a feel for the car. He and many others in the insurance and automotive industries believed that all drivers, both young and old, needed to be regularly assessed on how well they physically operated a motor vehicle. Their reaction times, knowledge of law, physical dexterity, and vision could be scientifically measured. A driver's psychological state, too, was equally subject to quantification. Driving competence, not civic adjustment, remained Whitney's goal. Payne believed, by contrast, that driver *education* fit within the context of a well-rounded responsible citizenry. Payne wrote, in *Education in Accident Prevention,* that driver education existed "as a means of securing to the individual the right sort of social action, and of developing in the individual the right kind of feelings, attitudes, points of view, and ideals. We look upon the various subjects in the curriculum as means to these ends."[73]

But while their educational philosophies differed significantly, both pedagogies—driver training and driver education—shared certain moral values about the drivers involved in accidents. To Whitney, while even the most careful driver might eventually be involved in an unavoidable accident, this was very rare. More typical were the ill-suited, ill-tempered drivers who needed to be weeded from the roads by the sure yet hidden hand of the marketplace. These included "accident-prone" individuals who have "accidents quite as consistently as others avoid them." Citing Sidney Williams's work in the NSC, Whitney targeted those without "the necessary fundamental capacities for safe driving" including the weak, the partially blind, those whose "intelligence is sub-normal." Even after "proper education," those who "cannot judge speeds and distances; [who] are unable to concentrate; [who] react too slowly; [and who] are clumsy and awkward" must be culled. Those *incapable* of correcting past mistakes and those with "bad mental attitudes" remained. Similarly, for Payne the accident signified poor "adjustment" to the realities of modern living. According to both educators, "accidents [were] caused by bad people being bad, and safety [was] created by good people being good. . . . The primary problem [was] a problem of soul, or right attitude."[74]

This view, espousing good citizenship, proper manners, and the ultimate perfectability of the modern driver, dominated early driving instruction manuals. On the first page of the Texas Department of Public Safety's 1943 training plan for "Youthful Drivers" is the warning that "traffic safety has emerged as one of the major social problems of the twentieth century. The home must not be expected to cope with the problem alone. The public schools must evolve a long range safety educational program that will eventually produce a more enlightened, a more skillful and a more social driving public."[75]

The moralizing and prescriptive tone of early driver education does support the charge, made by many historians, of debilitating utopian idealism. Rather than concentrate on the rules of the road, early educators spent countless hours in the pursuit of the perfect citizen. In 1925, Whitney went so far as to suggest that safety education acted as a form of Darwinian natural selection. In the NSC journal *Safety Education* he wrote,

> There is no reason why we should not produce a generation which will possess the attitudes of mind which will make it possible to survive even on our modern highways. Stranger accommodations have been made in nature even by the use of such a crude method as the survival of the fittest. The survival of the fittest is still operating, for some of the worst drivers are being killed off even before they have left descendants.

Yet this criticism needs to be kept within the context of the times. Progressive reformers of all stripes hoped to identify and bolster the values that best reflected an orderly and democratic modern society. Anger, aggression, and recklessness represented immature behaviors that most activists felt they could change. Their trust in the corrective powers of an American consensual code of ethics, rather than stiff legal or economic penalties, reflected a creed in which individual self-control formed the basis of modern progressivism. Moreover, within the auto safety community, the faith in the perfectibility of the driver was coupled with concurrent pronouncements about the perfection of the car and highway. In the end, it was the reformers' reliance on a flawed business model, a lack of national uniformity, and, more importantly, the weakness of enforcement that doomed their efforts to end automobile-related accidents.[76]

In 1938, the city of Dallas, in conjunction with the police department and the traffic engineering arm of the Works Project Administration, released a four-year study titled "A Survey of Traffic Conditions." Observing, recording, and assessing the behavior of thousands of motorists and pedestrians from 1933 to 1937, the research fit well within the contours of the era's auto safety reform efforts. Released under the auspices of Dallas city manager Hal Moseley, the report praised the leadership of the NSC, the hard work of traffic and highway engineers, and the educational principles of the city's public school teachers. Even the general philosophy of the study mirrored the citizenship initiatives and assumptions of "perfectibility" that coursed through the broader reform community. In the study's front piece, Citizen's Traffic Commission chair Carl Rutland confirmed that, for these investigators, auto safety existed as the "nation's leading civic problem," exceeding even the problems of fire, disease, and crime.[77]

Two policemen conduct a traffic survey near Washington and Canal Streets, Chicago, Illinois, in 1929. Such surveys showed the conflicted nature of American drivers and the essential role of law enforcement in automobile safety. (Chicago History Museum, DN-0088645)

The 130-page study remains a testament to the hard work and dedication of safety engineers, investigators, educators, and administrators. Hal Moseley's mute response, in January 1937, to the plea of those three Dallas schoolgirls stands in stark contrast to the findings of the study, which condensed thousands of hours of monotonous observations and recorded tens of thousands of everyday driving decisions made by Dallas motorists. To assuage their fear, Moseley could have cited the fact that, over the previous thirteen years, just two children had died from injuries incurred while walking to or from their schools. Researchers chronicled the activities of over 21,000 children at dozens of schools and found a remarkably similar pattern: they *were* living.[78]

While Moseley, Rutland, and the other authors of the report credited safety education, good roads, and better drivers as the likely source of this blessed survival rate, the study suggests a more direct cause. At each of the schools observed, pedestrian traffic was tightly controlled by safety officers, school crossing guards, mechanical devices, instructional signs for drivers, and police patrols. Within these highly enforced conditions schoolchildren of every age consistently "walked vigilantly" to their destinations. Under tight controls, and regardless of race or age, over 90 percent crossed at the correct location, over 90 percent observed the stop and go signals, over 70 percent kept within the official designated crosswalks, and less than 8 percent (of any population and under any form of traffic control) "walked heedlessly" of traffic. The conclusion of the report was clear: strict rules for the safe passage of children to and from school, when strictly *enforced*, proved effective. The report's wording appeared strikingly similar: "children [were] required to cross" at controlled intersections, "children should be required" to use only these crosswalks, officials must "enforce prohibition of roller skating in roadways," and that children should be penalized "extra time after school" for "violation of the safety rules." Armed with such a detailed analysis, Moseley could reasonably respond to the three girls' request for life with the stern demand: "you must follow the rules."[79]

But the perfectibility of the road and car beguiled reformers. Engineering and education methods required little federal oversight and reinforced the business model logic that worked so well for industry. Moreover, engineering and education solutions did little to offend existing drivers, a powerful public faction. Politicians might avoid the condemnation of millions, who feared the loss of their automotive freedoms, while appearing concerned (and downright scientific) in their reliance upon these hidden professionals. But just as with these Dallas schoolchildren, the key to automotive safety lay in enforcement. Reformers and American motorists alike needed a sober accounting of the true cost of auto safety. This debt could be paid only by willfully limiting America's beloved automotive freedoms.

6

The Mirrored Glasses: Enforcement and the Inevitable Auto Accident

Bonnie Parker and Clyde Barrow epitomized the reckless, motorized criminality of the modern age. In an era filled with intriguing hoodlums—such as Kate "Ma" Barker, Charles "Pretty Boy" Floyd, Lester "Baby Face Nelson" Gillis, and the infamous John Dillinger—the jail breaking, car stealing, bank robbing, and kidnapping exploits of Bonnie and Clyde stole the headlines and exposed a subcurrent of raw antiauthoritarian values, a depression-era conceit against social progress. Unlike the urban gangsters of the 1920s, when organized criminals used cars to solidify control over territory and gain legitimacy, the libertarian exploits of road warriors like Parker and Barrow resembled the reckless and random destruction of a high-speed car crash. While Barrow claimed he accidentally killed jewelry store owner John Bucher during a heist on April 13, 1932, the same cannot be said for the eleven lawmen (ranging from local constables and highway patrolmen to a Huntsville, Texas, prison guard) he murdered over the next twenty-four months. Officials never proved Parker's complicity to homicide, but Barrow's indifference to life made him an imminent public danger.[1]

While the misadventures of Bonnie and Clyde dominated the news, the response by state policing agencies to capture the motorized outlaws deserves closer attention. The Texas State Highway Patrol (TSHP) treated the pair as an invading army. Officers publicly compared the duo's skylarking to Pancho Villa's violent forays through Southwest Texas during the Mexican Revolution. Following Barrow's murder of two highway patrolmen, E. B. Wheeler and H. D. Murphy, on Easter Sunday, 1934, the TSHP instigated the "most extensive Texas manhunt" in living memory. For fifty-three days a third of all uniformed police officers traveled the state's streets, highways, and rural routes searching for the fugitives. They logged over 800,000 miles of travel and 24,000 man-hours of labor. TSHP Chief L. G. Phares charged his 105 highway patrolmen to "stick to this until the job's finished. [Our] patrol will mobilize into a pursuit army with the one task—getting Barrow, dead or alive, but preferably dead."[2]

But it was a former Texas Ranger, Frank Hamer, who ended the lives of the two Dallas lovers on May 23, 1934. Hamer had resigned from the storied agency in 1932, disgusted by the rampant corruption of the James and Miriam Ferguson gubernatorial administrations. But Lee Simmons, superintendent of the Hunts-ville penitentiary, begged the noted lawman to avenge the killing of his prison guard. Hamer accepted a special commission from the TSHP on February 10, 1934. He partnered with his friend and fellow ex-Ranger Mannie Gault.[3]

Barrow's mobility gave him his greatest edge over the lawmen. Education re-former Albert Whitney once complained that the car gave modern "criminals a new tool for their lawless work," one "of more advantage to them than the machine gun." Indeed, Phares claimed that his special six-man TSHP teams av-eraged over 150 miles of driving per day in pursuit. Hamer, too, recalled how "Barrow never holed up at one place; he was always on the go; and he traveled farther in one day than any fugitive that I have ever followed." He chased the pair across Texas, Oklahoma, and Louisiana. But the Ranger never established when they might appear along this triangular route.[4]

Ivan Methvin, father to one of the Huntsville convicts freed by Clyde Bar-row's daring raid, handed Hamer his big break. To secure immunity for his son, Methvin told of a location near Arcadia, Louisiana, where the Barrow gang of-ten left and received communications. In the early morning of May 23, Hamer, Gault, and four others staked out the drop. They used Methvin Sr. as bait, plac-ing him and his truck at the side of the road to feign mechanical trouble. Around 9:10 a.m., Parker and Barrow approached and slowed to examine the situation. Hamer claimed he emerged from the brush to identify himself. He ordered Bar-row to stop. When the officers saw the pair reach for their considerable arse-nal, Hamer opened fire. The lawmen discharged 167 bullets. Fifty struck the two criminals, who died instantly.[5]

No doubt Phares, Hamer, and Gault took great pride in stopping the willful lawlessness of Bonnie and Clyde and avenging the deaths of their fallen col-leagues. Barrow's stolen 1934 V-8 Ford Deluxe Sedan, perforated by dozens of bullet holes, toured numerous state fairs and other public attractions for the re-mainder of the decade. Mere participation in the dragnet made many lawmen local heroes. Hamer was glorified by historian Walter Prescott Webb in *The Texas Rangers: A Century of Frontier Defense* as a model Ranger and prototype for the modern enforcement officer.

Phares, himself a former Ranger, used the spectacular ending of the Parker-Barrow crime spree to champion the professionalism and businesslike efficiency of the TSHP. Informed by Gault of the shootings, Chief Phares announced the deaths of Bonnie and Clyde to a grateful public. In a carefully crafted statement, Phares highlighted the extensive mileage, man-hours, and commitment that his agency had applied to the problem. His force, affectionately termed T-Men, pa-trolled "every part of Texas, watched every car on the highways, scanned the features of every person they saw . . . keyed to the job at last of finding Barrow and his woman." Phares correctly, if disingenuously, claimed that the reassigned agents, Hamer and Gault, were "Texas officers," not Rangers. He minimized other Ranger contributions as well, noting that "an unknown number" of the special force "gave a part of their time to the one big job of finding Barrow." As a back-handed compliment, Phares added that Rangers "resorted to the strategy of taking Barrow's mother in custody as a taunt to the desperado." But this mean-spirited gesture—the apprehension of a blameless citizen (on Mother's Day, no less)—stood in stark contrast to the cool professionalism of his T-Men.[6]

The chief labored for years to cultivate this hard-nosed, no-nonsense reputation for the TSHP. As new head of the patrol in 1929, Phares added a mandatory eight-week crime fighting curriculum at Ft. Mabry, near Austin. He required his men to master modern automotive criminal investigation techniques, such as those pioneered by the Northwestern University Training Institute (NUTI) and the Evanston (IL) accident investigation squads. By the mid-1930s, 68 of Phares's 138 officers boasted of a college education (all held high school diplomas). Phares also developed complementary police training courses at Texas A&M University, hired external forensic consultants, and inaugurated the use of unmarked police cars. He intended to shift the role of the Highway Patrol from a redundant and largely ineffective branch of the Highway Department to a critical and creative force for social order in a motorized world. The violent end to Clyde Barrow's murderous reign provided the chief with dramatic justification for his new rolling shock troops, the essential enforcement arm of the NSC's "three E's."[7]

In retrospect, Phares also nurtured a new *attitude* in traffic law enforcement. The stereotype of the officious, tough-minded highway patrolman favored at the TSHP—the type of official who approaches the car with an impassive stare behind mirrored sunglasses—stood in stark contrast to the original ideal of the traffic cop. The earlier model offered citizens a friendly face, one that promised protection from the vicissitudes of the highway: more of a safety monitor than actual law enforcement official. Drivers praised these early sentinels for *not* "issuing tickets in wholesale lots" or "bawling out" motorists for simple driving infractions. Even the Hoover commission believed that such "even-handed treatment" was critical to "instill in the public respect for the traffic laws and regulations." Traffic court judge John Maher agreed. Aggressive policing only "irritates good drivers and defeats cooperation" in highway safety.[8]

But Phares, like most other modern law enforcement officials, held a less tolerant view of motor law violators. To his agents the speed limits, directional signs, and reckless driving ordinances were the unequivocal law of the land. Habitual law avoidance was both criminal and a leading source of highway accidents. As such, lawless behavior simply could not coexist with a rational plan for street and highway safety. An outspoken delegate to the national Accident Prevention Conference in 1935, Phares regretted that "too much emphasis had been placed on courtesy" and vowed that, for his force at least, "severity of enforcement was superior to courtesy." The motorist should expect no mercy if they broke the law in Texas.[9]

Phares found a willing ally in the young new governor, James V. Allred. Elected in 1934, Allred promised Texas a wide-ranging "New Deal from a New Deck." He moved aggressively to institute a "sweeping reorganization of [all] departments under his immediate control" and proposed "major reforms in taxation, public utility regulation, [and] crime control." Speaking to the Texas Bar Association, Allred claimed that habitual law breaking on the roadway "breeds disrespect for other laws until it is small wonder that the vicious, violent element finds consolation and encouragement for the commission of major crimes." In the summer of 1935, Allred proposed a new, strengthened, and centralized state law enforcement agency, titled the Department of Public Safety (DPS). His friend L. G. Phares not only helped draft the bill, enacted on August 10, 1935, but was named to head the agency later that year.[10]

As with the TSHP, Phares found most existing state policing practices unsound, outdated, and illogical. For example, the Texas Rangers, now under the direct control of the DPS, suffered from widespread corruption and cronyism. Individuals like Hamer, Gault, and indeed Phares despaired at the blatant politicization of the force. Where the state once accredited only 36 select lawmen, by the time of Allred's election more than 1,600 "special" Ranger commissions existed. These included local thugs and political musclemen. One Austin dispatch categorized the force as "official gun-toters" who served as "bouncers in night clubs" and "officers in gambling houses . . . and dog race tracks." At Phares's direction, Allred revoked all special commissions. Phares retained 35 Rangers, but merged them with the 140 elite T-Men of the State Highway Patrol.[11]

The public expressed mixed reactions to the sudden reforms. On the one hand, many grudgingly agreed that the "book closed" on the fabled Ranger force. One editorial contrasted the old frontier lawmen, "a small number of men [who patrolled] the wild border country on horseback," with Phares's modern and "younger men . . . equipped for speed and mounted on motorcycles." In the face of the motorized criminality of sociopaths like Barrow, the heroic myth of "one riot, one Ranger" no longer reassured.[12] Phares's recent headline-stealing announcement only accentuated the need for more modern law enforcement techniques. In contrast to the lone Ranger doggedly pursuing his prey, "it took the entire state patrol, local and special officers working together, to put an end to the Clyde Barrow–Bonnie Parker raids." Even Webb's glowing account, published immediately after Bonnie and Clyde's demise, appeared more as a eulogy.[13]

But the aggressive policing tactics of the DPS spurred new, equally problematic questions in the minds of many motorists. Constructed within the progressive and self-validating context of the automotive love affair, many drivers saw their performance behind the wheel as evidence of their civic virtue and personal independence. Good driving showed good citizenship and responsible freedom. Policing, within this framework, served only to identify those who willfully violated the spirit of laws; the irresponsible activities of the flivverboobs and motor morons (or possibly violent criminals like Barrow) reflected their lack of civic consciousness. By contrast, modern enforcement rejected this loose compact in favor of a much stricter legal interpretation. Phares and his agents believed and behaved as if most motorists habitually broke the law. They were petty criminals who needed to be held to task. As such, strict motor law enforcement challenged Americans' basic assumptions about automobility. It generated a new aggressive police force, wearing those damned mirrored glasses, who hoped to terminate the nation's rampant lawlessness as convincingly as Hamer ended the lives of Bonnie and Clyde. In Phares's words, agencies like the DPS emerged to "protect us from ourselves."[14]

But America's commitment to motorized freedom proved stronger than its desire for legal safety. Most traffic violators did not see themselves as "criminals" and rejected the policies that assumed they were. Revealingly, Phares and his new agency foundered on this very issue in Texas. Almost immediately, critics and municipal enforcement agencies fought the broadened mandate of the DPS. Others objected to the heavy-handed tactics of the Highway Patrol and questioned their efficacy. Here, Phares's earlier and exaggerated claims about the TSHP's role in killing Parker and Barrow returned to haunt him. Hamer, made even more famous by Webb's tribute, charged in late 1935 that Phares and the Highway Patrol played no substantive role in the Arcadia affair. Moreover, as Webb clearly showed, the two Rangers needed no fingerprinting, forensic science, or college training to stop the pair, just steely determination and instinctive cunning. Hamer claimed that "Phares did not have the slightest connection with this case, either in its planning or in the final result and elimination of these two persons." He quipped that "two days before the killing in Louisiana," Phares and his high-tech battalions "thought Barrow and Parker were in San Antonio." While the Highway Patrol technically bagged their trophy, it was in spite of its leadership, organization, and techniques.[15]

Having cast the first stone, the Rangers then unleashed a barrage of criticism against the vaunted Texas T-Men. Critics attacked Phares's use of outside, and mostly northern, consultants and his bureaucratic interference in local policing operations. Phares mounted a spirited defense, complaining to the Austin *Dispatch* that "one of the main charges against me is that I have tried to smother the Ranger force in favor of the motor patrol. A lot of that was due to a statement in a book by Walter Prescott Webb, University of Texas professor, in which he said that the number of the Rangers has been lowered and that they were gradually being crowded out." Phares argued "that is not so. I have had practically nothing to do with the Rangers for some time, making them responsible to the commission only, so as to prevent jealousy." But the damage was done. By the fall of 1936, senior officials within the Rangers, such as C. W. McCormick and D. D. Baker, threatened to resign if Phares did not step down. In September, Phares complied, leaving the DPS yet retaining control over the TSHP.[16]

The rise and fall of Phares, beginning with the dramatic pursuit of Bonnie and Clyde and ending with the termination of his commission, approximates the wider contemporary trends in national safety enforcement reform. As early as 1924, national reformers applauded the use of modern criminal investigation techniques, centralized state records, and the summary suspension of licenses for traffic offenders. Most demanded that state enforcement agencies "stop bungling" and "assume their responsibility for doing away with the causes of traffic accidents."[17] For its part, the motoring public appeared willing, at first, to accept this greater scrutiny. The *New York Times,* reporting on the new Texas law enforcement agencies, noted how "a militant public has been aroused" to justify the call for "strict enforcement." The normative values of America's early driving culture—where good driving reflected good citizenship—gave these reforms a didactic or crusading quality. Officials, like Phares, wanted the "fear of God . . . put into every murdering criminal" on the highway. "Let us be just and assume our part," one advocate sermonized. "No sidestepping. We are the masters of the machine. It is under our control and we must assume our full measure of responsibility. It may not be legal, but it is a moral responsibility."[18]

The zeal of these safety reformers, combined with the moralistic love affair and mounting number of auto fatalities, established a tone of righteous anger. Like L. G. Phares, frustrated citizens demanded that reckless motorists "be hunted down as vigorously as bank absconders." *Collier's* ran a sympathetic account of a grieving father whose six-year-old child was killed by a speeding truck. The desperate man sat near an open window armed with a shotgun "ready to shoot the first driver who passed his house at a reckless rate of speed." Private auto clubs, often in conjunction with local police, formed semi-official "monitoring committees" to patrol the streets and record instances of law breaking. The puritanical Henry Ford once policed Michigan's highways for the Detroit Automobile Club in just this way. The Dallas Citizens' Traffic Commission unleashed its own hidden army to supplement an "undermanned police department." While many applauded these local efforts, comparing them to the Rangers of old, others likened such vigilante justice to actions of the Ku Klux Klan. *Texas Parade* contributor Clitus Jones nervously cautioned the posses that "snooping or trouble making tactics had to be avoided" for the "machinations of certain hooded orders were still fresh in the minds of the citizenry."[19]

While, without doubt, most motorists did not approve of popular or summary justice, the roadway provided Americans with an open and contested arena for a new social order. Driving over congested streets and long, modern highways, the public established collective attitudes toward speed, recklessness, and other forms of civic manners. As the Omaha *Morning World-Herald* opined in 1924, "Nowhere else does the individual come into such intimate relationship with society as upon the public highway."

Here is the common meeting-ground of all the people. All of them share in its ownership, all of them contribute to its maintenance and all of them, regardless of station, must use it. It is no invasion of his personal rights to require that each shall use this common property in such a way as to make it reasonably safe and easy for every person to exercise his right to go upon it also.

Such high-minded civic idealism spurred near-utopian visions of a self-regulating citizenry. Even Maher, ever the pragmatic traffic judge, fantasized "there would be little need of the police if the public . . . would only respect the rights of others and lend a helping hand in the enforcement of all traffic rules."[20]

As with other aspects of reform, enforcement advocates grappled with the rival concepts of risk and safety, of avoidable and inevitable accidents, and with "good" and "bad" driving. Officials developed three distinct enforcement methods, each with its own limits and possibilities. Legal and market reforms restricted "bad" drivers through tougher licensing, testing, and insurance standards. Intended to deny access of a car to the worst offenders, this method sought to prevent accidents *before* they occurred. A second approach favored stricter policing of moving traffic. Here agencies like the DPS assumed that all motorists, even those pried from their wrecked autos, represented potential lawbreakers. These reforms did little to prevent accidents but they did establish the legal liability of those deemed responsible. Lastly, enforcement occurred after an infraction or accident. Arrest and trial, through special traffic courts, adjudicated the character of these drivers that both strengthened and weakened the parameters of civic participation.

As with education and engineering reforms, enforcement upset the balance between the individual liberties assumed by most motorists and the security desired by society. Through laws and financial incentives, initial enforcement reformers hoped to establish *preventative* safety measures that might limit access by "unqualified" drivers to the nation's highways. As such, these reforms did little to address the potentially dangerous conditions of the roadway or to guarantee the application of the law. Their positive (or negative) effects took hold long before a driver ever turned the ignition.

The juridic doctrine of prima facie provided the greatest tool of these early reformers. Prima facie evidence, literally "evidence on first appearance," includes all behavior observed by a law enforcement official that warranted a legal citation. For example, an officer's observation of speeding or an illegal U-turn is alone sufficient evidence of a crime. By itself, an officer's allegation of such "first appearance" criminal evidence can convict a driver in court. By 1915, most municipalities listed a wide variety of driving activities, from speeding to illegal parking, as "prima facie evidence of negligence." The celebrated Hoover Commissions supported the use of prima facie evidence. In 1924, its Committee on

A Denver police officer stands at a tramway boarding zone on 16th Street near California Street in Denver, Colorado, 1928. (Denver Public Library, Western History Collection, Harry M. Rhoads, Rh-171)

Regulations sought to extend the doctrine to mean that all *accidents* were "in themselves proof of guilt of either incompetence, carelessness, or recklessness." As such, an accident indicated driver negligence. Guilt was "presumed from the fact of a collision." By 1938, thirty-three of forty-eight states used similar "first appearance" provisions to define motorized criminality.[21]

The use of prima facie evidence insured high conviction rates. Citation alone provided courts with both the formal charge and the legal evidence necessary to convict the accused. By 1939, more than half of all cities reported traffic conviction rates in excess of 92 percent (the top third of cities, including the largest urban centers, exceeded 98 percent). In theory, elevated conviction rates offered evidence of the efficacy of reform. But in practice the policy cut against the grain of most individual's assumptions about American jurisprudence. Motorists resented the assumption of guilt and relative ease of conviction. Moreover, these resentments fueled fears that traffic cops and courts targeted the traditional freedoms that endeared so many to the open road.[22]

Under these conditions, it is no small wonder that traffic police and drivers developed an adversarial relationship. While no one enjoys having limits placed on their freedom, the level of opposition exceeded what one might expect from traditional nuisance or safety laws. Where citizens might habitually bend some municipal ordinances (e.g., limits to commercial activity to simple littering or loitering laws), they positively ignored efforts to rein in their driving freedoms.

San Diego's city manager, E. B. Lefferts, believed "motorists and the enforcement units were like two armies in daily combat." Instead of demonstrating a progressive mastery over the automobile, drivers acted like a "naughty boy . . . trying to do everything he can without being caught by his teacher." Lefferts wrote,

> I really believe this to be the truer simile, because so many men and women seem to have such a juvenile reaction toward the traffic regulations, in spite of the fact that their other attitudes show the maturity you would expect from persons of their age and position in the community. In their enthusiasm of playing the game of trying to outwit one another, both motorists and officers seem to have lost sight entirely of the safety motive that underlies our rules of the road.

These conflicting goals—between safe driving and personal freedom—proved difficult for early reformers to balance.[23]

Initial traffic enforcement reform appeared first in local communities. Cities, in particular, possessed clear and long-standing rights to regulate urban transit. Municipal road building, for example, eased the transition to mass automobility but also served the needs of a varied population. Urban traffic ordinances regulated the automobile, but also pedestrians, animal-powered hacks, jitneys, and baggage wagons in an effort to better manage the growing congestion. Their focus remained maximal traffic throughput and overall efficiency rather than safety or law observance.[24]

By 1919, the successful segregation of pedestrians and gradual retirement of animal-powered vehicles shifted the debate away from balancing multiuse patterns and toward more optimal conditions for auto transit. Many towns sponsored detailed investigations of local traffic conditions with the hope of decreasing congestion, rationalizing regulations, and beefing up enforcement. Studies in Chicago, Detroit, Grand Rapids, San Antonio, and Dallas, for example, targeted bottlenecks and dangerous intersections, set standards for rights of way, and further limited pedestrian access. By 1925, over twenty-seven other municipalities had followed suit. While reforms lowered the fatality rate of urban streets, particularly for pedestrians, their primary goal remained transit efficiency. Drivers and police officers alike ignored certain laws, such as speed limits, parking restrictions, and loading zones, in order to facilitate mass transit. As traffic engineer Miller McClintock observed, this often "resulted in violations by the public with the *consent and assistance* of the police officials, the latter being aware that a rigid enforcement would result in intolerable conditions."[25]

A good example of these new policies developed in San Diego. Working with the chief of police and the traffic enforcement division, city manager Lefferts proposed a radical shift in the nature of traffic law enforcement. Passed July 1, 1927, the "San Diego plan" shifted policing almost exclusively to congestion abatement. Officers enforced almost no speed limits, parking restrictions, or other typical traffic laws. As Lefferts noted, the policy charged motorists "with their *own responsibility* for avoiding traffic accidents, instead of attempting to have officers spy on drivers at all times." The law did require motorists to contact the police if an accident occurred. Only at that time, after the fact, did officers collect vital information, ascribe blame and, in all likelihood, summon the offending parties to court.[26]

The strength of the San Diego plan lay in how well it conserved public assumptions about good driving. While the enforcement remained passive—much like engineering and education—it assumed most motorists were capable of determining appropriate behavior. Lefferts proudly announced that the law "practically amounted to the San Diego Police Department's serving notice to the motorists that they were not going to lie in wait for them and pounce out and make an arrest whenever a technical violation of the Motor Vehicle Act was witnessed." Officials reported, in 1928, that the change significantly reduced congestion and auto-related injuries.[27]

But the passive nature of this type of reform ran counter to the progressive impulses of the broader safety movement. These initial enforcement methods simply picked up the pieces of a fractured society. They declined to use modern policing methods to reduce auto fatalities. To make matters worse, many assumed that little could be done to correct the damage from accidents that were considered the inevitable by-product of automobility. By the mid-1920s, traffic engineers and safety specialists claimed the chief fault with existing traffic ordinances was not what they omitted, but rather that "they have been made on a basis of opinion, rather than on the basic of fact." The "three E's" suggested active risk reduction. Centralized state control intended to shift the carnage (and debate) away from the inevitable collision to the avoidable accident.[28]

State reform certainly expanded the policing oversight on the roads. California's 1905 Motor Vehicle Act was the first in the nation to require specific automotive safety equipment, such as horns and headlights. Five years later, New York passed the Callan Automobile Law with similar provisions. These laws also required an annual licensing fee, published a complete rules of the road, established a statewide maximum speed limit (30 miles per hour), and authorized the secretary of state to administer the growing driver population. In 1914, under the influence of the national movement for greater legal uniformity, Wisconsin's "Model Automobile Law" established the supremacy of state law over local or municipal enforcement policies. Others followed Wisconsin's lead, making both state law and the subsequent state enforcement agencies the "supreme" law of the highway.[29]

The evolution of state hierarchical oversight merged with the broader trends in contractual citizenship during the Progressive Era. Driving was redefined as a legal privilege rather than an individual right. New Jersey's influential commissioner of motor vehicles, Harold G. Hoffman, argued that governments granted "the right to operate an automobile." Citizens, "in accepting a license," also "assumed certain obligations" that demanded drivers to act as "good citizens." Connecticut's 1924 statute classified twenty-one separate causes of driver criminality, all prima facie evidence of wrongdoing. These included "intoxication; speed too great for the conditions; cutting in; passing a standing trolley; passing on a curve, on a hill, on wrong side; trying to beat a train to the crossing; cutting corners; parking on the wrong side; failure to grant right of way; inattention; following too close; runaway car due to failed brakes; confusion; skidding; careless backing; inexperience." The statute offered, as one reporter keenly noted, a "pretty complete catalog of the motoring sins."[30]

Reformers recognized that the power to license remained their chief weapon in the war of safety enforcement. "The right to drive a car is not inherent," traffic judge Maher emphasized, "in reality, it is a grant of permit issued by the state and capable of being withdrawn for certain reasons. In fact, it is a privilege and not a right." Licensing laws often charged citizens with their own defense. As one driver surmised for Connecticut's new law, "if you don't report" yourself to the police after an accident, "the other party to the smash probably will, and then your goose is cooked" and one's license would be revoked. In this way, just as an unethical lawyer or incompetent teacher might lose their state license, a driver could forfeit the "privileges" of the open road. Others reasoned that "the present system of fine and imprisonment does not reach the worst offenders. The wealthy reckless driver cares nothing for a fine, but if he forfeited his right to own and run a car there is very little doubt that he would find it worth while to be careful."[31]

But the problem, as Maher again correctly noted, was that the motorist "isn't easily convinced that the authorities have the right to discipline him by the withdrawal of his license." To establish this "right to discipline," states instituted a series of escalating proofs of driver competency. Reformers wanted a method "whereby drivers of motor vehicles, or those who are about to become drivers, may be so graded and classified so that the reckless, the careless, and the incompetent are forbidden to even touch a steering wheel." Initially, this standard was a simple licensing fee. For a small sum, nearly anyone could receive an operator's license. Farmers and rural Americans registered the loudest opposition to the fees because, typically, multiple members of their families needed to drive.[32]

By the end of World War I, states expanded the qualitative restrictions to driving. They acted as gatekeepers, limiting access to those deemed incapable of exercising caution and good judgment. Officials, like New York City Traffic Magistrate Bruce Cobb, argued that the public deserved a full measure of "the applicant's character and physical and mental condition." Cobb praised the stringent competency exams administered in New York, Massachusetts, Connecticut, New Jersey, and Maryland. While their criteria varied, typically one needed to submit to either a written or driving test. Michigan gave its municipalities the freest hand in defining these exams. Detroit proved particularly strict. Five examiners (often members of the municipal traffic police) audited an average of 300 applicants per day. The bureau required all who failed the exam to take a remedial course in safe driving. The agency also maintained detailed records of operators who demonstrated a propensity for accidents or violations. They performed psychological examinations on many of these repeaters brought before the court. In 1923, New Jersey alone rejected over 15,000 applicants and revoked 1,700 licenses based on poor driving records. That same year, the District of Columbia rejected 6,857 of 26,605 prospective drivers. As one examiner explained, the unfettered use of the automobile proved too dangerous for "every person is not fitted to drive an automobile."[33]

Yet, enforcement advocates asked, "just how far is it practical to classify fit and unfit applicants for the privilege of driving?" Physical competency proved the easiest to measure. In 1920, the state of Pennsylvania first defined a physically "unfit" driver as one who "lost the use of one hand or both, or who has lost the use of both feet, or whose eyesight is so impaired that with the aid of glasses he cannot distinguish substantial objects clearly." Others tested for color-blindness and uncorrected defective vision. Drivers under the age of eighteen or suffering from inhibiting ailments, such as chronic high blood pressure, were also restricted. The NSC reported that, by 1938, twenty-five states conducted physical qualification exams. Based on physical liabilities, traffic bureaus rejected from 2 to 15 percent of all license applicants.[34]

Qualitative evaluations soon followed these objective physical exams. Reaction time tests, for example, supposedly measured a driver's decision-making skills during an emergency. Using a modified revolver attached to the undercarriage of a test vehicle, instructors shot a burst of red paint onto the street. Told to brake immediately after hearing the shot, drivers depressed the pedal to activate a second pistol which left a second mark on the roads. Administrators then calculated the reaction time by measuring the distance between the two points and dividing by the observed speed. Repeated testing found little or no difference in the "normal" applicant's response time; a little more than half a second. Many reports cited, to their amazement, that no gap existed between men and women or between the wealthy and the poor. Still, the data did not prevent others from drawing broader societal conclusions. Typically, as one report claimed, examiners perceived correlations between qualitative exams and "general intelligence."[35]

Clearly, qualitative exams opened the testing process to cultural and "scientific" bias. Given rising death tolls and heightened public fears over the motor menace, many clinicians simply attributed accidents to the deficient "mental equipment" of certain drivers. One Houston physician complained that while aged or physically impaired drivers were certainly troublesome, the motorist "with a mental aberration presents a more appalling menace." He knew of "many psycho-neurotic men and women who operate cars."

> As a rule they are self-centered, likely to disregard signals, and to be utterly oblivious of the rights of others. Some of them are in the grip of egoistic thoughts that elevate them to a plane of superiority where no law applies. They are convinced that the right-of-way is theirs. If an accident happens, the other fellow is to blame. If crippling injuries, or even death, results there is little or no remorse. They feel they are wholly justified in every situation.

Such "medicalization" of social deviance is a well-studied phenomenon. Scholars like Michel Foucault argue that the distinction between legitimate psychological maladies and socially "defective" behavior is often dangerously slim. Pseudo-psychological conditions, such as restlessness, nervousness, inattention, or other "irritations of the brain" arose as a convenient excuse to explain the growing auto accident problem. For Americans who readily equated good driving with progressive citizenship, psychological testing offered a practical and scientific means by which to justify their well-established fears.[36]

Psychiatric driving tests appeared first in private industry, lending the practice legitimacy because of its links to the business model of safety. Dr. A. J. Snow, of Northwestern University's Department of Psychology, for example, examined five thousand Chicago taxicab drivers in the early 1920s. He conducted tests to determine driver "intelligence, carefulness, and reaction time to sudden danger." To simulate the random lethality of the open road, Snow subjected the cabbies to a battery of bizarre experiments. One test strapped the men to a chair fitted with a series of menacing electrodes and several hand and foot controls. Darkening the room, a clinician "turns a switch to the high-frequency machine and a brilliant blue spark leaps across a gap a few inches from the startled chauffeur's nose. Another and larger spark sputters within the glass-fronted cabinet of the machine and a third darts toward the hand resting on the telegraph key." Researchers recorded the reactions of these startled cabbies, establishing both normal and abnormal responses to these outlandish conditions. T. D. Pratt, general manager for the Motor Truck Association of America, conducted similar examinations of the nation's truck drivers. These revealed that about 3 to 5 percent of all operators proved incapable of passing the psychological exams.[37]

With the endorsement of progressive scientists and businessmen, psychiatric testing opened the door for traffic bureaus to practice substantive social engineering. Reports of early "brain tests" bristled with startling conclusions. For example, men and women responded almost identically to a crisis. Class and ethnicity also proved impossible to identify in a laboratory. Scrutinizing the records of more than two thousand everyday drivers, Snow determined that marital status and the number of dependents were also meaningless safety factors, "upsetting the old belief that a married man was a steadier and more careful driver." Moreover, personal attributes, such as intelligence and critical thinking skills, seemed to matter little to good driving. Snow wrote that the typical motorist does "not need to be an intellectual heavyweight," only "able to carry out simple directions, recognize objects under unusual conditions, learn simple things, and have a normal memory."[38]

With the assurance that exams were not biased in favor of book-learning, enforcement officials embraced the opportunity that psychological testing offered. California's Levy Bill added "Harvard Intelligence Tests" to the state's licensing exams in 1929 to detect the "mental disability" of drivers. Psychologist Raymond Dodge, working through the National Research Council, suggested creating a "national blacklist for chauffeurs" based on these and other brain tests. Much like current lists of convicted sex offenders, the index would identify those who failed their exams and prevent them from going "over into another State [to] continue their homicidal practices." Detroit established a full psychopathic clinic in 1919 that began testing automobilists in 1921. The city's traffic court relied exclusively on the clinic to decide the driving fate of repeat offenders. Judge Maher reported in 1937 that fewer than ten of the one hundred fifty cases he personally sent to the clinic emerged with "clean bills of health." The remainder "all had a faulty attitude or were [deemed] dangerous, were insane, or were feeble-minded." The court revoked the driving privileges for every "failed" patient.[39]

Detroit's psychopathic clinic examined over fifteen thousand suspect drivers between 1936 and 1965. While the engineer perfected the road and car, these new "mental engineers" aimed to correct the deficiencies of the driver. Dr. Fred Moss, head of Department of Psychology at George Washington University and secretary of the Committee on the Causes of Accidents for the 1924 Hoover Commission, agreed. Unlike auto engineers, Moss wrote, "the human engineer has no lock-washers or cotter-pins to hold the human 'nuts' in the proper position, the result being the wrecks we read about daily." Leading clinicians, such as Snow, Dodge, Moss, Theophile Raphael, and Lowell Selling (all accredited physicians or psychologists), frequently linked their work to the popular hereditarian psychology of the eugenic movement. It was no small wonder, then, that the Detroit clinic distinguished African Americans, immigrants, and women as the likeliest carriers of mental illness. Nearly two-thirds of all patients returned to the court with a recommendation for license suspension or revocation were part of these demographic groups.[40]

Clinicians' strong scientific support of the troubled, "accident-prone" driver remains the greatest legacy of the psychiatric hospitals. Most, such as Detroit's psychopathic clinic, specifically targeted repeat offenders (those either cited for multiple driving infractions or involved in more than one collision). Dr. Selling concluded that the accident-prone driver was "not insane in the conventional sense," but "as unpredictable and dangerous as the usual insane person would be, for he has no more consideration of the rights of others than one who suffers from an actual serious mental disorder." The "repeater's" proven irresponsibility and lack of social conscience contrasted sharply with the values of personal restraint and collective safety that defined the automotive love affair. In 1933, Ohio State University's A. R. Lauer concluded that repeaters who represented less than 7 percent of the driving population accounted for more than half of all accidents.[41]

Reformers used these assumptions about the existence of an "accident-prone driver" to advance and sustain several key assumptions. The first was their confidence in the inevitable fate of these motorists. Selling concluded, for one such patient, that the "fact that he has had no previous accident record is a matter of luck, and he is bound to get into serious trouble in the future if he drives." Weeding society of these potential killers was as logical as quarantining those carrying an infectious lethal disease. This task soon materialized as the chief role of benevolent law enforcement.[42]

Second, the diagnosis of accident-prone behavior validated a link (already strong in terms of the love affair) between avoidable collisions and driver attitudes. Andrew Boone, reporting in 1939 on the broad psychiatric testing community, admitted that their approach "seems to harp on *attitude*" but that "the emphasis is wholly desirable, for *attitude* of the driver toward the law and his fellow man holds the key to success."[43]

Armed with this psychiatric data and a powerful consensus about proper driving attitudes, states moved aggressively to establish uniform standards, regulatory simplicity, and bureaucratic efficiency. Much as with engineering and education reform, the national Hoover Commission recommended improvements in data collection, record keeping, schedules of penalties, and consistent treatment for traffic offenders. It supported data collection as "ammunition for the war on accidents" and physical or psychological examinations to "weed out unfit drivers." The commission endorsed a "Standard Drivers' License Law" for all states. A 1939 summary of its recommendations cautioned that "the full benefit of such disciplinary measures is only realized when authorities follow a more aggressive plan of action, *seeking out* 'accident repeaters' and chronic offenders" and punishing them with suspension or revocation of their license. Federal reformers applauded state enforcement activities but added little to their efforts.[44]

In addition to state regulatory oversight, the free market emerged as another potential restriction of poor drivers. As with state reform, many assumed that auto liability insurance could limit access to automobiles in those deemed "unacceptable" risks. Automobile liability insurance developed rapidly in the first two decades of the new century. Carriers wrote the first auto policy in 1898. Ten years later, the product was common throughout the country. A typical early policy sold for a costly $500 annual premium, a $25 deductible, and, in case of an accident, guaranteed full indemnity for financial liability. Expanded coverage of more and more drivers lowered the collective risk for insurance carriers, who cut premiums nearly in half over the next decade. By 1919, the driver of a new low-cost runabout (under $800) paid a $45.00 annual premium while new luxury car owners could expect up to three times this fee. That year, Americans paid more than $150 million in auto liability insurance per year.[45]

The financial protections of insurance proved essential for mass automobility. Speaking before the Insurance Society of New York in 1919, Eugene Hord credited the "progressive growth" of the auto industry to insurers' willingness to assume "the burden of the inevitable toll of lives, injuries and destruction of property that might only naturally be expected to follow such a rapid absorption . . . of a powerful machine, capable of great speed and which, only a few years ago, was still regarded as an experiment."[46]

The business logic of private insurance—where private citizens assume the financial burden for the public risk that their actions create—supported the broader assumptions of early safety reform. Liability insurance reflected the good economic sense of the motorist, and higher insurance premiums promptly "hit the pocket" of the reckless motorists. One insurer lectured, "that which is good judgement and a sound principle for the business man is equally so for the individual." Individual policies proved the most direct route to personal financial responsibility and, therefore, greater accountability for safety on the streets.[47]

Many viewed liability insurance as the best hope for substantive progress in auto safety. William Cowles, vice president of Travelers Insurance, solemnly told his colleagues that insurers "cannot disregard unreasonably the moral obligation which falls upon them . . . to properly serve the public as a matter of good business sagacity as well as morality." Cowles believed the public wanted reform but "fails to get it from the governmental sources from which it might be expected." Vindicated by the free market, rate adjusters criticized the lack of meaningful progress from state enforcement efforts. Licensing and examinations offered "no protection of any moment" and lacked any "effective enforcement which is really protective." By 1929, the consensus held that insurers, not the state, offered the only realistic chance for improved public safety.[48]

Many state officials agreed. They proposed *mandatory* liability insurance laws that shifted the burden of safety enforcement from government to the free market. They reasoned "if persons prove to be reckless drivers" they must pay for their imprudence through higher annual rates. Quite simply, if "they can not get insurance . . . they can not drive." Others preferred the clean and direct financial relationship between rate-payers and insurers, rather than the diffuse obligations of the social contract. Jesse S. Phillips, general manager of National Bureau of Casualty and Surety Underwriters, advised the Hoover commissioners that this link "should not be underestimated. The relationship of insurer and insured is one which makes it possible for the insurance company's representative to bring home with great force the lessons of safety." Public opinion surveys found that 81 percent of car owners and 89 percent of nonowners agreed that motorists should be required to carry accident liability insurance. Massachusetts enacted the nation's first compulsory auto liability insurance law on January 1, 1927. California followed suit less than two years later.[49]

But deep flaws in this market-based enforcement solution went unexamined. As Hoover Commissioner George Graham noted, insurance was not a "panacea." For one, it did not make the streets any safer. While accident victims received financial compensation from universal coverage, it remained "doubtful whether such a law would reduce auto accidents." Moreover, Graham continued, "careless drivers might shelter under the protection of this insurance and be still more reckless." In the words of another, the insured driver "may feel entitled to run down a few pedestrians in order to get his money's worth."[50]

By the close of the decade, support for state-mandated liability insurance was on the wane. In 1927, a group of leading auto insurance executives formed the "Committee of Nine" to examine the "Financial Responsibility for Automobile Accidents." The conclave hoped to lead from above, like the high-powered educational council of the same name. The business community agreed that universal liability insurance did little more than increase the cost of driving for the average, conscientious driver. Their services remained "at best but a partial and ineffective answer to the question of how to protect the public." Significantly, the nine concluded, "the elimination of reckless and incompetent drivers from the public highways" remained the duty of "the police power of the State," and not of the free market. If governments were to "pass the problem over to private insurance companies," they argued, the public would simply shirk its essential civic responsibility to provide for collective security. Through mandatory insurance "the individual responsibility of the wrongdoers [is] ignored and the prevention and punishment of wrongdoing forgotten."[51]

In response to the concerns raised by the Committee of Nine, the American Automobile Association sponsored a campaign for new "safety responsibility" laws. Hoping to provide some guarantee of financial compensation and to stave off "the spectre of universal compulsory automobile liability insurance raised" by Massachusetts's actions, their proposal did not demand insurance before licensing, but merely "proof of financial responsibility." Significantly, under their plan, state enforcement kicked in only after an accident occurred and after a driver was found legally guilty of reckless, intoxicated, or hit-and-run driving. At that time, the convicted driver must provide evidence of financial responsibility in order to reinstate driving privileges. Failing to furnish this proof (in the form of a liability insurance policy or public bond) within fifteen to thirty days of judgment meant the immediate forfeiture of license. The severity of the accident or violation determined the amount of money to be set aside, ranging from $5,000 to $10,000. First proposed in 1929, by 1932 eight states (including Massachusetts) adopted the AAA model rather than mandate private liability insurance for all motorists. Sixteen other states appended portions of the "safety responsibility" provisions to their existing laws. The practice remained voluntary, but for those who believed in the business model (where safety and insurance reflected budgetary foresight rather than social or moral values) and had the necessary financial resources, liability insurance signified individual prudence and self-control. In the words of New Jersey's Commissioner of Motor Vehicles, drivers "owe it to yourself, your family, to the public, to maintain a degree of financial responsibility that will enable you to meet any emergency." Still, many drivers chose not to insure. Bad drivers could still acquire a license. Insurance did little to enforce safe driving conditions.[52]

Legislative and market reforms certainly limited *access* to the highways. But as safety enforcement measures these policies remained too passive to effectively contain unsafe motorists. While those convicted of chronically poor driving found it harder to reinstate their automotive privileges, the public was no better protected from the specter of "sudden death." Moreover, as Americans' reliance on the auto increased, judges and juries proved less willing to convict citizens of recklessness and permanently bar them from the roadway. While their compassion might be justified—was it fair to sentence a citizen to walk in an auto-based society?—the trend choked off the flow of convicted motorists made susceptible to driving restrictions.

It thus fell to motorized policing to take a more active role in protecting mobile citizens. Drivers and pedestrians, if left alone, will consistently disobey traffic laws. In large part this is simple human nature: interpreting social customs liberally to suit immediate needs. One should not assume, however, that citizens would drive madly if no laws existed. But the lack of law (or, more appropriately, of law *enforcement*) certainly encourages personal recklessness. Traffic engineer Miller McClintock reasoned "many users of the streets will be ignorant of the rules . . . a few will maliciously violate them," and all "require the assistance of some official moderator to determine their respective rights when traffic becomes dense." These three roles of traffic enforcement—educating the ignorant, arresting malicious intent, and resolving accidents—determined the shape of the emerging traffic enforcement community.[53]

Most reformers recognized that traffic congestion posed the greatest single variable to law observance. For the typical automobilist, snarled traffic often led to frustration and anger. Impatient drivers blamed others for their delay, often overreacting to perceived slights or hints of further inconvenience. Seeing open roads, or even slight gaps in the traffic, motorists compensated their frustrations with sudden speeding or aggressive and reckless driving. One 1929 driver noted, as a car "makes its way through congested streets and finally reaches open country, the person at the wheel is likely, in the very exuberance of spirit, to 'let 'er go!'" Street policing initially hoped to limit this common tendency toward situational or reactionary lawbreaking.[54]

In the earliest years, only a few mounted urban policemen patrolled the streets, largely to preserve the peace between "wrangling drivers" and pedestrians or to assist "some infirm persons or children over a dangerous crossing." Most of these officers were young beat cops temporarily reassigned to traffic duty, often for disciplinary reasons. But by the 1920s, it became clear that a dedicated force was necessary to uphold the law. In 1919, Boston permanently reassigned 154 men to create a steady traffic police force. They selected "the most fit" candidates and established a "semi-military type" of discipline that fostered a unique *esprit de corps*. One year later, the Minneapolis police department formed its own elite force of trained officers known locally as "the Specials." These forty-six men received focused training, followed exclusive patrols, and enjoyed legal support systems, in the form of a dedicated traffic court, to deal with the growing traffic menace. Periodically, the entire Minneapolis police department took to the streets, aiding the Specials in sweeps that netted over eleven hundred citations a month. The show of force also administered "a few jolts to the driving public," impressing upon them that "a force armed with authority has established . . . that the city streets do not belong to individual drivers." Reformers in other cities, such as Cleveland, Kansas City, New York, St. Louis, and Washington, D.C., established similar teams during these early years.[55]

Following the 1916 Federal Road Aid Act, states also acted to create rural highway patrols. One state patrolman recalled how, in the mid-1920s, the new Highway Patrol formed "to give more adequate protection to the traveling public—to you and to me, when we become careless and violate the rules of the road and the dictates of sound judgement." In 1927, Michigan's motor cops placed Detroit "virtually under martial law" to enforce state traffic laws during the Christmas holiday. Similar crackdowns around the country gave the new units greater standing within the law enforcement community and provided a very visible reminder of the national safety reform movement. By 1938, forty-five states operated state traffic police forces. In eleven, the force exceeded two hundred active patrolmen.[56]

The evolution of these distinct traffic enforcement squads occurred within the growth of other progressive municipal and state services. Urban traffic forces needed to merge with existing police structures. In Chicago and Pittsburgh, for example, the use of administrative districts simplified police coverage of street and beat patrols but did nothing to iron out the differences in policing authority or strategies. For states and large cities, enforcement contingencies, for park management and business or residential zones, or mixed jurisdictions, such as wholly absorbed self-governing suburban communities (like Brookline within the city Boston), only muddled effective reform. While highway patrols faced fewer conflicts with regional county sheriffs, the vast distance of rural highways and the relatively sparse coverage of officers limited protection and weakened their authority.

Traffic Police Sergeant Edwin Cowing directing cars in Chicago, Illinois, 1917. (Chicago History Museum, DN-0068612)

Still, by the close of the 1920s, most drivers had experienced at least one direct confrontation with these new traffic cops. On the whole, to those recording their views, the best motorized officers demonstrated an open and honest demeanor when dealing with the public. One writer praised local "Officer Bannerman" because "he believes in patrolling his beat constantly at a good lively clip—and not in hiding in bushes and coaxing folks to break the law." He targeted driving menaces, the "line-crowders and road hogs and fender crashers," rather than those who temporarily sped or occasionally rolled a stop sign. Patience and civility ranked high on the list of ideal traits. A talk with Bannerman, for instance, was "never a bawl-out. None of that raucous, snarling 'Hey you! Where's the fire? Whothell you think you are? Didn't yuh see me hand? Ain't yuh got eyes?"

The good patrolman issued warnings, not citations; gentle lessons in traffic law, not sermons. The ideal traffic cop even treated reckless motorists "as children to be curbed and not criminals to be clubbed." He never abused his legal power of arrest (which, due to prima facie, usually meant conviction). "That 'tell it to the judge,' stuff isn't his line," one reported,

> To [Bannerman] it means that having power, having the force of law behind him gives him the moral responsibility to use it justly and with intelligence. He feels that in acting as a traffic officer it's up to him to protect careful motorists from careless ones and to protect the careless ones from themselves. . . . He alters his rules according to the moment, realizing that it's just as much his task to keep traffic moving as fast as safety will permit, as it is to keep it from moving any faster than that.

In sum, the ideal traffic cop educated the driver, enforced the law, and engineered smooth-flowing traffic.[57]

Of course, no such ideal individual ever existed. Berton Braley's imagination created Officer Bannerman; "I made him up. But wouldn't it be grand if there were one like that?" T. D. Robinson, by contrast, was a very real Los Angeles traffic policeman. Unlike the mythical Bannerman, Robinson expressed an emphatic annoyance with the deadly cat-and-mouse games played between himself and motorized scofflaws. Disheartened by rising fatality rates, Robinson cautioned "if you'd cover my detail for twenty-four hours, you'd wonder why it is that two hundred people ain't killed every day in auto accidents, instead of only eleven." As for the powerful reforms issued by eager state legislators, the officer lamented that simply "makin' new laws for auto drivers is just given' them more laws to break!" Prima facie remained Robinson's greatest means of power and authority, for "when we stop you we got you dead to right, and what's more, you *know* it!" The officer listed thirteen "rules" of the highway as practical advice for the modern motorist. The first *and* last of his commandments was never to "argue with a cop." Rather than rely on patrolmen as paragons of motorized virtue, Robinson concluded, "everybody drivin' an auto ought to take the angle that there *ain't* no cops to watch over 'em, that they're their *own* cops, and the *only* traffic laws is carefulness, common sense, and a little less selfishness." These contrasting views—between the idealized public servant and the overworked cynic—reflected the widening gulf between traffic policing and law observance. If cops were to play a central role in automotive safety, they would have to demonstrate their ability to hold individuals accountable for collective safety.[58]

The lack of manpower, resources, and organization placed the greatest strains on traffic policing. In most regions, the new state and city traffic forces simply lacked the officers and squad cars to do the job (Table 6.1). Many took to the streets in outdated, underpowered autos or motorcycles. Most worked without

Table 6.1. State Policing Statistics, 1939

State	Number of Registered Cars	Number of Patrolmen	Miles of State Roadway	Miles per Patrolman
New York	2,584,123	517	12,652	24
California	2,510,867	780	12,097	15
Pennsylvania	1,976,466	1,461	26,084	17
Texas	1,548,343	200	24,000	120
Michigan	1,408,835	275	9,437	34
New Jersey	1,000,684	240	1,642	6
Oklahoma	535,399	113	7,146	63
South Carolina	287,913	98	5,762	58

Source: Report of the Investigation of Drunk Driving, Texas Safety Association. Presented at Texas Safety Conference, Austin, Texas, April 16, 1940.

police dispatch radios and under conflicting orders to enforce both the traffic and nonmotorized laws. The U.S. Bureau of Public Roads reported, as late as 1938, that most states were "unable to handle satisfactorily those duties related directly to highway matters because of other entirely justifiable but conflicting responsibilities."[59]

Again, the massive popularity of driving simply overwhelmed the safety mission of most enforcement agencies. Reformers understood it was "no small matter to enforce *any* sort of law against nine million drivers, each manning an instrument of great fleetness and wide radius of action with opportunities to break the law present every moment the vehicle is in motion." To most, it became an "impossible job" that "require[d] a multitude of officers with the ability to be omnipresent." Not only did the numbers not add up, but public expectations only intensified the patrolman's plight. As *Atlantic* contributor Seth Humphrey concluded in 1931, enforcement's "fatal weakness" lay in the "limit of public toleration for both the added expense" of policing and its resistance to the "intimate police regulation of all motorists."[60]

Undermanned, underfunded, and unappreciated, the patrol officers did what many other public safety agencies would do: they used their experiences and biases to profile "bad" drivers. By targeting certain motorists at specified locations, they established protocols to nab and prosecute those they (pre)judged to be likely criminals. Police reformers termed the practice "selective enforcement." The policy placed officers at prearranged locations, such as a busy intersection or a particular stretch of highway, where infractions or accidents commonly occurred. But the practice remained rooted in the confrontational assumptions of traditional law enforcement. Men trained to capture murderers and thieves have little regard for their prey. But, as Judge Maher summarized, selective enforcement "was designated to deal with criminals," not everyday motorists.[61]

Selective enforcement targeted three main types of violations: speeding, reckless driving, and driving under the influence of drugs or alcohol. Speeding remained the most common and therefore hardest to fairly enforce. In court, prima facie evidence of speeding generally sealed a conviction, but officers needed to support their observations with some form of physical proof. The police perfected several methods of accurately measuring speed. While engineers proposed a variety of ingenious devices based on oscillographs, the three methods employed by everyday traffic cops included stopwatch timing, matching the speed of a suspect using a trailing squad car, and experienced observation (such as considering an offender's rate of speed as compared to the rest of traffic). The first two methods provided officers the most effective courtroom evidence. Some municipalities even required more exacting measurements to secure a conviction. In Houston, the court demanded the testimony of two officers, riding together or on separate motorcycles, who both observed the speeder for at least two blocks, who followed no less than one-half block behind the suspect at all time, who never lost sight of the suspect, who could swear that the defendant was also the driver, and who had their police speedometer(s) checked within the last ninety days. As with most cases involving prima facie evidence, policemen soon learned how to correctly answer these questions to insure a conviction.[62]

The main problem remained the frequency of speed violations. A 1935 study of nearly two thousand Indiana drivers showed that three-fourths habitually exceeded posted speed limits; most by over 10 miles per hour (mph). Investigations in Rhode Island, Maryland, and South Carolina confirmed this behavior. Collectively, nearly 86 percent of all drivers exceeded limits set at 20 mph, 69 percent at 25 mph, 52 percent at 30 mph, and 39 percent at 35 mph. Significantly, fewer than one in nine drivers violated the law when the speed limit topped 45 mph. Drivers appeared most willing to break the law when constrained by slower speeds that the surrounding environment did not seem to justify or in areas of higher congestion. They did not appear interested in traveling at the highest speed possible.[63]

While statistics varied for driving under the influence, officers reported a steadily growing incidence of drunk driving throughout the period. Stories of foolish, inebriated drivers crowd the pages of popular journals. Their mood remained serious but with a humorous, even complicit tone. One Connecticut state trooper observed a driver who repeatedly pulled his vehicle to the side of the road as traffic approached. Viewing eight such detours (in less than three miles) the police stopped the driver who responded, "You fool, I'm drunk! I never drive this careful when I'm sober." A California police officer reported another drunk who bolted through four lanes of traffic, hit a streetcar, then plunged *into* a corner drugstore. The driver responded to the officer's questions by barking like a dog. In both cases, juries found it easy to convict the offenders.[64]

But for the vast majority of others, charges of driving while drunk required much stiffer evidence for a conviction. Texas lawmakers, frustrated by the success of defense attorneys and the overall lack of drunk-driving convictions, noted how direct police observation (in this case, the prima facie evidence of erratic driving) was "no longer adequate" to convince juries. To make their charges stick "scientific testing of inebriates must supplant personal opinion of [juries] frequently swayed by prejudice or friendship." Particularly in cases involving death or injury, the use of chemical analysis of breath, urine, saliva, or blood was essential to secure a meaningful sentence. Legal precision supplanted the officer's experienced observations, but did not constitute guilt in all cases. Section 54 of the Indiana Drunk Driving Law, for example, read that "evidence that there was, at the time, from five-hundredths percent to fifteen-hundredths percent by weight of alcohol in his blood is *relevant evidence* but is not to be given prima facie effect in indicating whether or not the defendant was under the influence of intoxicating liquor." In 1939, the *Journal of the American Medical Association* reported what was, by then, a widely accepted medical opinion that blood-alcohol content remained the only accurate indicator of intoxication. In the end, most police agencies agreed to use standardized breath tests, such as the Harger "Drunk-O-Meter," before charging a motorist with drunk driving.[65]

In addition to targeting hazardous drivers, enforcement reformers also improved the quality of their police reports. The U.S. Department of Agriculture complained that early police records proved "wholly unreliable" in most courts. The agency did not fault the officers but rather their training and the methods used to capture information. The administrative solution followed two distinct paths. One focused on changes to the existing municipal police force and was led by "internal reformers," such as Evanston police lieutenant Franklin Kreml. Kreml pioneered investigation methods used to diagnose the source of accidents. Skid marks, impact analysis (to assess the direction and force of a collision), on-the-spot interviewing, and other forensic tools, Kreml argued, must accompany a formal charge of lawlessness. While the Evanston police remained skeptical of Kreml's methods, hometown Northwestern University established a formal training curriculum, beginning in 1933, called the Northwestern University Traffic Institute (NUTI) using Kreml's approach. The sole purpose of improved accident reporting was to identify the likeliest locations, times, and driving behaviors that led to serious accidents. Armed with this validated information, the modern policeman could, according to Kreml and NUTI, target the most dangerous drivers at the most dangerous times and locations.[66]

The influence of Kreml and NUTI remains hard to gauge. Highway patrolmen, like L. G. Phares, soon converted to their cause. The promise of progressive, scientific criminal investigation techniques certainly encouraged reformers and their efforts to stem the flow of blood. Aggressive new policies in Cleveland, San Diego, Detroit, and, of course, Evanston significantly altered the relationship between the traditional "cop on the beat" and the general public. In 1930, Kreml distributed a filmstrip and training manual describing this new rapport. The text concluded that modern policing must *force* motorists to accept their safety responsibility. With effective investigation techniques, the poor driver would be held to task while indifferent motorists "will learn that an accident can not be dismissed by turning it over to an insurance company for settlement of claims." Under these new protocols, citizens "will learn that a criminal proceeding *must* also be faced. They will learn that the way to avoid trouble is to avoid accidents. The emphasis is placed, not on driving within a certain speed or obeying certain rules, but on driving safely."[67]

Rural highway police adopted many of Kreml's reforms, but modified their efforts in the face of extensive mileage and minimal personnel. The Michigan State Police offers a representative narrative of highway patrol techniques. Formed in 1916 and reorganized in 1921 and 1935, the agency divided the state's 18,000 miles of roadway into eight jurisdictional zones policed by 275 patrolmen. In District One, which covered East Lansing and its surrounding counties, nineteen officers used five patrol cars and five motorcycles to circuit more than 7,000 miles of road. In a single month, November 1936, the district issued thirty-six tickets, reported fifty-five accidents, conducted fifty "liquor inspections" (stopping motorists suspected of DUI), inspected nearly three hundred cars for defects, and assisted fraternal police organizations (both local and federal) on fifty occasions. In addition to these regular duties, the State Police remained responsible for all highway accident reporting. As with city cops, patrolmen standardized their routines in order to capture as much information as possible. Upon arriving and offering any necessary emergency assistance, the officer collected data, such as "marks on the road surface or shoulder, the actual point of impact, the position of the cars after impact, and the kind and extent of damage." After this, he examined and noted the working condition of the cars. Finally, the patrolman questioned the motorists; he "found out how much driving experience each operator had, whether city or rural, and his general driving habits, especially with respect to speed."[68]

Formal police investigative and reporting procedures significantly altered the relationship between the police, the driver, and driver safety. Where the officer once acted as a guardian angel for the good motorist, working to limit the destructive potential of the flivverboob, the modern force emerged as much less benevolent. Formal investigation procedures stripped the accident of its moral tone. Accidents now happened because of skidding, poor visibility, and, of course, poor driving. Where early enforcement policies hoped to restrain or intimidate careless drivers, the new professional forces focused their limited energies on an accounting of accidents after they occurred. These post hoc investigations accurately reconstructed the conditions of a crash (speed, location, mechanical defects) but did little to examine the attitudes or behavior of the drivers involved.

With the power of scientific data to prove their conclusions, those experiencing an auto accident became, prima facie, poor drivers. Significantly, these policing assumptions soon translated into new court procedures and legal responsibilities by the motorized public.

The final resolution of traffic law enforcement remained the courts. Adjudication of early traffic violations typically transpired in local criminal courts. The rise in auto use and traffic policing brought with it an equally rapid increase in the number of cases brought before the bench. As with policing, courts faced a growing problem in the perception of most offenders. While many could concede their guilt to speeding or rolling a stop sign, few liked being hauled before a criminal bench alongside "drunkards, murderers, wife beaters, and any of the other odd species of fish that fall into the seine of the law." As with other aspects of law enforcement, drivers found it hard to see their individual actions as criminal.[69]

Smaller cities and rural communities compensated for the crush by holding special sessions, often reserving one day a week for traffic offenders. In larger urban settings regulators established specialized traffic courts. By the 1920s, dozens of cities, including Chicago (which established the first traffic court in 1916), Memphis, Baltimore, Philadelphia, Mobile, St. Louis, Pittsburgh, Cleveland, and Detroit dedicated full-time judges and prosecutors to deal with the problem. In 1931, New York City prosecuted over three hundred thousand offenders a year. To expedite case resolution, state motor vehicle agencies often established "violations bureaus" to handle uncontested misdemeanor charges (such as speeding, illegal parking, and other violations not involving accident, injury, or property damage). Staffed by civilians, not judges or lawyers, these divisions allowed offenders to waive their legal rights, plead guilty, and pay a small scheduled fine. Many courts copied this approach, establishing what some termed "cafeteria style" justice. By the start of World War II the Automotive Safety Foundation estimated that nearly 4.5 million persons were "hauled before traffic courts" every year.[70]

The benefits of a dedicated traffic court extended beyond simple efficiency. While it was certainly possible to process larger numbers of offenders more simply and uniformly, the repetition also allowed more specificity and nuance. Many defendants used detailed diagrams, models, and other specialized exhibits to explain the unique (and hopefully exonerating) circumstances of their offense. Traffic police and investigation experts learned how to best present their cases before a magistrate and jury. Equally important, enforcement officials came to know local repeat offenders more intimately, allowing, many believed, for more effective punishment of those held responsible for the growing accident crisis.

As with all aspects of automotive safety reform, legal professionals struggled to balance the moral implications of "good driving" with laws that demanded safe driving. Moreover, the efficiency of cafeteria-style justice, where the accused reflexively admitted guilt and paid a small fine, actually undermined the deterrent purpose of law. Penalties remained too lenient to effectively modify driver behavior. By 1925, eleven of twelve municipal police chiefs recommended significant increases in the amount of fines if society hoped to see any safety improvements on the roadway.[71]

To be sure, serious offenses involving property damage, injuries, or fatalities merited stiffer punishment. Most courts recommended incarceration for repeated alcohol abuse or recklessness. Judge Maher argued that "jail time is necessary . . . [and] the best of all educational influences if used rightly." Cities like San Francisco and Chicago impounded vehicles, placing them under a heavy bond for a prescribed period, to deny the guilty access to their cars. A critical problem, addressed in only a few states, remained the court's inability to suspend or revoke drivers' licenses. Often reserved to state highway authorities, denying this privilege proved effective in forcing common motorists to respect the new morality of the streets. As Maher concluded, "the average motorist is a decent fellow, but he must learn that he has no *right* to drive. All he has is a *privilege* granted by the state, and that privilege can be revoked at any time when the motorist shows that he is unfit to have it. . . . The vital thing is that the motorist shall learn a new and more civilized mode of conduct when he is at the wheel of his car."[72]

But even for serious offenders, traffic courts established few uniform and just protocols for moral education. Where most agreed that judges should exercise personal discretion and that "no standing punishments should be adopted or followed," the inconsistency of local courts soon became legend. Stories circulated of Southern judges allowing violators to roll dice to determine their sentence, a distracted Western magistrate who accidentally sentenced a witness rather than the offender, an apathetic Midwestern judge who often left the bench while court was in session, or the Indiana jurist who decided twenty-six cases in under twenty minutes, a personal record. A New York City court broke into abandoned laughter after an accused repeat-speeder used the term "exhilarator" rather than "accelerator." The judge "got so much fun out of this excruciating bit of humor that he gave the defendant a suspended sentence." In an effort to teach motorists a "new and more civilized mode of conduct," judges even sentenced drivers to spend a day in the local morgue or by the side of ailing accident victims in the hospital.[73]

But poor justice did more than simply exonerate the guilty. By the 1930s, court congestion, corruption, and, predictably, professional boredom undermined the enforcement powers of state regulators. Court reporters, like R. L. Burgess, who toured traffic courts in twenty-one states, and Thomas Compere, who sat through thousands of hearing in New York City's traffic court, agreed that the situation was becoming "hopeless" and there was "ample justification for bitterness" by defendants. A veteran magistrate agreed, stating "you have about as much chance of getting justice in a traffic court. . . . as [a] smoke ring has of making a loop over the nose of the man in the moon. [Traffic] court is a madhouse; a disgrace to any civilized community." Compere noted that many defendants left feeling it was better to spend a day in jail than to again suffer the injustice of traffic court.[74]

As accounts like these suggest, the modern driving experience, including the new motor laws, aggressive policing, and specialized traffic courts, drained much of the social meaning from the civic tableaux of the roadway. Rather than participate within a community of motorists, drivers increasingly found themselves isolated within an impersonal bureaucratic machine. One Philadelphia defense attorney, who spent a considerable amount of time in traffic court, defined the experience as a growing "fatalism of the multitude." "The ever-increasing confusion and congestion," the lawyer continued, "undermin[ed] respect for law and moral responsibility of citizenship. I am convinced that the real blame, on the whole, cannot be charged directly to the individual officers entrusted with enforcement. Rather, it lies in the ill-conceived, unwieldy system of regulation which has sprung up hit-or-miss, along with the amazing growth of automobile travel." George Warren, who studied the nation's traffic courts for the National Conference of Judicial Councils in 1938, agreed that "almost all violations bureaus are run mechanically and tickets are paid for with the same attitude used for a grocery store purchase." Reform failed to conserve the collective and positive civic energies of the love affair. Moreover, it atomized the driver through a "confusion of an ill-digested and conflicting mass of traffic laws, rules, and regulations."[75]

Intensified reforms, combined with rising accident rates and congestion, forced a reevaluation of the driver's responsibility to public safety. While the broad values of the love affair remained—the easy, self-congratulatory feelings of personal freedom, driver equality, and progressive mastery—the driver's negative attitude toward law enforcement emerged as a critical new addition to America's driving culture. Public safety officials, like Michigan's James Sinke, held by 1926 that "the attitude of the individual towards law observance is a predominating influence upon accident frequency." A report of Connecticut auto accidents, sponsored by the NSC, found that no fewer than 14,559 (or 70 percent) of the state's 20,781 collisions resulted from the personal attitudes and controllable behaviors of the motorist.[76]

In an attempt to gauge the public's response to these changes, the Massachusetts Highway Department polled over twelve thousand motorists from December 12, 1933, to September 30, 1934. The demographics of their sample represented the "typical" driver of the era: over 90 percent male, most between 21 and 44 years old, and with at least five years of driving experience. The survey described the "attitude" toward safety and law enforcement by 97.3 percent of the respondents as "interested." The stated purpose of the study was "to deter-

mine the extent to which motor-vehicle laws are being violated and the preva-
lence of driving habits which might lead to accidents."[77]

The first part of the analysis proved relatively simple to document and painted
an equally clear picture of the typical driving experience. Using hundreds of
thousands of direct observations—451,410 vehicles were counted at intersections alone—the researchers found rampant lawlessness on the streets of the
commonwealth. Depending on the location, 85.0 to 98.5 percent of drivers never
signaled, did not stop at signs or lights, or habitually sped. One in two neglected
the right-of-way of others, one in three drove unsafe vehicles, one in four traveled over 15 miles per hour above the posted limit, and one in eight motorists
disobeyed all traffic signals entirely.[78]

The most fascinating finding, however, was not the predictable monotony of
public lawlessness but rather the conflicting safety values expressed by these
same drivers. They overwhelmingly supported stricter state enforcement measures, such as regular car inspections, increased police patrols, and more sophisticated traffic controls (such as automated stoplights and directional signs).
Three-fourths responded favorably when asked if Massachusetts should post and
enforce highway speed limits to slow traffic and reduce accidents. But they sum-
marily rejected most of the safety reforms enacted over the past fifteen years.
Half disdained license testing (of those who favored exams, 63 percent thought
the state should only consider physical qualifications). Fully 85 percent rejected
driver training (although 97 percent thought schools should "be required to teach
children accident prevention"). Most agreed to strict punishment for repeat offenders (license suspension or jail time), but four out of five thought that a reduction in insurance premiums was a better incentive for accident prevention.[79]

More than anything else, it was the accusatory tone of the law and the awkward means of administering justice that disconnected the mood of safety reform
from individual drivers' stated desire to change their behavior. R. L. Burgess, in
1932, found "throughout the nation, ample justification for a growing bitterness
among our millions of motorcar owners, who have come to resent and ridicule an
outrageous system of traffic law enforcement which violates almost every American principle of justice and equality." He witnessed

> automobile owners, hauled before tribunals for trivial violations of traffic
> rules, herded like dumb cattle to a practically inevitable doom. I saw oth-
> erwise respectable and law-abiding citizens driven to the surrender of their
> rights, to perjury, and even to bribery as the simplest way out of a maddening
> situation. I saw others exposed to official persecution, to the threats and 'fix-
> ings' of official racketeers—even to blackmail. And I witnessed the grossest
> kind of discrimination and favoritism—the rich and influential freed of real
> crimes of the road; the poor and powerless made to pay for trifling infractions
> of the rules.

Burgess interviewed "Mr. Davis," a local hardware merchant who patiently suffered harassing officers, indifferent judges, and inefficient bureaucrats in the pursuit of justice. Hoping to prove that his parked car was pushed into a no-parking zone by another motorist (a typical maneuver of many harried urban commuters), Davis waited most of the day to see the judge. In the end, he was denied a hearing. Frustrated, Davis lied to the court clerk, paid a fine, and left vowing to use his connections with the "district political leader" to fix any future summons. He concluded that the "law is a jackass [and] justice is a joke." Any man who trusts the cops or the courts to serve and protect motorists "is a sucker."[80]

Many agreed with Davis that the absurdity of traffic law enforcement justified their conscious disregard for the law. Unlike reforms aimed at straightening roads, perfecting automobiles, or educating the ignorant, law enforcement foundered on the lack of public cooperation. Like petulant preschoolers forced to follow the rules in kindergarten, many drivers complained that enforcement now took "all the joys out of motoring." New York traffic judge Frederick House observed "a subtle but very perceptible change" in the offenders brought before his court. Where public manners and civic justice once checked rude or antisocial behavior, the freedoms and social anonymity of driving amplified Americans' "perfectly natural instincts toward a certain amount of lawlessness." A 1931 study of over 81,000 New Jersey motorists found, as in neighboring Massachusetts, four-fifths of all drivers regularly disregarded the law. Indeed, much like Bonnie and Clyde, the driving public took great pride in avoiding most motor law enforcement. These values had a pronounced effect on the nature of early safety reform and helped define the contours of our modern risk society.[81]

Conclusion: Accidental Freedoms and the Risk Society

*There is something appalling about being gloriously well and exuberant
and carefree one moment, and in the next moment being part of a frantic,
struggling, bloody human mass writhing in a ditch or under an automobile, or
both, and having added to one's physical agony the intolerable mental anguish
of being unable to help loved ones in that mass. I know I shall never cease to
hear ringing in my ears the horrible groans of a man with a fractured skull,
lying near me in a pool of blood . . . mingled with my sister crying out loud,
"Won't you men help me with my mother?" . . . My head had been cut open,
both eyes were full of blood, and I was convinced that my left eye was lying
somewhere in the road. . . . It makes me feel "kind of sick" to recall it and to
write it.*

Elizabeth Jordan, "Automobile Collisions,"
Saturday Evening Post, 1926[1]

Elizabeth Jordan's recollection of a crash that injured eight people remains a rare published personal account of an automobile accident. To that point in her life Jordan had experienced five separate collisions (never once as the driver). Each produced multiple injuries. Her honest admission of terror, confusion, and helplessness stands in stark contrast to the optimistic forecast of the nation's auto reformers, who promised safety through improved engineering, education, and law enforcement. Jordan doubted that such an impersonal bureaucracy could convey the emotional horrors and personal loss necessary for effective deterrence. For her, the "majority of reckless drivers can learn only by the experience of hurting others or of being hurt." She shared her painful personal "lessons" so that others might avoid "weeks of mental and physical agony and thousands of dollars of expense."[2]

Few frank commentaries like Jordan's exist, both then and today. While journalists frequently wrote heart-wrenching narratives of accidental loss, they typically related these stories with an aloof, third-person detachment; one of sympathy but not empathy. Occasionally, narratives penned by professional auto racers proved the exception. While couched in the male bravado of competitive sports, their stories pierced the veneer of driver invincibility. Renault motorist

R. H. Bacon recalled how his short life flashed before his eyes as he "turtled" (i.e., somersaulted) his speeding car at the Delaware State Fair. Bacon nervously admitted that "usually no occupant was left alive with sufficient grasp of the situation to give a detailed account" of the experience. The famed American driver Barney Oldfield bitterly remembered how promoters profited by these vicarious thrills, drawing spectators to see accidents yet insulating them from the personal responsibility of a crash. It was all just a part of racing. Following a 1911 incident Oldfield admitted "I never realized my foolishness . . . until I was in the hospital with the doctors standing around and the nurses looking serious." Lying in bed, he acknowledged that "the dignity of motor racing [was] gone." "It has ceased to be racing" he surmised, but "merely a morbid and un-elevating spectacle."[3]

American publishers and the reading public certainly did not shrink from the horrors of accidental harm. First-person experiences from industrial catastrophes, violent crime, natural disasters, wars, and other transportation mishaps (such as the sinking of the *Titanic* or the capsizing of the Great Lake steamer *Eastland*) filled the periodicals. Even the stir caused by J. C. Furnas's 1935 *Reader's Digest* article "And Sudden Death," as noted in Chapter 4, had more to do with his blunt depiction of the physical aftermath of an accident, including decapitated or otherwise mangled bodies, than with developing empathy for crash victims. Furnas wrote in the same voyeuristic, omnipresent style of the newspapers. The sad events descended upon depersonalized and nameless victims.

Why this lack of apparent interest in the personal experiences of accident victims? Simple self-censorship is one answer. As contemporary sociologists Ulrich Beck and Anthony Giddens note, modern societies are risk societies. Individuals feel increasingly helpless to avoid the multiple threats of modernity. Whether from environmental pollution, violent crime, or auto accidents, citizens tune out the potential for disaster in order to limit the emotional impact on their daily lives.[4]

Our distressed relationship with roadside memorial markers, the spontaneous monuments placed by friends and family members to remember the victims of auto accidents, provides perhaps the best contemporary example of this phenomenon. Nothing better illustrates the sudden and violent finality of an auto accident than these informal cemeteries, oddly situated and deeply personal. Historian Erika Doss notes how public memorials reinsert the specter of death into an American culture that typically relegates mortality to the hospital and grieving to the home. One Maryland memorialist sounded much like Elizabeth Jordan, eighty years earlier, in expressing his hopes that the observance "will just slow [other drivers] down to realize that someone was killed there." In 2006, the *New York Times* reported that roadside markers were now "so numerous, *and so distracting and dangerous* . . . that more and more states are trying to regulate them." As author Ian Urbina observes, while the markers are "poignant reminders" of the personal anguish of survivors, most Americans simply see them as "macabre eyesores and dangerous distractions."[5]

Flipping the question on its head yields another plausible reason for the relative lack of public empathy. As this study makes clear, Americans did pour a great deal of energy into the bureaucratic response intended to ameliorate the automobile accident crisis. Based on falling fatality rates, reformers could report progress. Moreover, the safety bureaucracy garnered public support through its endorsement of scientific, rational, and efficient laws. Its very purpose was to circumvent the irrational ambiguities of America's driving culture. Accordingly, the dampened emotional response to accidents could be the consequence of a practical choice to focus on bureaucratic solutions rather than painful realities. Paraphrasing Abraham Lincoln's Gettysburg Address, perhaps Americans reasoned they could do little to honor the accident victims. On the other hand, they could do much to take from their loss a greater dedication to safety.[6]

But these explanations, while plausible, avoid the honesty, eloquence, and reproving gaze of Elizabeth Jordan or roadside memorialists. Why, Jordan asked, mere days after her accident, it appeared as if her neighbors had forgotten her suffering? Indeed, she claimed, "in most instances the sympathy of the community appears to go out to the driver who is on trial for being a menace." Cautioning the millions who would soon join her as accident survivors, Jordan warned of an irrational yet "natural suspicion" that society "desired him, the victim, to be killed off" rather than answer the victim's lonely calls for justice.[7]

While Jordan's paranoia is evident, automobile scholars suggest her claim has merit. Clay McShane records a noticeable "shift to callousness" toward accident victims in the first decades of the twentieth century. The editors at *Commonweal* magazine came to the same conclusion in 1931. They held that efforts to instill empathy in fellow motorists "fail[ed] notoriously." Accounts intended to stir indignation left most Americans "relatively cold."[8]

This book argues that the automotive love affair represents an underappreciated variable in explaining America's odd early response to auto safety. The love affair emerged as a shared visceral and intellectual acknowledgment of the freedoms of driving. The love of speed and mobility, the sense of equality and freedom, and the prideful validation of controlling a high-tech, high-cost consumer good sustained the twentieth-century transportation revolution. The love affair was real and its presence greatly eased America's transition to an automotive nation.

But the salient qualities of the love affair also shielded many from the dire costs of automobility. By personalizing the car's many benefits, consumers avoided collective responsibility for driver safety. According to this logic, only those unwilling or unable to adapt to the motor age caused accidents. While reformers concentrated on reducing collective risk and suggested the inevitability of collisions, drivers preferred to focus on the individual character traits that, they hoped, shielded one from disaster. From this perspective, then, the sorrowful personal stories of victims like Elizabeth Jordan had no place in American auto culture. Her response was, perhaps, too emotional for bureaucratic reformers and too culpable for the love affair. While the lack of these types of personal experience essays offers clues to this paradoxical relationship, negative evidence cannot substantiate the claim.

Americans did, however, record their responses to safety *reform*. As this text shows, from 1900 to 1940 public alarm over the rising accident crisis fed efforts to improve the engineering, education, and enforcement of the nation's roads, cars, and drivers. Yet even as these changes took hold motorists increasingly chaffed at even modest restrictions to their driving freedoms. Many claimed the new motor laws were unjust, ineffective, or simply foolish. They rejected the power ceded to the traffic police and expressed contempt for traffic courts. The appearance of this "natural lawlessness" undermined much of the potential for reform. While we are left to ponder the absence of personal accident narratives, we are awash in evidence indicating that most drivers considered themselves unfairly burdened, even oppressed, by efforts to curb their motorized liberties.

The public hesitancy to support restrictive driving laws cannot be attributed to overly aggressive policy makers; legislators passed traffic laws to serve motorists. Drivers "wrote the rules," McShane concludes, and shaped them "to help mobility, much more than safety." Nevertheless, critics turned against the seeming "hodge-podge of conflicting and overlapping enactments" and the lax efforts to coordinate and justly enforce these new rules.[9]

The primary public concern rested on the vagueness and lack of conformity in the new codes. On the one hand, reformers hoped to identify specific problem points—such as driver education, liability insurance, road and car improvements—that, once addressed, would gradually reduce the collective risk of automobility. For drivers, by contrast, the issue centered on correcting only *certain* motorists' derelict "attitude of mind." This cross-purpose, between specific criminal law and modified driver behavior, appeared most conspicuously in the courts. Traffic judges Frederick House and John Maher both noted the paradox that existed between legal violations of the law and the public's perception of safe or unsafe driving. House pondered,

How am I to regard that man? What is to be my attitude toward him? Is he, simply because he owns or drives a motor car, to be treated as an honorable, respectable, privileged member of an upper class who has been inconvenienced by a slight accident similar to bumping into another man in the subway? Or is he an offender who has willfully disregarded the law and, through his negligence, has committed an unwarranted assault upon another person?

Defendants facing more serious charges, such as manslaughter or drunk driving, frequently relied on this ambiguity to extricate themselves from their legal troubles. Defense attorneys argued that their clients' *victims* showed contributory negligence; a point of little concern to the state as it sought to prove the "defendant failed to observe a traffic law." The uncertain purposes of safety legislation, which abetted a shifting "sense of obligation [in other drivers] to exercise a degree of care commensurate with the increased risk," coupled with the inconsistencies of traffic laws and enforcement left the "whole framework" of safety reform "tottering."[10]

The public reserved its strongest and most unified opposition for the enforcement community. House believed this reaction was sustained by drivers' "perfectly natural instinct" toward lawlessness. Maher concurred, in 1937, admitting he was ashamed of Americans' traffic "crime record and general lack of law enforcement and law observance" as compared to other motorized countries. In 1942, George Warren marveled that "people whose sense of law and order would preclude their attempting to tamper with the administration of justice" in other fields would "not hesitate to do so in evading punishment for traffic offenses." While "human nature" accounts for some of these attitudes and behaviors, the public constructed strongly negative stereotypes of traffic cops and traffic courts to justify their behavior.[11]

Certainly no one enjoyed being caught nor the inconvenience and expense of settling a traffic violation. Still, public perceptions of the traffic police contrasted sharply with the benevolent (even glorified) image ascribed to safety engineers, educators, inspectors, and regulators. Unlike these more scientific progressives, many portrayed the traffic cop as a lazy or meddlesome jerk that intelligent citizens must learn to avoid. *Motor World* lamented the "fact" that peace officers "apparently lack the necessary poise, judgement and discretion that go to make up the ideal guardian of the law." Editorial cartoons depicted the motor police as overweight, dim-witted, and often asleep while on duty. In Ralph Barbour's 1936 educational safety novel *For Safety!* the teenage protagonists discuss their frustrations with the local traffic cop,

> "All I know is," said Henry disgruntledly, "if you park your car six inches inside a hydrant mark or more'n a foot away from the curb or leave it five minutes over the half-moon [mark on the parking meter] old 'Lump' Hanniford gives you a ticket, but if you wreck some one else's car or knock a kid down and bust his hip and two, three ribs it's okay. What I think, the cops ought to spend less time snooping around for minor infractions . . . and crack down on some of the crazy drivers in this town."

American Auto News laughed about a team of South American explorers who returned from the jungle with "two real cannibals." The editors suggested "starting them in on a few motor cops."[12]

Amidst popular negative stereotypes of foolish or arrogant traffic policemen, the growing awareness of real institutional abuse solidified public opposition to broadened police authority. Judge Maher warned in 1937 that the "low caliber of public officials" was a direct "contributing factor" to the nation's "lack of law observance." The apparent absence of professional ethics manifested itself in two ways. The first was petty corruption. The volume and arbitrary application of traffic violations meant that unscrupulous local officials could shake down just about any motorist. The result, for "a majority of car owners, in big cities and small," was an "accept[ance of] the belief that, once arrested, the cheapest and best thing to do is either attempt to 'fix' the officer or to plead guilty whether innocent or not." The problem was so widespread that reformers, scrambling to protect the legitimacy of their enforcement crusade, hoped to prohibit all "fees from the money collected from traffic convictions" from ever passing through the hands of the police. If this was not done, Earl Reeves predicted in a 1926 Collier's essay, the public would assume that all local officials were corrupt and stop all law observances. One deceitful constable, who recently snared Reeves in a speed trap, was dressed "in civilian clothes that were a great deal snappier than mine, he came down the steps of a $25,000 house, he had a $100 dog on leash, and he got into a $2,000 car. He draws $2,300 a year, and it seems pretty obvious that he is a crook—but it is I who belong to the criminal class."[13]

In addition to petty corruption, the public displayed anxiety over officers' abuse of the prima facie doctrine. In theory, the policy addressed a practical problem: most driving violations left no visible evidence of a crime. As noted in Chapter 6, the observations and testimony of trained law enforcement professionals solved this dilemma. Their opinions served as unassailable evidence in a court of law. In practice, drivers understood the doctrine to mean that they retained few legal rights if charged with a violation. It remained "the arresting officer, not the man on the bench" who acted as "the real judge." Some drivers responded by assuming the appearance of innocence rather than by changing their dangerous driving behaviors. The Literary Digest, in an essay titled "Avoid That Fine," cautioned drivers never to "appear" nervous or "look guilty" when pulled over. Earl Reeves, hauled to court four times in less than three weeks, offered several "axioms" for the American motorist, the first being that "when stopped, say nothing, . . . Even if you are guiltless, saying so is likely to insure arrest, while if you take a browbeating meekly you may escape." The national Accident Prevention Conference, in 1935, concluded that petty corruption and prima facie abuse were the primary obstacles for "building local public sentiment in favor of enforcement."[14]

Opposition to the "speed trap" combined these public resentments—toward police incompetency, corruption, and oppression—into a modern parable of legal abuse and civil disobedience. Motorists long understood and clearly demonstrated that their view of "excessive" speed remained highly contingent upon driving conditions, the self-assessed skill, experience, and common sense of the driver, not merely a number posted on a sign. The difference between a reckless and safe driver, in the mind of many, depended upon where, when, and how one drove. By contrast, municipal and state police forces often established protocols to snag every motorist who violated the letter of the law regardless of driving conditions. They set up "traps" that arbitrarily lowered limits in places where people would not expect them. Indeed, the very basis for their effectiveness was the natural sensibilities of the motorist, who assumed that road conditions allowed for a higher rate of travel. The public response to "speed traps" proved predictable. They saw them as "unfair," "unreasonable," and "worse than absurd."[15]

Autocamper Melville Ferguson, caught in an Ohio speed trap in 1925, illustrates an example of the public's general attitude toward law enforcement. Ferguson knew, through anecdotal evidence, of the frequent use of speed traps along the Lincoln Highway. His caravan of two cars, heavily laden with camping gear, traveled along a relatively empty yet straight and modern highway, "as smooth as a billiard-table." In spite of his caution, a concealed policemen emerged to cite both drivers for speeding. When stopped, the officer asked for no explanation nor offered any evidence of their speeding. Ferguson fumed that "the man on the motorcycle smirked with satisfaction" as he handed him the summons. Ferguson did not protest, knowing how it was "useless to argue with a traffic officer" and because he knew that he had broken no laws; there was no posted limit and the lack of traffic assured him that he was not driving recklessly. Unfortunately, the local judge did not agree. Based solely on the policeman's testimony (and disregarding all protest by the plaintiffs) the magistrate found both drivers guilty and fined each $9.95. Ferguson mused how the lack of "legal evidence" made it particularly difficult to accept the verdict. His rising cynicism showed when he wrote,

I was deeply touched by this evidence of hospitality to tourists from beyond the Ohio borders, because several cars bearing the licenses of that State had passed me on the road, going in the same direction at an even higher speed, just prior to this unpleasantness. But I felt relieved to be let off so lightly, and not a little puzzled, in view of the judge's cordiality, that he did not urge me to partake with him of the volatile medicament that imparted a genial odor to his breath.

Another frustrated offender beseeched, in 1935, "What has been accomplished? Absolutely nothing except resentment by the driver against what he considers dumb traffic rule enforcement and trickery on the part of the cop."[16]

As evident from Ferguson's experience, the public lumped the courts into its generally negative assessment of traffic law enforcement. According to American civic tradition, an independent judiciary will check unfair laws and overbearing executive authority. Law-abiding citizens trusted the courts to correct abuses of excessive or arbitrary government. Significantly, most people had few direct encounters with the law beyond traffic violations. As George Warren surmised, "what our fellow citizens see and hear (and in some instances smell) in our police courts, our traffic courts and in proceedings before our justices of the peace quite naturally determines their idea of American justice."[17]

Unfortunately, most found that these courts were designed to *process* offenders, not to review or assess the merits of their case. The summary force of prima facie evidence, routine speed traps, overly aggressive or corrupt officers, and absurdly high conviction rates rendered hope of an ethical legal defense meaningless. Moreover, petty corruption and ticket fixing undermined the entire purpose of deterrence. As one critic bitterly surmised, the "man who knows he has nothing to fear when violating the law and the state of mind of the offender who pays for his violations knowing others get away with the same offense, are destructive of both traffic law enforcement and public safety." Advised by his state motor vehicle commissioner to hire a lawyer to overturn his unjust speeding convictions, Reeves snapped "If I wanted to be restored to a state of lily-whiteness in the eyes of the law, I would [now] have to pay for the whitewash. . . . I would have to buy back my legal virtue!" He concluded that the public "conceded to traffic officers and traffic courts a dictatorship such as has not existed in this country." To Reeves, *both* enforcement arms "further weaken our respect for the law." Rather than appeal his convictions, he affirmed his moral superiority to the law. "If this were the state of things," Reeves surmised, "I was proud to belong to the criminal class."[18]

Many shared his pride. Traffic engineer Miller McClintock reported in 1925 that "gross favoritism" and "improper attitudes" of policemen and justices alike led to a condition where all traffic enforcement was "held in disrepute." Many used the term *justice mills* to describe the new sad reality. Cross-country tourists found that wherever "a greedy justice of the peace, unprincipled constables, and a large number of transitory motor-tourists exists, there the justice mill shows to the best advantage." Some lamented the impenetrable legal privileges of the arresting officer. Others condemned the prevailing climate of bureaucratic ineptitude and corruption, where litigants waited hours to be informed of their guilty verdict. At one Atlanta "cafeteria" traffic court, where motorists were allowed to "save delay by going up to a window and shoving money through to a clerk," drivers who challenged their citations waited an additional four to five hours only to receive the same summary justice, along with added court costs. One prosecuting attorney marveled, "Human nature is perverse. A lot of them insist on a hearing." Reporting on the scene, R. L. Burgess exclaimed, "what an amazing commentary on American justice is contained in that single phrase, '*A lot of them insist on a hearing!*'"[19]

Compounding the problem, courts and juries routinely showed what seemed to be excessive leniency toward menaces that the public *did* fear: drunks, reckless speeders, and repeat offenders. Although it proved relatively easy to charge and convict the average leadfoot, the same was not true for more aggressive forms of recklessness. Eyewitness testimony, even from the cops, rarely carried the same weight with criminal court juries as prima facie assumptions did in traffic court. Estimates about the rate of speed, distance, and other presumptions about "safe" motoring provided grist for defense attorneys to establish reasonable doubt. Moreover, the high incidence of everyday traffic law breaking made it difficult for prosecutors to convince juries that the accused was willfully negligent. One 1931 study estimated that less than a fifth of all drivers (who comprised most juries) always observed posted traffic notices like stop signs. Attorneys readily conceded that "most jurors both drove and drank." Judges and juries proved all too willing to suspend sentences or simply fine "drunken drivers lucky enough to be arrested before they have hit something." Even when juries *convicted* defendants of hit-and-run or drunk driving offenses, judges often proved unwilling to suspend or revoke their licenses.[20]

In 1938, the U.S. Bureau of Public Roads called the "astonishingly light character of punishment" the most "disturbing feature" of American jurisprudence. As a result, the "irresponsible driver usually figures he can 'get away with it'" in a court of law. Elizabeth Jordan reasoned that juries empathized more with the violator than the victim because

> by the time the case comes on, the victims are out of danger. The driver is not. He is in the clutches of the law—a serious situation to the lay mind, and seemingly one more stimulating to the imagination that the situation of the victims in the hospital. Moreover, and this may be the gist of the matter, collisions are becoming so frequent the pleaders fear that they themselves, being drivers of their own cars, may sometime, though a hazard of the road, figure in a collision and need the sympathy they are hastening to offer.

Seeing repeat offenders freed from justice coupled with the public "outpouring of solicitude for the reckless driver," Jordan felt threatened by the very safety community she depended on to protect her. She cited the example of a pardoned reckless driver who crashed again only days later, killing his mother and crippling his aunt, as a "particularly flagrant example of the leniency of the law and misguided community sympathy."[21]

The logical response for many was to further insulate themselves from a seemingly unresponsive and deceitful enforcement system. Motorists carried cameras, notepads, and measuring tapes to personally document their traffic difficulties, hoping to provide some legal counterweight to the prima facie powers of the police. Predictably, most looked to secure favorable witnesses or to "carefully point out to his witnesses any feature of the accident that seem to him to indicate his own blamelessness." One suggested that it was essential "to establish the fact that [your] car was not being driven at an excessive rate of speed, and the car owner should be sure that his witnesses have this fact firmly implanted in their minds." Jordan was outraged when the driver who struck her did just that. Following the maxim that the best defense was a good offense, attorneys routinely countersued the victims of a crash, claiming contributory negligence. Jordan mockingly surmised that

> in his first collision, the victim does not expect this, and so does not prepare for it. In the second he may be unconscious and unable to respond to the stimulus of the knowledge. But in any collision after then, if he is able to stagger about on his legs, he learns to lay his fellow victims in a more or less neat row by the roadside and to hustle about among the spectators with a notebook and pencil, jotting down the names and addresses of witnesses who will testify in his behalf when the case comes up in court.

Driver advocacy groups, like the American Automobile Owners Association, offered bond money and legal assistance as a regular benefit to dues-paying members. Their journal published chilling accounts of their constituents easily acquitted on charges ranging from drunk driving to vehicular manslaughter. One, who claimed it was *his* misfortune "to run over a seven year old girl," boasted of being out on bond less than ten minutes after the police booked him.[22]

Perhaps no comments better illustrate the troubled relationship between motorists and law enforcement than these statements of pride in eluding the traffic bureaucracy. Repeatedly, motorists indicated their great satisfaction in beating the "game" of law enforcement. As early as 1910, civil disobedience included breaking speed limits, evading local police, and ignoring summonses. Many rationalized that safety regulation was "taking all the joys out of motoring." Others drove with the "deliberate intention of violating the laws, as a means of adding a little spice to an otherwise humdrum life." A common opinion "considered [it] rather smart to be hauled up in a station-house and fined." The Canton *News* reported in 1922 that most motorists felt "justified in boasting of the number of times they have been fined for speeding—it is assumed by them to set them apart from the common kind" of driver. Others enjoyed "laughingly telling the officer who made the arrest . . . that next time he won't be caught so easily." By 1942, one in eight summoned violators simply refused to appear in court. Melville Ferguson assuaged his conscience (and his lighter wallet) by taking "pride to think that [his] car, which had tipped the scale loaded at 5,800 pounds, dragging a trailer which weighed 1,400 pounds, could be legally attested to have made forty-two miles an hour."[23]

Meanwhile, others expressed outrage at the widespread lack of "shame and humiliation in being arrested for endangering the lives of his fellows by his rate of travel over a highway." One reformer lectured, "Don't be proud to tell how fast you made a certain forty-mile run. Be ashamed to tell it, and then there will be some hope." This widespread and "frivolous attitude on the part of traffic law violators" undermined respect for the law, frustrated the law-enforcement community, and "exacted a terrible toll" in its failure to check recklessness.[24]

But while drivers might comfort themselves by assuming a defiant stance toward "unjust" motor laws and corrupt traffic enforcement, they could not ignore the growing reality of traffic accidents. Here again the powerful individual values of the automotive love affair helped many to deny their obligations to reduce collective risk. Citizens viewed accidents not as the inevitable by-product of an inherently dangerous technology but rather as the wholly avoidable consequence of individual driver apathy, laziness, and ineptitude. To this view, collisions indicated "careless and inefficient driving" or a "failure of the person behind the wheel to carefully consider all the factors involved." New and dangerous personal freedoms did not cause accidental death, the "stupidity, self-indulgence, and in no small degree exaggerated sense of importance" of bad drivers did.[25]

Unlike the conflict generated over legal and enforcement reforms, this public view merged seamlessly with the prevailing expert opinion before 1940. As noted in Chapters 4, 5, and 6, all agreed that the "accident-prone" driver was the principal problem. Psychiatric professionals and medical doctors, like Dana Hubbard, diagnosed the accident prone as those who exhibited "fidgets, restlessness, unnecessary hurrying" and other "irritations of the brain." In 1939, Charles Lawshe, a prominent auto safety advocate, summarized what represented well-accepted qualities of "the repeater." These included "the 'ne'er-do-well,' the paranoiac and hot-headed, the timid soul, the drug addict and alcoholic, the insane, the older man and the very young man, the person under unusual physical or mental strain, persons with intelligence quotients under 75 or 80 and between 110 and 125, and [all other] 'reckless persons.'" Judges sanctioned these views by describing many traffic offenders as "physically and mentally unfit to drive" and a "new enemy" of the republic. By 1940, safety reformers reassured drivers troubled by speed traps, bossy cops, and justice mills that future legislation "for accident prevention ought to be launched, not against the entire driving population, but against this dangerous minority."[26]

Fortunately for native-born male drivers, the dominant social biases helped define this "dangerous minority" in terms of nationality, class, and gender. While, as Chapters 2 and 3 show, the road was not limited by these qualities, the concept of a good driver certainly was. Researchers stretched small or biased data sets to argue that women were three times more likely to suffer from "nervousness" behind the wheel. Other studies highlighted how women performed "poorer as a group than the men on the tests involving muscular quickness and accuracy," even if they appeared statistically safer behind the wheel. Predictably, experts also asserted that immigrants, the poor, and the undereducated lacked the normative (and redemptive) qualities that constituted the love affair.[27]

Once cataloged, accident-prone drivers lost much of the public's sympathy for their "natural lawlessness." For these miscreants, law enforcement must be swift, sure, and severe. Where judges once agonized over the proper sentence for the "honorable, respectable, privileged member of an upper class," they readily agreed that those "falling under this [new] classification should be eliminated from our highways." John Maher reasoned, "if we send the confirmed criminal to prison for the protection of society in general, why shouldn't we remove from the highway the chronic reckless and negligent driver? There is only one answer: we should." As noted in Chapter 5, from 1930 to 1940, courts thus called upon scores of psychiatrists, medical doctors, jurists, reformers, and social scientists to confirm the biased assumptions of the "accident-prone" analysis. They assuaged the conscience of the American driving public, who knew all along that "the problem" resided with the other guy.[28]

Within this context—the widespread presumptions of excessive or unfair enforcement, the powerful normative values of "good" driving, and the professional acknowledgment of the accident-prone menace—it is no wonder that public confessions of personal responsibility for auto accidents remained rare. Admitting culpability confirmed one's dubious status as a flivverboob; as a childish motor moron in need of constant supervision; or as a "new enemy" of the automotive republic. Furthermore, the Great Depression, the resulting political activism of the New Deal, and World War II validated authoritative, top-down hierarchical solutions. Donning their grey flannel suits, many Americans willfully deferred to the axioms of technical experts, the order of rational bureaucracies, and the fiscal logic of big business.

During World War II, industry produced tangible benefits to sustain this faith. President Franklin Roosevelt relied on auto executives, like GM's William Knudson, to maximize America's potential as the arsenal of democracy. Automakers quickly converted to wartime production, efficiently funneling billions of public dollars into tanks, trucks, and munitions. Given the industry's wholehearted adoption of Fordism in the previous decades, James Flink concludes, the "Axis powers stood no chance of winning a war of logistics in which the motor vehicle and mass production played the key roles."[29]

Domestic concerns over auto accidents and highway safety faded from public view. Given the magnitude of the war this hardly seems surprising. But auto-related fatalities also fell dramatically during the conflict. From a high of 38,142 deaths in 1941, the nation saw a 40 percent drop in auto fatalities, to 22,727 deaths, only two years later. These gains had less to do with improved safety consciousness than with the realities of a wartime society. Roosevelt suspended domestic auto production in February 1942, which meant fewer new cars on America's already overcrowded streets. Rationing of gasoline, rubber, and oil lowered the total number of vehicle miles traveled, thereby decreasing the potential for accidents. The administration established a national speed limit of 35 miles per hour in an effort to further conserve fuel. Lowered speeds diminished the severity of the collisions that resulted. Finally, millions of young men now found themselves in boot camp rather than behind the wheel.

The immediate postwar period took many of these fortuities for granted, producing a uniquely promiscuous, even hedonistic, period in American car culture. The era spanning from 1946 to 1966 saw both consumer and producer extravagance and a willful repudiation of personal responsibility for auto accidents. In terms of manufacturers and auto engineers, General Motors, Ford Motor Company, and Chrysler Corporation enjoyed unparalleled success and freedom from regulation. Once refitted for peacetime production, the "big three" controlled over 94 percent of the massive American market. The lack of significant competition (from either new arrivals or imports) allowed Detroit to shift resources away from product innovation and toward the satisfaction of limitless consumer desire.

Scholars have long noted the self-indulgent absurdities in auto design from 1946 to 1966. From the elongated tail fins of the Cadillac to the protruding chrome "Dagmars" and miscellaneous "gorp" attached to other makes and models, the new styling did little more than pad the bottom line. Larger, more muscular cars added a dose of virility to earlier, more respectable models. While arguably attractive in their unapologetic excess, the slapdash ornamentation and the Buck Rogers "forward look" design (that sacrificed visibility and safety for a sleek resemblance to an airplane fuselage) reflected and underscored the marketing delirium of the age.[30]

Pent-up consumer demand generated a seller's market. But local dealers operated at significantly closer margins. In the highly competitive retail arena, dealers placed intense pressures on consumers to spend lavishly for lucrative aftermarket improvements and services. Compelled by manufacturers to accept millions of "new" models every year (as GM's John DeLorean later admitted, most were simply last year's vehicles with "new wrinkles in the sheet metal"), dealers adopted hard-sell tactics, used bait-and-switch promotions, or simply cheated their customers to close the sale. By the late 1950s, consumers esteemed dealers with the same scornful contempt once reserved for officious highway cops or corrupt traffic court judges. Indeed, consumer resentment over the "scandalous treatment" by dealers sparked the revival of safety reform in the 1960s.[31]

Predictably, expressions of the automotive love affair changed dramatically under these conditions. The cultivated taste for showy auto exteriors and the diminished concern for accident safety accentuated the strengthening individualistic aspects of America's postwar culture. Sounding more like an anthropologist than the country's premier writer, William Faulkner observed that the postwar "American really loves nothing *but* his automobile: not his wife his child nor even his bank-account first." Designers, advertisers, and consumers reveled in the stimulating excess and sexual overtones of cars and driving. Critics wrote of "marketing binges" driven by an "orgy of nonfunctional styling." Art critic Robert Hughes christened the bloated and bejeweled passenger car of the 1950s the "great symbol of America's new post-war life," one "packed with the symbolism of sex and power." Armed with high-compression V-8 engines "they had the tails of rockets . . . chromium breasts like Jane Mansfield, and when you hit the brakes the rear end [lit] up like a robot animal in heat."[32]

Detroit's temporary market dominance and its ability to sidestep federal oversight shifted the national auto safety debate in significant ways. On the one hand, sensing a profit, automakers took the lead in *selling* basic safety engineering as a new marketable feature. Ford and Chrysler, to their credit, offered optional "safety packages"—which included a padded dashboard, sturdier door locks, seatbelts, and a collapsible steering column—in the mid-1950s. The public, convinced of their own good driving, showed little interest in paying for these upgrades or in substituting safety for faddish styling. Unlike in earlier decades, motorists did not chide Detroit for advertising larger, heavier, faster, and more dangerous cars from 1950 to 1970.[33]

In addition, private medical professionals replaced public officials as a leading voice in the safety reform community. Unlike the 1920s and 30s, when doctors joined a broad coalition of safety advocates that included engineers, businessmen, insurers, educators, and enforcement professionals, in the 1950s most medical professionals approached the accident problem as outsiders. Their primary concern did not center on how to prevent avoidable accidents or identify accident-prone drivers but on how to limit the severity of the collisions that inevitably occurred. In 1948, Detroit plastic surgeon Claire Straith gathered statistical data on various auto injuries. He noted that serious lacerations and traumas arose when passengers were thrown against the instruments, dials, and other projections within the confines of the cabin. That same year, Dr. Fletcher Woodward compared these "second crash" injuries to those of other high-energy wrecks, such as airplane disasters. He too found that simple restraints, used regularly by pilots but rarely by motorists, often made the difference between life and death. Aided by the work of Hugh DeHaven, an engineer who plotted the range of impact forces and their effect on the human body, these and other physicians shifted the public debate away from the moral character of the road and driver toward the objective physical characteristics of the accident.[34]

The term "crashworthiness" describes the intended goal of their work. The concept assumed the inevitability of transit collisions. Even in a perfect world, they argued, accidents happened and injuries ensued. This new paradigm conserved the hard-edged views of inevitability expressed earlier by the courts and police. Moreover, crashworthiness placed no responsibility on the driver involved in an accident. Their decisions might influence the immediate cause of a crash, but the sheer number of situational probabilities rendered the search for accident-prone miscreants a wild goose chase.[35]

Crashworthiness also describes the prevailing attitude toward auto safety today. Rather than rely on regulatory bureaucracies, their rules, and training to improve conditions or driver behavior, most Americans now admit that engineers alone can protect motorists from themselves. Television commercials enthusiastically reenact collision impact tests, including slow-motion footage of flailing crash dummies, crumpled molding, and showering glass, as a reassuring gesture to this resigned public consensus about the inevitability of auto accidents.[36]

In tandem with the appearance of crashworthiness, modern consumer culture also propelled auto safety reform in new directions. Fittingly, present-day federal oversight emerged as a variation of consumer protection. In 1958, Senator Mike Monroney spearheaded efforts to rein in the hard-sell tactics of dealers and their suppliers. The Automobile Information Disclosure Act (or Monroney Act) required every new car to carry a sticker clearly indicating the manufacturer's suggested retail price and all standard and optional features available for that specific vehicle. These "Monroney stickers," still in use today, offer consumers minimal contractual guarantees. As historian Paul Gikas concludes, safety reform was reborn through consumption, where security became "synonymous with safe *packaging*" not safe driving.[37]

The combination of crashworthiness, consumer rights, and the smoldering dissatisfaction with Detroit's marketing and design policies banded into a "perfect storm" of regulatory reform in the early 1960s. These efforts coincided with what James Flink labels the third (and final) stage of American automotive consciousness. Beginning at that time, citizens appeared less willing to define automobility in progressive, laudatory, or economically beneficial terms. The accumulated frustrations with accidents, congestion, pollution, poor industry leadership, and outright larceny reversed the perceived benefits of the love affair. Where the relationship once validated individual characteristics of the driver, the heightened costs no longer justified these luxuries. Resigned to living with auto accidents, the public demanded the least deadly consequences. Again using the language of consumer protection—where precaution emerged as a basic *right* of individual consumers not the *duty* of a democratic society—critics like Bishop G. Bromley Oxam, Lewis Mumford, John Keats, Jeffrey O'Connell, and Ralph Nader spearheaded the attack on a complacent and arrogant auto industry.

Daniel Patrick Moynihan's 1959 essay, titled "Epidemic on the Highway," built upon the anxieties of medical professionals and the consumer and led to a national re-examination of auto safety legislation. Aided by the dogged committee work of Senators Abe Ribicoff (D-NY), Warren Magnuson (D-WA), and Gaylord Nelson (D-WI) and Representatives Kenneth Roberts (D-AL), John Beamer (D-IN), Harley Staggers (D-WV), and James MacKay (D-GA), the expanding federal investigation focused mostly on industry abuses and the obvious lack of self-discipline in engineering safe cars. Notably, they made little effort to highlight the responsibilities of drivers.[38]

The rise of Ralph Nader as consumer safety advocate reflects the volatility of the historic moment. A 1958 graduate of Harvard Law School, Nader studied the history of safety engineering and the early efforts of the U.S. auto industry. As with previous generations, national periodicals like *The Nation, Time* magazine, and the *Christian Science Monitor* brought added attention to safety engineering and publicized the indifference shown by the Big Three. In "The Safe Car You Can't Buy," Nader charged that Detroit ignored the loss of life simply because automakers saw no profit in building safer cars. He released a book-length investigation, *Unsafe at Any Speed,* in 1965, that focused on the well-known design flaws of GM's over-powered compact car, the Chevrolet Corvair. In spite of clear evidence that the vehicle suffered from excessive oversteer (the car's heavy rear end swerved out of control during high-speed cornering), company executives refused to recall the defective model or even make simple and low-cost corrections. GM under-scored its own disdain for public criticism by launching a secret (yet "routine") investigation of Nader's personal life to dig up compromising dirt in the hope of discrediting Nader's charges. When the scandal broke, and GM was found guilty of unlawfully invading Nader's privacy, the public mood shifted, setting the stage for the most sweeping auto safety legislation in American history.[39]

The resulting National Traffic and Motor Vehicle Safety Act and the Highway Safety Act, passed in 1966, fundamentally altered the motoring responsibili-ties of both the private and public sectors. For the first time, federal regulators required manufacturers to include specified safety features, such as seat belts, head rests (to reduce whiplash), collapsible steering columns, and shatterproof safety glass. The seventeen specifications expanded to twenty-eight by 1969. The acts established the National Highway Safety Bureau (now the National Highway Traffic Safety Administration) to examine road and car design, required manu-facturers to institute recalls of defective products, and formally tied highway appropriations to the states' effective enforcement of these federal safety provi-sions. Supporting Flink's contention of a new "auto consciousness" in America, John Graham notes how the legislation "radical as it was—occurred swiftly and without serious opposition."[40]

In addition to unifying safety standards under a centralized federal agency, the new reforms officially absolved individual drivers of their responsibility for both accidents and collective safety. Perhaps the greatest irony of Ralph Nader's advocacy (often nostalgically remembered as a form of "Sixties" grass-roots so-cial activism) lies in the fact that citizens became passive consumers of safety—like intelligent crash dummies—rather than active agents of reform. Indeed, the laws ignored driver behavior completely. Enforcement officials now expect reck-less driving just as motorists expect safety protection as a consumer right. As Daniel Albert concluded, the 1966 National Traffic and Motor Vehicle Safety Act "ushered in a *new* era in the history of traffic safety with a *new* network of experts who have a *new* strategy for reducing traffic injuries and death."[41]

Placing more recent changes in automotive safety within the broader historical arc of the twentieth century remains problematic on a number of fronts. Our closeness to the subject makes it difficult, if not impossible, to contain contemporary biases. Nor can we know the long-term efficiency of current policies. Will "zero tolerance" of inebriation or universal passive restraint systems make permanent inroads into America's driving culture? Ulrich Beck's *Risk Society* proposes both useful and compelling reasons to speculate on the changes to come.[42]

Beck's approach in *Risk Society,* first published in 1992, could easily be termed postmodern or postindustrial, but it differs in significant ways. The heart of his inquiry concerns the collapse of a public consensus over the costs and benefits of modernity. The world lurched, in recent decades, as a result of global social realignments and mass migrations, a technological and information revolution that we are only just beginning to understand, the rapid expansion of individualism (and desire for individual agency), and the deeply conservative reaction by institutions and values under assault. In his first sentence, Beck admits his theme "is the unremarkable prefix 'post'. . . . the key word of our times." But the terms *postmodern* and *postindustrial* are already in wide circulation. These words imply a variety of cultural responses to late modernity (many deeply qualified by race, gender, class, and ethnicity). Vague yet provocative concepts, like simulacras, hyper-reality, and deconstruction, suggest to scholars the difficulty of studying, much less generalizing about, shared social trends. Nor was Beck willing to accidentally append his theory to the triumphant assumptions of postindustrial scholars, who argued at the end of the Cold War that western liberalism and industrial capitalism now represented the lone operating ideologies on the planet; it was the end of history. While Beck could have used the terms *postmodern* or *postindustrial* to accurately describe his thesis, the resulting confusion and intellectual enmity would have rendered his ideas to bits.[43]

Beck's assumptions are indeed grounded in the firm realities of modern life. Like Karl Marx and Max Weber, who first proposed material and rational explanations for the rise of modern societies, Beck looks to the key institutions responsible for maintaining the dominant social, economic, and political structures: family, work, business, government, and, above all, bureaucratic experts and hierarchical authority. Beck follows these lines, but he is not a materialist. His focus is on new shared social values and the social capital they generate.[44]

Marx and Weber looked to industrial production as the primary means of understanding and defining modernity. Both recognized that the central paradox of industrial capitalism lay in the way it unfairly distributed goods, especially capital. For Marx this led (or will lead) to an eventual conflict between those who produce wealth and those guilty of robbing laborers of a fair share. Scandals like Enron or Teapot Dome can make this scenario attractive. By contrast, Weber argued that those concerned with the asymmetrical distribution of goods turned to and empowered democracy, central governance, and especially the neutral hands of bureaucratic experts. These institutions could check the growing power of capital and ameliorate the worst excesses of modern societies. While Marx seemed doubtful about the efficacy of traditional social institutions and cultural values (e.g., gender or nationalism), both Weber and neo-Marxists saw how the family, the corporation, unions, political parties, race, and gender were used by groups to retain some control over the distribution of goods.[45]

Beck relies on these founding academic principles with one central shift in emphasis. Whereas modern societies evolved to address the unequal distribution of "goods," postmodern societies were increasingly driven by the need to address the very universal distribution of "bads." These drawbacks include corporate downsizing, globalization, the loss of power by the nation-state, and, for Beck, the spread of universal risk. Industrial pollution has emerged as the most obvious example of this type of risk. Once confined to poorer sections of town and rationalized (by the middle class and above) as merely the "latent side-effect" of progress, the costs of pollution now weigh on us all. Asthma, emphysema, and chronic allergies affect everyone regardless of race, gender, ethnicity, or class. One's reliance on family, unions, party affiliation, or job status may assist them in acquiring *goods* but are meaningless in protecting them from *bads*. Moreover, the technical experts and bureaucracies once trusted to propose rational solutions to society's ills have emerged as the primary culprits. Like the auto accident, modern risk is man made. Beck notes, as risks become "globalized, and subject to public criticism and scientific investigation, [risks] come, so to speak, out of the closet and achieve a central importance in social and political debates."[46]

Beck's proposal, that postindustrial societies practice "reflexive modernization" to deal with risk, returns us to the modern response to auto accidents. Where citizens once heedlessly trusted extended social networks and institutions (family, business, and so on) to protect them from the vicissitudes of the marketplace, they now intently and privately reflect upon the individual risks that they could control. The ease of access to and explosion of public information—via mass media and now the internet—short-circuits the public's reliance on privileged experts. Quitting smoking is a perfect example. While once widely accepted in popular culture and (dishonestly) validated by the business and medical communities, smoking is seen today as an improperly risky personal choice. One can greatly reduce their susceptibility to disease by controlling personal behavior. Again, traditional associations appear as meaningless relics of a producer-obsessed past. The strength of *Risk Society* is in Beck's ability to clearly yet powerfully articulate these changes. As he writes,

> The driving force in the [old] class society can be summarized in the phrase: *I am hungry!* The movement set in motion by the risk society, on the other hand, is expressed in the statement: *I am afraid!* The *commonality of anxiety* takes the place of the *commonality of need.* The type of risk society marks in

this sense a social epoch in which *solidarity from anxiety* arises and becomes a political force.

Beck honestly admits that we do not know how this social capital accumulates. "It is still completely unclear" for example, "how the binding force of anxiety operates, even whether it works." How, under these assumptions, will "risk communities" withstand traditional social stress caused by racism, war, or economic depression? What about the once-pervasive assumptions of liberal utilitarianism, where governments exist to provide the greatest good for the greatest number? As Gabe Mythen writes of the risk society hypothesis, solutions are "keenly contested by politicians, scientific experts, media professionals and the general public." But this lack of consensus is what "makes risk such a fascinating topic of inquiry."[47]

Beck's theory of a risk society conditioned by reflexive modernity explains many of the changes seen in American auto safety over the past thirty years. Increasingly, citizens relied on their own personal resources to understand and respond to the threat of accidental death. In a risk society, individual behavior again plays the central role in avoiding accidents. Zero-tolerance laws, which mandate harsh penalties for drunk or otherwise impaired drivers, remove the doubt from traffic courts and law enforcement. Mandatory seat belt and child-restraint statutes, as well as the growing pressures on industry to maximize passive safety systems like airbags and computerized braking, eliminate the uncertainties of the secondary crash (unrestrained bodies striking the interior of the vehicle). State-mandated auto inspections and liability insurance (as well as the growing popularity of accident-free discounts) rein in the distrusted promises of industry executives. Restrictions applied to inexperienced or aged drivers—such as laws requiring a parent or legal guardian to accompany all drivers under the age of sixteen—and the appearance of aggressive safety advocacy groups like Mothers Against Drunk Drivers (MADD) solidify the perception that individual citizens are deeply engaged in maximizing their personal safety within a risk-laden future.

But the ambiguity of a risk society remains an open question. Why is it that modern Americans live longer today than ever before yet they feel less secure? What drives the country to fixate on the threat of terrorism, which in 2001 cost nearly three thousand lives, while ignoring threats posed by more common and possibly more controllable threats like auto accidents, which led to over 42,000 deaths that same year? Part of this paradox rests in the transitional state of the risk society. The residual trust and confidence placed in bureaucratic solutions remains strong. For example, the administration of President George W. Bush effectively employed concepts of public risk and personal safety to promote or enhance centralized political authority following the September 11 attacks. Clearly we stand unwilling to abandon all collective bureaucracies in the search for personal security.

A second wrinkle remains in the personal construction of risk and safety. One case study testing Beck's hypothesis, by sociologists John Tulloch and Deborah Lupton, examined ways that people describe risky behaviors. Not surprisingly, perceptions of risk rested upon a number of variables. The pair found many middle-aged respondents who now regretted, or at least admitted, foolish behavior in their youth, including drunk driving and sexual promiscuity. Women more frequently exhibited concerns over physical risks than men. Males, on the other hand, tended to worry more about material threats, such as unemployment and debt. Tulloch and Lupton conclude that "it was clear from the interviews that the risks to which people felt they were exposed were very much phrased through their own position in the life course, their gender, age, sexual identity, occupation, and so on."[48]

Such personal relativity exposes a bias in risk analysis that this study has sought to correct for early auto safety. In terms of American automobility, the irrational and emotional love affair factored very large in the construction of "safe" motoring. On the one hand, the uncertainty and novelty of driving clearly placed people in harm's way. But on the other hand, many recognized these risks and turned them into personal challenges to be conquered. For Tulloch and Lupton's interviewees, who sounded very much like the early defenders of the automotive love affair, these modern risks added a "heightened degree of emotional intensity that [was] pleasurable in its ability to take [respondents] out of the here-and-now, the mundane, everyday nature of life." In conceptualizing risk this way—not as an irrational fear of the unknown but as a negotiated contest between the perceived costs and anticipated benefits—modern societies prioritize and, when needed, detach the fears of accidental loss. Tulloch and Lupton conclude that "people tend to see familiar or voluntary risks as less serious than risks that are new or imposed upon them, and that they are more likely to be concerned about risks that are rare and memorable than those that are seen as common but disastrous." In this way, and in spite of the probabilities, we fear airplane crashes or terrorist attacks more than the everyday automobile accident.[49]

Risk societies also display a profoundly new and combative stance toward rational bureaucratic solutions. Where we once trusted risk management experts, like educators and engineers, to solve the problems of automobility, today's legislative solutions appear to banish or severely curtail the powers of "the system." Indeed, zero tolerance is not just a catchphrase for anti–drunk driving campaigns but rather the motto of the risk society. As Beck writes, "the calculation of risk as it has been established so far by science and legal institutions *collapses*" under these new assumptions. Bureaucracies, like the National Safety Council or federal safety commissions, "no longer [grasp] this late modern reality."[50]

Beck's thesis offers an interesting vantage to speculate about the changes and continuities in the cultural and legal response to auto safety in contemporary America. Clearly, drivers today place less trust in the pronouncements of safety experts who, before 1940, effectively defined this country's response to the accident crisis. The "three E's" appear today as simplistic and hopelessly outdated largely because the notion of risk contained within this solution no longer resonates with the driving public. When asked to define risk, few of Tulloch and Lupton's interviewees presented "risk in technical terms as a probability, approximating the 'official' definition which represents risk as a neutral phenomenon." These formal and "dispassionate definitions" lacked the immediacy and emotional impact of risks understood by those experiencing them. In the risk society, Elizabeth Jordan now earns a hearing from an empathetic public.[51]

Ironically, with the lessened influence of technical safety specialists and risk managers comes a heightened deference to enforcement officials. Certainly drivers still resent being ticketed, but the trend toward zero tolerance and the cultural renaissance of enforcement officials into (post-9/11) "heroes" appears to have significantly altered the public's relationship to policing bodies. Perhaps because of the personalized assumptions of reflexive modernity we see these officials as agents of *our* bidding rather than the meddlesome bureaucrats of the NSC. Where Hoover's safety councils might today trigger politicized denouncements about the heavy hand of government's bloated bureaucracies, the execution of Bonnie and Clyde by Phares's T-Men would surely be placed in the permanent rotation on America's cable news channels. Today, enforcement clearly eclipses education and engineering as the preferred public response to auto accidents.

While these changes contrast sharply with the assumptions of the driving public before 1940, perceptions of the automotive love affair seem to be returning to their origins. Certainly American advertisers and manufacturers have not stepped away from highlighting the pleasures of driving as opposed to the logic of safe and efficient transportation. Moreover, the conquest of risk (even if only perceptional) validates and strengthens the core components of the automotive love affair. Tulloch and Lupton found that "voluntary risk-taking" like driving "is often pursued for the sake of facing or conquering fear, displaying courage, seeking excitement and thrills, and achieving self-actualization and a sense of personal agency." The pair found "evidence in many people's accounts of positive meanings associated with risk: adventure, the emotions of excitement, elation and enjoyment, the opportunity to engage in self-actualization and self-improvement." Moreover, engaging modern risks allows individuals the "means of conforming to gender attributes that are valued by the participants, or, in contrast, as a means of challenging gender stereotypes that are considered restrictive and limiting of one's agency or potential." If these observations are accurate, then pronouncements of the death of the automotive love affair appear premature.[52]

Finally, a risk society returns citizens back to the original paradox posed by mass automobility. If driving represents an act of personal freedom—one strongly supported by cultural values, the marketplace, governance, and technology—then what do motorists owe each other as they exercise these liberties?

In the years before World War II, such obligations split between the personal morality of the motorist and the rational utility of mass society. With the relative loss in prestige of bureaucratic solutions and the heightened insulation of personal responsibility from consumerism, who now owns the responsibility for safety? In arguing against the omniscience of bureaucratic risk managers (who he sees at the heart of the "system concept"), Beck notes, "The causes [of risk] dribble away into a general amalgam of agents and conditions, reactions and counter-reactions, which brings social certainty and popularity to the concept of system. This reveals in exemplary fashion the ethical significance of the system concept: *one can do something and continue doing it without having to take personal responsibility for it. . . . this is the way the 'hot potato' is passed.*"[53]

Addressing the strengths and weaknesses of risk remains a compelling and largely unexamined feature of modernity. The work of Beck, Anthony Giddens, and others offers useful starting points by which historians can reexamine social, cultural, and technological change in the twentieth century.

Unfortunately, in terms of the public's response to automotive risks, one returns again and again to the unsatisfactory conclusion that ambiguity, uncertainty, and expediency define our relationship with the car. While we want accidents to end (or at least decline to the minimal number predicted by inevitability) we appear unwilling to enact measures that might insure a "perfected" transportation system. The primary reason for this apparent schizophrenia, I contend, remains the ceaseless appeal of the automotive love affair. Auto safety advocate J. O. Munn, who wrote the opening quote for a 1924 driver instruction manual, titled *Safety for Twenty Million Automobile Drivers,* understood this powerful and bewitching twentieth-century symbiosis between man and machine. It remains a fitting conclusion, even an explanation for why Americans struggled in vain to solve the dilemma of the car's accidental freedoms from 1900 to 1940. Munn wrote, "I am speed made subject to human will. I give mankind dominion over distance. I open the avenues of all the world to humanity. I enlarge the radius of human life. . . . I give to his body the speed and mobility of his ambition. . . . I give supremacy of locomotion to man whom nature made slower than the beasts. I am individual transportation free of all laborious limitations. *I am the Automobile.*"[54] Realizing this psychological predicament—between the love of freedom, power, and excitement and the threatening physical risks that come with modernity—remains a necessary prerequisite in understanding our own relationship to the automobile and our ability to establish a just system of public safety.

Notes

Introduction

1. Sinclair Lewis, "Adventures in Automobumming: Want a Lift?" *Saturday Evening Post* (December 27, 1919): 70.

2. Sinclair Lewis, *Babbitt* (New York: Harcourt, Brace and World, 1922), 23.

3. Ibid., 150, 152.

4. Ibid., 26, 29.

5. Sinclair Lewis, "Adventures in Automobumming: The Great American Frying Pan," *Saturday Evening Post* (January 3, 1920): 25; Lewis, "Adventures in Automobumming: Gasoline Gypsies," *Saturday Evening Post* (December 20, 1919): 5; Lewis, "Adventures in Automobumming: Want a Lift?" 70.

6. Lewis, "Adventures in Automobumming: Want a Lift?" 66.

7. Ibid.

8. Mark Schorer, *Sinclair Lewis: An American Life* (New York: McGraw-Hill, 1961), 241, 291, 300–301.

9. Peter Steinhart, "Our Off-Road Fantasy," in David L. Lewis and Lawrence Goldstein, eds., *The Automobile and American Culture* (Ann Arbor: University of Michigan Press, 1980), 346. Fans of Federico Fellini's 1963 film *8½,* which used this image at the start of the movie, can appreciate the sense of claustrophobia and purposelessness contained in Steinhart's allusion.

10. "Deaths: Final Data for 2001," *National Vital Statistics Reports* 52, no. 3 (September 18, 2003); Rajesh Subramanian, "Motor Vehicle Crashes as a Leading Cause of Death in the United States, 2001," U.S. Department of Transportation, National Highway Traffic Safety Administration, December 2003; U.S. Department of Transportation, National Highway Traffic Safety Administration, "Motor Vehicle Traffic Fatalities and Fatality Rates," July 23, 2003.

11. Ulrich Beck, *Risk Society: Towards a New Modernity* (London: Sage Publications, 1992); Anthony Giddens, *The Consequences of Modernity* (Palo Alto, CA: Stanford University Press, 1991). Beck's German-language manuscript was published in 1986. For a more extensive treatment of "risk societies," see the concluding chapter.

12. "The Flurry of Anti-Speed Legislation," *Horseless Age* 9, no. 65 (January 15, 1902), cited in James J. Flink, *America Adopts the Automobile, 1895–1910* (Cambridge, MA: MIT Press, 1970), 184; John Farson, "The Rights of the Automobilist," *World To-Day* 10 (March 1906): 308.

13. Flink, *America Adopts the Automobile,* 184; Thomas H. Russell, *Automobile Driving Self-Taught: An Exhaustive Treatise on the Operation, Management and Care of Motor Cars* (Chicago: Charles C. Thompson, 1914), 224.

14. Harlan C. Hines, "Morons on the Macadam," *Scribner's Magazine* 82 (November 1927): 596, 599, 600; John J. Maher, *Mind over Motor* (Detroit: n.p., 1937), 21.

15. For more on *Death on Ridge Road,* see Anedith Jo Bond Nash, "Death on the Highway: The Automobile Wreck in American Culture, 1920–1940," Ph.D. dissertation, University of Minnesota, 1983, 100–125.

16. For an excellent overview of Weber's ideas and intellectual indebtedness, see Fritz Ringer, *Max Weber: An Intellectual Biography* (Chicago: University of Chicago Press, 2004). Weber quoted in ibid., 221. Emphasis in original.

Chapter 1. The Car and American Life, 1900–1940

1. See Warren J. Belasco, *Americans on the Road: From Autocamp to Motel: 1910–1945* (Cambridge, MA: MIT Press, 1979). Two popular movies of the day—*It Happened One Night* and *The Grapes of Wrath*—show just how charming these camps, at their best, could be. Of course, Steinbeck also shows how dehumanizing camping can become when the amenities of home and community are absent. See also "What Cities Think of Their Tourist Camps," *Literary Digest* 105 (April 12, 1930): 46–48.

2. For an account of the Ford-Firestone-Edison-Harding trip, see *New York Times,* July 23, 1921, 7; *New York Times,* July 24, 1921, 1, 2; *New York Times,* July 25, 1921, 1, 3.

3. *New York Times,* July 24, 1921, 1.

4. Ironically, while Harding was clearly the least accomplished of the *Übermenschen* (or supermen), he was also the only one to join a white supremacist organization, the Ku Klux Klan.

5. Belasco, *Americans on the Road,* vii, ix; John C. Long and John D. Long, *Motor Camping* (New York: Dodd, Mead, 1923), 1–2.

6. *New York Times,* July 24, 1921, 1.

7. Clay McShane, *Down the Asphalt Path: The Automobile and the American City* (New York: Columbia University Press, 1994), 125.

8. Examples of pioneers and practitioners of a technology system approach include Thomas Parke Hughes in his study of Edison and electric power, *Networks of Power: Electrification in Western Society, 1880–1930* (Baltimore: Johns Hopkins University Press, 1983); Harold Platt, *The Electric City: Energy and the Growth of the Chicago Area, 1880–1930* (Chicago: University of Chicago Press, 1991); David Nye, *Electrifying America: Social Meanings of a New Technology, 1880–1940* (Cambridge, MA: MIT Press, 1990); and Merritt Roe Smith and Leo Marx, eds., *Does Technology Drive History: The Dilemma of Technological Determinism* (Cambridge , MA: MIT Press, 1995). James J. Flink, "Three Stages of American Automobile Consciousness," *American Quarterly* 24, no. 4 (October 1972): 457; Daniel M. Albert, "Order out of Chaos: Automobile Safety, Technology and Society, 1925 to 1965," Ph.D. dissertation, University of Michigan, 1997, 22.

9. "Automobility" is a term that Flink credits to John C. Burnham, "The Gasoline Tax and the Automobile Revolution," *Mississippi Valley Historical Review* 48 (December 1961): 435–459. Contingency and technological change is evident in most leading works, including Flink, Rae, McShane, Paul Barrett, and Belasco; see also Michael Berger, *The Devil Wagon in God's Country: The Automobile and Social Change in Rural America, 1893–1929* (Hamden, CT: Archon, 1979); Norman Moline, *Mobility and the Small Town, 1900–1930: Transportation Change in Oregon, Illinois,* Department of Geography Research Paper no. 132 (Chicago: University of Chicago Press, 1971); Blaine Brownell, "Symbol of Modernity: Attitudes towards the Automobile in Southern Cities in the 1920s," *American Quarterly* 24 (March 1972): 20–44, and David L. Lewis, *The Public Image of Henry Ford* (Detroit: Wayne State University Press, 1976).

10. French quote in Tom Lewis, *Divided Highway: Building the Interstate Highways, Transforming American Life* (New York: Penguin Books, 1997, 1999), 33. James J. Flink, *The Automobile Age* (Cambridge, MA: MIT Press, 2001), viii. See also Howard Preston, *Automobile Age Atlanta: The Making of a Southern Metropolis, 1900–1935* (Athens: University of Georgia Press, 1979); Paul Barrett, *The Automobile and Urban Transit: The Formation of Public Policy in Chicago, 1900–1930* (Philadelphia: Temple University Press, 1983); Scott Bottles, *Los Angeles and the Automobile: The Making of the Modern City* (Berkeley: University of California Press, 1988); Corey T. Lesseig, *Automobility: Social Change in the American South, 1909–1939* (New York: Routledge, 2001).

11. James J. Flink writes, "Whereas 44 percent of American families did not own cars in 1927, 41 percent still lacked personal automobility in the form of a family car as late as 1950. This contrasts with only about 13 percent autoless American households at present." *Automobile Age,*

131. See also Joel A. Tarr, *Transportation Innovation and Changing Social Patterns in Pittsburgh, 1850–1934* (Pittsburgh: Public Works Historical Society, 1978).

12. Dorothy Childs Hogner, *South to Padre* (Boston: Lothrop, Lee, and Shepard, 1936), 23–24; Herbert H. Harrison, "The Automobile as a Social Factor," *American Homes and Gardens* 12 (July 1915): 239. James J. Flink, "Three Stages of American Automobile Consciousness," *American Quarterly* 24, no. 4 (October 1972): 460, 472. For comparative numbers see McShane, *Down the Asphalt Path*, 105; for saturation point and the Great Depression, see Flink, *Automobile Age*, 130–131, 189, 192–193.

13. The obvious contradictions, embodied so neatly by Henry Ford—America's only millionaire folk hero, a man of the people obsessed with dictatorial control—were left for the generations following World War I to resolve. Michael McGerr, *A Fierce Discontent: The Rise and Fall of the Progressive Movement in America* (New York: Oxford University Press, 2003), xiv. McGerr, like others, sees the legacy of the Progressive Era stretching all the way to the present. The debate over progressivism and modernization is, of course, extensive and unresolved. For a recent discussion of the former, see McGerr; for an introduction to the latter, see Daniel Joseph Singal, "Towards a Definition of American Modernism," *American Quarterly* 39, no. 1, Special Issue: Modernist Culture in America (Spring 1987): 7–26. 1936 quote in *Texas Parade* 1, no. 7 (December 1936): 2. For a succinct treatment of Ford's contradictory legacy, see Flink, *Automobile Age*, 40–55.

14. *Recent Social Trends in the United States*, Vol. 1 (New York: McGraw-Hill, 1933), 186. As discussed in later chapters, these progressive or modernist values established America's initial relationship with the car and informed the public debate over how best to solve the problem of automobile safety.

15. McShane, *Down the Asphalt Path*, 119.

16. Michael Furman, *Motorcars of the Classic Era* (New York: Henry A. Abrams, 2003), 11; James J. Flink, *America Adopts the Automobile, 1895–1910* (Cambridge, MA: MIT Press, 1970), 29–31. The most obvious legacy of these pioneer days is the way that automotive terminology has retained a certain continental flair: l'automobile, le garage, le chauffeur, le tonneau (enclosed rear seats), and le coupé (two-door closed car).

17. Furman, *Motorcars of the Classic Era*, 11, 12.

18. McShane, *Down the Asphalt Path*, 136–137; Furman, *Motorcars of the Classic Era*, 255. Oddly, the Jordan "Playboy" was intended for the female consumer (McShane, *Down the Asphalt Path*, 140). See also Pamela Walker Laird, "'The Car without a Single Weakness': Early Automobile Advertising," *Technology and Culture* 37, no. 4 (October 1996): 796–812.

19. In terms of sales, the largest manufacturers of automobiles before 1940 were General Motors, Ford, Chrysler, Hudson, Packard, Willys-Overland, Studebaker, and Nash. The Hudson Motor Car Company executive is quoted in Flink, *Automobile Age*, 41; see also ibid., 40–42, 56, 70.

20. Ralph Epstein, *The Automobile Industry: Its Economic and Commercial Development* (Chicago: A. W. Shaw, 1928), 75–77.

21. David A Kirsch, *The Electric Vehicle and the Burden of History* (New Brunswick, NJ: Rutgers University Press, 2000), 203. See also Gijs Mom, *The Electric Vehicle: Technology and Expectations in the Automobile Age* (Baltimore: Johns Hopkins University Press, 2004). Joel Eastman notes how safety concerns prompted Cadillac to examine the electronic self-starter. "Around 1910, Henry M. Leland of Cadillac Motor Car Company was moved to attempt to devise a safer method of starting automobiles as the result of the death of his friend and fellow automobile manufacturer, Bryon Carter. Carter died of gangrene after suffering a broken jaw when a crank handle kicked back while he was attempting to start a stalled automobile for a woman motorist." Joel Webb Eastman, "Styling vs. Safety: The American Automobile Industry and the Development of Automobile Safety, 1900–1966," Ph.D. dissertation, University of Florida, 1973, 46.

22. McShane, *Down the Asphalt Path,* 81–101. Steamer racing was clearly an effort to attract publicity and renew interest in the fading technology. The explosion of the Stanley car in one test actually reinforced public fears of the danger of steam. Steamers also suffered from internal clogging of the steam apparatus from contaminated water. The use of internal condensers was suggested but came relatively late in the product's life cycle, offering little incentive to those weighing the alternatives to internal combustion devices.

23. William Kaszynski, *The American Highway: The History and Culture of Roads in the United States* (Jefferson, NC: McFarland, 2000), 46–48; McShane, *Down the Asphalt Path,* 113–124. David A. Kirsch notes how the historiography of the automobile *assumes* that one of these three power systems must win out. This assumption has led to an approach that places a bias against the steam and electric cars. We look for the reasons that they "failed" relative to the internal combustion engine. See Kirsch, *Electric Vehicle,* 19–25.

24. German manufacturer Nicolaus Otto developed the 4-cycle engine in 1876. Unlike the 2-cycle engine, which introduces and ignites gasoline vapor on one stroke of the piston and produces power and releases the exhaust on the "down" stroke, the 4-cycle engine takes two additional steps. In the Otto engine the cylinder (1) takes in the vapor, then (2) compresses the mixture, then (3) ignites it, releasing the power, finally (4) it vents the exhaust. The design increases the efficiency and reduces the noise of each cylinder, but requires twice the number of cylinders and valves to produce the same power.

25. Flink, *Automobile Age,* 51–55; McShane, *Down the Asphalt Path,* 100.

26. McShane, *Down the Asphalt Path,* 126–127; C. H. Claudy, "Learning to Drive a Motor Car," *Country Life in America* 14 (September 1908): 470.

27. For early autos, other problems arose from a "lack of attention to proper lubrication," "dirt in the water circulation system," "yanking [the] throttle open," or ignoring the settings of the "fan, front wheel, steering connection, spring link, and various lever bearings." Frederic F. Van de Water, *The Family Flivvers to Frisco* (New York: D. Appleton, 1927), 19; "Automobile Troubles That May Be Avoided," *Country Life in America* 14 (May 1908): 59–61; see also Sinclair Lewis, "Adventures in Automobumming: Want a Lift?" *Saturday Evening Post* (December 27, 1919): 24.

28. Thomas H. Russell, *Automobile Driving Self-Taught: An Exhaustive Treatise on the Operation, Management and Care of Motor Cars* (Chicago: Charles C. Thompson, 1914).

29. McShane notes that the "constant utilization of gender stereotypes" in American car culture suggested the strong biases inherent in early automotive values. McShane, *Down the Asphalt Path,* 149; Lee Meriwether, "The Adventures of an Average Man with a Motor-Car," *Outlook* 87 (October 5, 1907): 247, 252.

30. Mrs. Andrew Cuneo, "Why There Are So Few Women Automobilists," *Country Life in America* 13 (March 1908): 516; Virginia Scharff, *Taking the Wheel: Women and the Coming of the Motor Age* (Albuquerque: University of New Mexico Press, 1992), 25; see also Charles L. Sanford, "'Woman's Place' in American Car Culture," pp. 137–152 in David L. Lewis and Lawrence Goldstein, eds., *The Automobile and American Culture* (Ann Arbor: University of Michigan Press, 1980).

31. Flink, *Automobile Age,* 34. Physical strength still limited certain women and their ability to drive. At the New York Auto Show, Will Rogers observed that "you can take any sedan in the display and lock a frail woman up in it, or shut the door on her, and she'll starve to death before she can get out." Quoted in Katherine Allen, *Bleeding Hearts: A Solution to the Automobile Tragedy* (San Antonio: Naylor Company, 1941), 102. For engineers and their role in making the car both easier to operate and safer to drive, see Austin A. Lescarboura, "Cross-Examining the Automobile: What Organized Research Work Is Doing for the Present and Future Automotive Industry," *Scientific American* 131 (July 1924): 8–9, 59.

32. Flink, *Automobile Age,* 34; Berton Braley, "Noodlebeak on Experts," *American Auto News* 1 no. 4 (November 1929): 11–13. In a lament that would resonate throughout the century, Braley cursed the thick operator's manuals, written in unintelligible techno-jargon, that he was expected to learn. Refusing this, he reasoned "I know my car has an engine that will run, and any time it doesn't I get an expert to fix it." For additional examples of the benefits of consumer-friendly automobiles, see "Motor Car Emergencies," *Scientific American* 107 (September 8, 1917): 184; H. S. Whiting, "Saving the Car by Careful Driving: Some of the Evils of an Excess of Caution," *Scientific American* 114 (January 1, 1919): 18.

33. Tom Lewis, *Divided Highway: Building the Interstate Highways, Transforming American Life* (New York: Penguin Books, 1997, 1999), 22.

34. Many scholars, like Richard C. Wade, Sam Bass Warner, Kenneth T. Jackson, and Joel Garreau, focus on the functional characteristics of automobility, or how individuals used cars, as the most compelling explanation for this transition. Other historians, such as McShane, Barrett, Eric Monkkonen, Blaine A. Brownell, and Mark S. Foster, look more to the conditional application of automobiles by urban planners and developers, or how societies privileged car use, to explain the change. Neither view rejects the influence of the other, and both represent essential precursors to the growth of America's dependency on the auto. In addition to Flink, Rae, McShane, Barrett, Bottles, Mom, Tarr, and Preston, cited above, see Charles W. Cheape, *Moving the Masses: Urban Public Transit in New York, Boston, and Philadelphia, 1880–1912* (Cambridge, MA: Harvard University Press, 1980); Kenneth T. Jackson, *Crabgrass Frontier: The Suburbanization of the United States* (New York: Oxford University Press, 1985); Sam Bass Warner, *Streetcar Suburbs: The Process of Growth in Boston, 1870–1900* (Cambridge, MA: Harvard University Press, 1962); Robert Fishman, *Bourgeois Utopia: The Rise and Fall of Suburbia* (New York: Basic Books, 1989); Clay McShane, *Technology and Reform: Street Railways and the Growth of Milwaukee, 1887–1900* (Madison: State Historical Society of Wisconsin, 1974).

35. Barrett, *The Automobile and Urban Transit,* xi; McShane, *Down the Asphalt Path,* 78.

36. Needless to say, the benefits of the suburbs were not shared by those left behind in the cities or those prohibited by race from moving. The most direct safety-related consequence of suburbanization was in segregating children and play areas from the roadway. Lawns, backyards, and low-traffic cul-de-sacs significantly lowered the risk of children being struck by a car while playing on busy streets. See Clay McShane and Gijs Mom, "Death and the Automobile: A Comparison of Automobile Ownership and Fatal Accidents in the United States and the Netherlands, 1910–1980," paper presented at the ICOHTEC Conference, August 2000.

37. These benefits were specifically intended for the affluent and middle-class Americans who were escaping from the inner city; see Eric H. Monkkonen, *American Becomes Urban: The Development of U.S. Cities and Towns, 1780–1980* (Berkeley: University of California Press, 1988), 81, 158–162.

38. Mark S. Foster, *From Streetcar to Superhighway: America City Planners and Urban Transportation 1900–1940* (Philadelphia: Temple University Press, 1982), 44.

39. Lewis Mumford, *The Highway and the City* (New York: Harcourt, Brace and World, 1964), 244–245; see Foster, *From Streetcar to Superhighway,* 44; Monkkonen, *America Becomes Urban,* 158–181. Warren Belasco quoted in Robert C. Ackerson, "Some Milestones of Automotive Literature," in Lewis and Goldstein, eds., *Automobile and American Culture,* 403. Even the term *automobile* projects this sense of individual choice. For a comparison of the terms *automobile* and *motor car* and observations on how Americans tended to prefer the former, see Joseph Anthony Interrante, "A Movable Feast: The Automobile and the Spatial Transformation of American Culture, 1890–1940," Ph.D. dissertation, Harvard University, 1983, 12.

40. Following the lead of Tarr, *Transportation Innovation,* Interrante argues that the growth of the Pullman luxury coaches eased the early criticism of the automobile as a toy of the rich.

Given their lavish spending on personal Pullman cars, a luxury automobile was not much of a stretch. As the costs of automobiles fell, many middle-class Americans thought that they too could now afford to live like the Carnegies, Mellons, and Dukes. See Interrante, "A Movable Feast," 20, 28–38, 49.

41. Flink, *Automobile Age,* 4–6.

42. Flink, *Automobile Age,* 6; George E. Latham, "The Automobile and Automobiling," *Munsey's Magazine* 29 no. 2 (May 1903): 164; John B. Rae, *The American Automobile Industry* (Boston: Twayne Publishers, 1984), 6.

43. John B. Rae, *The Road and Car in American Life* (Cambridge, MA: MIT Press, 1971), 32; *Recent Social Trends,* Vol. 1, 176; Lewis, *Divided Highway,* 9–11; Flink, *Automobile Age,* 169.

44. Lewis, *Divided Highway,* 10–11; Percy H. Whiting, "Motoring Conditions in the South," *Country Life in America* 21 (January 1, 1912): 37.

45. Epstein, *Automobile Industry,* 17. It appears that the industrialized East and urban Middle-West found reasons to improve their roadways that were independent of the auto. In the South, rural Middle-West, and Far West, however, it was "Automobilists, not enlightened leaders in government and industry [who] determined the goals and directed the massive road building programs initially undertaken in the years between the First and Second World Wars." Lesseig, *Automobility,* 69.

46. During the New Deal, 1933–1940, $1.8 billion was spent. Lewis, *Divided Highways,* 18–23; Reginald M. Cleveland and S. T. Williamson, *The Road Is Yours: The Story of the Automobile and the Men Behind It* (New York: Greystone Press, 1951), 86–89.

47. Flink, *Automobile Age,* 171; an additional $615 million in federal money was spent on road development between 1916 and 1925. See also John Chynoweth Burnham, "The Gasoline Tax and the Automobile Revolution," *Mississippi Valley Historical Review* 98 (December 1961): 433–456; Hogner, *South to Padre,* 24. In a reversal of GM chairman Charles Wilson's 1955 statement, what was deemed good for American automobility proved to be good for the auto industry. Charles "Engine Charlie" Wilson said "For many years, I thought what was good for our country was good for General Motors and *vice versa*." Cited in Kenneth Hey, "Cars and Films in American Culture, 1929–1959," in Lewis and Goldstein, eds., *Automobile and American Culture,* 198.

48. Albert, "Order Out of Chaos," 34.

49. Lewis, *Divided Highways,* 8, 12.

50. William Phelps Eno, *The Story of Highway Traffic Control, 1899–1939* (Saugatuck, CT: Eno Foundation for Highway Traffic Control, 1939), 2; McShane, *Down the Asphalt Path,* 186–189.

51. Flink, *Automobile Age,* 188; Ford cited in Rae, *Road and Car,* 55. References to the faddishness of cars were more common in the early years, but safety experts frequently (and wildly inaccurately) suggested that the car could be easily abandoned by the public should the safety problem go unchecked. For example, see Frederick Dwight, "Automobile: The Other Side of the Shield," *Independent* 65 (December 3, 1908): 1299–1303. Others seemed more confident of the long-term viability of the car. George Latham thought talk of faddishness would soon fade. "It may not be in the next five years, nor even in the next ten years, but before the new century is out of its teens [such ideas] will look like ancient history, and whoever stumbles across it will wonder whether it was intended seriously or as a joke." Latham, "Automobile and Automobiling," 162.

52. Epstein, *Automobile Industry,* 57–58; Will Barry, "The Automobile as the Agent of Civilization: California and Good Roads," *Overland Monthly* 53 (March 1909): 244–245. As Flink notes, by the time Ford Motor Company was founded, in 1903, "No industry in history developed a more favorable climate of public opinion. . . . the belief that the automobile would soon supercede the horse was commonplace." Flink, *Automobile Age,* 27.

53. Rae, *American Automobile Industry,* vii, 14.

54. Flink, *Automobile Age,* 24–25.

55. That year, Dr. H. Nelson Jackson and Sewall K. Crocker drove a Winton from San Francisco to New York City in sixty-three days. Tom Fetch then made the same distance in fifty-three days in a Packard. Finally, Eugene Hammond and L. L. Whitman drove the inexpensive Curved Dash Olds from San Francisco to Detroit in only thirty-two days.

56. Flink, *Automobile Age,* 29, 44; Zirbes quoted in the *New York Times,* April 10, 1910, 4.

57. Flink, *Automobile Age,* 27. Ford biographies include Reynold M. Wik, *Ford and Grass-Roots America* (Ann Arbor: University of Michigan Press, 1973); Keith Sward, *The Legend of Henry Ford* (New York: Russell and Russell, 1948); David L. Lewis, *The Public Image of Henry Ford* (Detroit: Wayne State University Press, 1976); Allan Nevins and Frank Ernest Hill, *Ford: The Times, the Man, the Company* (New York: Charles Scribner's Sons, 1954); Allan Nevins and Frank Ernest Hill, *Ford: Expansion and Challenge, 1915–1933* (New York: Charles Scribner's Sons, 1957); Allan Nevins and Frank Ernest Hill, *Ford: Decline and Rebirth, 1933–1962* (New York: Charles Scribner's Sons, 1963).

58. One indication of the saturation of the market was the increased availability of used cars. By the early 1920s, essayists were already remarking about a "plague" of used cars bringing crisis to many dealerships. In 1923, one industry insider wrote that "The used-car plague has proven the ruin of 25 per cent of the automobile dealers annually. No automobile factory can thrive when its dealer organization is suffering the high mortality rate it has for the past three years." See "Used Cars Ruining Dealers," *Literary Digest* 78 (July 14, 1923): 59–61; see also chapter two.

59. Flink, *Automobile Age,* 37; Meriwether, "Adventures of an Average Man," 253.

60. D. W. Webb, "Henry Ford," *System* 28 (September 1915): 297.

61. Clay McShane, *The Automobile: A Chronology of Its Antecedents, Development, and Impact* (Westport, CT: Greenwood Press, 1997), 61.

62. Epstein, *Automobile Industry,* 132–152; in fact before 1913 the Model T was available in black, green, blue, red, or gray; Rae, *American Automobile Industry,* 56–57; Flink, *Automobile Age,* 84–85.

63. Flink, *Automobile Age,* 85, 230–231; Rae, *American Automobile Industry,* 57–60.

64. Flink, *Automobile Age,* 232; for Durant quote, see ibid., 68–69.

65. The appreciation of the value for automotive common stock had a subtle effect on the minds of analysts and, no doubt, aided in the availability of further capital. One analyst wrote in 1916, "The day when the automobile industry was regarded with suspicion from a commercial standpoint and its securities occupied the same plane as 'wildcat' mining shares has long gone by. The industry is as stable as any." "The Craze for Automobile Securities," *Review of Reviews* 54 (November 1916), 574–576.

66. Epstein, *Automobile Industry,* 102–110. Alfred Du Pont Chandler and Stephen Salsbury, *Pierre S. Du Pont and the Making of the Modern Corporation* (New York: Beard Books, 2000); David R. Faber, *Sloan Rules: Alfred P. Sloan and the Triumph of General Motors* (Chicago: University of Chicago Press, 2002).

67. GM was not alone in weathering the Great Depression. As Rae notes, "Even at the bottom of the depression in 1932, total motor vehicle registrations were only about 5 percent lower than they had been in 1929. The same phenomenon appeared in later downswings of the economy. Americans did not give up their cars when hard times came; they simply deferred the purchase of new ones." Rae, *American Automobile Industry,* 74; by 1955, GM controlled 50 percent of U.S. market, Ford 27 percent, and Chrysler 17 percent.

68. Eastman, "Styling vs. Safety," iii, 62, 124; see also A. Ludlow Clayden, "Automobile Engineer: Is He Falling Down on the Job?" *Automotive Industries* (November 19, 1925): 871, quoted

in Eastman, 68. Often, technological "improvements" led to unexpected losses in average safety. Such was the case, for example, of Studebaker's "freewheeling" transmission, which placed the engine in neutral when the throttle was released. While this innovation conserved fuel, it lost the braking power of the engine used to slow cars coasting down hill. See Rae, *American Automobile Industry,* 76; Flink, *Automobile Age,* 215–216.

Chapter 2. Auto Use and Auto Accidents, 1900–1940

1. David L. Lewis and Lawrence Goldstein, eds., *The Automobile and American Culture* (Ann Arbor: University of Michigan Press, 1980); Blaine A. Brownell, "A Symbol of Modernity: Attitudes toward the Automobile in Southern Cities in the 1920s," *American Quarterly* 24 (March 1972): 42. Songwriters penned tunes like "Take Me Out for a Joy Ride," "In Our Little Love Mobile," or "Tumble in the Rumble Seat," and profited by the sexual liberation promised by the car.

2. Julian Smith, "A Runaway Match: The Automobile in the American Film, 1900–1920," in Lewis and Goldstein, eds., *Automobile and American Culture,* 182; Clay McShane, *Down the Asphalt Path: The Automobile and the American City* (New York: Columbia University Press, 1994), 144.

3. Kalton C. Lahue and Terry Brewer, *Kops and Custards: The Legend of Keystone Films* (Norman: University of Oklahoma Press, 1968).

4. F. Scott Fitzgerald, *The Great Gatsby* (New York: Scribner's Paperback Fiction, 1925, 1992), 68; Fitzgerald records the accidents in the typical detached yet sensationalized prose of the newspapers, see ibid., 144; Cynthia Golomb Dettelbach, *In the Driver's Seat: The Automobile in American Literature and Popular Culture* (Westport, CT: Greenwood Press, 1976). As literary critic David Laird concludes, the "mood" of the novel was one of "bitter disenchantment." The car "reflect[ed] the material world of spoiled success, of moral bankruptcy and careless anonymity which conspire[d] to corrupt the values and aspirations with which that world was initially endowed." David Laird, "Versions of Eden: The Automobile and the American Novel," in Lewis and Goldstein, eds., *Automobile and American Culture,* 253.

5. Laird, "Versions of Eden," 249.

6. For national comparisons, see James J. Flink, *The Automobile Age* (Cambridge, MA: MIT Press, 2001), 129, and Ralph Epstein, *The Automobile Industry: Its Economic and Commercial Development* (Chicago: A. W. Shaw, 1928), 321.

7. For a discussion of regional adaptation, see Flink, *Automobile Age,* 140–147.

8. Epstein, *Automobile Industry,* 73–76; to see how these ownership figures affected liability insurance rates, see A. Ryder, "Principles of Automobile Rate Making: Underwriting the Dollar. Read before the Insurance Society of New York, December 9 and 16, 1919," Widener Library, Harvard University. The seven counties include Bexar, Dallas, El Paso, Harris, McLennan, Tarrant, and Travis, representing the largest urban regions in the state. In contrast to low-end sales, sales of moderate to mid-cost models (De Soto, Pontiac, Buick, Hudson, Nash, Reo, Studebaker) decreased by 2 percent and sales of high-end cars (Cadillac, Packard, Pierce-Arrow, LaSalle) decreased by 7.3 percent. See Bureau of Business Research, University of Texas–Austin, "Ranking of New Passenger Car Registrations in Seven Texas Counties, October 7, 1929," Center for American History, University of Texas–Austin.

9. U.S. Bureau of the Census, *Historical Statistics of the United States, Colonial Times to 1957* (Washington, DC: Government Printing Office, 1960), 163, 91.

10. Flink, *Automobile Age,* 131–134; Epstein, *Automobile Industry,* 322.

11. Automobile Manufacturers Association, *A Factual Survey of Automobile Usage* (Detroit: New Center, c. 1941), 23–24.

12. For a discussion of auto clubs, see James J. Flink, *America Adopts the Automobile, 1895–1910* (Cambridge, MA: MIT Press, 1970), 144–170. European clubs mirrored American patterns,

see Gijs Mom, *The Electric Vehicle: Technology and Expectations in the Automobile Age* (Baltimore: Johns Hopkins University Press, 2004), 45; Flink, *Automobile Age,* 17–18, 27–28, 31.

13. Virginia Scharff, *Taking the Wheel: Women and the Coming of the Motor Age* (Albuquerque: University of New Mexico Press, 1992); Mom, *Electric Vehicle,* 59; McShane, *Down the Asphalt Path,* 155; see also Flink, *Automobile Age,* 162–164.

14. McShane, *Down the Asphalt Path,* 162; for San Antonio, see *Jules A. Appler's Log Book and Directory of Automobile Owners of San Antonio and Bexar County* (Soledad, TX: 1913), available at the Center for American History, University of Texas–Austin. One 1934 study found that 103 (16.9 percent) of 608 drivers in accidents were women; two 1940 studies of highway speeding placed the number of women closer to 8.4 percent; a 1934 state study of Massachusetts surveyed over 12,000 drivers and recorded 8.54 percent women drivers. See Charles Hubert Lawshe Jr., "A Review of the Literature Related to the Various Psychological Aspects of Highway Safety," *Engineering Bulletin* 23, no. 2a (April, 1939): 7–56; "Report on Massachusetts' Highway Accident Survey, 1934," Widener Library, Harvard University.

15. Lawshe, "Review of Periodical Literature," 32–33.

16. American Automobile Association, *State Rules and Regulations Governing Safety Education in the United States* (Washington, DC: AAA, 1939), 4.

17. "What Do Folks Use Their Cars For?" *Literary Digest* 79 (November 17, 1923): 66–69. Total sample size was 1,063 respondents to a questionnaire by National Automobile Chamber of Commerce.

18. Robert S. Lynd and Helen Merrell Lynd, *Middletown: A Study in Modern American Culture* (New York: Harcourt, Brace and World, 1956), 251–263; *Recent Social Trends in the United States*, Vol. 1 (New York: McGraw-Hill, 1933), 177; Flink, *Automobile Age,* 118–119, 132–134, 155.

19. Ronald R. Kline, *Consumers in the Country: Technology and Social Change in Rural America* (Baltimore: Johns Hopkins University Press, 2000), 57; Hal S. Barron, *Mixed Harvest: The Second Great Transformation in the Rural North, 1870–1930* (Chapel Hill: University of North Carolina Press, 1997), 195, 198–204.

20. The survey reported 274 billion passenger miles of necessity usage in more than 11 billion round trips. By comparison, "railroads, buses, Pullman cars, airplanes, and electric railways" accounted for 73 billion passenger miles. Automobile Manufacturers Association, *A Factual Survey,* 5.

21. Ibid., 15, 18, 13.

22. Much of the gain in auto safety rates in the past three decades, between 1970 and 2000, was due directly to improvements in passive restraint systems. The use of seatbelts, child car seats, air bags, and collapsible steering columns protected occupants and lowered the fatality rate but did little to affect the overall number of collisions.

23. David Shinar, *Psychology on the Road: The Human Factor in Traffic Safety* (New York: John Wiley and Sons, 1978), 112; John B. Rae, *The Road and Car in American Life* (Cambridge, MA: MIT Press, 1971), 347.

24. For fatality rates from 1940 to 1980, see Rae, *American Automobile Industry,* 138–139.

25. U.S. Department of Agriculture, Bureau of Public Roads, *Highway Accidents, Their Causes and Recommendations for Their Prevention* (Washington, DC: Government Printing Office, 1938), 2–3, 32; U.S. Department of Agriculture, Bureau of Public Roads, *Uniform Act Regulating Traffic on Highways* (Washington, DC: Government Printing Office, 1939).

26. Automotive Safety Foundation, *Priority for Traffic Safety* (n.p., 1941), 4, Widener Library, Harvard University; USDA, *Highway Accidents,* 21, 33.

27. James Sinke, *Think: An Analysis of Automobile Accident Causes* (Grand Rapids, MI: Department of Public Safety, 1926), 15; State of Ohio, Division of Vital Statistics, Department of Health, "Report of Fatal Accidents from 1910 to 1933," Library of Congress, Washington, DC,

13; Texas Department of Public Safety, Driver's License Division, *Texas Highway Accidents, 1938* (Austin, TX: n.p. 1938), subsequent study published in 1939; Travelers Insurance Company, *The Great American Gamble* (Hartford, CT: Travelers Insurance Company, 1934), 45; if one were unfortunate enough to be involved in a collision, the statistically safest conditions were found from 1:30 a.m–5:00 a.m., preferably on Tuesday or Wednesday morning, in February, and while the road was encased in fog.

28. Travelers Insurance Company, *Tremendous Trifles: Minor Decisions of Major Importance* (Hartford, CT: 1932).

29. State of Ohio, "Report of Fatal Accidents," 3–4; Travelers Insurance Company, *Great American Gamble*, 13; Dallas Bureau of Traffic Education. "Survey and Report of Pedestrian Traffic Accidents in the City of Dallas, Texas. A Complete Analysis Covering 1935, '36, '37, and together with 1938 Supplemental Summary," Center for American History, University of Texas–Austin.

30. Sinke, *Think*, 23; "Are Traffic Accidents Caused by Speed?" *American City* 44 (June 1931): 129; Travelers Insurance Company, *Great American Gamble*, 23, 45.

31. "Report on Massachusetts' Highway Accident Survey," 1, 3, 7, 8, 30–41, Widener Library, Harvard University.

Chapter 3. The Dysfunctional Love Affair

1. Robert Bruce, "The Place of the Automobile," *Outing* 37 (October 1900): 69, 65.

2. Ibid., 65–66.

3. Leading contemporary works avoid much direct mention of the "love affair," and it is rarely included in most indexes. Clay McShane, John B. Rae, and James J. Flink are more concerned with the long-term structural components of automobility (technology, industry, roads, and legislation) than with the shifting cultural perceptions of the car. Typical is Clay McShane's treatment of this relationship as a manifestation of popular culture. He acknowledges that the car "granted an *ersatz* sense of both economic and gender status," where "consumers obtained a feeling of control and liberation," and where "Cars symbolized escape from the constraints of family and neighborhood." *Down the Asphalt Path: The Automobile and the American City* (New York: Columbia University Press, 1994), 147–148. Flink sees the rising public support for the automobile before 1940 as a logical trade-off for the advantages provided over rail and not from supposed social or cultural affinities contained within the concept of a "love affair." Moreover, he is critical of the many myths, such as those surrounding Henry Ford or Detroit's safety record, that validate much of the public's faith in the car; Flink, *The Automobile Age* (Cambridge, MA: MIT Press, 2001), 51–55.

4. "Second-Hand Cars as Pitfalls and Pleasures," *Literary Digest* 81 (April 5, 1924): 63; Sinclair Lewis, "Adventures in Automobumming: Gasoline Gypsies," *Saturday Evening Post* (December 20, 1919): 6. Many accounts note how drivers often name their autos. For an example of the guilt associated with a trade-in from a trusted old friend to a new model, see Walter Pritchard Eaton, "The Passing of Elisa," *American Auto News* 9 (April 1930): 4–5.

5. Frederic F. Van de Water, *The Family Flivvers to Frisco* (New York: D. Appleton, 1927), 23–24; for Issachar, see Genesis 49:14–15.

6. James Ball Naylor, "The Song of the Motor Car," *Collier's* 42 (January 16, 1909): 22. See also Stuart Travis, *"Bubble" Jingles: The Jolly Side of the Automobile* (New York: Rohde and Haskins, 1901). For more on songs dealing with early automobile culture, see McShane, *Down the Asphalt Path*, 141–143, David L. Lewis, "Sex and the Automobile: From Rumble Seats to Rockin' Vans," pp. 123–133, in David L. Lewis and Lawrence Goldstein, eds., *The Automobile and American Culture* (Ann Arbor: University of Michigan Press, 1980); Warren Belasco, "Motivatin' with Chuck Berry and Frederick Jackson Turner," pp. 262–279 in Lewis and Goldsein, eds., *Automobile and American Culture.* Modern advertisers still prefer the emotional appeal of the

automobile over the rational. Catch-phrases like "We Built Excitement" (Pontiac), "Oh What a Feeling" (Toyota, complete with leaping drivers), or "Zoom Zoom" (Mazda) reflect these earlier and more romantic expressions.

7. Sidney Strong, "Looking Backward: The Influence of the Automobile upon the 'Funny Men' and This Sociological and Mundane," *Collier's* 50, no. 17, Automobile Section (January 11, 1913): 21 (emphasis added).

8. Walter Pritchard Eaton, "If Motor Cars Could Talk, What a Lot of 'Backfire' Most Drivers Would Get," *American Auto News* 1, no. 6 (January 1930): 15; *Oh, That Funny Ford!* (New York: Morris and Bendien, 1916), 27, 1, 3, 7.

9. Another bias, seen more commonly in book-length manuscripts, was the drama of long-distance travel, rather than the travails of everyday commuting. In addition to articles and books cited in the notes below, some of the better examples include Hugo Alois Taussig, *Retracing the Pioneers, From West to East in an Automobile* (San Francisco: privately printed,1910); Guy Woodward Finney, *Across the American Continent with the Ohio Pathfinder* (Cincinnati: Ohio Motor Car Company, 1911); Mary Crehore Bedell, *Modern Gypsies: The Story of a Twelve Thousand Mile Motor Camping Trip Encircling the United States* (New York: Brentano's, 1924). See also Cary S. Bliss, *Autos across America: A Bibliography of Transcontinental Automobile Travel: 1903–1940* (Austin, TX: Jerkins and Reese, 1982).

10. Melville F. Ferguson, *Motor Camping on Western Trails* (New York: Century, 1925), vi–vii.

11. Winifred Hawkridge Dixon, *Westward Hoboes: Ups and Downs of Frontier Motoring* (New York: Charles Scribner's Sons, 1924), 52.

12. Ironically, this is the opposite configuration of cars designed in the 1950s, which projected female qualities (headlights like breasts) in the front and male (projected fins and other "gorp") in the rear. See Karal Ann Marling, *As Seen on TV: The Visual Culture of Everyday Life in the 1950s* (Cambridge, MA: Harvard University Press, 1994). Dixon, *Westward Hoboes*, 58, 35, 2.

13. Dixon, *Westward Hoboes*, 18, 22.

14. In her charming and self-effacing style Dixon admitted that "those parts which commonly behaved themselves I left severely alone." Ibid., 2.

15. Herbert H. Harrison, "The Automobile as a Social Factor," *American Homes and Gardens* 12 (July 1915): 252; Henry Farrand Griffin, "The Motor Vagabond: His Wanderings at Home and Abroad," *Outlook* 107 (May 1914): 161; Leon Vandervort, "The Beginner and His Automobile," *Outing* 40 (August 1902): 615; "Second-Hand Cars as Pitfalls and Pleasures," *Literary Digest* 81 (April 5, 1924): 65. See also Emily Rose Burt, "Motoritis: An Agreeable Malady," *Delineator* 97 (October 1920): 110–113.

16. Vandervort, "Beginner and His Automobile," 616; Harrison, "Automobile as a Social Factor," 240; Julian Street, "Car Coming! Some Mental Snapshots of the Week before the Vanderbilt Cup Race," *American Magazine* 68 (July 1909): 252.

17. Henry Underwood, "Speed Mania and How to Cure It," *Harper's Weekly* 51 (March 30, 1907): 470; Harrison, "Automobile as a Social Factor," 240, 242; *Country Life in America* 12 (October 1907): 684.

18. "The New Romance of the Road," *Craftsman* 17 (October 1909): 52; Griffin, "Motor Vagabond," 161; D. Enville, "The Confessions of an Anti-Motorist," *Country Life in America* 13 (November 1907): 40.

19. Sinclair Lewis, "Adventures in Automobumming: Want a Lift?" *Saturday Evening Post* (December 27, 1919): 68; Ferguson, *Motor Camping*, vii.

20. Lewis, "Adventures in Automobumming, 70; Charles J. Finger, *Adventure under Sapphire Skies* (New York: William Morrow and Company, 1931), 6; Randall R. Howard, "The Automobile on the Frontier," *Collier's* 50 (January 1913): Supplement 66. Several diarists reported recurring dreams about wild animals, particularly after experiencing in their travels a harrowing

escape while at the mercy of the natural environment. After a particularly tough day on the road, Winifred Dixon "woke from a dream that a mountain lion had entered our shelter, when [her companion] Toby sat up excitedly. 'I just dreamed a bear was trying to get in,' she said." Dixon, *Westward Hoboes,* 2, 50–51.

21. Sidney Strong, "Looking Backward: The Influence of the Automobile upon the 'Funny Men' and Things Sociological and Mundane," *Collier's* 50 no 17, Automobile Section (January 11, 1913): 21; Ramiro de Maeztu, "Automobiles and National Character," *Living Age* 322 (September 20, 1924): 583.

22. Underwood, "Speed Mania," 470; *Country Life in America* 12 (October 1907): 684; "Time to Stop," *Outlook* 91 (April 17, 1909): 852.

23. Street, "Car Coming! Some Mental Snapshots," 251; Thomas H. Russell, *Automobile Driving Self-Taught: An Exhaustive Treatise on the Operation, Management and Care of Motor Cars* (Chicago: Charles C. Thompson, 1914), 240, 241.

24. Griffin, "Motor Vagabond," 161–169.

25. George Ethelbert Walsh, "Vacation by Motor Car," *Independent* 64 (April 16, 1908): 844; second quote from Warren Belasco, "Commercialized Nostalgia: The Origins of the Roadside Strip," in Lewis and Goldstein, eds., *Automobile and American Culture,* 107; Ferguson, *Motor Camping,* 20, 4. Contemporary road movies, like *Thelma and Louise,* capture this same sense of traveling without possessions.

26. Warren J. Belasco, *Americans on the Road: From Autocamp to Motel: 1910–1945* (Cambridge, MA: MIT Press, 1979), 22–23. In the words of historian Joseph Interrante, "Viewed against middle-class Progressive concerns, the freedom of automobility promised not only individual relief from some of the pressures of modern life, but also a collective solution to some of the worst effects of late nineteenth-century industrialization." Interrante, "A Movable Feast: The Automobile and the Spatial Transformation of American Culture, 1890–1940," Ph.D. dissertation, Harvard University, 1983, 20–38, 59. Middle-class tourists and commuters also decried the ugly scenery surrounding urban rail lines, their uncomfortable closeness with the working poor, and the way that long-haul rail systems bypassed much of the country.

27. Finger, *Adventure under Sapphire Skies,* 6; AAA, "Creed of the Open Road," in *Automobile Safety Lane Sponsored by the AAA, Police Department, and the Central Texas Auto Club* (Austin, TX: n.p., 1931), at the Center for American History, University of Texas–Austin.

28. Ferguson, *Motor Camping,* 7, 20; Walsh, "Vacation by Motor Car," 846; Van de Water, *Family Flivvers to Frisco,* 15; Griffin, "Motor Vagabond," 161–169.

29. Van de Water, *Family Flivvers to Frisco,* 34.

30. Ferguson, *Motor Camping,* 3; Sinclair Lewis, "Adventures in Automobumming: The Great American Frying Pan," *Saturday Evening Post* (January 3, 1920): 62; Belasco, *Americans on the Road,* 5.

31. Beth L. Bailey, *From Front Porch to Back Seat: Courtship in Twentieth-Century America* (Baltimore: Johns Hopkins University Press, 1988), 19; David L. Lewis, "Sex and the Automobile: From Rumble Seats to Rockin' Vans," in Lewis and Goldstein, eds., *Automobile and American Culture,* 124; Michael L. Berger, *The Devil Wagon in God's Country: The Automobile and Social Change in Rural America, 1893–1929* (Hamden, CT: Archon Books, 1979), 137–139.

32. Walsh, "Vacation by Motor Car," 844; Harrison, "Automobile as a Social Factor," 240; Ferguson, *Motor Camping,* 4, 46–47; Dixon, *Westward Hoboes,* 1–4. To Dixon, travel by auto "seemed luxurious in comparison . . . We pictured ourselves bowling smoothly along in the open air, in contrast with the stifling train; we pre-visioned no delays, no breakdowns, no dangers; we saw New Mexico and Arizona as motorist's Heaven, paved with asphalt and running streams of gasoline." For similar examples of beating the clock, see Norman Hayner, "Auto Camps in the Evergreen Playground," *Social Forces* (1930): 256–266; Griffin, "Motor Vagabond," 161–169.

33. A. G. Johnson, "Motor Car 'Don'ts,'" *Collier's* 50, supplement (January, 1913): 34; "Don'ts for the Autoist," *Illustrated World* 30 (October 1918): 288.

34 David Harvey, *The Condition of Postmodernity* (Cambridge, MA: Blackwell, 1990), 125–141.

35. Wilson cited in Clay McShane, *The Automobile: A Chronology of Its Antecedents, Development and Impact* (Westport, CT: Greenwood, Press, 1997), 34. Theodore M. R. von Keler, "Where Justice Mills Flourish," *Harper's Weekly* 57 (March 12, 1913): 12.

36. Harrison, "Automobile as a Social Factor," 239; de Maetzu, "Automobiles and National Character," 585. While elitism was minimized in shows put on by the Association of Licensed Automobile Manufacturers (ALAM), and commentary on runabouts and cheaper models became more common in the national press, much of the early coverage focused on the high end of the auto market. "The Seventh Annual Auto Show of the Automobile Club of America," *Scientific American* 95 (December 15, 1906): 442–443; "The Seventh Annual Automobile Show at Madison Square Garden," *Scientific American* 96 (January 12, 1907): 22–23; "The Automobile at the Recent Shows," *Scientific American* 97 (November 9, 1907): 320; "The Eighth National Automobile Show in Madison Square Garden," *Scientific American* 97 (November 16, 1907): 354; "The Ninth Annual Automobile Show in Madison Square Garden," *Scientific American* 100 (January 30, 1909): 94.

37. Van de Water, *Family Flivvers to Frisco,* 43; Griffin, "Motor Vagabond," 162.

38. Enville, "Confessions of an Anti-Motorist," 40; Harrison, "Automobile as a Social Factor," 241. Even before the first Model T was produced, enthusiasts argued that the cost of car ownership was lower than owning a horse. Largely because a car needs fuel only to operate, whereas a horse needs daily care regardless of its transit activities, it was found that "a family keeping a horse and trap can with little or no increased expenditures maintain a two-passenger run-about." See Harry B. Haines, "Automobiles for Everybody," *World's Work* 11 (March 1906): 7346.

39. R. H. Van Court, "The Automobile in Social Life," *American Homes and Gardens* 9, supplement (September 1912): ix.

40. *Texas Parade* 1, no. 4 (September 1936): 2 (emphasis added); Dixon, *Westward Hoboes,* 42; Van de Water, *Family Flivvers to Frisco,* 5, 7, 9.

41. John C. Long and John D. Long, *Motor Camping* (New York: Dodd, Mead, 1923), 1; Ferguson, *Motor Camping,* vii; George Ethelbert Walsh, "Vacation by Motor Car," 843.

42. Roland S. Wallis, "Tourist Camps," Bulletin no. 56 in *Iowa State College of Agriculture and Mechanical Arts Official Publication* 21, no 36 (February 7, 1923): 3, 5; Van de Water, *Family Flivvers to Frisco,* 48; Hayner, "Auto Camps," 256–266. Hayner reported that 77.2 percent of all camps now had cabins and basic amenities.

43. Ferguson, *Motor Camping,* 7; Lewis, "Adventures in Automobumming: The Great American Frying Pan," 65; Dixon, *Westward Hoboes,* 6; Dixon reported: "At the price of a fascinating morning and fifty-odd dollars, we parted from [the New York outfitter], owners of a silk tent, mosquito and snake proof, which folded into an infinitesimal canvas bag, a tin lantern, which folded flat, a tin biscuit baker which collapsed into nothing, a nest of cooking and eating utensils, which folded and fitted into one two-gallon pail, a can opener, a hunting knife, doomed to be our most cherished treasure, a flashlight, six giant safety-pins, and a folding stove." Dorothy Hogner's purchases were also typical: "a seven by seven wall tent, good old army style, clumsier than its silk relation, less durable, but the price was the thing—on sale for $10.00. Another special was a two burner gasoline KampKook stove at $3.95, to be fueled from the car tank. We added a couple of folding cots, a couple of pairs of blue jeans, a couple of khaki shirts for each of us, and, most important of all, a heavy mesh mosquito net. Our cooking outfit was Woolworth's best: two cook pans, a small coffee pot, two aluminum plates, two enamel cups, two each of knives, forks and spoons, the all important frying pan, one wash basin, one galvanized pail, and

one large, screw top oil can with a capped spout, for a water container." Dorothy Childs Hogner, *South to Padre* (Boston: Lothorp, Lee and Shepard, 1936), 15.

44. Hayner, "Auto Camps," 262–263; Belasco, "Commercialized Nostalgia," 120.

45. Dixon wrote that a traveling women needed, at a minimum, a three-piece suit of khaki, "composed of breeches, a short skirt split front and back, and many-pocketed Norfolk coat, worn with knee-high elk boots." She also advised that "A heavy and light sweater, two flannel and a half dozen cotton or linen shirts, and sufficient plain underwear suffice for a year's knocking about. Add to this a simple afternoon frock of non-wrinkling material, preferably black, and no event finds you unprepared." Dixon, *Westward Hoboes,* 7–8. Pamela Walker Laird, "'The Car without a Single Weakness,': Early Automobile Advertising," *Technology and Culture* 37, no. 4 (October 1996): 807.

46. Eugene Wood, "Do I Want an Automobile?" *Everybody's Magazine* 14 (January 1906): 35, 39. Wood believed what made cars so "desirable is that it is an advertisement of the fact that you have so much money you don't know what to do with it." Bozeman Bulger, "Making Owners Like Their Cars," *Saturday Evening Post* 195 (May 5, 1923): 32; See also *Texas Parade* 3, no. 8 (January 1939): 28; and Robert S. Lynd and Helen Merrill Lynd, *Middletown: A Study in Modern American Culture,* 254–255.

47. "The New Romance of the Road," *Craftsman* 17 (October 1909): 49; "Intensive Flivving," *Atlantic* 132 (August 1923): 278–279.

48. *Oh, That Funny Ford!* 10, 11, 21. Frank Capra's classic 1934 film, *It Happened One Night,* uses the Model T at the end of a long line of transportation options (yacht, train, plane, bus) to show the significant drop in class, style, and agency that his two main characters, portrayed by Clark Gable and Claudette Colbert, experience. Gable is left powerless, driving a twice-stolen Lizzie, when compared to the modern automobiles streaming past him.

49. Ferguson, *Motor Camping,* 59; Belasco, *Americans on the Road,* 116; Hayner, "Auto Camps," 263; Wallis, "Tourist Camps," 59; Van de Water, *Family Flivvers to Frisco,* 49.

50. Wallis, "Tourist Camps," 79–82.

51. Wallis, "Tourist Camps," 79–82; Hayner, "Auto Camps," 264; Ambrose continued: "With this advantage, [public camps] enter into competition with legitimate enterprise, and into ruinous competition with the citizens of the community. The tourist who knows anything about the world expects to pay his way, and a reasonable charge for camp privileges will not keep him away. He does not seek charity, but prefers to pay as he goes."

52. John Steinbeck, *The Grapes of Wrath* (New York: William Heinemann, 1939, 1976), 135, 200–202.

53. John R. Eustis, "Looking Forward: The Place of the Automobile in the Years to Come," *Scientific American* 118 (January 5, 1918): 45, 47.

54. Bruce, "Place of the Automobile," 66; Sinclair Lewis, "Adventures in Automobumming: Gasoline Gypsies," 6.

55. "Little Things about a Car That Every Women Who Means to Drive One Ought to Know," *Ladies' Home Journal* 34 (March 1917): 32; Stewart Ives De Krafft, "Motor-car Don'ts for Neophyte Owners," *Harper's Weekly* 54 (September 3, 1910): 25; A. G. Johnson, "Motor Car 'Don'ts,'" 33. See also Harry B. Haines, "'Don'ts' for the Driver: Wisdom and Warning for the Man behind the Wheel," *Harper's Weekly* 52 (January 4, 1908): 30; "Don'ts for the Autoist," *Illustrated World* 30 (October 1918): 288; Russell, *Automobile Driving Self-Taught,* 216–222; Emily Rose Burt, "Manners in a Motor," *Delineator* 98 (July 1921): 34; George Ade, "Do You Run a Motor-Car or a Moveable Madhouse?" *American Magazine* 92 (Spring 1921): 53–55.

56. Leon Vandervort, "Beginner and His Automobile," 616; C. H. Claudy, "Learning to Drive a Motor Car," *Country Life in America* 14 (September 1908): 469–470; C. H. Claudy, "Building Character with a Motor Car," *Country Life in America* 24 (August 1913): 80–84; C. H. Claudy,

"Power," *Country Life in America* 29 (March 1916): 110; H. S. Whiting, "Saving the Car by Careful Driving: Some of the Evils of an Excess of Caution," *Scientific American* 114 (January 1, 1919): 18; Harrison, "Automobile as a Social Factor," 241; John Chapman Hilder, "The Art of Automobile Driving," *Ladies' Home Journal* 37 (July 1920): 37; Julian Street, "Good and Bad Driving: The Pneumatic Peril of the Highway," *Collier's* 46, Supplement (January 7, 1911): 9–11. Street wrote that, in contrast to understanding the motorcar, clues of the road were "the simplest, [but] like the signs of the zodiac, they are influenced by other signs."

57. "Automobile Troubles That May Be Avoided," *Country Life in America* 14 (May 1908): 59, 60.

58. "Why Women Are, or Are Not, Good Chauffeuses," *Outing* 44 (May 1904): 158; C. H. Claudy, "Building Character," 80–84.

59. Mrs. Andrew Cuneo, "Why There Are So Few Women Automobilists," *Country Life in America* 13 (March 1908): 516; C. H. Claudy, "Building Character," 80–84; Virginia Scharff, *Taking the Wheel: Women and the Coming of the Motor Age* (Albuquerque: University of New Mexico Press, 1992), 13. In a related example, Philip J. Deloria shows how progress, race, and automobility affected Native Americans. Unlike whites, whose purchase of a car reflected progressive optimism, critics charged that Indians squandered their money. Deloria concludes "autos demonstrated the utter impossibility of Indian progress" in the minds of the majority. Deloria, *Indians in Unexpected Places* (Lawrence: University Press of Kansas, 2004), 136–182.

60. Fred Gilman Jopp, "Motoring's Most Deadly Menace: 'The Flivverboob,'" *Illustrated World* 38 (October 1922): 308; Mrs. Andrew Cuneo, "Why There Are So Few Women Automobilists," 516. As described in later chapters, women were repeatedly found to be safer and less reckless drivers than their male counterparts; Dr. Manion quoted in "Courting Danger in the Automobile," *Literary Digest* 82 (June 5, 1924): 35.

61. Cuneo, "Why There Are So Few Women Automobilists," 515–516; Kate Masterson, "The Monster in the Car: A Study of the Twentieth-Century Woman's Passion for the Motor Speed-Mania and Its Attendant Evils and Vagaries," *Lippincott's Monthly Magazine* 86 (August 10, 1910): 204; "Why Women Are, or Are Not, Good Chauffeuses," 159, 155.

62. Masterson, "Monster in the Car," 204; Montgomery Rollins, "Women and Motor Cars," *Outlook* 92 (August 7, 1909): 859–860. For further examples of prejudice, see W. Bruce Cobb, "Automotive Accidents—Their Cause and Prevention," *American City* 21 (August 1919): 125–128; Fred J. Wagner, "Safety First," *House Beautiful* 36, Supplement (June 1914): xxxvi, xxxviii, xl. One 1917 *Ladies' Home Journal* essay, titled "Little Things about a Car That Every Women Who Means to Drive One Ought to Know," referenced above, is a marvel of condensed sexism. It assumed that only men were capable of understanding automotive technologies and proclaimed "no doubt" that "the woman has not yet differentiated a motor from a horse and carriage." This was unfortunate, for "in the latter case a good deal could be left to the horse." The essay chided women on their unwillingness to adapt to the progressive needs of automobility and admonished "it is well for the woman driver to be familiar with what may be called the machine's essential surface requirements."

63. Margaret Emerson Bailey, "Motoring Manners, Whether You Drive Your Car or Go as Guest," *Woman's Home Companion* 50 (May 1923): 50; Cuneo, "Why There Are So Few Women Automobilists," 515–516; Ann Murdock, "The Girl Who Drives a Car," *Ladies' Home Journal* 32 (July 1915): 11.

Chapter 4. Avoidable Accidents and the Challenge of Automotive Citizenship

1. State of Texas, Governor's Special Traffic Accident Investigation Committee, *Official Traffic Investigation Report on [the] Collision That Killed Six People at the Crossing of State Highway*

No. 15 (U.S. No. 80) and Belt Line Road on May 5, 1938, Center for American History, University of Texas–Austin; *(Austin) American,* May 7, 1938, 1; *(Austin) American,* May 13, 1938, 1; Barrow quoted in Flink, *The Automobile Age* (Cambridge, MA: MIT Press, 2001), 230–231. The Model A Roadster weighed 2,350 pounds while the Model A Coupe was slightly heavier at 2,403 pounds. This compares roughly to a 2005 Honda Civic, which weighs 2,449 pounds.

2. *(Austin) American,* May 6, 1938, 5.

3. *Official Traffic Investigation Report,* 7; *(Austin) American,* May 13, 1938, 1.

4. *(Austin) American,* May 7, 1938, 3.

5. "St. Louis Monument to Children Killed by Cars," *Literary Digest* 79 (December 8, 1923): 52–55.

6. Allred's sister was killed in an auto accident in 1936; *Official Traffic Investigation Report,* 11; *(Dallas) Morning News,* May 9, 1938, 1.

7. *Official Traffic Investigation Report,* 3.

8. *Official Traffic Investigation Report,* 8–9; the report indicated nearly identical crashes occurring at the intersection on May 6, 1937, November 11, 1937, and December 22, 1937.

9. *(Dallas) Morning News,* May 5, 1938.

10. Emphasis added. Seth K. Humphrey, "Our Delightful Man-Killer," *Atlantic* 148 (December 1931): 730; see also Travelers Insurance Company, *Tremendous Trifles: Minor Decisions of Major Importance* (Hartford, CT: Travelers Insurance Company, 1932), 13–14.

11. U.S. Department of Agriculture, Bureau of Public Roads, *Highway Accidents, Their Causes and Recommendations for Their Prevention* (Washington, DC: Government Printing Office, 1938), 1; "The Murderous Motor," *New Republic* 47 (July 7, 1926): 190; Humphrey, "Our Delightful Man-Killer," 725, 728.

12. Julian Montgomery, "Death Never Takes a Holiday: Day by Day, the Grim Reaper Rides Rampant over the Roads," *Texas Parade* 3, no. 7 (December 1938): 14; N. K. Woerner, Head of Statistical Division of the Texas Department of Public Safety, in "Vertical Folders: Traffic Accidents," Center for American History, University of Texas–Austin.

13. "Wrecks That Come to the Repairman—and Why," *Literary Digest* 93 (May 21, 1927): 78–86; *American Auto News* 2 (December, 1930): 3.

14. Herbert L. Towle, "The Motor Menace," *Atlantic* 136 (July 1925): 98–107. For additional comments about the changing generational qualities of early drivers, see State of Connecticut, "The Human Factor Involved in Traffic Accidents Caused in Connecticut during the First Six Months of the Current Year, 1943," in the Widener Library, Harvard University.

15. Towle, "Motor Menace," 98–107. Like Towle, other critics charged that young women first willfully, then obsessively "sold her birthright of emancipation" to become "slave to the Motor-car." See Kate Masterson, "The Monster in the Car: A Study of the Twentieth-Century Woman's Passion for the Motor Speed-Mania and Its Attendant Evils and Vagaries," *Lippincott's Monthly Magazine* 86 (August 10, 1910): 204.

16. John J. Maher, *Mind over Motor* (Detroit: n.p., 1937), iii, iv, 1, 2.

17. Roger Cooter and Bill Luckin, "Accidents in History: An Introduction," in Roger Cooter and Bill Luckin, eds., *Accidents in History: Injuries, Fatalities and Social Relations* (Athens, GA: Rodopi, 1997), 4; Robert Campbell, "Philosophy and the Accident," in Cooter and Luckin, eds., *Accidents in History,* 21–22, 23; Joel Webb Eastman, "Styling vs. Safety: The American Automobile Industry and the Development of Automobile Safety, 1900–1966," Ph.D. dissertation, University of Florida, 1973, 157–158; Karl Dake, "Myths of Nature: Culture and the Social Construction of Risk," *Journal of Social Issues* 48 (1992), 21–37; Sheldon Krimsky and Dominic Golding, eds., *Social Theories of Risk* (New York: Praeger, 1992); Cooter and Luckin note that the theoretical ambiguities of accidents are particularly suited to our postmodern gaze: "It might be supposed that these tensions between providence and precaution, chance and predictability,

blamelessness and accountability, fate and intervention, the random and the structural, and the natural and the fabricated render the subject well suited to a postmodern gaze. Accidents, like wars, appear to challenge the logic of linear positivist explanations of progress and to mock the metanarratives of philosophy and sociology. Here, surely, are the fragments, contingencies and irreductions so beloved of post-structuralist discourse analysts. Not only is there no archive labeled 'accidents', but neither is there a stable subject." Cooter and Luckin, eds., *Accidents in History*, 4.

18. Masterson, "Monster in the Car," 206; Henry Farrand Griffin, "The Motor Vagabond: His Wanderings at Home and Abroad," *Outlook* 107 (May 1914): 161. The Frankenstein reference is common in essays critical of basing a solution to the accident problem on changing individual driver character; see "A Race of Frankensteins," *Independent* 119, no. 4048 (December 31, 1927): 644; Masterson, "Monster in the Car," 206; Charles E. Simons, "Sentinels of Safety: The Enlarged Texas Highway Patrol," *Texas Parade* 2 (November 1937): 3. The Travelers Insurance Company wrote: "Since no person of responsibility can picture himself or herself as the burglar or purposely setting a building on fire, by the same token why do so many use the streets and highways as drivers and pedestrians in ways that may—and often do—result in the loss of life—theirs included. Why this apparent Dr. Jekyll and Mr. Hyde in so vast a number of the public? A change in attitude toward the improper use of the streets and highways by motorists and pedestrians can make the careless use of them as unpopular as house-breaking and arson." Travelers Insurance Company, *Tremendous Trifles*, 5; for a similar reference to Jekyll and Hyde, see "What Does a Motorist Think About?" *Literary Digest* 80 (January 12, 1924): 54–56.

19. "Ten Thousand Automobile Deaths," *Literary Digest* 75 (November 18, 1922): 14; Kleberg Investigation, 11, 12; "Motor Fodder," *Outlook* 142 (March 24, 1926): 443–444; for similar examples of references to world war see "Consider the Other Fellow," *Collier's* 85 (June 21, 1930): 66; *Texas Parade* 3, no. 4 (September 1938): 7; *Texas Parade* 2, no. 7 (December 1937): 14; Maher, *Mind over Motor*, 3. One investigator wrote: "Christianity has its martyrs; every war takes its toll in life and suffering. These sacrifices have been presumably necessary for the advancement of civilization and the general welfare of humanity. . . . The soldiers died for a cause, as martyrs in defense of a Christian ideal. What have automobile victims died for? Have they left a heritage to humanity?" in James Sinke, *Think: An Analysis of Automobile Accident Causes* (Grand Rapids, MI: 1926), 35.

20. The Travelers Insurance Company, *Great American Gamble*, 4; S. Dana Hubbard, *Automobile Hazards: Keep Well Leaflet No. 20:* (New York: M. B. Brown Printing and Binding, 1922), 6, 9; "Curing Careless Drivers," *Literary Digest* 105 (April 12, 1930): 44–46. The Travelers Insurance Company held in 1933 that "If the automobile accident problem could be called hoof and mouth disease, if it were important as the corn borer evil or a crop-eating swarm of pests, if killing and injuring persons by automobiles happened to be as fearsome a menace as the infantile paralysis scare, then perhaps something might be done to stop the highway slaughter."

21. Julian Street, "Good and Bad Driving: The Pneumatic Peril of the Highway," *Collier's* 46, Supplement (January 7, 1911), 13.

22. J. C. Furnas, "And Sudden Death," *Reader's Digest* 27 (August 1935): 21, 26.

23. Furnas, "And Sudden Death," 21, 26.

24. Daniel M. Albert, "Order out of Chaos: Automobile Safety, Technology and Society, 1925 to 1965," Ph.D. dissertation, University of Michigan, 1997, 12; Eastman, "Styling vs. Safety," 175–182. For reference to grisly court penalties, see "Brain Tests for Drivers to Make Motoring Safe," *Literary Digest* Vol. 76 (January 20, 1923), 24–25; Elizabeth Jordan, "Automobile Collisions," *Saturday Evening Post* 198 (January 2, 1926): 16–17, 94, 96.

25. Hubbard, Cobb, and the others had begun to assemble a profile of the "accident prone" driver, or "repeater," that would factor quite significantly to the reform efforts of the times.

Hubbard, *Automobile Hazards,* 23; W. Bruce Cobb, "Automotive Accidents—Their Cause and Prevention," *American City* 21 (August 1919): 126; "When Accidents Are Not Accidental," *Literary Digest* 87 (October 17, 1925): 87; Street, "Good and Bad Driving," 11. For repeaters and accident-prone drivers, see "Driver Testing Results. Prepared under the Direction of Henry R. DeSilva and Theodore W. Forbes, Harvard Traffic Bureau," WPA Project No. 6246–12259 (1937), Widener Library, Harvard University; U.S. Department of Agriculture, *Highway Accidents*; "Brain Tests for Drivers to Make Motoring Safe," *Literary Digest* 76 (January 20, 1923), 24–25.

26. Michael McGerr, *A Fierce Discontent: The Rise and Fall of the Progressive Movement, 1870–1920* (New York: Oxford University Press, 2003), xiv.

27. McGerr, *Fierce Discontent,* 316–318.

28. "Curbing the Automobile Danger," *Hampton's Magazine* 24 (March 1910): 426; "What Does a Motorist Think About?" 55. See also "Automobile Killings, Pro and Con," *Literary Digest* 76 (February 3, 1923): 59.

29. "Automobile Killings, Pro and Con," 52, 57; Towle, "Motor Menace," 102; "Accidents—Increasing and Decreasing," *Literary Digest* 107 (November 22, 1930): 26; for similar comments on the public mood, see Price, "Automotive Industry Should Lead," 1188.

30. "Herod and the Innocents," *Commonweal* 14 (August 19, 1931): 375.

31. Masterson, "Monster in the Car," 210; Frederick Dwight, "Automobile: The Other Side of the Shield," *Independent* 65 (December 3, 1908): 1299–1303; Montgomery Rollins, "The Automobile Rowdy," *Collier's* 48 (January 6, 1912): 25; "Safety on the Road," *Literary Digest* 73 (May 20, 1922): 82; "Courting Danger in the Automobile," *Literary Digest* 82 (June 5, 1924): 35.

32. McGerr, *Fierce Discontent,* 114–116; see also Paul Boyer, *Urban Masses and Moral Order in America, 1820–1920* (Cambridge, MA: Harvard University Press, 1992).

33. A cousin to the flivverboob was termed the "parking pirate," who was "the nervy chap who sneaks up behind you as you are about to back into a parking place downtown and beats you to it." Fred Gilman Jopp, "Motoring's Most Deadly Menace: 'The Flivverboob,'" *Illustrated World* 38 (October 1922): 268–270, 308; Richard Sylvester, "The Selfishness of City Speeding," *Harper's Weekly* 51 (March 1907): 384. Jopp quipped of the speed maniac, "In writing of the early Norsemen, Emerson remarks that 'never were gallant gentlemen so anxious to put themselves or their fellows out of the world.' Perhaps the speed maniacs are the Norsemen of the Sagas reincarnated."

34. Ryland P. Madison, "Motor Idiots I Have Met," *Country Life in America* 22 (May 15, 1912): 43; *Texas Parade* 2, no. 4 (September 1937): 23.

35. Obviously, reformers of the period did not treat the "love affair" as a comprehensive set of qualities, as I do in this text, but rather focused on the individual components that I argue make up the "love affair." Hubbard, *Automobile Hazards,* 22; State of Connecticut, "The Human Factor," 1; Traffic Safety Primer, *The Law of the Road Is a Courtesy. Prepared by and Printed for the Streets and Safety Committee of the Austin Chamber of Commerce* (Austin, TX: 1944), 5; Travelers Insurance Company, *Tremendous Trifles,* 13, 14.

36. Norman G. Shidle, "All This Talk about Speed, Subject Much to the Fore Now among Motorists and Manufacturers and Scramble to Supply Demand for Fast Cars Has Led to Some Pretty Strong Performance Claims," *Automotive Industries* 56, no. 24 (June 18, 1927): 925–927; see also Fred J. Wagner, "Safety First," *House Beautiful* 36, Supplement (June 1914): xxxvi, xxxviii, xl; A. G. Johnson, "Motor Car 'Don'ts,'" *Collier's* 50, Supplement (January 1913), 33; for roads and enclosed car design, see Shidle, "All This Talk about Speed," 925; John Henshaw Crider, "Speed with Ease," *Scientific American* (December 1936), 331.

37. Shidle, "All This Talk about Speed," 926.

38. C. H. Claudy, "Building Character with a Motor Car," *Country Life in America* 24 (August 1913): 84.

39. Henry Underwood, "Speed Mania and How to Cure It," *Harper's Weekly* 51 (March 30, 1907): 470; Dwight, "Automobile," 1301; John T. Floherty, *Youth at the Wheel: A Reference Book on Safe Driving* (Philadelphia: J. B. Lippincott, 1937), 14. See also George Ade, "Do You Run a Motor-Car or a Moveable Madhouse?" *American Magazine* 92 (Spring 1921): 53–55; Ade wrote that "Attack is being made only on those motorists who are obsessed with the belief that because a car *can* hit up to fifty-five an hour, it is hanging back when it does a measly thirty-five, and who further count up the result of their tours by the miles instead of by the smiles. The main idea with the road whippets seems to be the necessity of registering at some far distant point within a highly sporting time limit."

40. H. F. Moorhouse, *Driving Ambitions: An Analysis of the American Hot Rod Enthusiasm* (Manchester, UK: Manchester University Press, 1991), 27–33. See also Robert C. Post, *High Performance: The Culture and Technology of Drag Racing, 1950–2000* (Baltimore: Johns Hopkins University Press, 2001).

41. Moorhouse, *Driving Ambitions*, 26, 29.

42. Ibid., 33–34, 35. In another trick, called "rotation," occupants changed position within the car while it was in motion. This also became a common prank while stopped at intersections.

43. Maher, *Mind over Motor*, 26–27; Crider, "Speed with Ease," 330.

44. "Wanted: Some Speedy Action on Speed Advertising," *Printers' Ink* (October 6, 1927): 93–94, 96.

45. The Eastern Conference of Motor Vehicle Administrators, held in Cleveland, in May 1928, condemned speed advertising and called for an examination of legal limits to speed. The Automobile Manufacturers Association in 1937 passed a resolution to stop all references of top speeds in auto advertising. Robert L. Cusick, "State Authorities Make an Issue of Speed Advertising," *Automotive Industries* 59, no. 5 (August 4, 1928): 145–148.

46. "Shall We Do Away with the Speed Limit for Motorists?" *Literary Digest* 95 (December 3, 1927): 62–66.

47. While widely expressed, for specific references to "prized idiots," stupidity, insanity, and fear of the other driver, see Travelers Insurance Company, *Great American Gamble,* 5; C. O. Morris, "The Cause of Automobile Accidents," *Country Life in America* 15 (February 1909): 375; "Are Traffic Accidents Caused by Speed?" *American City* 44 (June 1931): 129; Ryland P. Madison, "Motor Idiots I Have Met," *Country Life in America* 22 (May 15 1912): 43. Julian Street, "Good and Bad Driving," 9; for fears see Richard Sylvester, "The Selfishness of City Speeding," *Harper's Weekly* 51 (March 1907): 384; T. H. Parker, "Why Some People Don't Buy Automobiles" *Country Life in America* 21 (November 15, 1911): 43.

48. Travelers Insurance Company, *Great American Gamble,* 4; Street, "Good and Bad Driving," 10–11; Underwood, "Speed Mania and How to Cure It," 470. For other accounts of the inevitability of reckless driving, see Fred J. Wagner, "Needless Offenses of Motorists," *House Beautiful* 34, Supplement (June 1913): xxxii–xxxiii, xxxvi; Automotive Safety Foundation, *Priority for Traffic Safety* (n.p.: 1941), 3; State of Connecticut, "The Human Factor ," 2–3, Widener Library, Harvard University; "Ten Thousand Automobile Deaths," 14.

49. Maher, *Mind over Motor*, 5, 6, 8; Floherty, *Youth at the Wheel,* 20; *Texas Safety News* 1, no. 20 (December 11, 1936): 11.

50. Texas Safety Association, "Report of the Investigation of Drunk Driving," 7, located at the Texas State Library, Austin, Texas. Murfreesboro, Tennessee, paper cited in *Texas Parade* 3, no. 7 (December 1938): 22.

51. The Volstead Act was the enabling legislation for the 18th Amendment, which prohibited the manufacture, distribution, and sale of intoxicating beverages. Prohibition was federal law from 1920 until repealed in 1933. "Cause of Traffic Accidents—As Seen by Chiefs of Police," *American City* (May 1926): 542.

52. *Texas Safety News* 1, no. 20 (December 11, 1936): 1; for reference to problems with narcotics, see Richard E. Enright, "How State Licensing Menaces Safety in City Streets," *American City* 28 (January 1923), 3–4; U.S. Department of Agriculture, *Highway Accidents*, 11.

53. Travelers Insurance Company, *Great American Gamble*, 34; *American Auto News* 1, no. 2 (September 1929): 7.

54. Zero-tolerance and anti–drunk driving campaigns by groups like Mothers Against Drunk Driving (MADD) suggest that this approach is still accepted today. Curtis Billings, "Alcohol and Motors," *Atlantic Monthly* 155, no. 4 (April 1935): 451–458; Texas Safety Association, "Report of the Investigation of Drunk Driving," 10–11.

55. James O. Fagan, *What Price Safety? Some Practical Suggestions* (n.p.: 1927), 4; Travelers Insurance Company, *Great American Gamble,* 34; Accident Facts, Connecticut. Calendar Year of 1942, State Department of Motor Vehicles, 6, Widener Library, Harvard University.

56. Maher, *Mind over Motor,* 12; Texas Safety Association, "Report of the Investigation of Drunk Driving," 8.

57. Hoffman wrote for *American Magazine* in 1935, quoted in Katherine Allen, *Bleeding Hearts: A Solution to the Automobile Tragedy* (San Antonio, TX: Naylor Company, 1941), 118; What Does a Motorist Think About?" 54.

58. Barry Mulligan, *Collisions in Street and Highway Transportation* (Philadelphia: Dorrance, 1936), 20–21; Maher, *Mind over Motor*, 19–21.

59. John J. Shaw, "The Horn and the Pedestrian," *Outlook* 126 (November 3, 1920): 433; "Automobile Killings, Pro and Con," 57. See also Frederick Upham Adams, "'Heads Up' and 'Use Corners Only': A Practical Article Showing How We Must Learn to Adapt Ourselves to Motor-Crowded Streets," *American Magazine* 81 (June 1916): 58–59.

60. Hoffman cited in Allen, *Bleeding Hearts* (1941), 118; "Look before You Jay-Walk," *Saturday Evening Post* 195 (May 5, 1923): 28; see also Wagner, "Safety First," xxxvi, xxxviii, xl. Wagner went so far as to blame women carrying their babies as a public nuisance on the street, for "time after time we see women start to cross directly in the path of automobiles without looking up or down the street. If you think this statement is exaggerated just observe the next few weeks what percentage of women with infants and children you see trying to cross a street in careless fashion."

61. "Herod and the Innocents," 375; "St. Louis Monument to Children Killed by Cars," 54; see also, "Child Victims of the Auto," *Literary Digest* 100 (February 2, 1929): 34.

62. State of Texas, *First Biennial Report of the State Highway Commission* (Austin, TX: Von Boeckmann-Jones, 1917), 15

63. Humphrey, "Our Delightful Man-Killer,"727; P. H. Cameron, "Selfishness Rules Our Highways," *American Auto News* 1, no. 15 (November 1929): inside cover; "Where Road Wrecks Happen," *Scientific American* 126 (May 1922): 317.

64. Humphrey, "Our Delightful Man-Killer," 726–727.

65. Maher, *Mind over Motor,* 21–22; "Wrecks That Come to the Repairman," 84.

66. "A Little More Courtesy," *Literary Digest* 76 (May 24, 1923): 64–66; "'Stepping On the Gas'—And Results," *Literary Digest* 83 (October 4, 1924): 35–36.

67. Frank Wiggins, "Traffic Education to Supplement Traffic Legislation," *American City* 29 (September 1923): 273; "A Little More Courtesy," 64; see also *American Auto News* 1, no. 1 (August 1929): 12.

68. John J. Shaw, "The Horn and the Pedestrian," *Outlook* 126 (November 3, 1920): 433; *American Auto News* 1, no. 1 (August 1929): 12–13; see also Edward H. Holmes, "Better Be Sure Than Sorry," *Outlook* 126 (November 24, 1920): 561.

69. "Cars of Juggernaut," *New Republic* 60 (October 16, 1929): 232; Humphrey, "Our Delightful Man-Killer," 727; "Where Road Wrecks Happen," 317; "Death by Automobile," *Outlook* 146 (August 10, 1927): 462; "The Murderous Motor," *New Republic* 47 (July 7, 1926): 190; for

similar sentiments, see Charles B. Hayward, "Perils of the Country Road: The Dangers Behind the Coppice and Round the Bend That Lie in Wait for Careless Drivers," *Harper's Weekly* 54 (July 2, 1910): 16–17; "Motor Accidents," *Saturday Evening Post* 195 (March 24, 1923): 26; "The Demon Chauffeur," *Literary Digest* 77 (April 28, 1923): 12.

70. Charles E. Simons, "Teaching Highway Safety," *Texas Parade* 2, no. 2 (July 1937): 3–4.

71. Ray W. Sherman, *If You're Going to Drive Fast* (New York: Thomas Y. Crowell, 1935), 43–44.

Chapter 5. Perfection and Perfectibility in Auto Safety Reform

1. *(Dallas) Morning News*, January 8, 1937, Section 2, p.1, 10; *Texas Parade* 1, no. 9 (February 1937): 3–5, 23; Vertical File: Phares, L. G., Center for American History, University of Texas–Austin.

2. *(Dallas) Morning News*, January 8, 1937, Section 2, p. 1; This was the second state conference; see *Texas Safety News* 1, no. 20 (December 11, 1936): 1. In 1935, the NSC proposed the goal of reducing traffic fatalities by 7 percent per year. Five years later, traffic fatalities increased by over 35 percent.

3. *(Dallas) Morning News*, January 8, 1937, Section 2, p. 1.

4. For a good example of this criticism, see Robert F. Baker, *The Highway Risk Problem: Policy Issues in Highway Safety* (New York: Wiley-Interscience, 1971), vii, 2, 50, 103.

5. Clay McShane, *Down the Asphalt Path: The Automobile and the American City* (New York: Columbia University Press, 1994), 174–175, 177–179; John D. Graham, *Auto Safety: Assessing America's Performance* (Dover, MA: Auburn House Publishing, 1989), 7–9.

6. Baker, *Highway Risk Problem*, 15; Baker cites a 1962 study by the Ford Motor Company that showed that the statistically average driver makes more than two billion correct decisions before one that leads to an accident, ibid., 104; Shinar, *Psychology on the Road: The Human Factor in Traffic Safety* (New York: John Wiley and Sons, 1978), 2–4.

7. McShane writes, "the engineers measured their success much more by improvements in mobility than safety. Yet these improvements did not end congestion and, ultimately, their primary achievement was to improve safety." Clay McShane and Gijs Mom, "Death and the Automobile: A Comparison of Automobile Ownership and Fatal Accidents in the United States and the Netherlands, 1910–1980," paper presented at the ICOHTEC Conference, August 2000; McShane, *Down the Asphalt Path*, 202; James J. Flink, *The Automobile Age* (Cambridge, MA: MIT Press, 2001), 235–236.

8. Baker, *Highway Risk Problem*, 103; Daniel M. Albert, "Order out of Chaos: Automobile Safety, Technology and Society, 1925 to 1965," Ph.D. dissertation, University of Michigan, 1997, 29, 241, 270; Joel Webb Eastman, "Styling vs. Safety: The American Automobile Industry and the Development of Automobile Safety, 1900–1966," Ph.D. dissertation, University of Florida, 1973, 157–162.

9. William Kaszynski, *The American Highway: The History and Culture of Roads in the United States* (Jefferson, NC: McFarland, 2000); Albert, "Order out of Chaos," 27; Alfred E. Ommen, "The Right of the Road: An Aggravating Phase of Motoring," *Collier's* 41, Supplement (January 15, 1910): 11; National Conference on Street and Highway Safety, *First National Conference on Street and Highway Safety, Hon. Herbert Hoover, Secretary of Commerce, Chairman*, December 15–16 (Washington, DC: Government Printing Office, 1924), 8.

10. *(Dallas) Morning News*, January 8, 1937, Section 2, p. 10; Miller McClintock, *Street Traffic Control* (New York: McGraw-Hill, 1925), 166–167.

11. Fred J. Wagner, "Safety First," *House Beautiful* 36 (June 1914): xxxvi.

12. "Can't We Stop the Slaughter?" *Collier's* 75 (June 6, 1925): 24; "Consider the Other Fellow," *Collier's* 85 (June 21, 1930): 66; "'Gasoline Rabies'—A National Peril," *Literary Digest* 78 (September 8, 1923): 62; *Texas Parade* 2, no. 2 (July 1937): 14.

13. "Gasoline Rabies'—A National Peril," 60–65. The Cleveland *Plain Dealer* added, "Perhaps the best treatment for a sufferer from gas-madness would be to rusticate him on a turnip

farm in the mountains where the roads are too steep to be negotiated by even the most un-discourageable flivver. Under such treatment the recovery might be permanent." *Texas Parade* 1, no. 6 (November 1936): 20; Koehler quoted, emphasis added, in *Texas Safety News* 2, no. 3 (January 15, 1937): 2. See also Ray W. Sherman, *If You're Going to Drive Fast* (New York: Thomas Y. Crowell, 1935), 12.

14. Risk statistics show that in the year 2000, 1.53 Americans died per million VMT. Change the circumstances, by limiting the analysis to a certain age of the driver or the time of day, for example, and you change this probability. Safety, by contrast, is the *perception* by individuals that they have effectively limited the variables that produce risk. The increased visibility of airport security following the September 11, 2001, terrorist attacks, for example, provides some with a certain measure of perceived safety. Risk is statistical and comparatively easy to demon-strate through mortality rates. Safety is perceptional and relative to the observer. As a result, we can greatly influence our perceived safety but can do very little to change our exposure to risk. Using extreme examples to prove the point, we can be completely safe from death by automobile if we never drive nor come near a motor vehicle, but we will all eventually succumb to the risk of death. In early auto education, safety perceptions very frequently were linked to normative val-ues, of contributing a "positive good" to society. Driver education critic Edward Tenney wrote: "By some occult process, which [education advocate Albert W.] Whitney never describes, the human being who has acquired the safety soul-set is free to make the choice between good and evil, between the mean, low adventure and the high, noble one. The negative power of Safety enables one to throw out the evil; the positive power enables one to bring in the good." Edward A. Tenney, *The Highway Jungle: The Story of the Public Safety Movement and the Failure of "Driver Education" in the Public Schools* (New York: Exposition Press, 1962), 51–52.

15. Richard Shelton Kirby, "The Right to Drive," *Atlantic* 147 (April 1931): 442. During these same years annual auto fatalities rose from 13,253, in 1921, to 32,914, in 1940.

16. McShane, *Down the Asphalt Path*, 178–181; see also P. H. Cameron, "Human Element at Fault!" *American Auto News* 6, no. 9 (April 1930): inside cover.

17. Automotive Safety Foundation, *Standard Highway Safety Program for States: A Working Program to Increase Traffic Efficiency and Reduce Accidents* (New York: Automotive Safety Foun-dation, 1939), 5.

18. Historians Mark Aldrich, Price Fishback, and Shawn Kantor argue that the largest and most modern industries initially embraced risk reduction because of these inherent economic efficiencies. Mark Aldrich, *Safety First: Technology, Labor, and Business in the Building of Ameri-can Work Safety, 1870–1939* (Baltimore: Johns Hopkins University Press, 1997), 261–262, 275, 282; Price Fishback and Shawn Kantor, *A Prelude to the Welfare State: The Origins of Workers' Compensation* (Chicago: University of Chicago Press, 2000).

19. In 1911, 146 women workers died in a horrific factory fire at the Triangle Shirtwaist Com-pany, in New York City. The owners, warned by unions of on-the-job hazards and blocked exits, neglected to provide even basic fire prevention methods. Their neglect certainly contributed to the extensive fatalities. The resulting furor led to a dynamic combination between labor activ-ists, progressive businessmen, and state authorities that proved a forerunner of many pieces of Progressive Era and New Deal legislation. See Richard A. Greenwald, *The Triangle Fire, the Protocols of Peace, and Industrial Democracy in Progressive Era New York* (Philadelphia: Temple University Press, 2005).

20. Aldrich, *Safety First*; Fishback and Kantor, *Prelude to the Welfare State*; Tenney, *Highway Jungle*, 20–25.

21. Tenney, *Highway Jungle*, 22, 24.

22. Aldrich, *Safety First*, 282, Appendix 1–3; U.S. Department of Commerce, *Highway Statis-tics, Summary to 1955* (Washington, DC: Government Printing Office, 1957), 100.

23. John J. Maher, *Mind over Motor* (Detroit: n.p., 1937), 96.

24. C. W. Price, "Startling Figures for Automobile Fatalities," *American City* 25 (September 1921): 205–206; "Killings and Accidents as a Threat to the Whole Motorcar Industry," *Literary Digest* 80 (January 12, 1924): 60–64; *Texas Safety News* 2, no. 4 (March 20, 1937):1; State of Texas, Governor's Special Traffic Accident Investigation Committee, *Official Traffic Investigation Report on [the] Collision That Killed Six People at the Crossing of State Highway No. 15 (U.S. No. 80) and Belt Line Road on May 5, 1938,* Center for American History, University of Texas–Austin, 3; William Ullman, "Safeguarding America's Motor Transportation Interests," *Outlook* 134 (June 6, 1923): 143.

25. For examples of the concern that safety would reduce early auto sales, see "Time to Stop," *Outlook* 91 (April 17, 1909): 852; T. H. Parker, "Why Some People Don't Buy Automobiles," *Country Life in America* 21 (November 15, 1911): 43, 54; "Killings and Accidents as a Threat," 60–64; C. W. Price, "Startling Figures," 205–206; C. W. Price, "Automotive Industry Should Lead in Safety Movement," *Automotive Industries* 49, no. 24 (December 13, 1923): 1187–1189.

26. Tenney, *Highway Jungle*, 25; "Untangling Our Automobile Laws: How the Motor Vehicles Commissioners of Ten Eastern States are Working Together toward Uniformity," *Scientific American* 130 (April 1923): 232. Tragically, the rapid increase in public spending for modern roads and highways only encouraged greater speeding. As safety scholar Joel Eastman concludes, the process was "an invitation to chaos." See Eastman, "Styling vs. Safety," 8–9.

27. In addition, the second act designated that these funds be spent on the principal arteries of local and state commerce, limited to not more than 7 percent of the total rural mileage. Flink, *Automobile Age*, 170–171; Tom Lewis, *Divided Highway*, 12–22; U.S. Department of Commerce, *Highway Statistics, Summary to 1955*, 58, 139, 149. Congress authorized $500,000 for rural post-road construction in 1912, which acted as a case study for the 1916 legislation. Lewis, *Divided Highway*, 22–23. For the entire reporting period from 1921 to 1940: $3,235,659,000 came from federal sources, or 30.5 percent of the total; $2,483,369,000 came from state or local bonds, or 23.4 percent of the total; $4,901,610,000 came from user revenues, or 46.2 percent of the total.

28. U.S. Department of Commerce, *Highway Statistics, Summary to 1955*, 78; Corey T. Lesseig, *Automobility: Social Change in the American South, 1909–1939* (New York: Routledge, 2001), 60; Texas State Highway Commission, *First Biennial Report of the State Highway Commission* (Austin, TX: Von Boeckmann-Jones, 1918), 41, 43; Texas State Highway Commission, *Second Biennial Report of the State Highway Commission for the Period December 1, 1918, to December 1, 1920* (Austin, TX: Von Boeckmann-Jones, 1921), 28–29; Texas State Highway Commission, *Third Biennial Report of the State Highway Commission for the Period December 1, 1920, to December 1, 1922* (Austin, TX: Von Boeckmann-Jones, 1923), 44; Texas State Highway Commission, *Fourth Biennial Report of the State Highway Commission for the Period December 1, 1922, to September 1, 1924* (Austin, TX: Von Boeckmann-Jones, 1925), 77; U.S. Census Bureau, *Statistical Abstract of the United States: 2003* (No. HS–41. Transportation Indicators for Motor Vehicles and Airlines, 1900 to 2001), Mini-Historical Statistics, 77–78.

29. U.S. Department of Commerce, *Highway Statistics, Summary to 1955* (Washington, DC: Government Printing Office, 1957), 77, 151; Lewis, *Divided Highway*, 11, 14–16.

30. Lewis, *Divided Highway*, 13; Texas State Highway Commission, *Third Biennial Report*, 18. Texas Department of Transportation, Minute Orders (Red Book), 1917–1948, Reel 41-MIN.0–1.

31. An ancillary yet important development to highway funding was the source of the local and state matching monies. Typically, most states avoided using or issuing property taxes to pay for road improvements. But because the 1916 and 1921 bills specifically provided only matching funds, and only to selected rural routes, it was important for states to establish a system of finance broad enough to generate the necessary revenues to pay for these expensive projects. The rapid growth of automobility provided the solution. User fees from licensing, gasoline, and

oil furnished an almost limitless supply of local revenue. In 1924 alone, Texas officials estimated revenues of nearly $10.7 million for licensing and $3.8 million in gas taxes. The State Highway Department added, parenthetically, that they would see only $10.5 million from these sources due to diversion of funds. The concern over the diversion of revenues—to local projects ineligible for federal matching funds—was a source of constant concern for many auto advocates. Texas State Highway Commission, *Fourth Biennial Report*, 12–17. The shift from licensing to gasoline taxes was pronounced during these years. By 1937, the state reported earnings of $5.8 million from registration fees and $17.7 million from gasoline taxes; *Texas Parade* 1, no. 6 (November 1936): 27. Minnesota passed the first state constitutional amendment prohibiting diversion in November 1920, followed by Kansas and Colorado. These acts made "outright prohibition against the use of road-user taxes for purposes other than the construction, maintenance, and administration of highways." *Highway Statistics, Summary to 1955*, 48. The U.S. government passed its own antidiversion law with the Federal Aid Highway Act and Highway Revenue Act of 1956, removing these funds (including auto-related excise taxes) from the general use funds and placing them into a segregated highway trust fund. For auto-related federal taxes, 1917–1956, see *Highway Statistics, Summary to 1955*, 142. Texas did not pass a diversion law until November 1946. For reactions to the problem of diversion in Texas, see *Texas Parade* 1, no. 1 (June 1936): 2; *Texas Parade* 1, no. 6 (November 1936): 22; *Texas Parade* 1, no. 10 (March 1937): 15, 18.

32. "Motor Laws That Make Lawbreakers," *Literary Digest* 77 (May 12, 1923): 58, 61; "Unmuddling Our Motor Regulations," *Literary Digest* 75 (November 18, 1922): 73; John A. Harriss, "What Automobile Drivers Want," *Collier's* 69 (May 20, 1922): 14, 27.

33. T[yman] O. Abbott, "The Lawmaker and the Automobile," *Outing Magazine* 54 (August 1909): 614; Tyman O. Abbott, "What a Law-Abiding Motorist Found Out in a Tour of the United States," *Country Life in America* 18 (August 1910): 468; "The New Law in New Jersey," *Literary Digest* 44 (May 11, 1912): 1000–1001; Charles Johnson, "The Motorist and the Law," *Harper's Weekly* 54 (September 3, 1910): 12–13.

34. Abbott, "Lawmaker and the Automobile," 614; Abbott, "What a Law-Abiding Motorist Found Out," 468. States represented at the 1921 conference included Ohio, Pennsylvania, Maryland, New York, New Jersey, Connecticut, Maine, Vermont, and Massachusetts. "Motor Laws that Make Lawbreakers," *Literary Digest* 77 (May 12, 1923): 60; "Prevention of Automobile Accidents," *Scientific American* 129 (October 1923): 228; "One Law Versus Forty-Eight: The Practicability and the Necessity of Uniform Motor-Vehicle Legislation in All the States," *Scientific American* 130 (February 1924): 96, 140–142. See also Eastman, "Styling vs. Safety," 175. For additional calls for legal uniformity, see Edgar Jenkyns, "A Little Law for the Motorist," *Outing Magazine* 59 (January 1912): 479–480; "More Than One Hundred Automobile Bills," *Literary Digest* 48 (March 28, 1914): 714; A. B. Barber, "How the States Are Working towards a Uniform Motor Vehicle Code," *American City* 35 (December 1926): 851–854.

35. For Coolidge, see National Conference on Street and Highway Safety, *First National Conference*, 5–6; for Hoover, see National Conference on Street and Highway Safety, *Ways and Means to Traffic Safety. Recommendations of National Conference on Street and Highway Safety, Including Findings of All Conference Committees and of General Meetings of Conference Held in 1924, 1926, and 1930, as Summarized and Approved by Third National Conference, May 27–28–29, 1930* (Washington, DC: Government Printing Office: 1930), 5; for Roper, see "How to Stop Accidents: Summary of Opinions Developed at a Conference of Contact Men, Operating in Connection with the Accident Prevention Conference, as a Two-day Meeting in the Department of Commerce, Washington DC, 1935," Library of Congress, Washington, DC, 5. Business representatives were active participants in all four conferences (as well as the regional meeting that preceded them). These included the American Automobile Association, the American Electric Railway Association, the American Mutual Alliance, the American Railway Association, the Chamber of Commerce of

the United States, the Motor and Equipment Association, the National Association of Taxicab Owners, the National Automobile Chamber of Commerce, the National Bureau of Casualty and Surety Underwriters, and the Rubber Manufacturers' Association.

36. Forrest Crissey, "Speed Cop," *Saturday Evening Post* 197 (March 28, 1925): 10. By the time of the third national conference, in 1930, the organization standardized on six specific areas of reform. These were titled: Uniform Traffic Regulations, Enforcement of Traffic Laws and Regulations, Education of Highway Users, Traffic Accident Records, Construction and Maintenance of Motor Vehicles, and Street and Highway Traffic Facilities.

37. "The Murderous Motor," *New Republic* 47 (July 7, 1926): 190; National Conference on Street and Highway Safety, *Ways and Means to Traffic Safety*, 10. U.S. Department of Agriculture, Bureau of Public Roads, *Highway Accidents, Their Causes and Recommendations for Their Prevention* (Washington, DC: Government Printing Office, 1938), 2.

38. National Conference on Street and Highway Safety, *First National Conference*, 10. *Washington Star* quoted in Eastman, "Styling vs. Safety," 168; "How to Stop Accidents," 19.

39. National Conference on Street and Highway Safety, *First National Conference*, 9–10; Eastman, "Styling vs. Safety," 183–188.

40. Automotive Safety Foundation, *Standard Highway Safety Programs for States*, 2–3.

41. "How to Stop Accidents," 2, 5; U.S. Department of Agriculture, *Highway Accidents*, 14–16; Automotive Safety Foundation, *Standard Highway Safety Programs for States*, 5–6. See also Barber, "How the States are Working," 851–854.

42. For example, see John T. Floherty, *Youth at the Wheel: A Reference Book on Safe Driving* (Philadelphia: J. B. Lippincott, 1937), 13.

43. For these critical years, see Eastman, "Styling vs. Safety," 53–68.

44. Maher, *Mind over Motor*, 38. For early problems with brakes, see "Two Cures for Motor Accidents," *Literary Digest* 74 (July 1, 1922): 60–62; M. Worth Colwell, "The Worst Roads in America," *Outing Magazine* 51 (November 1907): 246–249; for headlamps, see Joseph Tracy, "Suggestions on Automobile Driving," *Country Life in America* 12 (October 1907): 684; for tires, see Wagner, "Safety First," xxxviii, xl; for headlamp testing, see Texas State Highway Commission, *First Biennial Report*, 25. See also National Conference on Street and Highway Safety, *Ways and Means to Traffic Safety*, 26–27.

45. For responsiveness, see Norman G. Shidle, "All This Talk About Speed, Subject Much to the Fore Now among Motorists and Manufacturers and Scramble to Supply Demand for Fast Cars Has Led to Some Pretty Strong Performance Claims," *Automotive Industries* 56, no. 24 (June 18, 1927): 925–927; Walter P. Chrysler, "The Only Cure for Auto Accidents," *Outlook* 145 (April 27, 1927): 531–533; Maher, *Mind over Motor*, 38; Austin A. Lescarboura, "Cross-Examining the Automobile: What Organized Research Work Is Doing for the Present and Future Automotive Industry," *Scientific American* 131 (July 1924): 8–9, 59.

46. Lescarboura, "Cross-Examining the Automobile," 8; Floherty, *Youth at the Wheel*, 20; Maher, *Mind over Motor*, 43; National Conference on Street and Highway Safety, *Ways and Means to Traffic Safety*, 26; see also "When Will Automobiles Be Perfect?" *Scientific American* 128 (February 1923): 82; Albert W. Whitney, *Man and the Motor Car* (New York: J. J. Little and Ives, 1936), 10; Cameron, "Human Element at Fault!" inside cover.

47. Eastman, "Styling vs. Safety," 62–68, 89, 97.

48. Emphasis in the original, Maher, *Mind over Motor*, 40; "Human Nature vs. the Motor Vehicle," *American City* 45 (September 1931): 117; "Taking the 'Un' out of 'Unavoidable,'" *Literary Digest* 78 (July 14, 1923): 57; "Motor Accidents," *Saturday Evening Post* 195 (March 24, 1923): 26; see also "Motor Car Emergencies," *Scientific American* 117 (September 8 1917): 184; H. S. Whiting, "Saving the Car by Careful Driving: Some of the Evils of an Excess of Caution," *Scientific American* 114 (January 1, 1919): 18; Eastman, "Styling vs. Safety," 157–158.

49. Accident Prevention Conference, "How to Stop Accidents," 6.

50. "Automobile Killings, Pro and Con," *Literary Digest* 76 (February 3, 1923): 59; "Shall We Do Away with the Speed Limit For Motorists?" *Literary Digest* 95 (December 3, 1927): 64.

51. "Device Self-Convicts Speed Law Violators," *Illustrated World* 34 (January 1921): 822; "Automatic Collision-Dodger," *Scientific American* 127 (October 1922): 243; John Henshaw Crider, "Speed with Ease," *Scientific American* (December 1936): 332; Norman G. Shidle, "All This Talk about Speed," *Automotive Industries* 56, no. 24 (June 18, 1927): 927.

52. "What Shall be the Cure for Speed Mania?" *Illustrated World* 34 (September 1920): 85–86; "Two Cures for Motor Accidents," 60–62; *Texas Safety News* 1, no. 20 (December 11, 1936): 1; Shidle, "All This Talk About Speed," 927; "Speed and Control to Stop Auto Deaths," *Literary Digest* 104 (March 1, 1930): 16. See also Frederick Dwight, "Automobile: The Other Side of the Shield," *Independent* 65 (December 3, 1908): 1301; "St. Louis Monument to Children Killed by Cars," *Literary Digest* 79 (December 8, 1923): 52–55; Anedith Jo Bond Nash, "Death on the Highway: The Automobile Wreck in American Culture, 1920–1940," Ph.D. dissertation, University of Minnesota, 1983, 50–51.

53. For example, see Cameron, "Human Element at Fault!" inside cover.

54. National Conference on Street and Highway Safety, *Ways and Means to Traffic Safety*, 34–35.

55. M. Worth Colwell, "The Worst Roads in America," *Outing Magazine* 51 (November 1907): 248; for other health concerns, see P. G. Heinemann, "The Automobile and the Public Health," *Popular Science Monthly* 84 (March 1914): 284–289. For examples of poor roads and auto accidents, see Will Barry, "The Automobile as the Agent of Civilization: California and Good Roads," *Overland Monthly* 53 (March 1909): 244–248; Charles F. Barrett, "The 'Blind Turn': Its Dangers and Various Methods of Solution," *Scientific American* 114 (January 1, 1916): 24. For economic efficiency and examples of business safety model of good roads, see John R. Eustis, "Haste Makes Waste," *Independent* 94 (May 4, 1918): 216.

56. "Prevention of Automobile Accidents," 228; National Conference on Street and Highway Safety, *Ways and Means to Traffic Safety,* 28–35; Albert, "Order out of Chaos," 61–62.

57. Albert, "Order out of Chaos," 30–75; on traffic engineers, Albert writes that, as a discipline, they were "inchoate and undifferentiated from municipal management . . . engaged in the kind of 'apolitical' management known and celebrated at the time as social engineering. They represented the evolution of the liberal progressives, from softhearted idealists before World War I into hard-headed social engineers in the interwar period," ibid., 44.

58. Albert, "Order out of Chaos," 36–42; McShane, *Down the Asphalt Path,* 185–187. By contrast to auto flow efficiency, railroad officials promoted changes that dramatically slowed car travel: One Long Island Railroad engineer proposed, for grade crossings, a series of sharp turns and one-way lanes "calculated to check the speed of motorists to a safe point, if not to force a full stop, before permitting machines to cross the tracks." See "One Way to Cut Down Crossing Accidents," *Literary Digest* 79 (November 17, 1923): 69.

59. Albert wrote, "Highway engineers took from Eno the mantle of continuous flow, offering cloverleafs as more elaborate expressions of Eno's rotary. They were far less interested in his traffic rules. That effort to control behavior through regulation was taken up by early traffic engineers. Although they adopted his methods, however, traffic engineers did not embrace the dream of uninterrupted motor traffic. Instead, they pursued the effective governing of traffic." Albert, "Order out of Chaos," 43.

60. McClintock, *Street Traffic Control,* 168; Albert, "Order out of Chaos," 50–52; McShane, *Down the Asphalt Path,* 200–202.

61. Albert concludes that traffic engineers' "effort to gain prestige and power through the rhetoric of science and engineering backfired." Albert, "Order out of Chaos," 32, 74–75. For rejection by ASCE, see ibid., 59–64; for rejection by Harvard and Yale, see ibid., 68–70.

62. *Texas Parade* 2, no. 2 (July 1937): 4; Maher, *Mind over Motor,* 71.

63. Richard Hofstadter, *Anti-Intellectualism in American Life* (New York: Vintage Books, 1962), 323–339.

64. The NEA, for example, valued accident prevention education largely because it unified their new curriculum. Michael McGerr, *A Fierce Discontent: The Rise and Fall of the Progressive Movement, 1870–1920* (New York: Oxford University Press, 2005), 109–110, 237; Hofstadter, *Anti-Intellectualism,* 336, 340, 341.

65. For Bibliography, see Tenney, *Highway Jungle,* 60; *Texas Parade* 2, no. 2 (July 1937): 3, 28–30.

66. American Automobile Association, *State Rules and Regulations Governing Safety Education in the United States* (Washington, DC: American Automobile Association, 1938).

67. Robert Chancellor, "Everybody Hates a Bad Driver," *American Magazine* 99 (June 1925): 66–67, 145–149; "The Fight for Safer Motoring," *Literary Digest* 85 (May 16, 1925): 70; National Conference on Street and Highway Safety, *Ways and Means to Traffic Safety,* 19, 21.

68. *Texas Parade* 2, no. 2 (July 1937): 28; Cameron described how "child training in safety is found in the 95 Junior Safety Councils now functioning in 74 public schools and 21 parochial schools in Kansas City. Twelve thousand school children under the age of fourteen are voluntary members of these councils. They hold rousing safety meetings, with programs, songs, yells and addresses on various safety subjects. Any Kansas City schoolchild knows the jay-walker for what he is; they inflict penalties on one another in regular courts for playing in streets, crossing streets not at corners; ignoring traffic signals; running in front of moving automobiles." In "Fight for Safer Motoring," 70–71.

69. Roy Rutherford Bailey, *Sure Pop and the Safety Scouts* (New York: World Book, 1915).

70. Ralph Henry Barbour, *For Safety!* (New York: D. Appleton-Century, 1936), 11–22, 42–43, 55.

71. Whitney, *Man and the Motor Car,* xi, xii, xiii.

72. E. George Payne, "Education in Accident Prevention," *Journal of Educational Sociology* 11 (September 1937): 20–21.

73. Payne quoted in Tenney, *Highway Jungle,* 36, 37, 39.

74. Whitney, *Man and the Motor Car,* 64. Whitney also cites the problems from youth culture, particularly jazz music, ibid., 64; Payne quoted in Tenney, *Highway Jungle,* 42–44. For Tenney, ibid., 68.

75. "Your Driver Training Plan. A Brief Concise and Practical Approach to Training Youthful Drivers." Issued by Department of Public Safety in Cooperation with State Department of Education (Austin, TX, 1943), 1; State of Texas, Department of Public Safety. Traffic Safety Quiz, Compiled by Safety Division, 1943; for a similar moralizing tone see also Floherty, *Youth at the Wheel.*

76. Whitney quoted in Tenney, *Highway Jungle,* 54.

77. "A Survey of Traffic Conditions in the City of Dallas Texas with Checks of Obedience to Traffic Laws," Works Progress Administration, Project No. 1065, sponsored by the Dallas Police Department, Field Work, 1933–1937, ii. Center for American History, University of Texas–Austin.

78. The study noted that problems in underreporting may bias this conclusion. "While all accidents involving school children during school hours are reported to the Board of Education, no permanent record is kept by that body. Records in the Police department are not broken down to show accidents to children en route to schools separate from accidents to children not en route to school." Ibid., 1.

79. Ibid., 11–15, 21.

Chapter 6. The Mirrored Glasses: Enforcement and the Inevitable Auto Accident

1. Barker, Floyd, Nelson/Gillis, and Dillinger were each killed in 1934 or 1935. For criminal attitudes and the car, see Blaine A. Brownell, "A Symbol of Modernity: Attitudes towards the

Automobile in Southern Cities in the 1920s," *American Quarterly* 24 (March 1972): 36–42. Greg DeBenedictis argues that Chicago gangsters often used the automobile as symbols of their respectability and social status, see Gregory DeBenedictis, "Gangster Funerals in Chicago," MA Thesis, Loyola University, Chicago, 1996. The official number of Bonnie and Clyde's victims varies. Barrow was likely to have killed two police officers in August 1932, two more by April 1933, and six more, including a guard at the Eastham Prison Farm in Huntsville, Texas, by April 1934. In December 1934, the FBI believed the pair responsible for thirteen murders. See E. R. Milner, *The Lives and Times of Bonnie and Clyde* (Carbondale: Southern Illinois University Press, 1996); U.S. Department of Justice, Federal Bureau of Investigation, "Clyde Champion Barrow, Bonnie Parker," December 14, 1934, I.C. #26–31672.

2. *Austin American,* May 24, 1934, 1.

3. Walter Prescott Webb, *The Texas Rangers: A Century of Frontier Defense*, 2nd ed. (Austin: University of Texas Press, 1935, 1965), 539. For an updated and much less sympathetic view of Hamer, see Benjamin Heber Johnson, *Revolution in Texas: How a Forgotten Rebellion and Its Bloody Suppression Turned Mexicans into Americans* (New Haven, CT: Yale University Press, 2003), 174–175. Given rumors of Clyde Barrow's impotence, the term *lovers* may not be literal.

4. Albert W. Whitney, *Man and the Motor Car* (New York: J. J. Little and Ives , 1936), 14.

5. Parker and Barrow probably outgunned the agents. After the two were killed, Hamer found three Browning automatic rifles, two sawed-off shotguns, nine Colt automatic pistols, a Colt revolver, one hundred machine gun clips of twenty cartridges each, three thousand rounds of ammunition, and fifteen license plates in their car. Webb, *Texas Rangers,* 543. Hamer reportedly later told Phares, "There [wasn't] much to it. . . . They just drove into the wrong place," quoted in Anedith Jo Bond Nash, "Death on the Highway: The Automobile Wreck in American Culture, 1920–1940," Ph.D. dissertation, University of Minnesota, 1983, 83.

6. *Austin American,* May 24, 1934, 1. One Texas newspaper later reported, "Phares was head of the state highway patrol at the time. Hamer held a commission as a state highway patrolman to facilitate his work. Mannie Gault, a highway patrolman, was given him as an assistant at his request. Properly they reported the Louisiana killing to Phares. He recognized its public interest and the importance of letting both the officers and the public know. Naturally he was quoted as authority for announcement, though he asked no credit." See Clippings File, 1935–1936, Texas Department of Public Safety, Archives and Information Services Division, Texas State Library and Archives Commission; Webb, *Texas Rangers,* 540.

7. Charles E. Simons, "Sentinels of Safety: The Enlarged Texas Highway Patrol," *Texas Parade* 2, no. 7 (December 1937): 3–4. The 138 new patrolmen commissioned on October 15, 1937, were the largest class in national history. Of these, 42 were from the military, 20 of these were above PFC, 68 of total had attended college, 16 of these graduated, all candidates had high school diplomas.

8. John J. Maher, *Mind over Motor* (Detroit: n.p., 1937), 61; National Conference on Street and Highway Safety, *Ways and Means to Traffic Safety. Recommendations of National Conference on Street and Highway Safety, Including Findings of All Conference Committees and of General Meetings of Conference Held in 1924, 1926, and 1930, as Summarized and Approved by Third National Conference, May 27–28–29, 1930* (Washington, DC: Government Printing Office, 1930), 18.

9. *Texas Parade* 2, no. 8 (January 1938): 30; Records, Texas Department of Public Safety, Archives and Information Services Division, Texas State Library and Archives Commission. Phares quoted at Accident Prevention Conference report titled "How to Stop Accidents: Summary of Opinions Developed at a Conference of Contact Men, Operating in Connection with the Accident Prevention Conference, as a Two-day Meeting in the Department of Commerce, Washington DC, 1935," Library of Congress, Washington, DC, 17; *(Corpus Christi) Caller,* September 1, 1935, 1. For polite troopers, see *(Corpus Christi) Caller,* June 26, 1935.

10. *(Corpus Christi) Caller,* January 13, 1935, 1–2; *(Corpus Christi) Caller,* February 9, 1935, 1–2.

11. *(Corpus Christi) Caller,* January 13, 1935, 1; *(Corpus Christi) Caller,* February 9, 1935, 1.

12. Briefly, the legend holds that, following a local disturbance, one Texas Ranger, Captain Bill McDonald, was sent to quell the uprising. As McDonald arrived at the train station, to the obvious disappointment of local law enforcement officials, he was asked why only a single ranger was sent. McDonald reportedly replied "what difference does it make; you only got one riot." See Albert Bigelow Paine, *Captain Bill McDonald, Texas Ranger: A Story of Frontier Reform* (Austin, TX: State House Press, 1986).

13. *(Corpus Christi) Caller,* August 9 1935, 5; Webb, *Texas Rangers.*

14. *Texas Parade* 2, no. 6 (November 1937): 3; Maher, *Mind over Motor,* 130.

15. Clippings File, 1935–1936, Texas Department of Public Safety; Webb, *Texas Rangers,* 541.

16. At the Dallas NSC conference, where the three girls pled "we want to live" (see Chapter Five), the highway patrolmen sat in conspicuous isolation from the Rangers and Dallas police authorities. The investigation of the Darst-Mullins crash, in May 1938, proved the final blow to Phares. Following the damning conclusions of the committee, which cited lax highway police enforcement as the leading source of the disaster, Phares resigned from the TSHP. Clippings File, 1935–1936, Texas Department of Public Safety.

17. National Conference on Street and Highway Safety, *Ways and Means to Traffic Safety,* 18; Automotive Safety Foundation, *Standard Highway Safety Programs for States* (New York: Automotive Safety Foundation, 1939), 11; Curtis Billings, "Accidents Don't Happen," *Atlantic Monthly* 149 (June 1932): 700.

18. *New York Times* quoted in Katherine Allen, *Bleeding Hearts: A Solution to the Automobile Tragedy* (San Antonio, TX: Naylor Company, 1941), 228; *Texas Parade* 2, no. 7 (December 1937): 14; "'Stepping on the Gas'—And Results," *Literary Digest* 83 (October 4, 1924): 35; S. Dana Hubbard, *Keep Well Leaflet No. 20: Automobile Hazards* (New York: M. B. Brown Printing and Binding Company, 1922), 22.

19. Julian Street, "Good and Bad Driving: The Pneumatic Peril of the Highway," *Collier's* 46, Supplement, (January 7, 1911): 11; "Can't We Stop the Slaughter?" *Collier's* 75 (June 6, 1925): 24; John R. Eustis, "Haste Makes Waste," *Independent* 94 (May 4, 1918): 216; *Texas Parade* 2, no. 10 (March 1938): 12. For public vigilantism, see also Pierce Atwater, "A Phase of Public Safety," *American City* 23 (September 1920): 321. During the Texas DPS controversy, state auto clubs formed scores of "secret police" forces, complete with unmarked cars and summons forms. Corpus Christi police chief Lee Petzel worried that these vigilantes did more harm than good, ironically undermining the laws they set out to enforce. Petzel believed it was impossible "to secure a conviction on a complaint filed by a secret officer as testimony in open court will be necessary." *(Corpus Christi) Caller,* May 23, 1935, 1.

20. George M. Graham, "Safeguarding Traffic: A Nation's Problem—A Nation's Duty," *Annals of the American Academy,* 116 (November 1924): 185; "Ten Thousand Automobile Deaths," *Literary Digest* 75 (November 18, 1922): 14; Maher, *Mind over Motor,* 61.

21. Traffic Ordinances Governing the Operation of Automobiles, Hacks, Rent Cars, Jitneys and Baggage Wagons in the City of Houston, Effective October 15, 1915. Texas State Library; *First National Conference on Street and Highway Safety, Hon. Herbert Hoover, Secretary of Commerce, Chairman* (Washington, DC: December 15–16, 1924), 11. See also Ordinance No. 2808, Governing Vehicular and Pedestrian Traffic, City of Dallas, 1938, Texas State Library.

22. U.S. Department of Agriculture, Bureau of Public Roads, *Highway Accidents, Their Causes and Recommendations for their Prevention* (Washington DC, Government Printing Office, 1938), 12–13; Traffic Safety, Austin, "How to Put a 'Hex' on Austin's Traffic Accidents," Center for American History, University of Texas–Austin, Texas.

23. E. B. Lefferts, "A Year's Experience with the 'San Diego Plan' of Traffic Law Enforcement," *American City* 39 (December 1928): 141–142.

24. Traffic Ordinances Governing the Operation of Automobiles. As traffic judge John Maher observed, in 1937, urban "traffic codes are the result of the conditions which have grown up during the past 20 years. The increase in the number of automobiles on the city streets; the congestion resulting from their increased use; and the hazards created by more speedy type of transportation, rendered the former ordinances passed for the control of horse-drawn vehicles entirely inadequate, and new codes have been drafted." Maher, *Mind over Motor,* 173–174. Forrest Crissey recalls Chicago in 1899 as a city of animal-powered vehicles. "Now Chicago has 310,000 motor vehicles, and pedestrians cross the lake-front boulevard at the wink of an automatic stop-and-go signal. Only two horse-drawn hacks now survive in the city whose harness traffic threw such a scare into the old frontiersman. This incident always helps me to realize the fact that the automobile has been the most revolutionary physical element that has yet touched the life of man." See Forrest Crissey, "Speed Cop," *Saturday Evening Post* 197 (March 28, 1925): 10.

25. "Report of the Committee of Nine on 'Financial Responsibility for Automobile Accidents,'" 12–13, Widener Library, Harvard University; Miller McClintock, *Street Traffic Control* (New York: McGraw-Hill, 1925), 175, emphasis added.

26. E. B. Lefferts, "A Year's Experience with the 'San Diego Plan,'" 141–142.

27. Ibid.

28. McClintock, *Street Traffic Control,* 177–178.

29. *American Auto News* 1, no. 5 (December, 1929): 20. For Callan Law see "A New Automobile Law," *Outlook* 96 (September 24, 1910): 147–148; Charles Johnson, "The Motorist and the Law," *Harper's Weekly* 54 (September 3, 1910): 12–13. For Wisconsin see "Wisconsin's Model Automobile Law," *Literary Digest* 47 (August 30, 1914): 328; "Traffic and Other Regulations for Wisconsin," *Literary Digest* 46 (March 8, 1913): 539.

30. Dave H. Morris, "The Automobilist and the Law," *Harper's Weekly* 50 (January 1906), 47; "The Regulation of Automobiles," *Outlook* 82 (February 24, 1906): 388–389; for early New Jersey law see also "The New Law in New Jersey," *Literary Digest* 44 (May 11, 1912): 1000–1001. Harold G. Hoffman in "Are You Financially Responsible?" (n.p., 1932), 1, Widener Library, Harvard University; "When, Where, Why? How Connecticut Gathers the Data of Her Automobile Accidents, and the Use She Makes Thereof," *Scientific American* 130 (May 1924): 312, 360–361.

31. C. I. Dorrian, "Better Automobile Laws," *Country Life in America* 19 (April 15, 1911): 467. See also T. H. Parker, "Why Some People Don't Buy Automobiles" *Country Life in America* 21 (November 15, 1911): 43, 54; "Automobile Fatalities Becoming One of Our Deadliest Scourges," *American City* 35 (September 1926): 342.

32. Maher, *Mind over Motor,* 58; Ernest Greenwood, "Grading Human Beings," *Independent* 115 (December 26, 1925): 737–739. For opposition to fees, see Maher, *Mind over Motor,* 56; *Texas Parade* 1, no. 10 (March 1937): 18; Crissey, "Speed Cop," 10–11, 162, 168.

33. W. Bruce Cobb, "Automotive Accidents—Their Cause and Prevention," *American City* 21 (August 1919): 127; "What Does a Motorist Think About?" *Literary Digest* 80 (January 12, 1924): 55; McClintock, *Street Traffic Control,* 168–172; Crissey, "Speed Cop," 162; Greenwood, "Grading Human Beings," 737–739.

34. Greenwood, "Grading Human Beings," 737–739; Charles Hubert Lawshe, "A Review of the Literature Related to the Various Psychological Aspects of Highway Safety," *Engineering Bulletin—Purdue University* 23, no. 2a (April 1939): 35–39; Maher, *Mind over Motor,* 53; McClintock, *Street Traffic Control,* 166–168. Optometrist Harry Pine claimed that "about twenty-five per cent of automobile accidents can be attributed to speeding and recklessness, and about fifty per cent to *defective vision*." See Harry E. Pine, "Are Your Eyes Fit to Drive a Car?" *Illustrated World* 38 (December 1922): 545–547, 620.

35. Greenwood, "Grading Human Beings," 738. For additional accounts of reaction time tests, see Theophile Raphael, Alfred C. Labine, Helen L. Flinn, and L. Wallace Hoffman, "One Hundred Traffic Offenders," *Mental Hygiene* 13, no. 4 (1929): 809–824; "Brain Tests for Drivers to Make Motoring Safe," *Literary Digest* 76 (January 20, 1923): 24–25; Lawshe, "A Review of the Literature," 37–39.

36. Hubbard, *Keep Well Leaflet No. 20,* 26; Allen, *Bleeding Hearts,* 95. See also Michel Foucault, *Madness and Civilization: A History of Insanity in the Age of Reason* (New York: Pantheon Books, 1965); Daniel M. Albert, "Order out of Chaos: Automobile Safety, Technology and Society, 1925 to 1965," Ph.D. dissertation, University of Michigan, 1997, 147–149.

37. McClintock, *Street Traffic Control,* 168–169; "Mind Tests Given Automobile Drivers," *Popular Mechanics Magazine* 42, no. 5 (November 1924): 705–708; T. D. Pratt, "Psychological Tests to Prevent Motor Vehicle Accidents," *American City* 31 (July 1924): 58–59; "Brain Tests for Drivers," 24–25. Psychological testing gained considerable prestige during World War I. Accounts such as these provide compelling reminders of why we now have national standards for social experiments involving human subjects.

38. "Mind Tests Given Automobile Drivers," 708; McClintock, *Street Traffic Control,* 169. Judge Maher concurred, writing "The individual with average intelligence is usually a better driver than one who is highly intelligent. The college professor does not necessarily make a good driver." Maher, *Mind over Motor,* 53.

39. *American Auto News* 1, no. 1 (August 1929): 7; "Brain Tests for Drivers," 24–25; Maher, *Mind over Motor,* 55.

40. Albert reports that "a statistical analysis of clinic records supports the conclusion that diagnoses and recommendations were highly dependent upon assumptions about the patient's racial or ethnic background, as well as to a lesser degree upon his or her gender and age." Daniel M. Albert, "Psychotechnology and Insanity at the Wheel," *Journal of the History of the Behavioral Sciences* 35, no. 3 (1999): 291–305; F. A. Moss, "Standardizing Our Automobile Drivers," *American City* 34 (January 1926): 46–49; Lowell S. Selling, "The Psychiatric Findings in the Cases of 500 Traffic Offenders and Accident-Prone Drivers," *American Journal of Psychiatry* 97 (July 1940): 68–79.

41. Andrew R. Boone, "Insanity at the Wheel," *Scientific American* (October 1939): 199–201; Lawshe, "A Review of the Literature," 30–33. Using the logic of the habitual, accident-prone driver, the Yellow Cab Company of Chicago instituted a testing policy that included the following evaluations: "1. Their knowledge of regulations, customs, and how to drive. 2. Actual skill and competence in driving. 3. Adequacy of vision and hearing. 4. Judgement of distance and speed of other vehicles. 5. Reaction time. 6. Accuracy of designation. 7. Constitutional inferiority of intellect or feeble-mindedness. 8. Temperamental and emotional characteristics. 9. Evidence of mental diseases of the type that produce a proneness to accident, such as paresis [paralysis often brought on by syphilis] or epilepsy." See Greenwood, "Grading Human Beings," 737–739. See also Albert, "Order out of Chaos," Chapter 4; Daniel Albert, "Psychotechnology and Insanity at the Wheel," 291–305.

42. Lawshe, "A Review of the Literature," 40.

43. Boone, "Insanity at the Wheel," 201.

44. McClintock, *Street Traffic Control,* 176–178; National Conference on Street and Highway Safety, *Ways and Means to Traffic Safety,* 17–18; Automotive Safety Foundation, *Standard Highway Safety Programs,* 10, emphasis added.

45. A. Ryder, "Principles of Automobile Rate Making," A Paper Read before the Insurance Society of New York, December 9 and 16, 1919 (n.p.:1919), 5–9, Widener Library, Harvard University.

46. Eugene F. Hord, "History and Organization of Automobile Insurance," delivered before the Insurance Society of New York, November 11, 18, 1919, 2–3, Widener Library, Harvard

University. See also A. Ryder, "Principles of Automobile Rate-Making: Underwriting the Dollar," read before the Insurance Society of New York, December 9 and 16, 1919, Widener Library, Harvard University.

47. James O. Fagan, *What Price Safety? Some Practical Suggestions* (n.p.: 1927), 5, Library of Congress, Washington, DC; *American Auto News* 1, no. 1 (August 1929): 8; William Ullman, "Safeguarding America's Motor Transportation Interests," *Outlook* 134 (June 6, 1923): 143.

48. Insurance Society of New York, *What Is the Matter with Automobiles?* (New York: Travelers Insurance Company, 1921), 5–6; "A Crusade against Motor Accidents," *Hygeia* 7 (May 1929): 507.

49. "Taking Arms against the Auto Killer," *Literary Digest* 97 (April 7, 1928): 70; Herbert L. Towle, "The Motor Menace," *Atlantic* 136 (July 1925): 98–107; "The Fight for Safer Motoring," *Literary Digest* 85 (May 16, 1925): 66–71; *Texas Parade* 3, no. 8 (September 1938): 28. For California's Levy Bill, see *American Auto News* 1, no. 1 (August 1929): 6–8.

50. Graham, "Safeguarding Traffic," 185; Harlan C. Hines, "Morons on the Macadam," *Scribner's Magazine* 82 (November 1927): 597.

51. The Committee of Nine included representatives from the U.S. Casualty Company, the National Association of Casualty and Surety Agents, the Maryland Casualty Company, the Continental Casualty Company, Globe Indemnity Company, Aetna Life Insurance Company, Travelers Insurance, and Employers' Liability Assurance Company. "Report of the Committee of Nine: A Financial Responsibility for Automobile Accidents," 3, 5, 7, 28, Widener Library, Harvard University.

52. As one advocate reminded lawmakers, "in the last analysis the success and popularity of the law depends upon the character of its administration." Hoffman, "Are You Financially Responsible?"; R. Leighton Foster, "International Aspects of Automobile Safety-Responsibility Laws," 1931, both housed at Widener Library, Harvard University; Maher, *Man over Motor*, 127–128. See also "Report of the Committee of Nine," 6.

53. McClintock, *Street Traffic Control,* 185.

54. "Place of Accident, Not Place of Death, Important in Traffic Accident Statistics," *American City* 41 (July 1929): 152.

55. U.S. Department of Agriculture, *Highway Accidents,* 14; Atwater, "Phase of Public Safety," 325; "Taking Arms against the Auto Killer," 71.

56. *Texas Parade* 2, no. 2 (July 1937): 14; Simons, "Sentinels of Safety," 3–4; McClintock, *Street Traffic Control,* 186–188; Clay McShane, *Down the Asphalt Path: The Automobile and the American City* (New York: Columbia University Press, 1994), 184–185.

57. Bannerman characterized in Berton Braley, "Noodlebeak Describes an Officer and a Gentleman," *American Auto News* 1, no. 5 (December 1929): 4–5. For a similar account, see Crissey, "Speed Cop," 10–11, 162, 168.

58. H. C. Witwer, "Pull Over to the Curb," *Collier's* 69 (January 7, 1922): 11–12, 38.

59. Bob L. Blackburn, "Law Enforcement in Transition: From Decentralized County Sheriffs to the Highway Patrol," *Chronicles of Oklahoma* 56 (Summer 1978): 194–207. U.S. Department of Agriculture, *Highway Accidents,* 37.

60. "Two Cures for Motor Accidents," *Literary Digest* 74 (July 1, 1922): 60; Crissey, "Speed Cop," 10; Seth K. Humphrey, "Our Delightful Man-Killer," *Atlantic* 148 (December 1931): 730. Humphrey wrote "every child born to Uncle Sam in these days begins to grab for a steering wheel about as soon as it ceases to strain for the nursing bottle."

61. Maher, *Mind over Motor,* 130.

62. For speed measurement devices, see C. H. Lawshe, "Two Devices for Measuring Driving Speed on the Highway," *American Journal of Psychology* 53, no. 3 (July 1940): 435–441; Houston statutes in Box 2000/080–1, Training records, Personnel and Staff Services Division, Texas De-

partment of Public Safety, Archives and Information Services Division, Texas State Library and Archives Commission.

63. Studies cited in Lawshe, "A Review of the Literature," 15–19.

64. Crissey, "Speed Cop," 165; Witwer, "Pull Over to the Curb," 38.

65. Report of the Investigation of Drunk Driving, Texas Safety Association, Inc., presented at Texas Safety Conference, Austin Texas, April 16, 1940, 10–11, 23. Center for American History, University of Texas–Austin, Austin, TX.

66. Albert, "Order out of Chaos," 100–113. For use of statistics, see "When, Where, Why? How Connecticut Gathers the Data," 312, 360–361.

67. "Getting Convictions for Traffic Accidents," *American City* 42 (May 1930): 140–144.

68. U.S. Department of Agriculture, *Highway Accidents,* 28–30.

69. R. L. Burgess, "Can You Get a Square Deal in a Traffic Court?" *American Magazine* (December 19, 1932): 11–13, 111–115.

70. McClintock, *Street Traffic Control,* 221–225; Automotive Safety Foundation, *Priority for Safety* (Washington, DC: Automotive Safety Foundation, 1940), 4.

71. "Is the Motorist a Criminal?" *Collier's* 65 (January 3, 1920): 48; see also McShane, *Down the Asphalt Path,* 198–199; McClintock, *Street Traffic Control,* 223–224.

72. Burgess, "Can You Get a Square Deal in a Traffic Court?" 114.

73. Maher, *Mind over Motor,* 68, 69; Automotive Safety Foundation, *Priority for Safety,* 10; Elizabeth Jordan, "Automobile Collisions," *Saturday Evening Post* 198 (January 2, 1926): 17; Burgess, "Can You Get a Square Deal in a Traffic Court?" 111. Safe-driving schools also emerged as a variable sentence; see "Chicago Sends Traffic Violators to School," *Literary Digest* 97 (April 7, 1928): 72.

74. Thomas Compere, "Telling It to the Judge: A Survey of the Traffic Courts," *Forum* 84 (August 1930): 79–85; Burgess, "Can You Get a Square Deal in a Traffic Court?" 11–13, 111–115. For similar accounts of Texas traffic courts, see "Traffic Court Conferences, Held at Camp Mabry, Austin, TX," Training Records, Personnel and Staff Services Division, Box 2000/080-1, Texas Department of Public Safety, Archives and Information Services Division, Texas State Library and Archives Commission.

75. Defense attorney Ervin in Burgess, "Can You Get a Square Deal in a Traffic Court?" 12; George Warren, *Traffic Courts* (Boston: Little, Brown, 1942), 57.

76. James Sinke, "Department of Public Safety Analyzes Automobile Accidents Causes," *American City* (August 1926): 227; "Fight for Safer Motoring," 66–71. See also H. I. Phillips, "On Which Side of the Windshield Do You Do Your Cussing?" *American Magazine* 103 (May 1927): 58–59, 98, 100; E. B. Lefferts, "A Year's Experience with the 'San Diego Plan,'" 141–142.

77. Report on Massachusetts Highway Accident Survey, 1934, Widener Library, Harvard University, 1–2, 30.

78. Ibid., 4–14.

79. Ibid., 30–41.

80. Burgess, "Can You Get a Square Deal in a Traffic Court?" 11, 12.

81. There exists a wide variety of literature discussing this early public antipathy toward motor law enforcement. See "Motor Laws That Make Lawbreakers," *Literary Digest* 77 (May 12, 1923): 62; Kate Masterson, "The Monster in the Car: A Study of the Twentieth-Century Woman's Passion for the Motor Speed-Mania and Its Attendant Evils and Vagaries," *Lippincott's Monthly Magazine* 86 (August 10, 1910): 209; for similar expressions of pride at lawlessness, see "Death Toll of the Automobile," *Literary Digest* 72 (February 4, 1922): 13; Street, "Good and Bad Driving," 9, 11. For outrage over laws, see Herbert M. Baldwin, "The Speed Problem," *Country Life in America* 16 (June 1909): 200; T. O. Abbott, "The Lawmaker and the Automobile," *Outing Magazine* 54 (August, 1909): 618; "Is the Best Speed Limit Merely 'Good Judgement'?" *Literary*

Digest 83 (October 11, 1924): 69; "Eighteen Per Cent Obedience to 'Stop' Signs," *American City* 45 (September 1931): 117.

Conclusion: Accidental Freedoms and the Risk Society

1. Elizabeth Jordan, "Automobile Collisions," *Saturday Evening Post* 198 (January 2, 1926): 16.

2. Jordan, "Automobile Collisions," 16–17, 94, 96. Ironically, where the Darst-Mullins crash described in Chapter 4 involved a man hurrying home from a sporting event, this accident was caused by a young man "hurrying to a ball game." It led to the permanent crippling of Jordan's sister and mother. Jordan was involved in five other crashes at the time of that publication.

3. "How It Feels to Turn Turtle at Top Speed," *Literary Digest* 51 (October 2, 1915): 739–740; "Commercial Murder," *Outlook* 99 (September 30, 1911): 258–259. Ironically, Oldfield recalled that his celebrity was predicated on the death of two racing fans. He claimed "I was never famous until I went through the fence at St. Louis and killed two spectators. Promoters fell over one another to sign me up."

4. Ulrich Beck, *Risk Society: Towards a New Modernity* (London: Sage Publications, 1992); Anthony Giddens, *The Consequences of Modernity* (Palo Alto, CA: Stanford University Press, 1990).

5. Daniel de Vise, "Roadside Tributes Wear Out Their Welcome," *Washington Post,* May 2, 2006, emphasis added. http://www.washingtonpost.com/wp-dyn/content/article/2006/05/01/; Ian Urbina, "As Roadside Markers Multiply, a Second Look," *New York Times,* February 6, 2006, http://www.nytimes.com/2006/02/06/national/06shrine.html. Erika Doss, "Death, Art, and Memory in the Public Sphere: The Visual and Material Culture of Grief in Contemporary America," *Mortality* 7, no. 1 (2002): 62–82.

6. Writers attributed the apparent apathy to a host of unrelated or conflicting factors. Many claimed that the car itself transformed normal law-abiding citizens into motor fiends. Others suggested that the problem was too big to comprehend, while yet others claimed it was too personal. Engineers suggested that the dilemma was too new, while traffic judges suggested deep social patterns that dated back to the Revolution. *The Literary Digest* noted the lack of "imaginative prudence," meaning that citizens seemed incapable of anticipating the dangers that were just past the windshield. Elizabeth Jordan modified this argument to suggest that the "American mind is incurably optimistic. . . . They simply cannot grasp the possibility that anything unpleasant can happen to them." For these and other rationalizations, see George M. Graham, "Safeguarding Traffic: A Nation's Problem—A Nation's Duty," *Annals of the American Academy* 116 (November 1924): 176; "Is the Motorist a Criminal?" *Collier's* 65 (January 3, 1920): 48, 82, 87, 90; John J. Maher, *Mind over Motor* (Detroit: n.p., 1937), 11–12; "Taking the 'Un' out of 'Unavoidable,'" *Literary Digest* 78 (July 14, 1923): 56–58; Automotive Safety Foundation, *Standard Highway Safety Program for States* (New York: Automotive Safety Foundation, 1939), 11; "To Chicago Motorists—And Others," *Literary Digest* 78 (September 29, 1923): 64–65; Elizabeth Jordan, "Automobile Collisions," *Saturday Evening Post* 198 (January 2, 1926): 17. For a discussion of the social support for bureaucracies, see Fritz Ringer, *Max Weber: An Intellectual Biography* (Chicago: University of Chicago Press, 2004), 220–221.

7. Jordan, "Automobile Collisions," 16.

8. Clay McShane, *Down the Asphalt Path: The Automobile and the American City* (New York: Columbia University Press, 1994), 183; "Herod and the Innocents," *Commonweal* 14 (August 19, 1931): 375. For similar observations about callousness, see Frederick Dwight, "Automobile: The Other Side of the Shield," *Independent* 65 (December 3, 1908): 1299–1303; John J. Maher, *Mind over Motor* (Detroit: n.p., 1937), 12. Others, like Paul Gikas, conclude that the "gravest charge that can be made against a culture is that it is indifferent to human suffering, that it lacks the will to regulate or control the violent elements within itself." American car culture "raises this

moral issue in its broadest form." Paul W. Gikas, "Crashworthiness as a Cultural Ideal," pp. 327–339, in David L. Lewis and Lawrence Goldstein, eds., *The Automobile and American Culture* (Ann Arbor: University of Michigan Press, 1980), 327.

9. McShane, *Down the Asphalt Path*, 189; "Is the Motorist a Criminal?" 48, 82, 87, 90; George Warren, *Traffic Courts* (Boston: Little, Brown, 1942), 14–15. Others admitted that "legislative fiat" would not act as "a cure-all for every fundamental ill." See Frederick Upham Adams, "'Heads Up' and 'Use Corners Only': A Practical Article Showing How We Must Learn to Adapt Ourselves to Motor-Crowded Streets," *American Magazine* 81 (June 1916): 58; Dave H. Morris, "The Automobilist and the Law," *Harper's Weekly* 50 (January 1906), 46–48; "Motor Laws that Make Lawbreakers," *Literary Digest* 77 (May 12 1923): 58–62.

10. "Is the Motorist a Criminal?" 48; Warren, *Traffic Courts*, 107; Maher, *Mind over Motor*, 11–12. For similar responses, see Dwight, "Automobile: The Other Side of the Shield," 1300; C. O. Morris, "The Cause of Automobile Accidents," *Country Life in America* 15 (February 1909): 375; Richard Sylvester, "The Selfishness of City Speeding," *Harper's Weekly* 51 (March 1907): 384; "Is the Best Speed Limit Merely 'Good Judgement'?" *Literary Digest* 83 (October 11, 1924): 67–71; C. I. Dorrian, "Better Automobile Laws," *Country Life in America* 19 (April 15, 1911): 467; "Motor Accidents," *Saturday Evening Post* 195 (March 24, 1923): 26.

11. "Is the Motorist a Criminal?" 48; Maher, *Mind over Motor*, 11–12; Warren, *Traffic Courts*, viii–ix.

12. "If You Are Arrested, Remember Your Rights," *Literary Digest* 78 (September 29, 1923): 60; Ralph Henry Barbour, *For Safety!* (New York: D. Appleton-Century, 1936), 3–4; *American Auto News* 1, no. 1 (August 1929): 14.

13. Warren, *Traffic Courts*, 121; Maher, *Mind over Motor*, 13; National Conference on Street and Highway Safety, *Ways and Means to Traffic Safety. Recommendations of National Conference on Street and Highway Safety, Including Findings of All Conference Committees and of General Meetings of Conference Held in 1924, 1926, and 1930, as Summarized and Approved by Third National Conference, May 27–28–29, 1930* (Washington, DC: Government Printing Office, 1930), 18; Automotive Safety Foundation, *Standard Highway Safety Programs for States*, 11; Earl Reeves, "Tell It to the Judge," *Collier's* 77 (May 22, 1926): 52. In an era where Progressives routinely compared themselves to the bad old days of the late-nineteenth century, the contemporary traffic police appeared modeled "after the fashion of the robber baron."

14. "Avoid That Fine," *Literary Digest* 75 (November 18, 1922): 66–73; see also *American Auto News* 1, no. 8 (March 1930): 9. Reeves, "Tell It to the Judge," 26, 52. How to Stop Accidents: Summary of Opinions Developed at . . . the Accident Prevention Conference, as a Two-day Meeting in the Department of Commerce, Washington DC, 1935, Library of Congress, Washington, DC, 17, 20. For another account of a driver advising motorists simply to agree to any and all police demands, see H. C. Witwer, "Pull Over to the Curb," *Collier's* 69 (January 7, 1922): 11–12, 38.

15. S. Dana Hubbard, *Automobile Hazards: Keep Well Leaflet No. 20* (New York: M. B. Brown Printing and Binding, 1922), 32; Miller McClintock, *Street Traffic Control* (New York: McGraw-Hill, 1925), 93. In 1923, the California Motor Vehicle Act was the first to demand officers to "remain in plain sight" and be dressed in "distinctive uniforms" when making arrests for speed violations.

16. Melville F. Ferguson, *Motor Camping on Western Trails* (New York: Century, 1925), 36; Ray W. Sherman, *If You're Going to Drive Fast* (New York: Thomas Y. Crowell, 1935), 13.

17. Warren, *Traffic Courts*, vii.

18. R. L. Burgess, "Can You Get a Square Deal in a Traffic Court?" *American Magazine* (December 19, 1932): 13; Earl Reeves, "Tell It to the Judge," 52.

19. McClintock, *Street Traffic Control*, 221; Theodore M. R. von Keler, "Where Justice Mills Flourish," *Harper's Weekly* 57 (March 12, 1913): 12; emphasis in original, Burgess, "Can You Get a Square Deal in a Traffic Court?" 13.

20. McShane, *Down the Asphalt Path*, 179; Warren, *Traffic Courts*, 63, 77, 170; for an example of the high burden of proof, see Thomas Russell, *Automobile Driving Self-Taught* (Chicago: Charles C. Thompson, 1914), 246–251; Maher, *Mind over* Motor, 22; *Texas Parade* 2, no. 8 (January 1938): 4, 29; "Eighteen Per Cent Obedience to 'Stop' Signs," *American City* 45 (September 1931): 117.

21. U.S. Department of Agriculture, Bureau of Public Roads, *Highway Accidents, Their Causes and Recommendations for their Prevention* (Washington DC, Government Printing Office, 1938), 23; Herbert L. Towle, "The Motor Menace," *Atlantic* 136 (July 1925): 103; Jordan, "Automobile Collisions," 16–17. Warren concluded, in 1942, "it is felt that a great deal of the conviction difficulty in jury trials can be attributed to the severe penalties applicable in those cases wherein a jury is usually demanded. Since the offense is either very common or very close to home in the sense of stimulating the fear of jurors that they might have committed the same violation, the thought of large fines and possible jail terms in addition to the loss of driving privileges augments an already enlarged consideration for the defendant." Warren, *Traffic Courts*, 77.

22. Alexander Johnson, "In Case of Accident," *Country Life in America* 36 (October 1919): 94; Jordan, "Automobile Collisions," 94; *American Auto News* 1, no. 5 (December 1929): 8. For similar practices, see Warren, *Traffic Courts*, 108–109.

23. "Motor Laws That Make Lawbreakers," 62; Kate Masterson, "The Monster in the Car: A Study of the Twentieth-Century Woman's Passion for the Motor Speed-Mania and Its Attendant Evils and Vagaries," *Lippincott's Monthly Magazine* 86 (August 10, 1910): 209; *(Canton) News* cited in "Death Toll of the Automobile," *Literary Digest* 72 (February 4, 1922): 13; Ferguson, *Motor Camping on Western Trails*, 33. For additional examples of public pride at ticketing, see Julian Street, "Good and Bad Driving: The Pneumatic Peril of the Highway," *Collier's* 46, Supplement (January 7, 1911): 9, 11; "Is the Best Speed Limit Merely 'Good Judgement?'" 67–71; "Motor Accidents," 26; T. O. Abbott, "The Lawmaker and the Automobile," *Outing Magazine* 54 (August 1909): 618; "Eighteen Per Cent Obedience to 'Stop' Signs," 117. For more examples of outrage, see Herbert M. Baldwin, "The Speed Problem," *Country Life in America* 16 (June 1909): 200.

24. Frederick Dwight, "Automobile: The Other Side of the Shield," 1300; Warren, *Traffic Courts*, 66–67, 147.

25. *Texas Parade* 1, no. 8 (January 1937): 26–27; George M. Graham, "Safeguarding Traffic: A Nation's Problem—A Nation's Duty," *Annals of the American Academy* 116 (November 1924): 183; *(Omaha) Morning World-Herald* cited in "'Stepping on the Gas'—And Results," *Literary Digest* 83 (October 4, 1924): 36. See also Barry Mulligan, *Collisions in Street and Highway Transportation* (Philadelphia: Dorrance, 1936), 19–20; Joel Webb Eastman, "Styling vs. Safety: The American Automobile Industry and the Development of Automobile Safety, 1900–1966," Ph.D. dissertation, University of Florida, 1973, 159.

26. Hubbard, *Automobile Hazards*, 26; Charles H. Lawshe, "A Review of the Literature Related to the Various Psychological Aspects of Highway Safety," *Engineering Bulletin—Purdue University* 23, no. 2a (April 1939): 30; Maher, *Mind over Motor*, 1; Burton M. Parks, "Reducing Automobile Accidents by Municipal Control of Operators: Practical Preventative Methods for Discovering and Handling Accident-Repeaters," *American City* 46 (April 1932): 92. For other forms of accident scapegoating, see John B. Rae, *The Road and Car in American Life* (Cambridge, MA: MIT Press, 1971), 347.

27. Lawshe, "A Review of the Literature," 33; Driver Testing Results. Prepared Under the Direction of Henry R. DeSilva and Theodore W. Forbes, Harvard Traffic Bureau. WPA Project No. 6246–12259 (1937), 35; Richard Shelton Kirby, "The Right to Drive," *Atlantic* 147 (April 1931): 443; Towle, "Motor Menace," 101. For additional reports on women drivers, see R. Clair, "Again the Woman Driver," *Journal of American Insurance* 8 (1931): 13–15; M. S. Viteles and H. M. Gardner, "Women Taxicab Drivers," *Personnel Journal* 7 (1929): 349–355.

28. Maher, *Mind over Motor,* 54; James Sinke, "Department of Public Safety Analyzes Automobile Accidents Causes," *American City* (August 1926): 225, 227–228; Walter V. Bingham, "Psychology and Highway Safety," *Scientific Monthly* 31 (December 1930): 552–556; "Curing Careless Drivers," *Literary Digest* 105 (April 12, 1930): 44–46. For a good review of the scores of studies related to the accident-prone driver, see Charles H. Lawshe, "A Review of the Literature," 30–35. Some of the more interesting works include, Theophile Raphael, Alfred C. Labine, Helen L. Flinn, and L. Wallace Hoffman, "One Hundred Traffic Offenders," *Mental Hygiene* 13, no. 4 (1929): 809–824; J. S. Baker, "What Can We Do for High Accident Drivers?" *National Safety News* 25 (June 1932): 19–20; R. C. Eddy, "Interesting Phases of the Massachusetts Highway Accident Survey," *Proceedings Institute of Traffic Engineers* 5 (1934): 78–82; E. Farmer, "Accident Proneness," *Journal of the American Medical Association* 105 (December 1935): 113–125; C. A. Drake, "Accident-Proneness: A Hypothesis," *Character and Personality* 8 (1940): 335–341; U.S. House Document No. 462, *Motor-Vehicle Traffic Conditions in the United States, Part 6: The Accident-Prone Driver* (Washington, DC: Government Printing Office, 1938); A. P. Weiss and A. R. Lauer, *Psychological Principles in Automobile Driving* (Columbus, OH: Ohio State University, 1931).

29. James J. Flink, *The Automobile Age* (Cambridge, MA: MIT Press, 2001), 273–275

30. Thomas Frank, *The Conquest of Cool: Business Culture, Counterculture, and the Rise of Hip Consumerism* (Chicago: University Press of Chicago, 1997), 60–67. With the exception of American Motors's Rambler, no American firm built smaller more economical styles—leaving these runts to the struggling Japanese and German firms. For more on the era of massive profits far in excess of the business risk, see Flink, *Automobile Age,* 278–279; Jane Holtz Kay, *Asphalt Nation: How the Automobile Took Over America and How We Can Take It Back* (Berkeley: University of California Press, 1997), 235–236.

31. See Eastman, "Styling vs. Safety"; Flink argues that manufacturing and engineering innovations proved a "competitively neutral factor" in new car sales during these years; Flink, *Automobile Age,* 278, 281–293.

32. Faulkner quoted in Ted Ownby, "The Snopes Trilogy and the Emergence of Consumer Culture," pp. 95–128 in *Faulkner and Ideology,* Donald M. Kartiganer and Ann J. Abadie, eds. (Jackson: University Press of Mississippi, 1992), 103; Frank, *Conquest of Cool,* 60–62; Flink, *Automobile Age,* 286; Robert Hughes quoted in "The Empire of Signs," American Visions, VHS directed by John Bush (New York: PBS Home Video, 1997). James J. Flink, *America Adopts the Automobile: 1895–1910* (Cambridge, MA: MIT Press, 1970), 100–103, 107–112.

33. Eastman, "Styling vs. Safety," 9; John D. Graham, *Auto Safety: Assessing America's Performance* (Dover, MA: Auburn House, 1989), 16; McShane, *Down the Asphalt Path,* 172.

34. Eastman, "Styling vs. Safety," 188; Graham, *Auto Safety,* 18–19; Fletcher D. Woodward, "Medical Criticisms of Modern Automotive Engineering," *Journal of the American Medical Association* (October 30, 1948): 627–631.

35. Graham, *Auto Safety,* 18; As Flink notes, previous "concern over automotive safety shifted its focus from road conditions and driving skills to the designed-in dangers of the car itself." Flink, *Automobile Age,* 383.

36. Paul W. Gikas, "Crashworthiness as a Cultural Ideal," pp. 327–339 in Lewis and Goldstein, eds., *Automobile and American Culture;* Graham, *Auto Safety.*

37. Flink, *Automobile Age,* 282, emphasis added; Gikas, "Crashworthiness as a Cultural Ideal," 328.

38. Daniel Patrick Moynihan, "Epidemic on the Highway," *Reporter* (April 30, 1959).

39. Flink, *Automobile Age,* 288, 290–291.

40. Flink, *Automobile Age,* 384–385; Graham, *Auto Safety,* 16–17.

41. Daniel M. Albert, "Psychotechnology and Insanity at the Wheel," *Journal of the History*

of the Behavioral Sciences 35, no. 3 (1999): 302, emphasis added; David Shinar, *Psychology on the Road: The Human Factor in Traffic Safety* (New York: John Wiley and Sons, 1978). Lyndon Johnson announced the Safety Act before the American Trial Lawyers Association on February 2, 1966. Like his earlier Texas counterparts, Johnson declared war against "slaughter on the highways," believing auto accidents the "gravest problem facing this nation—next to Vietnam." Unlike earlier reform efforts, however, the president enjoyed the strong backing of federal legislators. Johnson quoted from Graham, *Auto Safety*, 26. Robert F. Baker, *The Highway Risk Problem: Policy Issues in Highway Safety* (New York: Wiley-Interscience, 1971) vii, 50. Baker added that early moralizing was "'tolerated' by specialists, primarily because it was politic and more helpful in the long run to ignore the suggestion than to agitate or to discourage the well-intentioned advisors. It is now essential that such procedures be reexamined." Ibid., 38.

42. Described as an academic best-seller, Beck's work is better appreciated as part of a broader scholarly interest in the production, cultural appreciation, and societal response to risk in the postmodern age. All italics are in the original. See Ulrich Beck, *Risk Society: Towards a New Modernity* (London: Sage Publications, 1992); Scott Lash, Sociology of Postmodernism (New York: Routledge, 1990); Giddens, *Consequences of Modernity*; Anthony Giddens, *Modernity and Self Identity* (Palo Alto, CA: Stanford University Press, 1991).

43. In the spirit of the Yankees-Red Sox or Kentucky-Duke, I prefer to see the "provocative" rather than "vague" qualities of postmodern scholarship. Beck, *Risk Society*, 9, 11; John Tulloch and Deborah Lupton, *Risk and Everyday Life* (London: Sage Publications, 2003), 206. See David Harvey, neo-Marxist critique of these theories.

44. Broadly speaking, Marx and Weber form the basis for most "critical theory" historical scholarship *not* connected to postmodernism or postindustrialism.

45. Clearly these are broad generalizations about historical theories fundamental to over a century of historical scholarship. For a more detailed comparison, see Gabe Mythen, *Ulrich Beck: A Critical Introduction to the Risk Society* (London: Pluto Press, 2004), 2, 3, 26; Fritz Ringer, *Max Weber: An Intellectual Biography* (Chicago: University of Chicago Press, 2004).

46. Beck, *Risk Society*, 13.

47. Beck, *Risk Society*, 49; Mythen, *Ulrich Beck*, 2. Critics point to several other shortcomings of Beck's thesis. His focus is largely on society's response to risk management not in society's construction of what constitutes risk. Beck fails to effectively account for voluntary risk taking (like smoking) as well as variations caused by race, class, gender, ethnicity, and residency. He is imprecise in his definition of the all-important and ascendant force of individualism. While strong supporters of the central thrust of *Risk Society*, John Tulloch and Deborah Lupton write, "Beck prioritises the information-bearing role of institutional experts and counter-experts within science, government, media and the legal system . . . [which] causes Beck to neglect the aesthetic and cultural drivers of reflexivity. In many respects, the risk society argument follows the trajectory of Weber's theory of social action, with epochal changes being related to transitions in human behavior." John Tulloch and Deborah Lupton, *Risk and Everyday Life* (London: Sage Publications, 2003), 147.

48. Tulloch and Lupton, *Risk and Everyday Life*, 19, 25.

49. Moreover, this behavior explains much of the "irrationality" of risk contained in paradoxes discussed above (i.e., fear of rare terror attacks verses common auto accidents). Tulloch and Lupton, *Risk and Everyday Life*, 8, 34. Tulloch and Lupton also note the inherent bias in many risk studies. Scholars tend to view all unnecessary risks as "foolhardy, careless, irresponsible, and even 'deviant', evidence of an individual's lack of ability to regulate the self." The pair go on to write "much of the academic literature on risk represents individuals in late modernity as living in fear, constantly dogged by feelings of anxiety, vulnerability and uncertainty in relation to the risks of which they are constantly made aware. The notion that risk-taking may be inten-

tional and rational seems unacceptable to the psychometric approach." They are critical of Beck who assumes that "the human actor is portrayed as anxious about and fearful of risk, eager to acquire knowledge in order to best avoid becoming the victim of risk." Ibid., 10.

50. Beck, *Risk Society,* 22. As some reviewers have noted, Beck's work is primarily an attack on the risk specialists who claim privilege as buffers between citizens and risk. According to Beck, in a risk society these specialists are increasingly irrelevant and counterproductive.

51. Tulloch and Lupton, *Risk and Everyday Life,* 18.

52. Ibid., 11, 19.

53. Beck, *Risk Society,* 33.

54. Munn quoted in Joseph Grondahl, *Safety for Twenty Million Automobile Drivers: Avoid Accidents and Escape the Traffic Court* (New York: Safety First League, 1924), 3.

Bibliography

Unpublished Primary Sources

Accident Facts, Connecticut. Calendar Year of 1942, State Department of Motor Vehicles. Widener Library, Harvard University, Cambridge, MA.

Automobile Club of Michigan, Meeting of the Safety and Traffic Club, Wednesday, August 2, 1939. Widener Library, Harvard University, Cambridge, MA.

Automobile Red Book. Official Automobile Red Book, Vol. D, 1924. Texas State Archives and Library, Austin, Texas.

Automobile Safety Lanes Sponsored by AAA, Police Department–Central Texas Auto Club, 1931. Center for American History, University of Texas–Austin.

Automotive Safety Foundation, Priority for Traffic Safety. n.p., 1941. Widener Library, Harvard University, Cambridge, MA.

Bureau of Business Research, University of Texas, Ranking of New Passenger Car Registrations in Seven Texas Counties, October 7, 1929. Center for American History, University of Texas–Austin.

Commission Minute Orders, Red Minute Books, Official Minutes, Books #1, June 4, 1917–Dec. 16, 1919. Texas State Archives and Library, Austin.

Dallas Bureau of Traffic Education. Survey and Report of Pedestrian Traffic Accidents in the City of Dallas, Texas. A complete analysis covering 1935, '36, '37, and together with 1938 supplemental summary. Center for American History, University of Texas–Austin.

Driver Testing Results. Prepared under the Direction of Henry R. DeSilva and Theodore W. Forbes, Harvard Traffic Bureau. WPA Project No. 6246–12259, 1937. Widener Library, Harvard University, Cambridge, MA.

Hord, Eugene F. History and Organization of Automobile Insurance. Delivered before the Insurance Society of New York, November 11, 18, 1919. Widener Library, Harvard University, Cambridge, MA.

Houston Traffic Regulations. Compliments of the Houston Young Men's Business League, n.d. Center for American History, University of Texas–Austin.

How to Stop Accidents: Summary of Opinions Developed at a Conference of Contact Men, Operating in Connection with the Accident Prevention Conference, as a Two-day Meeting in the Department of Commerce, Washington DC, 1935, Library of Congress, Washington, DC.

Jules A. Appler's Log Book and Directory of Automobile Owners of San Antonio and Bexar County, Containing the No. of Machine, Name of Owner, Their Address, Make of Machine and Its Color, Also about 3,000 Miles of Logs. Center for American History, University of Texas–Austin.

Official Traffic Investigation Report on Collision that killed six persons at the crossing of State Highway No. 15 (U.S. No. 80) and Belt Line Road on May 5, 1938. Conducted by a committee appointed by Governor James V. Allred of Texas to investigate this collision and submit recommendations for the prevention of similar accidents in Texas. Hearing held in Dallas on May 12, 1938, by members of the committee. Center for American History, University of Texas–Austin.

Ordinance No. 2808. Governing Vehicular and Pedestrian Traffic. City of Dallas, 1938. Center for American History, University of Texas–Austin.

Report of the Committee of Nine: A Financial Responsibility for Automobile Accidents. n.p., 1927. Widener Library, Harvard University, Cambridge, MA.

Report of the Investigation of Drunk Driving, Texas Safety Association, Inc. Presented at Texas Safety Conference, Austin, Texas, April 16, 1940. Center for American History, University of Texas–Austin.

Report on Massachusetts' Highway Accident Survey, 1934. Widener Library, Harvard University, Cambridge, MA.

Ryder, A. Principles of Automobile Rate-Making: Underwriting the Dollar. Read before the Insurance Society of New York, December 9 and 16, 1919. Widener Library, Harvard University, Cambridge, MA.

State Board of Insurance, Correspondence and Reports, 1929–1952. Texas State Archives and Library, Austin.

State Board of Insurance, Property hearings, 1910–1957. Texas State Archives and Library, Austin.

State of Connecticut. The Human Factor Involved in Traffic Accidents Caused in Connecticut during the First Six Months of the Current Year, 1943. Widener Library, Harvard University, Cambridge, MA.

State of Ohio, Division of Vital Statistics, Department of Health. Report of Fatal Accidents from 1910 to 1933, Library of Congress, Washington, DC.

State of Texas, Department of Public Safety. Traffic Safety Quiz, Compiled by Safety Division, 1943. Center for American History, University of Texas–Austin.

State of Texas, State Highway Department. History of Texas roads and the Highway Department. Texas State Archives and Library, Austin.

A Survey of Traffic Conditions in the City of Dallas Texas with Checks of Obedience to Traffic Laws. Works Progress Administration, Project No. 1065, Sponsored by the Dallas Police Department, Field Work, 1933–1937. Center for American History, University of Texas–Austin.

Texas Department of Public Safety, Records, 1935–1995. Texas State Archives and Library, Austin.

Texas Traffic Accidents, 1937, 1938, 1939, Compiled by Accidents Section Driver's License Division, Department of Public Safety, Austin, Texas. Center for American History, University of Texas–Austin.

Thompson, John T. City Traffic Law Enforcement in Texas. Institute of Public Affairs, Austin: University of Texas, 1957. Center for American History, University of Texas–Austin.

Traffic Ordinances Governing the Operation of Automobiles, Hacks, Rent Cars, Jitneys and Baggage Wagons in the City of Houston, Effective October 15, 1915. Texas State Library.

Traffic Safety Primer, The Law of the Road is a Courtesy. Prepared by and Printed for the Streets and Safety Committee of the Austin Chamber of Commerce (1944). Center for American History, University of Texas–Austin.

Your Driver Training Plan. A Brief Concise and Practical Approach to Training Youthful Drivers. Issued by Department of Public Safety in Cooperation with State Department of Education, Austin, Texas, 1943. Center for American History, University of Texas–Austin.

Periodicals

American Auto News

American City

American Homes and Gardens

American Journal of Psychiatry

American Magazine

American Motorist

Annals of the American Academy of Political and Social Science

Automotive Industries

Atlantic

Chauffeur

City Manager Magazine

Collier's
Commonweal
Country Life in America
Craftsman
Current History
Delineator
Everybody's Magazine
Forum
Hampton's Magazine
Harper's Weekly
Horseless Age
House Beautiful
Hygeia
Human Factor
Illustrated World
Independent
Ladies' Home Journal
Lippincott's Monthly Magazine
Literary Digest
Living Age
Journal of Educational Sociology
Mental Hygiene
Motor
Motor Age
Motor Camper
Motor Life
Motor Travel
Motor World

Munsey's Magazine
Nation
National Safety News
New England Magazine
New Republic
Outing Magazine
Outlook
Overland Monthly
Playground
Popular Mechanics
Popular Science Monthly
Printers' Ink
Public Safety
Reader's Digest
Proceedings of the Institute of Traffic Engineers
Review of Reviews
Saturday Evening Post
Scientific American
Social Forces
Social Psychology
Scribner's Magazine
Texas Parade
Texas Safety News
Traffic Quarterly
Traffic Digest
World To-Day
World's Work
Woman's Home Companion

Published Primary and Secondary Sources

Albert, Daniel M. "Order out of Chaos: Automobile Safety, Technology and Society, 1925 to 1965." Ph.D. dissertation, University of Michigan, 1997.

————. "Psychotechnology and Insanity at the Wheel." *Journal of the History of the Behavioral Sciences* 35, no. 3 (1999): 291–305.

Aldrich, Mark. *Safety First: Technology, Labor, and Business in the Building of American Work Safety, 1870–1939.* Baltimore: Johns Hopkins University Press, 1997.

Allen, F. L. *The Big Change.* New York: Harper and Brothers, 1952.

Allen, Katherine. *Bleeding Hearts: A Solution to the Automobile Tragedy.* San Antonio: Naylor Company, 1941.

Alvord, Katie. *Divorce Your Car! Ending the Love Affair with the Automobile.* Gabriola Island, B.C., Canada: New Society Publishers, 2000.

American Automobile Association. *Official Manual of Motor Car Camping.* Washington, DC: AAA, 1920.

American Automobile Association. *State Rules and Regulations Governing Safety Education in the United States.* Washington, DC: AAA, 1939.

Ansted, Harry B. "The Auto-Camp Community." *Journal of Applied Sociology* 9 (1924): 136–142.

Automobile Manufacturers Association. *Automobile Facts and Figures,* 23d. ed. New York: AMA, 1941.

Automobile Manufacturers Association. *A Factual Survey of Automobile Usage.* Detroit: New Center, c.1941.

Automotive Safety Foundation. *Standard Highway Safety Programs for States: A Working Program to Increase Traffic Efficiency and Reduce Accidents.* New York: Automotive Safety Foundation, 1939.

Bailey, Beth L. *From Front Porch to Back Seat: Courtship in Twentieth-Century America.* Baltimore: Johns Hopkins University Press, 1988.

Bailey, Roy R. *Sure Pop and the Safety Scouts.* New York: World Book, 1915.

Baker, Robert F. *The Highway Risk Problem: Policy Issues in Highway Safety.* New York: Wiley-Interscience, 1971.

Barger, Harold. *The Transportation Industries, 1889–1946.* New York: National Bureau of Economic Research, 1952.

Barrett, Paul. *The Automobile and Urban Transit: The Formation of Public Policy in Chicago, 1900–1930.* Philadelphia: Temple University Press, 1983.

Beck, Ulrich. *Risk Society: Towards a New Modernity.* London: Sage Publications, 1992.

Bedell, Mary Crehore. *Modern Gypsies: The Story of a Twelve Thousand Mile Motor Camping Trip Encircling the United States.* New York: Brentano's, 1924.

Behling, Laura. "'The Woman at the Wheel': Marketing Ideal Womanhood, 1915–1934." *Journal of American Culture* 20 (Fall 1997): 13–30.

Belasco, Warren J. *Americans on the Road: From Autocamp to Motel: 1910–1945.* Cambridge, MA: MIT Press, 1979.

Belloc, Hilaire. *The Highway and Its Vehicles.* London: Studio, Ltd., 1926.

Bennett, Dianne, and William Graebne. "Safety First: Slogan and Symbol of the Industrial Safety Movement." *Journal of the Illinois State Historical Society* 68, no. 3 (June 1975): 243–256.

Berger, Michael L. *The Devil Wagon in God's Country: The Automobile and Social Change in Rural America, 1893–1929.* Hamden, CT: Archon Books, 1979.

Bexar County, Texas. *Highway League's Official Log Book For Texas, 1914–1915. A Touring Hand Book of the Principle Automobile Routes in the State of Texas.* San Antonio: Bexar County Highway League, 1914.

Bliss, Carey S. *Autos across America: A Bibliography of Transcontinental Automobile Travel.* Austin, TX: Jerkins and Reese, 1982.

Borg, Kevin. "The 'Chauffeur Problem' in the Early Auto Era: Structuration Theory and the Users of Technology." *Technology and Culture* 40 (October 1979): 797–832.

Bottles, Scott. *Los Angeles and the Automobile: The Making of the Modern City.* Los Angeles: University of California Press, 1988.

Brimmer, F. E. *Autocamping.* Cincinnati: Stewart Kidd, 1923.

———. *Motor Campcraft.* New York: Macmillan, 1923.

Brownell, Blaine. "A Symbol of Modernity: Attitudes toward the Automobile in Southern Cities in the 1920s." *American Quarterly* 24 (March 1972): 20–44.

———. "The Urban South Comes of Age, 1900–1940." In *The City in Southern History,* ed. Blaine Brownell and David Goldfield. Port Washington, NY: Kennikat Press, 1974.

Bureau of Public Roads, U.S. Department of Commerce. *Highways and Economic and Social Changes.* Washington, DC: Government Printing Office, 1964.

Burnham, John Chynoweth. "The Gasoline Tax and the Automobile Revolution." *Mississippi Valley Historical Review* 48 (December 1961): 435–459.

Cary, Norman Miller. "The Use of the Motor Vehicle in the United States Army, 1899–1939." Ph.D. dissertation, University of Georgia, 1980.

Cerullo, Margaret, and Ewen, Phyllis. "'Having a Good Time': The American Family Goes Camping." *Radical America* 16 (January–April 1982): 13–43.

Chandler, Alfred D., Jr. *Giant Enterprise: Ford, General Motors, and the Automobile Industry*. New York: Harcourt, Brace and World, 1964.

Chandler, Robert Adams. *Questions and Answers on the Automobile, A Quiz Manual for Students*. Boston: n.p., 1911.

Clark, Neil M. *Seven Roads to Safety: A Program to Reduce Automobile Accidents*. New York: Harper and Brothers, 1939.

Cleveland, Reginald M., and S. T. Williamson. *The Road Is Yours: The Story of the Automobile and the Men Behind It*. New York: Greystone Press, 1951.

Cohn, David. *Combustion on Wheels: An Informal History of the Automobile Age*. Boston: Houghton Mifflin, 1944.

Cooter, Roger, and Bill Luckin, eds. *Accidents in History: Injuries, Fatalities and Social Relations*. Athens, GA: Rodopi, 1997.

De Santis, Hugh. "The Democratization of Travel: The Travel Agent in American History." *Journal of American Culture* 1 (Spring 1978): 1–17.

Dearing, Charles L. *American Highway Policy*. Washington, DC: Brookings Institution, 1941.

Deloria, Philip J. *Indians in Unexpected Places*. Lawrence: University Press of Kansas, 2004.

Dettelbach, Cynthia Golomb. *In the Driver's Seat: The Automobile in American Literature and Popular Culture*. Westport, CT: Greenwood, 1976.

Dixon, Winifred Hawkridge. *Westward Hoboes: Ups and Downs of Frontier Motoring*. New York: Charles Scribner's Sons, 1924.

Doolittle, James R., et al. *The Romance of the Automobile Industry*. New York: Klebold Press, 1916.

Eastman, Joel W. *Styling Versus Safety: The American Automobile Industry and the Development of Automobile Safety, 1900–1966*. Lanham, MD: University Press of America, 1984.

Economos, James P. *Traffic Courts*. Chicago: American Bar Association, 1942.

Eldridge, Maurice O. *Public Road Mileage, Revenues, and Expenditures in the United States in 1904*. U.S. Department of Agriculture, Office of Public Roads, Bulletin No. 32. Washington, DC: Government Printing Office, 1907.

Eno, William Phelps. *Fundamentals of Highway Traffic Regulation*. Washington, DC: Eno Foundation for Highway Traffic Regulation, 1926.

———. *The Story of Highway Traffic Control, 1899–1939*. Saugatuck, CT: Eno Foundation for Highway Traffic Control, 1939.

Epstein, R. C. "The Rise and Fall of Firms in the Automobile Industry." *Harvard Business Review* 5 (January 1927): 157–174.

Epstein, Ralph. *The Automobile Industry: Its Economic and Commercial Development*. Chicago: A. W. Shaw, 1928.

Evans, Leonard, and Richard C. Schwing, eds. *Human Behavior and Traffic Safety*. New York: Plenum Press, 1985.

Fagan, James O. *What Price Safety? Some Practical Suggestions*. n.p.: 1927. Library of Congress.

Ferguson, Melville. *Motor Camping on Western Trails*. New York: Century, 1925.

Finger, Charles J. *Adventure under Sapphire Skies*. New York: William Morrow, 1931.

Fischer, Claude S., and Glenn R. Carroll. "Telephone and Automobile Diffusion in the United States, 1902–1937." *American Journal of Sociology* 93, no. 5 (March 1988): 1153–1178.

Fitzgerald, F. Scott. *The Great Gatsby*. New York: Charles Scribner's Sons, 1925.

Flagg, James Montgomery. *Boulevards All the Way*. New York: George H. Doran, 1925.

Flink, James J. *America Adopts the Automobile, 1895–1910*. Cambridge, MA: MIT Press, 1970.

———. "Three Stages of American Automobile Consciousness." *American Quarterly* 24, no. 4 (October 1972): 451–473.

———. *The Car Culture*. Cambridge, MA: MIT Press, 1975.

———. "The 'Car Culture' Revised: Some Comments on the Recent Historiography of Automotive History." *Michigan Quarterly Review* 19, no. 4 (1980).

———. *The Automobile Age*. Cambridge, MA: MIT Press, 2001.

Floherty, John T. *Youth at the Wheel: A Reference Book on Safe Driving*. Philadelphia: J. B. Lippincott, 1937.

Foley, Thomas C. *The Pace That Kills: Speed as a Factor in Motor Accidents*. London: Public Affairs News Service, 1934.

Foster, Mark S. "The Model T, the Hard Sell, and Los Angeles' Urban Growth: The Decentralization of Los Angeles during the 1920s." *Pacific Historical Review* 44 (November 1975): 459–484.

———. *From Streetcar to Superhighway: America City Planners and Urban Transportation 1900–1940*. Philadelphia: Temple University Press, 1982.

Frank, Thomas. *The Conquest of Cool: Business Culture, Counterculture, and the Rise of Hip Consumerism*. Chicago: University Press of Chicago, 1997.

Franz, Kathleen Gail. "Narrating Automobility: Travelers, Tinkerers, and Technological Authority in the Twentieth Century." Ph.D. dissertation, Brown University, 1999.

French, Patterson H. *The Automobile Compensation Plan: A Solution for Some Problems of Court Congestion and Accident Litigation in New York State*. New York: Columbia University Press, 1933.

Garvey, Ellen Gruber. "Reframing the Bicycle: Advertising-Supported Magazines and Scorching Women." *American Quarterly* 47, no.1 (March 1995): 66–101.

Gladding, Effie Price. *Across the Continent by the Lincoln Highway*. New York: Brentano's, 1915.

Glasscock, Carl B. *The Gasoline Age*. Indianapolis: Bobbs-Merrill, 1937.

Graham, John D. "Automobile Safety: An Investigation of Occupant-Protection Policies." Ph.D. dissertation, Carnegie-Mellon University, 1983.

———. *Auto Safety: Assessing America's Performance*. Dover, MA: Auburn House, 1989.

Greenleaf, William. *Monopoly on Wheels: Henry Ford and the Selden Patent Suit*. Detroit: Wayne State University Press, 1961.

Greenwald, Richard A. *The Triangle Fire, the Protocols of Peace, and Industrial Democracy in Progressive Era New York*. Philadelphia: Temple University Press, 2005.

Gubbels, Jack L. *American Highways and Roadsides*. Boston: Houghton Mifflin, 1938.

Heaney, Thomas Michael. "The Call of the Open Road: Automobile Travel and Vacations in American Popular Culture, 1935–1960." Ph.D. dissertation, University of California–Irvine, 2000.

Hill, Frank. *The Automobile: How It Came, Grew, and Has Changed Our Lives*. New York: Dodd, Mead, 1967.

Hoffman, Harold G. "Are You Financially Responsible?" n.p., 1932.

Hoffman, Paul G. *Seven Roads to Safety: A Program to Reduce Automobile Accidents*. NY: Harper and Brothers, 1939.

Hogner, Dorothy Childs. *South to Padre*. Boston: Lothrop, Lee, and Shepard, 1936.

Hood, Clifton. *722 Miles*. New York: Simon and Schuster, 1994.

Hubbard, S. Dana. *Automobile Hazards: Keep Well Leaflet No. 20*. New York: M. B. Brown Printing and Binding, 1922.

Hulme, Kathryn. *How's The Road?* San Francisco: n.p., 1928.

Interrante, Joseph. "You Can't Go to Town in a Bathtub: Automobile Movement and the Reorganization of Rural American Space, 1900–1930." *Radical History Review* 21 (1979): 151–168.

———. "The Road to Utopia: The Automobile and the Spatial Transformation of American Culture." *Michigan Quarterly Review* 19 (Fall 1980–Winter 1981): 502–517.

———. "A Movable Feast: The Automobile and the Spatial Transformation of American Culture, 1890–1940." Ph.D. dissertation, Harvard University, 1983.

Jakle, John A., and Keith A. Sculle. *Fast Food: Roadside Restaurants in the Automobile Age*. Baltimore: Johns Hopkins University Press, 1999.

Jarvis, George Kirkham. "The Diffusion of the Automobile in the United States, 1895–1969." Ph.D. dissertation, University of Michigan, 1972.

Jessup, Elton. *The Motor Camping Book*. New York: G. P. Putnam's Sons, 1921.

Jordan, John. *Machine-Age Ideology: Social Engineering and American Liberalism*. Chapel Hill: University of North Carolina Press, 1994.

Joseph, Gregory Anthony. "Pride and Profit: The Dilemma of Quality and Quantity in the Early Automobile Luxury Industry." Ph.D. dissertation, Claremont Graduate School, 2000.

Karolevitz, B. F. *This Was Pioneer Motoring*. Seattle: Superior Publishing, 1968.

Kaszynski, William. *The American Highway: The History and Culture of Roads in the United States*. Jefferson, NC: McFarland, 2000.

Kennedy, E. D. *The Automobile Industry: The Coming of Age of Capitalism's Favorite Child*. New York: Reynal and Hitchcock, 1941.

Kern, Stephen. *The Culture of Time and Space, 1880–1918*. Cambridge, MA: Harvard University Press, 1983.

Kirby, Richard Shelton. *A Study of Motor Vehicle Accidents in the State of Connecticut for the Years 1924 and 1925*. New Haven, CT: Yale University Press, 1926.

——. *Third Study of Motor Vehicle Accidents in the State of Connecticut Including Those for the Year 1926*. New Haven, CT: Yale University Press, 1927.

——. *Fourth Study of Motor Vehicle Accidents in the State of Connecticut Including Those for the Year 1927*. New Haven, CT: Yale University Press, 1928.

Kirsch, David A. *The Electric Vehicle and the Burden of History*. New Brunswick, NJ: Rutgers University Press, 2000.

Kline, Ronald R. *Consumers in the Country: Technology and Social Change in Rural America*. Baltimore: Johns Hopkins University Press, 2000.

Kline, Ronald, and Trevor Pinch. "Users as Agents of Technological Change: The Social Construction of the Automobile in the Rural United States." *Technology and Culture* 37 (October 1996): 763–765.

Laas, William, ed. *Freedom of the American Road*. Detroit: Ford Motor Company, 1956.

Labatut, Jean, and Wheaton J. Lane, eds. *Highways in Our National Life: A Symposium*. Princeton, NJ: Princeton University Press, 1950.

Laird, Pamela Walker. "'The Car without a Single Weakness': Early Automobile Advertising." *Technology and Culture* 37, no. 4 (October 1996): 796–812.

Lansing, John B. *Transportation and Economic Policy*. New York: Free Press, 1966.

Lave, Charles. "Speeding, Coordination, and the 55-MPH Limit." *American Economic Review* 75, no. 5 (December 1985): 1159–1164.

——. "Speeding, Coordination, and the 55-MPH Limit: Reply." *American Economic Review* 79, no. 4 (September 1989): 926–931.

Leisseig, Corey. *Automobility and Social Change in the American South, 1909–1939*. New York: Routledge, 2001.

Leuchtenberg, William E. *The Perils of Prosperity, 1914–1932*. Chicago: University of Chicago Press, 1958.

Levine, Lawrence. "Progress and Nostalgia: The Self Image of the Nineteen Twenties." In *The American Novel and the Nineteen Twenties*, ed. Malcolm Bradbury and David Palmer. London: Edward Arnold, 1971.

Lewis, David L. *The Public Image of Henry Ford*. Detroit: Wayne State University Press, 1976.

Lewis, David L., and Lawrence Goldstein, eds. *The Automobile and American Culture*. Ann Arbor: University of Michigan Press, 1980.

Lewis, Sinclair. "Adventures in Automobumming: Gasoline Gypsies." *Saturday Evening Post* (December 20, 1919): 5–7, 138.

———. "Adventures in Automobumming: Want a Lift?" *Saturday Evening Post* (December 27, 1919): 24–25, 66, 69–70.

———. "Adventures in Automobumming: The Great American Frying Pan." *Saturday Evening Post* (January 3, 1920): 20–21, 62, 65–66.

———. *Babbitt*. New York: Harcourt Brace, 1922.

Lewis, Tom. *Divided Highway: Building the Interstate Highways, Transforming American Life*. New York: Penguin Books, 1997, 1999.

Liebs, Chester. *Mainstreet to Miracle Mile*. Baltimore: Johns Hopkins University Press, 1995.

Lincoln Highway Association. *Complete Official Road Guide of the Lincoln Highway*. Detroit: n.p., 1915.

Long, J. C., and John D. Long. *Motor Camping*. New York: Dodd, Mead, 1923.

Longstreth, Richard. *The Drive-In, the Supermarket, and Transformation of Commercial Space in Los Angeles, 1914–1941*. Cambridge, MA: MIT Press, 1999.

Lubove, Roy. *Community Planning in the 1920s: The Contribution of the Regional Planning Association of America*. Pittsburgh: University of Pittsburgh Press, 1963.

Lynd, Robert S., and Helen Merrell. *Middletown: A Study in Modern American Culture*. New York: Harcourt Brace, 1929.

———. *Middletown in Transition*. New York: Harcourt Brace, 1937.

MacManus, Theodore F., and Norman Beasley. *Men, Money, and Motors*. New York: Harper, 1929.

Maher, John J. *Mind over Motor*. Detroit: n.p., 1937.

Marley, Paul H. *Story of an Automobile Trip From Lincoln, Nebraska, to Los Angeles*. n.p., 1911.

Martin, Richard. "Fashion and the Car in the 1950s." *Journal of American Culture* 20 (Fall 1997): 51–66

Mason, Philip P. *The League of American Wheelmen and the Good Roads Movement, 1880–1905*. Ann Arbor: University of Michigan Press, 1958.

Massey, Beatrice. *It Might Have Been Worse*. San Francisco: Harr, Wagner, 1920.

Maxim, Hiram Percy. *Horseless Carriage Days*. New York: Harper, 1936.

May, Lary. *Screening Out the Past: The Birth of Mass Culture and the Motion Picture Industry*. New York: Oxford University Press, 1980.

McClellan, Grant S., ed. *Safety on the Road*. New York: H. W. Wilson, 1966.

McConnell, Curt. *Coast to Coast by Automobile: The Pioneering Trips, 1899–1908*. Palo Alto, CA: Stanford University Press, 2000.

McGerr, Michael. *A Fierce Discontent: The Rise and Fall of the Progressive Movement, 1870–1920*. New York: Oxford University Press, 2003.

McGill, Vernon. *Diary of a Motor Journey from Chicago to Los Angeles*. Los Angeles: Grafton Publishing, 1922.

McIntyre, Stephen L. "The Failure of Fordism: Reform of the Automobile Repair Industry, 1913–1940." *Technology and Culture* 41 (April 2000): 269–299.

McShane, Clay. "Transforming the Use of Urban Space: A Look at the Revolution in Street Pavements, 1880–1924." *Journal of Urban History* (May 1979): 291–296.

———. *Down the Asphalt Path: The Automobile and the American City*. New York: Columbia University Press, 1994.

Meyer, John A. "Transportation Today: The U.S. Experience in a World Context." *Annals of the American Academy of Political and Social Science* 553 (September 1997): 17–29.

Michigan Quarterly Review 19/20 (Fall 1980–Winter 1981): Special Issue on "The Automobile and American Culture."

Middleton, Jack. "Early Automobiles in Nevada: Registrations and License Plates, 1913–1937." *Nevada Historical Society Quarterly* 40 (Fall 1997): 307–318.

Moline, N. T. *Mobility and the Small Town, 1900–1930: Transportation Change in Oregon, Illinois.* Department of Geography Research Paper no. 132. Chicago: University of Chicago, 1971.

Monroe, D. L., et al. *Family Expenditures for Automobile and Other Transportation: Five Regions. Consumer Purchases Study, Urban, Village, and Farm Bureau of Home Economics*, Misc. Pub. no 415. Washington, DC: Department of Agriculture, 1941.

Moorhouse, H. F. *Driving Ambitions: An Analysis of the American Hot Rod Enthusiasm.* Manchester, UK: Manchester University Press, 1991.

Mulligan, Barry. *Collisions in Street and Highway Transportation.* Philadelphia: Dorrance, 1936.

Mumford, Lewis. *The Highway and the City.* New York: Harcourt, Brace and World, 1964.

Mythen, Gabe. *Ulrich Beck: A Critical Introduction to the Risk Society.* London: Pluto Press, 2004.

Nash, Anedith Jo Bond. "Death on the Highway: The Automobile Wreck in American Culture, 1920–1940." Ph.D. dissertation, University of Minnesota, 1983.

National Conference on Street and Highway Safety, *First National Conference on Street and Highway Safety, Hon. Herbert Hoover, Secretary of Commerce, Chairman.* December 15–16, Washington, DC: Government Printing Office, 1924.

National Conference on Street and Highway Safety, *Ways and Means to Traffic Safety. Recommendations of National Conference on Street and Highway Safety, Including Findings of All Conference Committees and of General Meetings of Conference Held in 1924, 1926, and 1930, as Summarized and Approved by Third National Conference, May 27–28–29, 1930.* Washington, DC: Government Printing Office, 1930.

National Safety Council. *Too Long at the Wheel: A Study of Exhaustion and Drowsiness as They Affect Traffic Accidents.* Chicago: National Safety Council, 1935.

Nevins, Allan, and Frank Ernest Hill. *Ford: The Times, the Man, the Company, 1865–1915.* New York: Charles Scribner's Sons, 1954.

———. *Expansion and Challenge, 1915–1933.* New York: Charles Scribner's Sons, 1957.

———. *Ford: Decline and Rebirth, 1933–1962.* New York: Charles Scribner's Sons, 1963.

Neyhart, Amos E. "Past Present and Future of Driver Education." *Journal of Traffic Safety Education* 30, no. 3 (April 1983): 13–14.

Oh, That Funny Ford! New York: Morris and Bendien, 1916.

Owen, Wilfred. *Automotive Transportation. Trends and Problems.* Washington, DC: Brookings Institution, 1949.

Owen, Wilfred, and Charles L. Dearing. *Toll Roads and the Problem of Highway Modernization.* Washington, DC: Brookings Institution, 1951.

Partridge, Bellamy. *Fill 'er Up: The Story of Fifty Years of Motoring.* New York: McGraw-Hill, 1952.

Paxson, F. L. "The Highway Movement, 1916–1935." *American Historical Review* 51, no. 2 (January 1946).

Pennybacker, J. E., Jr., and Maurice O. Eldridge. *Mileage and Cost of Public Roads in the United States.* Office of Public Roads, Bulletin No. 41. Washington, DC: Government Printing Office, 1912.

Pomeroy, Earl. *In Search of the Golden West: The Tourist in Western America.* New York: Alfred A. Knopf, 1957.

Post, Emily. *By Motor to the Golden Gate.* New York: D. Appleton, 1916.

President's Research Committee on Social Trends. *Recent Social Trends in the United States. Report of the President's Research Committee on Social Trends.* New York: McGraw-Hill Book Co., 1933.

Preston, Howard L. *Automobile Age Atlanta: The Making of a Southern Metropolis, 1900–1935.* Athens: University of Georgia Press, 1979.

———. *Dirt Roads to Dixie.* Knoxville: University of Tennessee Press, 1991.

Public Roads Administration. *Highway Statistics Summary to 1945.* Washington, DC: Federal Works Agency, 1947.

Rae, John B. *American Automobile Manufacturers: The First Fifty Years.* New York: Chilton, 1959.

———. *The American Automobile: A Brief History.* Chicago: University of Chicago Press, 1965.

———. *The Road and Car in American Life.* Cambridge, MA: MIT Press, 1971.

———. *The American Automobile Industry.* Boston: Twayne Publishers, 1984.

Raitz, Karl. "American Roads, Roadside America." *Geographical Review* 88 (July 1998): 363–387.

Raucher, Alan R. "Paul G. Hoffman, Studebaker, and the Car Culture." *Indiana Magazine of History* 79, no. 3 (1983): 209–230.

Russell, Thomas H. *Automobile Driving Self-Taught: An Exhaustive Treatise on the Operation, Management and Care of Motor Cars.* Chicago: Charles C. Thompson, 1914.

Safety First League. *Safety for Twenty Million Automobile Drivers: Avoid Accidents and Escape the Traffic Court.* New York: The Safety First League, 1924.

Scharff, Virginia. *Taking the Wheel: Women and the Coming of the Motor Age.* Albuquerque: University of New Mexico Press, 1992.

Sculle, Keith A. "The Best of Both Worlds: Home and Mobility in Motel Postcard Iconography." *Material Culture* 31 (Fall 1999): 21–32.

Sears, Stephen W. *The America Heritage History of the Automobile in America.* New York: American Heritage, 1977.

Seely, Bruce E. *Building the American Highway System: Engineers as Policy Makers.* Philadelphia: Temple University Press, 1987.

Setzer, Lawrence H. *A Financial History of the American Automobile Industry.* New York: Houghton Mifflin, 1928.

Sharp, Dallas Lore. *The Better Country.* Boston: Houghton Mifflin, 1928.

Sherman, Ray W. *If You're Going to Drive Fast.* New York: Thomas Y. Crowell, 1935.

Shinar, David. *Psychology on the Road: The Human Factor in Traffic Safety.* New York: John Wiley and Sons, 1978.

Sinke, James. *Think: An Analysis of Automobile Accident Causes* (Grand Rapids, MI: n.p., 1926).

St. Clair, David. "Modernization and Decline of Urban Public Transit, 1935–1950." *Journal of Economic History* 41 (1981): 579–600.

State of Texas. *First Biennial Report of the State Highway Commission.* Austin, TX: Von Boeckmann-Jones, 1918. Texas State Archives and Library, Austin.

———. *Second Biennial Report of the State Highway Commission for the Period December 1, 1918, to December 1, 1920.* Austin, TX: Von Boeckmann-Jones, January 1921.

———. *Third Biennial Report of the State Highway Commission for the Period December 1, 1920, to December 1, 1922.* Austin, TX: Von Boeckmann-Jones, February 1923.

———. *Fourth Biennial Report of the State Highway Commission for the Period December 1, 1922, to September 1, 1924.* Austin, TX: Von Boeckmann-Jones, January 1925.

Steinbeck, John. *The Grapes of Wrath.* New York: Viking Press, 1939.

Swanson, Wesley Alan. "The Automobile in the American Imagination, 1889–1929." Ph.D. dissertation, University of California–Los Angeles, 1996.

Taussig, Hugo Alois. *Retracing the Pioneers from West to East in an Automobile.* San Francisco: privately printed, 1910.

Taylor, George R. *The Transportation Revolution.* Economic History of the United States, Vol. 4. New York: Rinehart, 1951.

Tenney, Edward A. *The Highway Jungle: The Story of the Public Safety Movement and the Failure of "Driver Education" in the Public Schools*. New York: Exposition Press, 1962.

Tobin, Gary Allan. "The Bicycle Boom of the 1890s: The Development of Private Transportation and the Birth of the Modern Tourist." *Journal of Popular Culture* 8 (Spring 1974): 838–849.

Travelers Insurance Company. *Tremendous Trifles: Minor Decisions of Major Importance*. Hartford, CT: Travelers Insurance Company, 1932.

———. *The Great American Gamble*. Hartford, CT: Travelers Insurance Company, 1934.

Travis, Stuart. *"Bubble" Jingles: The Jolly Side of the Automobile*. New York: Rohde and Haskins, 1901.

Tulloch, John, and Deborah Lupton. *Risk and Everyday Life*. London: Sage Publications, 2003.

Twin Mutual's Primer of Automobile Insurance. Boston: Pinkham Press, 1920.

U.S. Department of Agriculture, Bureau of Public Roads. *Highway Accidents, Their Causes and Recommendations for Their Prevention*. Washington, DC: Government Printing Office, 1938.

Usselman, Steven W. "The Lure of Technology and the Appeal of Order: Railroad Safety Regulation in Nineteenth Century America." *Business and Economic History* 21 (1992): 290–299.

Van de Water, Frederic F. *The Family Flivvers to Frisco*. New York: D. Appleton, 1927.

Wallis, Roland S. "Tourist Camps." Bulletin no. 56 in *Iowa State College of Agriculture and Mechanical Arts Official Publication* 21, no. 36 (February 7, 1923).

Warren, George. *Traffic Courts*. Boston: Little, Brown, 1942.

Webb, Walter Prescott. *The Texas Rangers: A Century of Frontier Defense*, 2nd ed. Austin: University of Texas Press, 1935, 1965.

Whitney, Albert W. *Man and the Motor Car*. New York: J. J. Little and Ives, 1936.

Wik, Reynold M. *Henry Ford and Grass-Roots America*. Ann Arbor: University of Michigan Press, 1972.

Willey, Malcolm M., and Stuart A. Rice. "The Agencies of Communication." In *Recent Social Trends in the United States*. 2 vols. New York: McGraw-Hill, 1933.

———. *Communication Agencies and Social Life*. New York: McGraw-Hill, 1933.

Wisely, Harold Martin. "Personal Characteristics of Commercial Bus Drivers Related to Accident Proneness." Ph.D. dissertation, Northwestern University, 1947.

Works Projects Administration. *Texas: A Guide to the Lone Star State. Compiled by Workers of the Writers' Program of the Works Projects Administration in the State of Texas, American Guide Series*. New York: Hastings House, 1940.

Ziff, Larzer. *Return Passages: Great American Travel Writing, 1780–1910*. New Haven, CT: Yale University Press, 2000.

Index